THIS BOOK BELONGS TO

Roselyn Benon

MEMOIRS OF AN AESTHETE 1939-1969

MEMOIRS
OF AN AESTHETE
1939–1969

Harold Acton

New York   The Viking Press

Published in England under the title of More Memoirs of an Aesthete
Copyright © 1970 by Harold Acton
All rights reserved
Published in 1971 by The Viking Press, Inc.
625 Madison Avenue, New York, N. Y. 10022
SBN 670–46816–9
Library of Congress catalog card number: 74–138490
Printed in Great Britain
Bound in U.S.A.

To the memory of my mother
and to my friend John Cullen, who
prompted me to write these memoirs

Contents

MEMOIRS OF AN AESTHETE 1939–1969

Illustrations

Acknowledgements

I have many friends to thank and I hope to be forgiven by those I might have overlooked. I am especially grateful to Mr Christopher Sykes for allowing me to print his account of a visit to Gertrude Stein; to Mr A. D. Peters for permission to quote from Evelyn Waugh; to Mr Francis Sitwell for permission to quote from his aunt, Dame Edith; to Mr Islay Lyons for letting me reproduce his photograph of Norman Douglas, as well as to the latter's literary executor, Mr Kenneth Macpherson. Grateful thanks are due to the Earl of Rosse, Mr Maurice Cranston, and Mr and Mrs John Sutro for critical suggestions; to Mr Hamish Hamilton and the Rev. Victor Stanley for reminders; to Mr Alexander Zielcke for his excellent photographs; and above all to Mr John Cullen who jogged my memory and encouraged me to write this record.

H.A.

Explanatory and Apologetic

My first book of *Memoirs* was written in self-defence. In the time of my youth the Chinese were commonly considered peculiar to say the least, and the Europeans, apart from Christian missionaries who elected to live among them, were regarded as even more peculiar. Ignorant prejudice was rife in this respect. The myth of Mr Wu, Doctor Fu Man-chu, and sinister bogies of that ilk, still survived in popular fiction and cinema films. So many Chinese customs were the reverse of ours and their very refinement seemed a symptom of depravity. Instead of swilling beer they smoked opium, and so forth: they belonged to a creepy-crawly species. . . . Consequently it was easy to believe that an Oxford aesthete of ephemeral fame had settled in China for the purpose of wallowing in vice.

The rumour of my moral decline had assumed such concrete shape as to become a stumbling-block when, hoping to be of service to my country during the 1939–1945 war, I joined the R.A.F. By chance I was to read accusations against me that stung me like a corrosive acid. I saw myself described as a scandalous debauchee and there was nothing I could do about it since the typewritten screed emanated from an official, *ergo* a respectable source. So instead of being sent to Chungking where I might have been useful, I was detained at Barrackpore in a lowly secretarial capacity, answering telephones and filing documents which anybody without my linguistic qualifications could have done more efficiently than I. (In Peking I had no telephone and in Florence I seldom answer it.) And the documents I had to file were couched in execrable English which I was not allowed to correct.

On account of a malicious slander my few talents lay fallow until an enterprising Wing Commander came to my rescue, but of this more anon. Mindful of the adage that there is no smoke without fire, I have seldom been so discouraged. I still believe that even as a junior R.A.F. officer in that dark hour I might have done some good in China where I was not without influence and close connections. My Chinese friends trusted me. They paid me the compliment of treating me as one of themselves and our affection was mutual. 'We do not look upon you as a *wai-kuo-jen*,' they used to say. I knew they did not feel the same about most of my compatriots. But I was as helpless against an anonymous scrap of paper as Senator McCarthy's victims in later years. I could not challenge its author to a duel. Who was he? Evidently some epicene dunderhead from the Foreign Office. His rage against my independent way of life was that of the perennial snake in the grass, the envious Philistine. In time of peace I was beyond his bite; in time of war I was poisoned by it and the wound continued to fester. My *Memoirs* was an act of vindication.

Seven lean years were to follow the seven fat years I luxuriated in Peking, but even they had their moments of illumination. I shall dwell on these rather than on the hours, days, months of dreariness and frustration. For my amiable publisher has prevailed on me to write a sequel to *Memoirs of an Aesthete*. At first I faltered. Tame, all too tame, such sensations as I had to offer: a mere *susurrus* in comparison with the shocks provided by a Fleming. Surely my voice would be drowned in the multitude of those who have led 'eventful' lives and travelled in outer space . . .

Then I remembered those letters, sheaves of them, which continue to arrive from the readers of my previous volume. Some belong to the fan-mail category, but many come from thesis writers and biographers soliciting impressions, anecdotes, personal appreciations of Edith Sitwell, Norman Douglas, George Moore, Lady Cunard and her daughter Nancy, Reginald Turner, Ada Leverson, Gertrude Stein, Evelyn Waugh, Brian Howard, and other absent friends. At first I responded readily, but after a while I began to weary of contributing not only paragraphs but whole pages to publications of which I seldom received a complimentary copy. My *Memoirs* were already at their disposal, my brains exist to be picked, and I am willing enough to be drawn out in friendly conversation. But why devote further time and trouble to padding out other people's books for them? *Basta!* Let me write my own book in my own good time and manner. I refuse to be jostled and garbled and exploited.

One always has more to say about old friends, many of whom are more vital than yesterday's acquaintances. Is this because one grows atrophied, dulled by age? I suspect it is rather because my old friends were more striking as individuals. They would have made a singular impression wherever they went. Edith Sitwell, for instance, was in every detail unique. There was nothing vague or vaporous about her. Her presence imposed itself on any gathering even when she was silent. Others, less distinguished in appearance, imposed themselves by the brilliance of their speech. Reggie Turner, whose wit had cheered Oscar Wilde as he lay dying, would have passed unnoticed in a crowd. He needed winding up, as it were, but once he was wound up what a dazzling variety of fireworks he set off!

Another reason for continuing my *Memoirs* is the crop of reminiscences containing references to myself. Albeit kindly and veracious they crystallize images of forty years ago, as if I were embedded in a glacier. Yet I trust I have moved since then, though like Monkey Sun whose exploits were so vividly translated from the Chinese by Arthur Waley, I may not have travelled farther than the palm of Buddha's hand.

Memoirs of an Aesthete was published in 1948 but the book ended in 1939, which seemed the end of an era when many Englishmen 'thought imperially'. After a prelude of ominous calm another dance of death began that autumn.

During the Japanese occupation of Peking in 1937, one after another of my friends departed, but I decided to remain as long as possible, being enamoured of my second home and deploring the increased limitations of my home in Italy. The victorious Japanese campaign had ended in a stalemate. The Chinese Government were entrenched in Chungking and only bands of guerrillas harried the enemy, who could seldom detect or destroy them as they were apt to vanish among the anonymous peasantry. A few foreigners clung dutifully to their engagements, diplomatists, doctors, journalists and teachers; social institutions like Mrs Calhoun who had settled there during the twilight of the Manchu dynasty, and 'old China hands' like L. C. Arlington.

Fortunately I could still cultivate a circle of Chinese familiars who had not joined the general exodus. I dare not print their names for fear of compromising them with the present regime, if they have survived it. They were too deeply rooted in their native soil to transport themselves elsewhere, dedicated scholars in the classical tradition with a sound respect for their own literature and a keen curiosity about ours. I enjoyed the novelty of their comments as well as their instinctive subtlety. In our discussions poetry had no national boundaries: Wordsworth and Po Chü-i were birds of a feather. To them I owe some of my pleasantest hours. Where are they now, these voluptuaries of scholarship? One cannot conceive of them swallowing the slogans which prevail today or ploughing the fields with peasants. They had plenty of moral stamina but they were not brawny.

Chairman Mao has announced: 'We wish to eradicate the old Chinese culture.' Hence history, philosophy and literature are to be blotted out by robots. History repeats itself after a thousand years. When the ruler of Ch'in proclaimed himself First Emperor in 221 B.C. he decreed that all existing literature save that dealing with agriculture, medicine and divination was to be destroyed. But a few brave scholars concealed the Confucian Canon at the risk of their lives.

The Peking theatre had become my chief pastime and hobby, and I spent half the day translating the plays I preferred with my teacher Mr Chou who knew no English. Having lost most of his foreign pupils he was glad of this employment. A stout volume of these translations was to have been published by Henri Vetch of the French Bookstore, but beyond correcting some proofs just before the outbreak of war I have not seen or heard of them since. The manuscript must count as a war casualty. This was a grief to me at the time as the plays I had selected were in many respects superior to those I had rendered in condensed form with L. C. Arlington. With their lilt in my ears and the lithe actors leaping before my eyes I fancied I could convey some of their charm to Western playgoers, though the texts were the mere framework of many an exquisite performance.

In China as in Europe supreme theatrical instinct was the test of a great actor. 'She whose movements are disciplined, she who is a living harmony, a lyric in flesh and blood,' wrote Sarcey of Sarah Bernhardt. Alter the pronoun and this applied to Mei Lan-fang. I doubt if he has any successors in the China of Chairman Mao. Paradoxically, the role of heroine was best interpreted by males who created an illusion of ultra-femininity, whereas women on the stage were apt to rely on their intrinsic charm. This was a genuine triumph of art over nature.

Since the leading actors sang in falsetto to shrill accompaniment the music was not easy for foreigners to appreciate. When I invited the American poet Harriet Monroe to hear Ch'êng Yen-ch'iu she confessed that she could not endure the noise: pressing her fingers to her ears she tottered out in the middle of a stirring drama. Many others suffered from the same disability. Once the prejudice against falsetto singing was overcome such vocal agility aroused wonder and admiration. The European vogue for *bel canto* might seem equally strange and artificial. When we consider that in the eighteenth century the major roles of *opera seria* were soprani and that corpulent eunuchs fantastically garbed – for they insisted on choosing their own costumes – flaunted themselves as Alexander or Julius Caesar, the Chinese penchant for falsetto need not surprise us. Italian audiences of that period must have been similar to the Chinese when I lived in Peking, for when Farinelli sang his cadenza it is recorded that 'the orchestra stopped and left the field entirely to him, the audience ceased chattering or playing cards or eating supper in their boxes, and every man, woman and child in the building held his or her breath and stared in delight and admiration'.

The Chinese audience would chatter, sip tea or munch sweetmeats during a performance until hypnotized by vocal virtuosity, and I was told that Mei Lan-fang was bewildered by the unaccustomed silence when he played in Europe. Apart from his personality, one of his valuable contributions to the Chinese drama was his revival of ancient dances, such as the Sleeve Dance, the Flute and Feather Dance, the Spear Dance, the Fan Dance, and the thrilling sword dance in *Pa Wang's Parting with his Favourite*, which raised a trite melodrama to the highest level of art.

It was my love of what seemed permanent in Chinese culture that attracted me to the theatre in spite of occasional tedium, for the stage reflected the life and thought, the customs and costumes of China through the centuries. Wang Kuo-wei, the most learned authority on the subject, traced its origin to the songs and dances of primitive magicians to entice beneficent spirits and to exorcise evil ones. Something similar could be seen when the so-called Devil Dance was performed in the Lama Temple of Peking.

Dance and drama were blended in such plays as *Wu Sung's Combat with the Tiger*, wherein the jovial bandit, who is invincible under the influence of wine, destroys a ferocious tiger – an episode also described in the thirteenth-century novel *Shui Hu*

3

Chuan, translated by Pearl Buck as *All Men are Brothers*. Having swallowed twelve bowls of wine, Wu Sung laughs at the innkeeper's warning not to cross the mountain ridge where a tiger had already devoured a number of citizens. The local magistrate had posted proclamations forbidding travellers to cross it except at certain hours in compact groups. 'Silence!' shouts Wu Sung, his eyes blazing. 'If you hadn't mentioned the tiger I might stay here, but your words have challenged me. My hair is bristling and I shall certainly go.'

The innkeeper tries to dissuade him but Wu pushes him roughly aside and tells him to mind his own business. 'Alack', sighs the innkeeper, 'he has broken all my bones. The tiger will crunch you like a melon seed but I don't care what happens to you now.'

Supremely elegant in a close-fitting black costume, Hou Yung-k'uei gave an electric performance as Wu Sung reeling on his journey, singing and miming: 'I travel swiftly along the road by the setting sun's last rays. My eyes are blurred, I cannot see distinctly. Where is the cursed tiger? It's all nonsense, the magistrate's proclamation must be a joke. I'll march straight on. (Swaying.) Ai-ya, the wine is going to my head. Luckily there's a pillow of rock near by. I'll take a nap before going any farther. (He overturns a chair and lies down to sleep against it. The blast of a trumpet evokes a gust of wind and an acrobat disguised as a tiger climbs in on all fours.) What a bracing breeze! How now, the bug arrives! (Stands up and sings.) The thick-skinned beast looks pretty powerful. (Breaking his club in the ensuing struggle.) Ya, my club which was like a great wolf's fang is the very first thing to snap. (The tiger takes three leaps and Wu dodges it, singing as he swerves aside.) Now I spring forward to attack, and now I ward it off. The cursed brute jumps at me clawing and baring its fangs. (The tiger continues to pounce but each time Wu dodges it singing.) We are like peals of thunder. As soon as he turns his body round he leaps into empty space. In a twinkling he cannot find my whereabouts. Surely this beast is bent on destroying mankind. We meet as foes, oh tiger: now show your mettle!

4

Today your life is doomed since you have met the mighty Wu Sung. No matter what your strength, "the flower can't keep its hue a hundred days".' (He jumps on the tiger's back, seizes it by the scruff of the neck and pummels it with his fists till it falls dead.)

Two clownish huntsmen appear on the scene who ask the hero: 'Are you a man or a devil to venture alone across this ridge at night?' Wu Sung proceeds to describe his adventure without false modesty and shows them the dead tiger. The huntsmen insist on escorting him to the magistrate for his reward though he protests that he did not expect one. Carrying the carcass, they cross the ridge together, politely prompting each other to go first as if to a formal dinner.

The beauty of such a performance was in the miming, so rhythmically precise, the co-ordinated twists and turns of body, face and voice. One gathered strength from such graceful sinewy motions. It was unlike anything seen in our theatre: opera is not the right term for it and our ballet contains no singing or dialogue. For me it was the most exhilarating art that China could produce and I cannot help regretting its dissolution. There was already a trend towards realism in the thirties but now the most deplorable Western influence is paramount. The so-called 'bad influence of the past' was purely indigenous. While some Confucian virtues may still be respected under different names, filial piety is no longer mentioned, and one wonders if couples have time for conjugal fidelity when so many are compelled to live apart.

More and more I relied on my Chinese friends and the theatre for aesthetic nourishment. On the surface Peking was tranquil, yet we were all in a chronic state of nervous tension. Feverishly I tried to live in the present, inseparable here from an idealized past, but I was haunted, as few of my friends were, by dread of the future. Certain intellectuals monotonously harp on being 'committed'. Who was not committed while Hitler was spreading his snares, and what could the average individual do about it when the statesmen in power were so wobbly?

5

I began to taste everything as if for the last time and I felt rather guilty when the taste was ambrosial. At moments I was conscious of being an escapist in a vacuum from which all jarring elements were excluded. Why not, when there was so much vileness to escape from? The manifest signs and symptoms pointed to another war in Europe. A German acquaintance had urged me to read *Mein Kampf*: surely that was clear enough. He could not help being dazzled by Hitler. Germans of Jewish blood were losing their posts in Chinese universities and even in firms and hospitals, owing to the persistent intrigues of their Aryan rivals. Most of them attached swastika flags to their private rickshaws. Even with the seemingly anglicized Adam von Trott I never felt sure of his intimate convictions. The German Embassy was a hotbed of sinister denunciations and the amiable Ambassador Trautmann, an old-fashioned diplomatist, was eyed askance by his subordinates as insufficiently Nazi.

After the partition of Czechoslovakia I decided to go to England. If there was time before war broke out I hoped to visit my parents in Florence. In June, 1939, I started packing. As nobody could have predicted Japan's assault on Pearl Harbor I left my treasured possessions in Peking, expecting to return there. My house in Kung Hsien Hutung, a group of one-storey pavilions between spacious courtyards, was full of the ancient scrolls and furniture I had collected and arranged according to the season until the harmony seemed perfect. They belonged here absolutely and I could not imagine them in any other setting. Where else could I hang my long silk scrolls of birds and flowers or place my pre-Chippendale chairs and tables of *hung-mu*, my lacquered stools, wooden carvings, brush pots of carved bamboo, and gleaming assemblage of bronze mirrors, nearly all of them pre-T'ang?

My memory dwells fondly on certain objects, each of which had some intimate meaning, some unique association: a withered lotus leaf beside a blossom which glowed like ruddy amber though it was made of bamboo to serve as a water container for some scholar of the Ming dynasty, a wine cup of rhinoceros horn

6

carved in relief with a gnarled prunus branch in blossom, and others of pale green jade. Those anonymous artists were Cellini's equals with a greater refinement of taste. Why repine at their loss when they have yielded me so much pleasure? Perhaps it is sinful to attach excessive importance to objects, yet I confess to pangs of regret – the penalty, some will say, of selfish acquisitiveness. At least these symbols of a bygone civilization would have been safer in my hands than in those of the Red Guards. But I had no home in England, and the villa in Florence was crowded with my father's collection of Italian works of art.

From room to room I wandered, intent on each tangible record of my prolonged treasure-hunt through Chinese highways and byways, caressing their forms and colours with my eyes, while the water trickled on in my clepsydra. My emotions were akin to Mrs Gereth's in *The Spoils of Poynton*: 'There isn't one of them I don't know and love – yes, as one remembers and cherishes the happiest moments of one's life. Blindfold, in the dark, I could tell one from another. They're living things to me: they know me, they return the touch of my hand.' I did not suppose I should never see them again. For aught I know they have gone up in smoke like Poynton in Henry James's story.

The behaviour of the Japanese soldiery had prejudiced me against their country, but in the heat of summer it seemed more sensible to cross the Pacific than to swelter through the Indian Ocean. The train for Tangku left at six o'clock in the morning and I was deeply touched to find a group of Chinese friends who had come to see me off at this early hour. Most of them lived far from the station and they must have risen with the birds, almost as early as I in the frenzy of last minute packing after a sleepless night. Moreover they had brought parting gifts which they could ill afford, pots of ginger, preserved lychees, French cognac, and scrolls with auspicious characters, pressed upon me with such warmth that I could only stammer my thanks with an effort of Confucian control. I had received endless proofs of their courtesy, a virtue I prize above all, but this final proof will never be forgotten. I promised to return. We would all celebrate victory

7

together, but when? My Cantonese servant believed in a world-war lasting ten years and a reversal to primitive conditions. At the moment, surrounded by Japanese officers all boot and spur, and tough little guards with bestial faces, this victory looked remote. But my Chinese friends knew how to wait. The worst news failed to discourage them. With smiling stoicism they struggled to support their families and keep up appearances. The Japanese war machine hurtled hither and thither, but the Chinese had devised ways and means of neutralizing its effect. The descendants of Amiterasu the Sun Goddess on the station platform did not exist for them; they were so many mongrel dogs. Above the cacophony of travellers scrambling for places on the train my friends waved '*Tsai chien!*' and '*I lu p'ing-an!*' as slowly the engine crawled away from that city which had widened my vision and fortified my spirit. The grey and golden roofs seemed winged as if to take flight in the blue transparency of that June morning.

Chinese poets have expressed the poignancy of separation more frequently than our poets. Po Chü-i, so sensitively translated by Arthur Waley, often reminds me of the friends who saw me off: they, too, 'seemed to be regretting that joy will not stay:

That our souls had met only for a little while,
To part again with hardly time for greeting.'

It was ten o'clock when I boarded the S.S. *Tyozyo Maru* in a blanket of muggy heat. A sluttish sister of an old Channel steamer, she looked almost as tired as I felt. As soon as I found my cabin I stripped and flopped down on the nearest bunk. It was clammily close and infested with neurotic flies, but I covered my eyes with a black band and allowed my fatigue to overpower me, flooding my veins like an opiate. I was dozing off when I heard a shrill cry and a voice protesting: 'Mercy on us, a naked man in my cabin!'

Blinking, I beheld a stout elderly lady transfixed with horror at the threshold. 'This is monstrous. You can't put me in with a man,' the voice expostulated.

A pudding-faced cabin boy peered in, grinning from ear to ear with those gold tusks so favoured by the Japanese, but he did not seem to understand the lady's objections. As for me, I was too sleepy to collaborate. With a capacious yawn I turned my back on the intruders. The plaintive voice reverberated down the corridor.

The steward pretended to consider it normal that this female and I should share the same sleeping quarters. All the other cabins were reserved and he refused to gratify the whim of a fussy foreigner. I was no more pleased than the interloper, but when I spoke to the steward he said with a stubborn smile: 'Sorry, no can do.' Fortunately a chivalrous Frenchman came to our rescue. Though he was travelling with a winsome wife he exchanged bunks with the missionary spinster and moved into my cabin. His wife sulked, and I could hear her mutter something about an *emmerdeuse*.

We did not sail till early next morning when at last a breeze filtered through the stuffy cabin. Flying fish appeared to be racing each other through the phosphorescent waves: at least they were enjoying themselves. The Frenchman was severely critical of our foreign policy. Mr Chamberlain, he averred, would next be flying to Tokyo to reach an agreement with Japan about her 'New Order in Greater East Asia'. Prince Konoye would double-cross him just like Hitler. The French wife continued to sulk, and the missionary complained of her smoking habits. 'She smokes one cigarette on top of another and my, how they smell. Our cabin reeks of that terrible tobacco. I'm afraid it will get into my hair.' Conversation at meals was stifling.

At Moji four days later there was a long dismal ceremony on the jetty. A procession of widows and orphans had come to bow before the ashes of soldiers killed in 'the China Incident'. 'I guess those ashes make up most of the cargo,' the missionary remarked. 'Why don't all the women rise and put a stop to the war?' A steward scuttled up and asked us not to look, so we drifted back into the saloon with the stereotyped pictures of Fuji-yama. A Canadian who attempted to photograph the scene had his camera snatched from him by an irate officer. He in turn lost his temper and started swearing. The officer clutched one arm, a steward clutched the other, and together they dragged him out of sight. As it was rare to find a Japanese without a camera this episode proved how sensitive they were about their casualties.

I had qualms about the customs examination since my friend Tom Handforth had had many of his drawings confiscated on the pretext that they were obscene, a pretext somewhat hypocritical when a notorious 'Sex Shop' was tolerated in Kobe which specialized in all sorts of artificial stimuli for the frigid, the impotent and the widowed of both sexes: the catalogue of its wares advertised in preposterous English was a literary curiosity. Jacques Bardac put a few specimens in his powder-room for lady guests in order to study their reactions. Nearly all of them had the giggles, but a kleptomaniac removed the 'musical balls'.

After quarantine and passport inspection the customs required a list of all my books. Only one book was confiscated, *Twilight in Italy* by D. H. Lawrence, which might have been interpreted as the twilight of Mussolini. Apparently the others contained no 'dangerous thoughts'. Mindful of Tom Handforth's experience I put my luggage in bond except for two suitcases. These were turned inside out and all their contents were scrutinized to an accompaniment of hisses through masks of white gauze as if they were infectious. How courteous was the quiet 'Anything to declare, sir?' of the English customs officer in comparison. This was more like a police station: one had a sensation of being under arrest. I am told it is different now, thanks to an enlightened tourist industry, but there were few tourists in the June of 1939 and Englishmen were not popular. I could not help smiling over Lafcadio Hearn's raptures. Had he not written: 'everybody describing the sensations of his first Japanese day talks of the land as fairy-land, and of its people as fairy-folk'? I had never encountered a genuine fairy, but if these were specimens I would rather meet some other kind of being.

Allowed three days for rambling before the *Empress of Canada* sailed, I caught a train to Kyoto for another glimpse of the temples and gardens that had charmed me on a former visit. Soon I was sauntering through the Chion-in whose massive gate and noble proportions evoked a grander Japan akin to ancient China. After Peking the small scale of most Japanese buildings and the overcrowded landscape are apt to give one a cramping, shrinking feeling: 'the tiny groves of dwarf trees, and lilliputian lakes, and microscopic brooks,' so dear to Lafcadio Hearn, make one long for an Asian steppe. But in Kyoto there is spaciousness. The temple of the 33,333 images of Kwannon is immense, and Chion-in is like a castle on a hill where the gilt lotuses in the main building rise twenty-one feet high, half-way to the ceiling. Behind it are rooms with sliding screens by artists of the Kanō school: these are painted with cranes and pines, plum and bamboo, abundant snow scenes, the inevitable chrysanthemum, sparrows so life-like that they were said to have flown away, more pine-trees – so realistic that they were reputed to have oozed resin – and still more snow powdering willows and plum-blossoms. Flamboyant decorations remarkable for their boldness of design. Yet something was lacking which I nearly always find in Chinese paintings of similar subjects. A Chinese artist of the eleventh century wrote: 'The wise man creates with the help of his spirit and thereby has the same active force as heaven and earth.' These screen painters seem to have created with the help of mere manual skill. The emotions of the heart had been sacrificed to virtuosity. But one should not cavil when taste is so refined and when everything is kept so neat and clean. The Japanese are the Swiss of the Orient, I said to myself, and they deserve credit for their phoenix resurrections from ashes, from earthquakes, from cyclones throughout the ages.

In Kyoto one forgot the fascist feudalism of their military leaders, the insolence of their petty officials. Apart from priests with shaven pates, males were in the minority and the piled-up hair of the women contrasted with their glossy baldness. In the Hongwanji temple cables woven of 'a woman's crowning glory' were hanging as ex votos. I watched them clap their hands before bending their elaborate coiffures in prayer, some with babies on their backs; then off they toddled in their resonant wooden clogs. I imagined that they were praying for husbands in China.

My keenest regret was that I had nobody to converse with: nobody could understand my adaptations of a Japanese phrase-book. Surfeited with *fusuma* and *kakemonos* which required more leisure for contemplation, I strolled through the garden of Awata Palace to visit the azaleas that flourished there *en masse* with peculiar fragrance. Their silken bugles of pale orange and coralline pink were silent in the heat of midday. It was too soon for the cicadas to orchestrate the trees.

Very like crickets, however, were the sounds I heard in the Minamiza theatre that afternoon. One could only guess the meaning of the play, the plot of which was extremely complicated, but during the monotonous dialogue which alternated with frenzied action there was more than enough to captivate the eye, a medley of revolving scenes and costumes of extraordinary sumptuousness; and the music was weird and otherworldly. The actors moved as in some religious rite. Suddenly a dancer would shoot up from a hole in the stage or slide forward on a dais while the musicians sat rigidly in rows on either side plucking the strings and thumping the bodies of their *samisens*, which were like barometrical instruments capable of registering violent changes of temperature. The dancer swayed to the rhythm of the plectrum with a robe trailing behind him, for he was a female interpreter. The succession of graceful poses with hieratic outlines and gleaming patterns of brocade; the collaboration of body and costume in continuous rhythm, sleeves whirling to and fro or over the elaborate head-dress; the symbolical flutter of the fan, accompanied by drums and flutes – all this swept one back into an age that combined barbarity with sophisticated art.

Fukusuke Nakamura the Second was the dancer-heroine's name and he was sixty-four years old, but age had not withered him nor custom staled the variety of his poses. He was descended from a long line of famous Kabuki interpreters who had been trained with a religious respect for their profession. In a sense they were true scholars, for their art required systematic study and concentration, and though its rules were exacting they made it appear spontaneous.

The rival heroine of the matinée, Kichiemon Nakamura, was about ten years younger, and his performance was beautiful to watch even though its full meaning escaped me. No masks were worn as in the Nō drama, but many technical details were derived from Nō, which deals more with phantoms than with creatures of flesh and blood. And the music was ghost-like, keening for a dead lover or husband or child, lamenting a love unrequited. Spirits of water, moonlight, flowers and trees, malignant or hungry demons, were evoked by the musician-mediums. The *hana-michi* or flower ways, raised gangplanks prolonging the stage and serving for the entrances and exits of the actors, enabled one to inspect the latter in all their panoply as at a fashion parade.

Having brought the theatre programme into my hotel dining-room, I caused a twitter of curiosity among the swallowlike maids who hovered round my table. 'You like?' chirped one much bolder than the rest, perhaps due to her slight knowledge of English. 'Very much. *Banzai!*' I replied, which sent the girls into a chorus of giggles. Perhaps my pronunciation of Kichiemon and Fukusuke Nakamura made them giggle even more. Their amusement lightened an otherwise dull repast. They were cuddly little creatures, I thought, and they seemed to know it. It was easy to understand that they might be habit-forming.

The matinée had given me a glimpse of the world described in *The Tale of Genji*. It was also Utamaro's prints in slow and rapid motion. The floating sleeves and patterns of the dancers reminded one how much Toulouse-Lautrec and Art Nouveau had borrowed from Japanese designs. Their acme of refinement was a thing to cherish amid the squalor of industrial progress. Reverting to *The Tale of Genji*, it was not surprising that Arthur Waley, whose translation had made it live for non-Japanese, could not face the drab reality of modern Japan. Why embark on such a voyage when he carried the atmosphere of its golden age within himself?

Much as I had enjoyed it visually the theatre alone could not compensate for the militant psychosis whose miasma poisoned the social and political background, and I was not sorry to sail

13

away on the *Empress of Canada*. Not sorry yet none too happy, for I expected war in Europe at any moment. I might not arrive in time.

The posse of merrymakers on board who danced the oafish Lambeth Walk and thumped the piano till the early hours kept me awake as much as my gloomy thoughts. I spent the day writing introspective letters which I hope were destroyed by their recipients. I began to miss the presence of Chinese people around me as if I were short of oxygen. The sights and sounds of their old capital rose before me like a mirage when I gazed at the mono-tonous sea, which was hard to recognize as the Pacific Ocean from this floating hotel.

Midway across we stopped at Honolulu, which I have always associated with my favourite cousin Louise. She entertained half the world at her La Pietra, named after my home in Florence where she had married Walter Dillingham. Many Hawaiians wished to visit our La Pietra purely on her account, and some imagined that our villa was a replica of hers or vice versa. In fact there was a difference of some six hundred years between the two structures. Hers was built by David Adler, the Chicago architect, of pale pink stone on one side of Diamond Head, a volcano long extinct, and the garden was graced with Venetian statues found by my father: its effect was Italianate. Formerly there had been a temple dedicated to Ku, the Hawaiian god of power, on the slopes of Diamond Head, and Louise enjoyed her power as a hostess. Blessed with exceptional energy, she required a minimum of sleep. Soon after her marriage a friend remarked: 'Louise will make a trip round the island before breakfast, but what will she do after that?' Her husband, a pioneer of local railroads, dredging and engineering construction as well as a fine horseman, was a perfect mate for her but even he could not keep pace with her social activities.

La Pietra was described in the Press as 'an international celebrity centre' from which Walter often played truant at a distant ranch where he could indulge his passion for polo with-out interruption. Louise could only appear at this ranch by special invitation. Whereas Walter hated leaving Hawaii, Louise paid frequent visits to Europe. If she had a failing, it was an inability to relax, an itch to be in half a dozen places at once, a fear of missing something more sensational round the corner. She rose at six with a pile of letters for the post, dived into the swimming-pool and played a brisk round of tennis before breakfast, then off and away to her various engagements such as the Parks Board, the Garden Club, Outdoor Circle, Hawaii Citizens Council for Community Service to International Visitors, and others in which she let off superfluous steam.

In my despondent mood Louise would have been a tonic, but she had flown to London and taken Walter with her. Their Japanese factotum Sigita looked after me while their eldest son Lowell held the family fort. Sigita drove me to Mount Tantalus to enjoy the spectacular view and he loaded me with juicy mangoes. I gathered that he had no desire to return to his native land. The mixed population diffused an air of placid contentment. The pure Hawaiians excelling in aquatic sports assembled in the vicinity of Waikiki beach where the tourists pullulated. They rode the surf with hibiscus in their hair and taught blond Americans to do the same. They strummed on ukuleles and light-heartedly broke hearts. Not ineptly were they called the gigolos of the sea.

Again the aquarium thrilled me, especially the Samoan reef fish, deep blue with golden dorsals, the flat silvery moon-fish and grotesque balloon-fish, but the names of other creatures with iridescent spots and ruby eyes, with pink and yellow stripes, with huge fins and long-drawn filaments have slipped my memory, though they are the most marvellous of their kind and to painters, one might suppose, a source of inspiration. Very soothing after the sea voyage were the banyans, palms and jacaranda trees in the park surrounding the aquarium. Their green beauty flourished without self-consciousness yet their foliage and blossom seemed individual, even friendly, and I wished there were chlorophyll in human beings to make them flourish at regular intervals. As for me, I felt jaded and faded. Evidently I appeared so to my cousins, athletic Lowell, heir to the Dillingham Corporation, and his slender little wife. Lowell reminded me of the industry and enterprise behind Honolulu's frivolous façade. It must require great mastery of mind over matter to set one's nose to the grindstone where the whole of nature conspired to tempt one to idle contemplation. I fear I should soon become a beachcomber in such a place.

Departures from Hawaii are traditionally theatrical, with a band playing *Aloha Oe* and everybody wreathed in necklaces of flowers, some six in a row – so absurd on paunchy business men in goggles – handkerchiefs waving and wiping tears: adieu to the taste of undiluted honey! For all was scent and sweetness in that indolent air – on the surf-riding surface, remote from war and rumours of war, its great harbour named after a pearl. Yet in spite of the opulence of flora it struck me that the freedom and ease of daily life had less flavour here than in a colder clime, though Somerset Maugham would have picked up plenty of material for stories on the beach of Waikiki. The atmosphere was too loaded with languor for creative art to flourish. It was the realm of the picture postcard in excelsis. Tourists were necessary to the economy of the island and they were glutted with illusions of nostalgic romance.

As we slid away from the wharf, the men cracked jokes and the women smiled ruefully. The rest of the voyage to Vancouver was enlivened by extrovert friends who had joined the ship. I watched the daily log with growing interest: day's run 484 miles, average speed 20·61 knots. Clocks were advanced thirty minutes at midnight. There was still the whole of Canada and the Atlantic to be crossed before I reached London and I spent most of the time revising the Chinese plays I had translated with Chou I-min, an occupation that seemed futile in view of the inevitability of war. Who would bother about Chinese plays when the bombing started? Yet I clung to my task as to a floating spar: through its medium my mind could range in the China my body had left.

Having associated Canada with coolness I was astounded by

16

the heat of Vancouver. I caught a train to Banff which was relatively cool, but the scenery, perhaps because it was too virginal, made less impression on me than the huge bears which assembled near a rubbish dump at evening. There they scooped empty tins with long tongues and gambolled with each other so happily that it was hard to believe in their ferocity. More ferocious must have been the popular baiting of these animals chained to stakes and worried by dogs – 'a sport very pleasant to see', according to an Elizabethan. From Calgary I flew to Montreal where the heat became more oppressive; thence to Quebec to board the *Empress of Britain*.

I was amazed by the complexity of many Canadians who appeared quite simple and straightforward on the surface: their mixed or varied British, American and French strains had confused their sense of national identity. Like chameleons they could assume the colour of their background yet they seemed basically insecure, with sympathies shifting between England, France and the U.S.A. and curious chips on their shoulders. The speech of the French Canadians sounded quaintly provincial, a survival, perhaps, of early Colonial days.

2

Except for a short interval I had been absent from London for seven years, but it might have been since yesterday, so little change could I detect in my friends, all of whom were easily accessible.

Evelyn Waugh had remarried and settled down to the domesticity he had always wanted. His wife seemed hardly more than a child with celestial trusting eyes; she preferred country to town life and she belonged to the Catholic communion. Hers was the tranquil charm of an early Millais portrait. This marriage restored Evelyn's equanimity, which had been rudely shaken through a period of sour celibacy.

He had travelled to distant lands during the last restive decade and had produced sparkling books of impressions which were distilled with more subtle art through the medium of his novels. *Remote People* was the rough canvas for *Black Mischief*. *A Handful of Dust* was the consummate fruit of that period. He took his fame for granted without the vanity of most successful authors. Avoiding the publicity of literary congresses, he preferred the society of his Oxford cronies, whose foibles continued to amuse him. His personal privacy was sacrosanct and he made no effort to court popularity with strangers. He was his sprightly self again though stouter in build and his Catholicism, a rather special brand, had made him more uncompromising.

Morals mattered more to Evelyn than to certain other religious novelists of our age: he did not dissociate them from faith. Hence his vigour as a satirist. During his vagrant years the Church had been his only solid anchor. Perhaps because we had been best men at his first ill-fated wedding, Robert Byron and I had fallen from grace when he wished to cancel its memory. Now that the wound was healed he recovered his original bonhomie and we laughed as happily together as in our undergraduate days.

John Sutro was immersed in film production. Many of us regretted the absorption of so life-enhancing a companion in a milieu too coarse to appreciate the extraordinary versatility of his talents. Was he not too sensitive to cope with the ruthless paladins of the film industry? However, the complicated negotiations and intrigues of that hectic underworld appealed to his temperament: they split his existence but not his personality. Whenever he could spare time for his friends it was a feast of delightful surprises. He sang, he extemporized, he invented Rabelaisian fantasies and created new heroes of fiction, he conducted imaginary orchestras, radio discussions and farcical dialogues by telephone. So spontaneous was his genius that he could seldom repeat himself. Much depended on his mood. He was the first to forget his extravagant inventions, and alas, the recording angel was too submerged in laughter to record them for posterity.

My brother William, sociable and gregarious by fits and starts, had settled in a large studio in Tite Street to paint portraits of all the reigning beauties who would pose for him, and I stayed with him there till my presence became irksome.

So strong was the desire for peace that the subject of war was avoided, yet the cloud was above us growing blacker every day. Robert Byron was the loudest Cassandra among my friends. Since his visit to the Nuremberg Rally he had no illusions about the Nazi menace: he could talk of little else. Tiresomely tactless, scoffed Chamberlain's supporters, cry havoc, wolf wolf! Bleached and baggy-eyed with exasperation, he was building an air-raid shelter in his garden. Already he had provided himself with a tin helmet and a gas-mask. This brought one back to reality with a jolt. In Federal Union he saw hope for the future and he embraced the idea with his usual energy, addressing cosmopolitan gatherings like a hot gospeller. Unfortunately he was too choleric to make a good speaker: a calmer delivery would

19

have been more persuasive. The federal solution seems more plausible now, since even in Africa groups of states are in process of organization.

My old friend Miss Constable who frequented mediums with 'clairvoyant' powers and firmly believed in a sixth sense which she shared with blind bats – such a contrast with her majestic self – smiled incredulously when I mentioned war. 'Thoughts are things,' she retorted. 'If nobody thinks of war there will be no war. After all these years – why, it's at least ten years since I last saw you – I happened to be thinking of you this morning and here you are back from China! So it's all crystal clear and perfectly simple. Don't even dream of such a thing as war.' And it was futile to argue with one who imagined that Hitler was a misunderstood idealist and that we should 'go to meet him half-way'. The majority seemed to share this delusion.

The porter of my brother's studio held séances in the basement which he invited me to attend. Here too a Cockney spirit announced a long period of peace. 'I see doves, 'undreds and 'undreds of white doves, over Germany like over Britain', it said. 'The air is thick with them, and all of them cooing for joy. Peace in our time. No fear of Armageddon.'

When I called on Robin de la Condamine, who lived round the corner from Tite Street, he assured me with his emphatic stammer that war had gone the w-way of the ich-thyo-s-saurus. Robin, whose stage name was Robert Farquharson, was our last great actor in the Irving tradition. His house reminded me of *À Rebours*, for it was crammed with objects reflecting his curious temperament. Some of these I remembered from his Florentine apartment, alabaster bowls of semi-precious stones, rose quartz and smoky topaz and iridescent black amber from Catania illuminated by electric bulbs. The amber he described as resin from Hell's volcanoes – 'I bought it when I was down there on a visit.' He would stroke it sensuously and make purring sounds.

'Wh-why do you keep cut flowers in v-vases?' he had asked my mother. 'Cut flowers are such dead things. You should scatter stones on your dinner-table. Stones are so p-palpitatingly alive!'

20

He had given a performance as Herod in Wilde's *Salomé* which had won the eulogies of Max Beerbohm, Robert Ross, and other friends of the author; and Herod's catalogue of the jewels he promised the perverse princess must have haunted him when he indulged in such paradoxes. My mother thought him a fearful *poseur* but I was thankful for the strange variety he introduced. At least he was consistent in his poses. He delighted in causing embarrassment, as when he limped up to Mrs George Keppel in the street and exclaimed: 'Thank you, thank you so much!' 'What on earth for?' Mrs Keppel asked him curtly. 'For being you,' he replied with a libidinous leer.

Some people maintained that his lameness and his stammer were affectations and it was rumoured that he had collected club-foot boots until he developed a club-foot himself – or was it a hidden hoof? Neither his stammer nor his lameness was noticeable on the stage. He specialized in difficult psychotic roles. His Count Cenci was a terrifying monster of Renaissance corruption; his Emperor Paul of Russia was a memorable recreation of that sadistic tyrant, yet I have never seen a more moving Uncle Vanya.

Vividly real in the theatre, in private life he had an air of unreality. Not an easy person to live with, one inferred, yet his servants adored him in London as in Florence, where a toothless crone who waited at his table called him the *Signorino* or young master. Partly in order to shock his guests – he cultivated the prim and proper for the pleasure of shocking them – he would cover her with kisses while she wriggled and protested with the shrillness of a ravished virgin. Her withered cheeks were stained with lipstick in consequence. '*Che birichino!*' she would croak as if he were a naughty urchin. His pranks were often childish. A small ante-room adjoined his drawing-room. 'Let's pretend that this is the *salone*,' he said, 'as I'm expecting John Audley.' Mr Audley was very fat and when he was ushered in he was invited to sit on a tiny chair, puffing and panting with evident discomfort.

'How do you like my apartment?' Robin inquired.

'Very pretty,' spluttered Mr Audley, squinting with startled eyes. Then Robin flung open the double doors into a spacious room fragrant with Oriental incense. He played a brisk air by Scarlatti before luncheon was served. Robin could sing as well as play the piano, and his rendering of German *lieder*, Scottish border ballads and the songs of Yvette Guilbert was supremely dramatic.

He had published a single book, *The Upper Garden*. It begins: 'In those days which are consecutive, so as to give light or memory to each other, and to which men give one name of Life or another name of Death, beyond the garden bright with tulip-cups or poised with the gloom of rose-bowers, there is, in some moods, a new delight of dark trees and dark ponds, or tangled colours that were not set against each other in the war of the known gardens – a competition that often gives no greater suggestion to a garden than the war of life.' And it rambles on in the same strain for 264 close-written pages. How or why he accomplished this *tour de force* is a mystery I have never been able to solve. It was a book, he explained, not about gardening but rather about what a garden means to the artist, the wanderer, the saint and the student, since the time of the Garden of Eden. Perhaps it will be resurrected by some student of recondite literature who may unravel its message. Combining the sound of Walter Pater with the sense of Gertrude Stein, it is unquestionably a book for the few.

Robin had the charm of novelty, for one could not foretell how he would behave. The novelty was also due to the fact that he was a complete anachronism. He belonged to the eighteen-nineties and he had scarcely changed since his stuttering had given me the giggles in early childhood. His hair was fluffed out and dyed and his cheeks were improbably pink yet he wore shaggy suits of homespun with crinkly silk shirts and Liberty ties he purchased at Oxford, perhaps because they made him feel like an undergraduate. After a fitting at Hall's he would limp to the botanical garden opposite Magdalen to ponder among the cacti.

Though it was rumoured that he had sold his soul to the Devil to preserve his youth, one could not guess his age. He could look thirty or seventy. His best friends were of the same vintage: Courtenay Thorpe and Tom Kennion, copartners with the actress May Pardoe in an antique shop called Parkenthorpe, were as *fin-de-siècle* as Robin. Courtenay Thorpe went about with a poodle attached by a pink ribbon to his gloved wooden hand. Bernard Shaw had admired his 'remarkable feat' of playing Helmer in *A Doll's House* in the afternoon and the Ghost in *Hamlet* the same evening: off the stage he resembled the ghost of a dandy drawn by Beardsley. He made generous bequests to Robin and Tom Kennion when he died. Tom told me that Robin had a profitable flair for deathbed visits. He grumbled about it with some bitterness, and there was a temporary rift between them after Thorpe's demise.

Death was often in Robin's conversation when his mood was merry. When a notorious tippler died Robin asked innocently: 'Will the funeral start from Doney's or from Giacosa's?' – the fashionable tea-shops in Via Tornabuoni where more whisky than tea was served to the best customers. 'What a comfort to survive one's chums,' he remarked. 'They sprouting daisies and we alive, alive oh!' He had survived a great many: the most devoted had been F. H. Balfour, an Old China Hand with a parchment complexion and occult interests. Balfour was said to receive messages from the moon in bamboo tubes which dropped out of the air wherever he happened to be. I believe it was Balfour who left him his Florentine apartment.

Kennion was like a giraffe with a wavy *toupet* and elaborate make-up. 'Some of the boys tease me about it,' he confessed in his languid drawl, fluttering his mauve-lidded eyes, 'but I tell them I do it for my pleasure, not for theirs. One's duty is to make the best of oneself for one's own sake, don't you agree?'

He had certainly succeeded in making himself conspicuous. His taste in furniture was more selective than Robin's but in other matters he was oddly puerile. He only cared to read novels written for boys: he devoured the works of Henty and *The Boys' Own Paper*. This preference was out of harmony with his

23

appearance and his bygone friendship with Oscar Wilde, who before taking him to dine with the Sphinx (Ada Leverson) had sent her a telegram describing him as 'tall as a young palm tree – I mean tall as two young palm trees'. But he was reticent about his juvenile escapades.

One of the attractions of his antique shop was its eclecticism: he had an entire Chinese bedroom. Old Lord Ripon was often to be found there dusting the porcelain and we would be offered jasmine tea in *famille rose* cups. If one admired an object he would answer modestly: 'Yes, it is rather amusing.' Amusing, intriguing, and jolly were the usual epithets he applied to his pieces – a form of understatement which must have been prevalent at the turn of the century. Now *objets d'art* are said to have 'authority', or to 'expand the senses', or 'compel the imagination', and a critic wrote recently of a producer of pop-art beer cans: 'For him the image is meaningful in its meaninglessness.'

Between Tom's weary lisp and Robin's urgent stammer one was transported to a sphere remote from Hitler's threats. I welcomed this reprieve from actuality. Kennion and Condamine were links with a less panic-stricken age.

'Why do you waste your time in London?' Robin asked me. 'The Medici claim you in Florence. Have you not noticed my resemblance to Lorenzo il Magnifico?'

'You have a rosier complexion,' I replied.

'He was young too. But tell me what brings you here?' I explained that I had returned to England to do my bit in the event of war.

'Your bit? What a desuete expression! You must have been reading Daddy Kipling. Surely we have discovered that victories are the same as defeats in their results.'

A pessimist in most matters, Robin was optimistic about the duration of peace.

My parents remained in Florence. As a lifelong resident my father was convinced that he would not be molested and his Italian friends thought Mussolini too canny to involve them in another war. His house, which was classified as a national monument, his art collection and the garden he had created were almost dearer to him than life, so he lent a willing ear to assurances that he could stay on in safety whatever happened. Having suffered no personal annoyance under the dictatorship he was vexed by my anti-Fascism, which might lead to trouble with the authorities. My mother shared my views but she was cautious for his sake. During the Czechoslovakian crisis she had flown to Switzerland but she had returned when the scare subsided. Her dependence on my father was complete.

Many foreign residents tolerated Mussolini in a 'live and let live' spirit. 'Let sleeping dogs lie . . .' But they would not lie: they shifted and snarled in their uneasy sleep. Mr Goad, the pious director of the British Institute, thought the Duce a grand fellow. When somebody objected that the brass tablet outside the Institute needed polishing he said it might be imprudent to provoke the young patriots. Mrs Strong, the *doyenne* of the British colony in Rome, had hailed Mussolini as another beneficent Caesar.

The British colony in Florence had dwindled since Sanctions, which had strengthened Fascist propaganda at home. The consequent growth of ill feeling was depressing for those of us who remembered our friendly relations with Italy since the Risorgimento.

While my father became more of a *campanilista*, indifferent to events beyond the vale of Arno, I felt more English in our predicament, but having spent most of my life abroad I could not feel at home in England. Fortunately I had no lack of social distraction. My friends gave me a festive welcome and the tradition of hospitality was intensely alive.

My translations of Chinese plays were being printed by Kelly and Walsh in Shanghai but I could not expect to interest my friends in them with such rare exceptions as Arthur Waley and Beryl de Zoete. Arthur was (and the pun is appropriate) the whale of Chinese translators: he was also a poet whose versions of Chinese and Japanese texts could be enjoyed for their own sake

25

as if the soul of, say, Po Chü-i or Lady Murasaki had entered into him and guided his pen.

Scholars seldom write good prose, let alone good poetry, and Arthur Waley was a scholar of painstaking precision totally dedicated to his task; not only a linguist but a cultural historian familiar with the background of his subject throughout the centuries. An Assistant Keeper in the British Museum after graduating from Cambridge, he had taught himself without going to the Far East. Of average height, lean and clean-shaven with a mystical expression, he would gaze obliquely into the distance, and suddenly turn when one spoke to him. What he said was always to the point, a sharp arrow, but it often put a stop to conversation. His verbal output was minimal. Obliterating any kind of small talk, his staccato directness could be intimidating but I soon got used to it with Beryl de Zoete as a lightning conductor.

Beryl, who lived with Arthur on the top floor of 50 Gordon Square, seemed as ageless as Robin de la Condamine, who called her 'Baby Beryl', but she had travelled far while Arthur stayed at home. If Arthur went abroad it was to ski in Switzerland or Norway; Beryl roamed through Morocco, Bali, India and Ceylon in quest of the local dances for which her enthusiasm was unquenched and unquenchable. Her books about Indian and Balinese dancing are unique. Fully conscious of their merit, she was disappointed by their reception, but what could one expect of this Philistine age? The success of her beloved Arthur's books, which owed much to her critical sympathy, was a partial compensation. Though she did not care to be identified with Bloomsbury she was very much of it: Virginia, Vanessa, Duncan, Clive, Morgan, Lytton, Carrington, Bunny, Roger, were the protagonists of her private mythology. Nearly all of them had come from Cambridge like Arthur, who enjoyed their idiosyncrasies like a puppet show. Having met a few of them under the aegis of Lady Ottoline Morrell at Garsington when I was an undergraduate, I was amazed to hear of their amorous paroxysms. According to Beryl, they exchanged beds like musical chairs with a promiscuity unheard of in Florence or Peking. No doubt it was an expression of that frankness which they considered a social duty by reaction to their Victorian parents.

Beryl and Arthur lived so frugally that one might have thought them impecunious, which was far from being the case. Dr Hu Shih, the brilliantly bilingual philosopher who became Chinese Ambassador to Washington, told me of his astonishment when he was invited to dine with Arthur. Having donned full evening dress he found his host in shirt sleeves preparing a dinner, exiguous by Chinese standards, over a gas-ring. Beryl was absent, to Dr Hu's regret, and Arthur cross-questioned him about the sources of certain Zen Buddhist texts. Of the two I felt Arthur was the truer Buddhist, informal and other-worldly in his ways, and I was grateful to him for assuring me that my translations had not been a waste of effort. He asked me to read them aloud and offered crisp valuable suggestions.

When I rang the door-bell Arthur's head popped out of a top floor window and if he were busy he would throw out a key, but usually he ran down the stairs to let me in. The stairs were steep and I marvelled at his agility in racing up them without losing breath. He was a strenuous walker and skiing was his favourite sport. Eurhythmics kept Beryl limber: she had been a pupil of Dalcroze and taught his methods to children. Moreover she had won prizes at the Hammersmith Palais de Danse and vied with Moroccan dancing girls in the *Quartier Réservé* of Casablanca, where a friend assured me that her performance of the *danse de ventre* put the professionals to shame despite their disparity of age.

Since her sojourn in Bali, she was more attracted to the similar dances of South India and Ceylon than to those of the Western ballet companies she criticized in the *New Statesman*. Dancing is perhaps the most difficult of the arts to describe, especially when it is the expression of an alien culture, yet Beryl was so sensitive to its magic that she succeeded where most had failed.

While we crouched under the shadow of war Ram Gopal regaled us with a selection of Indian dances at the Aldwych. The music was mostly supplied by gramophone records but there was a drummer who extracted wonderful rhythms from his simple instrument, ranging from the soft patter of raindrops to rapid heart-beats and the rolling of thunder; there was also a veena player who created an ethereal mood. At present the Beatles are popularizing some of these sound effects, but even then I felt sure that Western music would be enriched by them. Some knowledge of the Hindu epics is required to absorb the full meaning of Indian dancing since Siva Nataraja 'danced the world into being'. The grace of Spanish fingers clicking castanets, the perfect timing of their heel-taps in limited space, is pure art for art's sake, but the eloquence of the Indian *mudras* is divine: here sexual and devotional symbolism is interwoven on a higher plane and the body becomes an instrument for the expression of something beyond itself. If rapture could be taught, that is what our dancers should learn from the Indians. Gravity too, the majestic gravity of supernatural beings. But Siva and Vishnu, Rama and Sita, seemed barbaric folk-lore figures to the devotees of Wagner's gods and goddesses. My friends who were pilgrims to Bayreuth were repelled by what they called 'indigestible Indian curry' and my efforts to convert them failed. But with Beryl and Arthur I often watched Krishna and listened to his flute in the heart of London. Sometimes we joined Ram Gopal for supper after the performance. With his lustrous jet-black eyes, flowing raven hair, his slender figure in a close-fitting Indian jacket, he was conscious of being a cynosure, but I doubt if he would attract attention among the longer-haired denizens of modern Chelsea.

In her own flat Beryl's diet was of the simplest; she and Arthur seemed mainly to subsist on Ovaltine and dry biscuits. But when she was taken to a restaurant Beryl was apt to be pernickety and exacting: invariably she demanded some dish not on the bill of fare or yak's milk as an aperitif. Most meat was anathema to her on the pretext that it was her 'totem animal'. At the Café Royal she ordered in vain those 'freshly-baked hoppers filled with honey' which she found so toothsome in Ceylon, and at a cocktail party she asked for 'a vivid heart-shaped leaf with one green orange' which had also refreshed her during Sinhalese ceremonies. Her aversion to meat was probably due to her horror of blood sports. When a big game hunter was boasting of a tiger he had shot she exclaimed: 'How despicable!' Wild life above all was worthy of preservation: Blake's tiger burning bright, the wise elephant, the graceful stag. . . . Though I ate meat I could not help sympathizing with her unsporting instincts.

Ram Gopal considered her too patronizing. Her repeated rhapsodies over Uday Shankar must have grated on him for they were ill-timed, however true. And Beryl was possessive: she tried to appropriate the people she liked and keep them under her wing. She was wont, as Berenson put it, 'to stake a claim'. If she liked a house, apart from its proprietor, she resolved to stay there indefinitely. Her charm wore off when she became a fixture. Paola Olivetti had to move out of her villa as a gentle hint, but Beryl lingered there unabashed till the cook announced it was time for his annual holiday.

Arthur's extreme patience with her struck me as angelic, especially when she grew older and more quixotic. But theirs was a happy and lasting attachment. They shared an intense curiosity about primitive cultures and sophisticated hybrids. They wished to preserve the primitive cultures while reforming their material conditions. Rather muddled by Marx, they spoke of 'the rich' with Biblical contempt, which did not prevent them from consorting with their most affluent votaries. Beryl dropped the names of Evan Tredegar, Stephen Tennant and the Elmhirsts with a special proprietary unction. Both were devout admirers of Edith Sitwell who said that Arthur was one of the three people who really understood her poetry, and it was in Edith's flat that I met them originally. Beryl's cooing voice covered Arthur's silences like a cloak.

I spent many an evocative hour in their Gordon Square eyrie. Here Arthur shook off his aloofness and discoursed on the abstruse subjects that absorbed him until they assumed topicality. Being partly Jewish, his anxiety about Hitler went too deep to endure the usual political palaver. 'A typhoid carrier, that is the thing to be,' he remarked of the Nazis and left it at that. Lion-hunting hostesses failed to tempt him from his ivory tower unless they could offer him music. He would leave a party to listen to a concert on the B.B.C. Third Programme.

Though I was no lion and too old for a cub, I was privileged to be treated like one by certain hostesses, perhaps because I was talkative by nature. The genuine lions are silent when they are not roaring. When I am told that I talk better than I write the compliment leaves me cold. I was brought up to contribute my share to conversation at the risk of uttering platitudes, and in China the exchange of platitudes was essential to social inter-course. *Il faut savoir s'ennuyer.*

I am inclined to think that these were the last days of the great London hostesses who preferred quality to quantity and ostentation, and I would choose Lady Cunard and Lady Colefax as their leading representatives. Both could blend politicians with poets, painters, novelists, economists and musicians, but they were very different. Since her husband's death and financial losses Lady Colefax had moved into a small house in Lord North Street where she still entertained her guests on a reduced scale. Like Madame Geoffrin, she was essentially kind and cosy, but one was too conscious of her hankering after the latest off-the-record news, whether of a divorce or what Hitler had really said to Mr Chamberlain, which induced restlessness rather than relaxation. She practised Wilde's dictum that conversation should touch on everything but should concentrate on nothing. If one happened to be engaged in a lively discussion she was bound to interrupt. 'You must come over and meet So-and-so. He has just flown back from Nepal.' Reluctantly one was whisked away.

To collect celebrities is hard work, involving the dispatch of invitations and reminders, of telegrams and frequent telephone calls, and Lady Colefax supplemented her income by other hard work as an interior decorator. She had penned so many postcards that her script had become a cursive shorthand which only initiates could decipher. But the celebrities of the moment thronged her house and she kept them on the hop. To me this was an amusing spectacle. I admired the drive and determination of our hostess, insatiable of every branch of knowledge. One left her house stimulated rather than appeased. For all her affability there was something impersonal about her, as if she invited one more for one's reputation – whatever that might be – than for one's real self.

With Lady Cunard one never had this sensation. I owed much to her. She had been at the centre of my existence before I went to China and she was far the most attractive of my older friends in London, imaginative, witty, warm-hearted and capable of profound affection. Like Horace Walpole she viewed the world as 'a comedy to those that think, a tragedy to those that feel'. Her appearance was exquisite in an original way, like a brilliant humming-bird. The bird simile is inescapable for she had, as George Moore wrote, 'the bright eyes of a bird, and she is instinctive and courageous as a sparrow-hawk'.

How mistakenly she was judged by people who only knew her superficially! Virginia Woolf described her in her diary as 'a ridiculous little parrokeet-faced woman; but not sufficiently ridiculous', and as 'a stringy old hop-o'-my-thumb'. 'Coarse and usual and dull these Cunards and Colefaxes are,' she exclaimed, 'for all their astonishing competence in the commerce of life.' Yet she admitted that Lady Cunard made her feel that she was 'now among the well-known writers' – surely a comfortable sensation. Those who caricatured her were eager enough to accept her invitations.

Harold Nicolson describes her in his diary as 'looking like a third-dynasty mummy painted pink by amateurs', and according to Lord Vansittart she was 'a small bright-coloured woman who had begun to enforce upon society the notice which she intended'. But George Moore, who had been an intimate friend for forty years, wrote of her: 'She had the indispensable quality of making me feel I was more intensely alive when she was by me than I was when she was away.' Throughout his letters to her one is aware of her enduring vitality, 'the magic apple which however much one eats of it never grows less'. And it was no small tribute to her 'genius to make a work of art out of life itself' that the ageing novelist, who was the most candid of beings, continued to pay her from first to last. When he died in 1933 he left her his most valued possessions.

No, neither Lady Cunard nor Lady Colefax, who was as Martha to her Mary, was ever coarse or dull, and Lady Cunard was certainly not usual. I agreed with George Moore, though I had not known her in her youth. For me too she was the incarnate spring. Paradoxically, the states of consciousness most esteemed by the 'Bloomsberries' and defined by their philosophical mentor G. E. Moore (no connection of the novelist) as the pleasures of human intercourse and the enjoyment of beautiful objects, were of equal importance to Emerald Cunard. If she succeeded in enforcing anything upon society, it was a wider appreciation of music, grand opera and ballet. She civilized those whom Matthew Arnold called The Barbarians (in *Culture and Anarchy*). And she achieved it so lightly that they were not aware of the transformation in themselves. To help the young writers she admired she would buy a dozen of their books at a time and recommend them to ambassadors and statesmen and others beyond their ken – an active form of encouragement all too rare.

The bias against her that trickles through memoirs and diaries may partly be due to her American origin, which is often resented by the British bourgeoisie. She flouted our insular prejudices and mocked the pomposities of our politicians whom she loved to tease and goad into indiscretions. Harold Nicolson relates a typical instance when she remarked to Eden, fresh from a Cabinet meeting in 1935: 'Anthony, you are all wrong about Italy. Why should she not have Abyssinia?' Such queries delivered in her sprightly manner might start the ball rolling in unpredictable directions and from what was said or not said one might guess which way the wind was blowing across the Channel. Nobody else could do this so spontaneously. 'Tiberius must have been charming. Why are so many historians against him?' I remember her asking.

Brisk yet belated – only her unpunctuality was usual – she

32

would flutter into a room and dispel the stuffiness and the fog which were in danger of settling on a mixed bag of prudent politicians and diplomats waiting like seals to be fed. She was always worth waiting for, a scented breeze of welcome.

> 'Like the notes of a fiddle, she sweetly, sweetly
> Raises the spirits, and charms our ears.'

'Very glad about everything' she seemed to Harold Nicolson. Even if she were not, she made her guests feel that she was pleased to see them and introduced them to each other in aphoristic phrases, putting each at his ease and creating a before-the-curtain atmosphere. Her door was open to the younger generation as well as to those who were established in their careers.

One of the few younger people of talent she failed to propitiate was her daughter Nancy, and the irony of it was that in many ways they were similar. Nancy became more like her mother as she grew older. But the society her mother adorned was hateful to her: in politics she became pro-Communist and anti-American, except for the coloured population whose rights she upheld with vehemence, vented in her diatribe *Black Man – White Ladyship* and in a massive *Negro Anthology*.

Perhaps the daughters of prominent hostesses are apt to feel like unwanted guests at home. Left to the care of governesses, they nurse grudges along with their dolls. I suspect that Emerald did not devote enough time to Nancy during her childhood and allowed her too much freedom as a débutante during the First World War. Freudians would offer other explanations but this one appears the most plausible. Emerald was not cast for a mother's role but I was sure that she loved her daughter and admired her talents. Doubtless she had dreamed of a different life for her, a common convention of the unconventional. Too late she woke up to realize that Nancy had developed a personality as strong as her own. In the Paris of Ernest Hemingway Nancy flung herself into a Left Bank *vie de Bohème* among writers and painters who exploited her generosity and, ultimately, Emerald's.

D

33

Her affair with Aragon brought her in contact with the Surrealists and the *avant-garde* of the twenties; and love led the way to a romanticized Communism. Abhorring the obvious, she detected beauty invisible to others; with rare exceptions she chose lovers whose virtues were only apparent to herself. In spite of her foot-loose-and-fancy-free existence she was more intolerant than her mother; she had the hard puritanical core of an extremist.

'It's a case of diamond cut diamond,' Norman Douglas used to say. But Emerald's hardness was superficial – a vizard worn against her enemies, who came out into open battle over the marriage of King Edward VIII. Being a friend of the controversial couple, she was accused of acting as go-between. Feeling ran so high that she was hissed at a private party. Nancy would have relished that occasion. The breach between mother and daughter was permanent. Yet Nancy's charm and grace, her manner, voice and speech, were all derived from 'Her Ladyship', whom she ridiculed but could not help resembling. In spite of the rupture each would ask me for news of the other in a seemly casual way, as if I were a subconscious link between them. During the civil war Nancy had been drawn to Spain and she was still agitating against Franco when I returned from China.

In the meantime Emerald was preparing to leave the mansion in Grosvenor Square where she had galvanized London society and she was distributing most of its contents among her friends with a premonition perhaps that the days of great hospitable houses were over. If she felt sad at the prospect she never betrayed it, and she continued to entertain the friends she really cared for. I could not but think of Madame Ranevsky in Tchekov's *Cherry Orchard* – a play which Emerald defended as a masterpiece against the dramatic critic of the *Daily Express*, who had dismissed it as silly, tiresome and boring.

How insipid were other London drawing-rooms compared to Emerald's! Here one was surrounded by the most vivid people, for Emerald made them vivid. That many belonged to the sphere of fashion was held against them by prigs, but fashion and art are related, as the Parisians were the first to realize. There was no gambling, but there was often music and always conversation. Her friends were too varied to be called a coterie and if they had influence it was chiefly in the realm of art. She was the only consistent patron of musical talent in London and she remained the strongest supporter of opera and Sir Thomas Beecham, who strove to make it a national institution.

Like Madame du Deffand she enjoyed the novels of Richardson and Fielding and eighteenth-century literature: she brought one as close to that polished age as it was possible to be in 1939. Her lightness of touch amid the general doldrums often struck me as heroic. Long after I had gone to bed I would be startled by her voice on the telephone quoting Theocritus from Grosvenor Square. Had anybody else done this I might have been nettled, but now that war was so ominously near the lilt of her voice was a comfort. She might have discussed the Nazi–Soviet pact or some topic equally futile since neither of us could affect the course of such events. Instead she discussed the style of Lord Hervey, the character of Queen Caroline, the translators of Greek poetry, reminding one at three o'clock in the morning that art was eternal.

To name the *habitués* of 7 Grosvenor Square who had the gift of dispelling black humours at this period would swell these pages into a social chronicle, yet some stand out in such high relief that they are essential to any evocation of Emerald's atmosphere, in particular those three Graces of superlative wit and beauty, Lady Diana Cooper, Venetia Montagu and Phyllis de Janzé.

Sir Thomas Beecham, humming to himself or tapping on a table, was the most privileged of the masculine visitors but he was a little too aloof to be popular with other guests. The immaculate Chips Channon buzzed in with the ultimate in gossip. Lord Berners bubbled over with private jokes and farcical inventions. A gleaming monocle livened the conventional mask he wore which might have belonged to a city magnate, and an abrupt manner concealed his shyness. Had he been less versatile he would have been less charming but more profound.

Constantly changing his skin, as it were, he revelled in mystification. In his Rolls-Royce he had installed a spinet and a porcelain turtle; in a crowded restaurant he blew soap bubbles which floated in iridescent swarms from table to table; and he dyed his family of doves at Faringdon bright pink.

Like Max Beerbohm he spent much time and ingenuity 'improving' illustrations in books of memoirs, adding beards and bulbous noses where they were least expected. His music was satirical and had something in common with Satie's *Airs à faire fuir*. The 'Three Little Funeral Marches', for instance, which I had heard originally played for the all-but-human marionettes of the Roman *Teatro dei Piccoli*, parodied public pomp for the statesman, ill-repressed joy for the rich aunt, and genuine sorrow for the death of a canary. The *Valses Bourgeoises* for piano duet and the *Fantaisie Espagnole* for orchestra were also exuberant pastiches. Among his songs he rendered *Du bist wie eine Blume* as if it were addressed to a snow-white pig, whose grunts interrupt the gushes of Teutonic sentiment. At one time a rubber pig in feminine garb adorned his chimney-piece. When squeezed this would squeak, and its likeness to a gluttonous woman of our acquaintance was so uncanny that it was hard to restrain one's laughter when she flounced into the room, picking up a sandwich before dumping herself in a chair.

At Eton an affable master used to entertain the boys with concerts of rollicking old English ballads. His partner, Miss Beatrice Spencer, was incomparably arch when she recoiled from 'Foxy' Ferguson's advances with a coquettish 'Oh no John, no John, no-o John, no!' And there was another which ran, 'Dashing away with the smoothing iron she stole my heart away.' Occasionally their refrains return to me in the bathroom and I find myself warbling, 'I did but see her passing by, And yet I love her till I die.' Which sets me chuckling on the dullest of mornings. Gerald Berners recaptured the mood of these ditties in which the folksy element had been whittled for drawing-room consumption, adding extra salt and pepper.

His writings, especially *First Childhood*, had the same fresh humour, and his paintings at best remind one of early Corots. He was an inspired amateur whose talents conspired against each other. His flights of fantasy were an escape from melancholy: he laughed in order not to weep.

Another *habitué*, Sir Robert Abdy, was a highly individual connoisseur, tall and handsome, frozen with exasperation at the vanities of the vulgar rich – an exasperation that only Emerald could melt. Nicknamed Sir Bertram the Absolute for his categorical manner, his taste was more French than English. According to him the Rothschilds were the last and purest representatives of European royalty since they served meals on perfect Sèvres with a separate vintage wine to accompany each course. An adventurous interlude as an art dealer in New York was cut short by his refusal to sell to clients of whose taste he disapproved. He could only enjoy books that were beautifully printed and bound since he had bought a third folio Shakespeare at the age of twenty, paying all his available cash for it. But as the finest book productions are seldom the finest literature he had nourished his mind on a Russian salad of subjects ranging from heraldry to horticulture. The stock of strange facts he assimilated enhanced his powers of appreciation and kept him youthful, and his passion for the arts enabled him to bear cruel misfortune.

But even the inner circle of Emerald's friends would fill a tome, for as Lytton Strachey wrote of Madame du Deffand's, 'they led an existence in which the elements of publicity and privacy were curiously combined'.

Only the mindless boast that they are entirely free from melancholy. When the cloud threatened to envelop me I would visit Emerald Cunard. More than any man or woman I knew she could dissipate it in a few sparkling sentences. The art of pleasing or doing good to one another, wrote Fielding, is the art of conversation. Emerald led the society she moved in because she was a consummate mistress of this art, which Fielding also identified with 'good-breeding'.

3

Towards the end of August, 1939, the radio had become a
dreaded but necessary drug. It told of conscription, the evacuation
of women and children, air-raid shelters, gas-masks, the blackout,
and prepared stunned listeners for the wrath to come. There was
a forced geniality among one's acquaintances, but when by
chance one crossed them in the street they had gloomy tense
expressions.

I had posted my application to the War Office and I had asked
my friend Frank Oliver, who represented Reuter's, to buy my
house in Peking on my behalf: fortunately its owner, an impoverished descendant of the imperial Manchus, refused my
offer, but I had a long lease and hoped to return there eventually.
This hope buoyed me up in moments of dejection. My thoughts
embellished that haven of bliss and the many good friends I had
left there. Though the Japanese intended to drive other foreigners
out of China I could not believe they would do so permanently. It
was chiefly the foreign concessions that they were eager to grab,
and they were waiting for their opportunity.

Nobody present will forget the 'Please stand by for an important announcement' on the morning of September 3rd and
Chamberlain's mournful speech, followed by those siren wails to
which our ears were to grow so familiar. This was our first air-
raid warning, but in the calm that ensued no crash was audible.
Even if it was due to an error it was a dramatic emphasis of the
fact that we were at war. Personally I had anticipated a massive
bombardment by the Luftwaffe. Even after the All Clear our
nerves were a-jangle. Air-raid wardens in tin hats with policemen's rattles paced the empty streets which wore the usual

38

solemnity of a Sunday morning. Oscar Wilde and Whistler had both lived in Tite Street and I wondered what they would have thought of the times we lived in, and what they would have said in the circumstances. With regard to Mr Chamberlain Wilde might have repeated his remark that it is always with the best intentions that the worst work is done. Whistler might have praised the silvery tones of the barrage balloons and the blue nocturnes of the blackout. At first I did not mind the lack of illumination. Night had recovered its mystery and beauty. Now and then a torch flashed on, now nearer, now farther, added a certain excitement, lit up a cubistic vista, a couple of lovers kissing or a hag with a bottle of gin. Soho became Hogarthian again. But after a while one missed the illusory warmth of electricity.

I settled down to a protracted period of waiting, of filling up forms for all sorts of national service just in case one might lead to some useful occupation. The period was to be much longer than I bargained for, and it made me realize that Norman Douglas's introduction to *Alone* was scarcely exaggerated: in this respect there had been little progress since the last world war, for my own experiences of kicking my heels in Government offices were similar to Norman's.

Sir John Pratt was exceptionally amiable at the Ministry of Information. He had a face worth studying, as he bore a distinct resemblance to his brother Boris Karloff. He complimented me on my writings and we chatted about China, but he could not offer me a job. He promised to communicate with me if something suitable turned up. Elsewhere I was dismissed with perfunctory words which failed to inspire me with confidence.

'Why not wait till you're called up?' I was told at the War Office. At the age of thirty-five this was hardly encouraging. I decided then and there to join the R.A.F., but even so I was advised to wait on account of my special knowledge of the Far East.

The large windows of my brother's studio were papered and darkened to shut out any chink of light. His portrait of the Duchess of Kent stood proudly on an easel; other beauties among cornucopias of flowers, coral and sea-shells looked through the twilight like summer mermaids stranded on a wintry shore. But his palette and brushes were dry and he was in no mood for painting. He never admitted that he had been disappointed in his work but this became evident as time wore on and he never touched a canvas. He had recently developed an enthusiasm for things Indian and Beryl de Zoete fanned the flame. They studied Urdu together, and Beryl inspired him with her accounts of Kathakali dancers and the marvels of Malabar. The idea that the world is an illusion, that we are ourselves illusory, which was a leitmotiv of Indian dance-drama, appealed to his imagination and nourished his natural fatalism. Hence I pleaded in vain that he should apply his skill to military camouflage like Oliver Messel and other friends who were painters. I felt sure that he would find such an occupation congenial. No, he would wait till he was called up and serve in the ranks, and he begged me to stop nagging him about it.

William's habits and mine were so dissimilar that I sought a flat elsewhere. For an artist it might be normal to turn night into day but I was a light sleeper accustomed to rise early. What I considered the best part of the day he spent in bed; he would breakfast with the blackout and write page after page of rambling letters home as if he were living in a more leisurely century. Stimulated by benzedrine and black coffee, he struck others as exuberantly cheerful, but I realized that he was far from happy, devoured by a nostalgia for Italy of which he never spoke. We both felt more English than American or Italian yet here we were exiles, *désorientés*. By temperament my brother was Italian. How delighted he was when an almost legendary figure from our childhood appeared in his studio, for Tony Gandarillas had brought the fabulous Marchesa Casati to visit him – she for whom Bakst and Poiret had designed their most characteristic costumes before the First World War.

In Capri and in Venice, where she had occupied the unfinished Palazzo Venier dei Leoni, her entertainments had been spectacular, the guests announced by temple gongs while scented flames arose from braziers refuelled by half-naked slaves in honour of each arrival, herself a living statue with huge eyes ringed with kohl, sometimes with a macaw on her shoulder or a gibbon on an arm, followed by a barbaric attendant with a panther on a leash. The latter was serviceable in dispersing crowds. The Marchesa might have been invented by D'Annunzio: she seemed a character from *Il Piacere*. But now she had fallen on evil days and a handful of friends clubbed together to support her. My brother saw her as one of the Fates, he could not decide which.

'Meaningless as her flatteries were, they made me feel at home,' he wrote. 'As soon as she saw my paintings she said I was the *one* painter she had been looking for, and so forth. After the horror that Beltran y Masses did of her I thought she might well hope for something more encouraging. I had not expected such a heroic figure. Having heard so much about her forbidding affectations I found her positively cosy.'

The shimmering witch-balls and shell-shaped furniture in his studio appealed to her immensely. Soon she proposed that he take her as a paying guest. 'The very idea of it struck me as so comically fantastic and madly inconvenient that I was almost tempted to try it as an experience,' he said.

I hoped that she might induce him to add her portrait to his collection, even as a tragic travesty of her former self. Now, as he wrote, 'she always wears the same clothes, grey and black, a loose tailor-made version of an eighteenth-century lady's riding habit. When she sits down and forgets the movements of her legs the skirt opens up to the thigh exposing a leg which can hardly claim to be stockinged as the stocking is a cobweb of ladders and holes. The only colour she wears is in her wine-red velvet gloves trimmed with gold lace. She can be a brilliant talker though I fear she depends on stimulants. Her culture has a French polish to its natural robustness. I pressed her to stay to dinner but whatever she had taken previously had worn itself out during an hour's conversation and she said she felt ill and she looked rather lost and depleted.'

In her social heyday she had spoken little: her ambiguous silences had bewildered her Latin swains, who asked themselves, like Andrea Sperelli, the hero of *Il Piacere*: 'What was the real essence of this creature? Was she aware of her continuous metamorphosis, or was she impenetrable to herself, excluded from her own mystery? In her expressions how much was artifice and how much was spontaneity?' With advancing age she had grown more spontaneous while her artifice had been absorbed into *les paradis artificiels*. Those charity bazaars evoked by D'Annunzio, where patrician beauties sold at a premium pomegranates into which their pearly teeth had taken a bite, or champagne to be lapped from their cupped white hands, charging extra to gentlemen who offered their beards as napkins and were challenged to duels by their clean-shaven rivals in consequence – those fabulous bazaars had been replaced by dowdy jumble sales. The Casati belonged to the vanished *belle époque*. Lord Berners told me that when he had invited her to stay his mother had been captivated by her charm. 'I like her much better than your other foreign friends,' she said. But his guest had brought a python in a box and when it was let loose in her boudoir his mother changed her mind.

My brother happened to share this sympathy for snakes. He had introduced a tribe of them into our garden and occasionally I meet their shy progeny basking in the sun. They destroy pests and are said to be co-operative, but I cannot prevent the gardeners from killing them.

The lack of any patriotic employment had begun to prey on my mind. Perhaps my seven years in China were a stumbling-block? My other associations had been with Italy and America, though these had been weakened by absence from both countries. I was never an adept in wire-pulling. Painfully aware that I was wasting time in England, I fancied I might be of some use in Italy. Our relations with Italy had deteriorated since the conquest of Albania. In spite of a flattering reception, Mr Chamberlain's visit to Rome had been as negative as his visit to Berchtesgaden. But in spite of Mussolini the people of Italy were peace-loving: the masses had no enthusiasm for Hitler. During the Risorgimento we had been their friends, the Austro-Germans their enemies, but the sanctions we had promoted during the Abyssinian campaign had made many Italians forget this. Shouldn't we remind them of the links that had held us together since Britain was a province of Rome?

As an Anglo-Florentine I thought of all the English men and women who had identified themselves with Florence, of the Brownings and Landor and the lyrical partisans of Italian liberty, of the influence of Italian literature on our own, of Italian painters and architects on those of England, of Castiglione and della Casa on manners and education. Hardly any department of our social and intellectual life had not been influenced by Italian example.

The Italian love of history was stronger than ours. The leading articles in their newspapers proved it. While they were neutral wouldn't it be opportune to stir the embers of their memory? Half my Florentine friends had some English ancestor or kinsman of whom they had cause to be proud.

In England where the Press was free the word propaganda was still unpalatable, but the minority who dealt with international relations had become aware of its importance, especially in countries where the Press was muzzled and our newspapers were banned. Even in these countries foreign literature and art were still open to discussion, and in Italy they had never ceased to exert a powerful attraction. Through our literature especially we could open alien eyes to our way of life. The truest facts may be doubted but poetry carries its own conviction: like music it can set the spirit free. And the free spirit soars above the barriers of race and nationality. Hence I believed and still believe that the British Council is our most effective Foreign Office. It was then in its infancy, but it was under the aegis of Lord Lloyd, a far-sighted man who understood the value of cultural ties. I went to him boldly and proposed to lecture in *lingua toscana* on England's cultural debt to Italy. Some of my friends were indignant at my choice of subject but Lord Lloyd did not turn a hair. 'I'm sure you'll do it well,' he said, and he agreed to send me on a lecture tour of Italy. It was late, but not too late.

Edward Hutton, the doyen of English writers about Italy, and Cecil Sprigge, who had been Rome correspondent of the *Manchester Guardian*, gave me sound advice and letters to Liberal colleagues who were still at large. Both were ardent Italophiles who had been obliged to leave the country owing to their critical candour. Luigi Barzini and Giannalisa Feltrinelli were then in London and their resentment at Italy's subordination to the Führer gave me a cue.

Though my Italian had rusted in China I managed to cover a great deal of ground in my lecture. I was tempted to quote Dr Johnson's remark: 'Almost everything that sets us above savages has come to us from the shores of the Mediterranean.' But on second thoughts a reference to *mare nostrum* were best avoided, since the cry of 'Tunis, Corsica, Nice' had been raised in the Italian Chamber of Deputies and resounded outside it. I should bear in mind a shrewd Italian's advice to Sir Henry Wotton: '*I pensieri stretti ed il viso sciolto*' — 'Thoughts close and an open countenance'.

I flew to Paris at the end of February, 1940, and caught the Simplon-Orient Express to Milan. Evidently the Maginot Line was a general tranquillizer, for there was less sign of strain in Paris than in London during this hiatus of the so-called 'phoney war'. The same type of gastronome studied the menu and discussed the appropriate wine with the *sommelier* of the Escargot; life on the boulevards, in the crowded cafés, seemed as confidently brisk as in peace-time; the swagger of bosoms evoked the Folies-Bergère.

My first lecture was given in Milan, which has never seemed quite Italian to me. The Austrians, whose ancestors had been evacuated after the frenzied *Cinque Giorni* of street fighting in 1848, were back in full force, or were they German 'tourists'? One heard as much German as Italian in the Galleria. But the British Institute, small but select, was a bastion of Old England where Miss Isopel May, a teacher by vocation who beamed with benevolence behind her spectacles, a little breathless with grammatical afflatus, was assisted by the humorous philosopher Richard Webster and the versatile Jim Barber. Perhaps I owed my warm reception to the goodwill these civilized people had created. If there were rabid Fascists in my audience they could not have been friendlier, and they were to grow friendlier with every lecture. In the little time at my disposal I rushed through the Brera and Poldi-Pezzoli galleries to wash my eyes, as the Chinese would say; marvelled again at the ghost of Leonardo's Last Supper; filled my lungs with the perfection of the Portinari chapel in Sant' Eustorgio; and I gazed for the last time at Tiepolo's airy frescoes in the Archinti and Clerici palaces, soon to be destroyed, like so many other treasures of the Milan dear to Stendhal, who wished the words *'Arrigo Beyle, Milanese'* to be engraved on his tomb.

No doubt we all love cities on account of their inhabitants apart from aesthetic or practical reasons, and Stendhal was drawn to Milan by that 'sublime wench' Angiola Pietragrua, in whom he saw a personification of Italy. With Angiola in mind he wrote that 'the art of enjoying life appears to me here to be two centuries ahead of Paris'; he raved over the iced coffee, superior in his opinion to anything to be found in Paris; he was even delighted by a certain smell of manure peculiar to its streets, which were 'as commodious as ours are disgusting'. The streets had been modernized by Eugène Beauharnais, but it was still a city of picturesque contrasts, of luminous cloisters and courtyards behind massive doorways, like Pompeo Leoni's, flanked by muscular Atlantides. Now the palaces which survived destruction are engulfed in concrete.

The anti-Fascist writers to whom Cecil Sprigge had given me introductions were oracles of impending disaster. Between those who blamed our selfish and indolent complacency and those who blamed us for throwing the Duce into the Führer's arms I was considerably embarrassed and could only repeat the truism that Mr Chamberlain had strained himself to bursting point for the sake of peace, and that nobody could accuse him of being a

45

warmonger. But when the ladies exclaimed: 'Dear, good Mr Chamberlain, let us hope that he will remain your Prime Minister for ever!' I bit my tongue, for he had been duped by the dictators once too often.

After spouting in Milan and Genoa I repaired to Florence with conflicting emotions. Not only was it my home but I had not seen my parents for four years. This visit was sprung upon them suddenly. They had never heard me lecture and, sensitive to the quips of their Florentine friends, they feared I would make a fool of myself and put them to shame– an unspoken fear with which I sympathized. Their nervousness affected me though I was satisfied that my theme was not banal. Many of my statements were pregnant with *sous-entendres*. When I spoke of Milton's progress through the Florentine academies, where he talked openly of his religion and politics and visited Galileo who was virtually a prisoner of the Inquisition, and of the influence of such exiles as Foscolo and Panizzi who produced a better understanding of the Italian national character in England, I hoped to evoke parallels between past and present. I could not say that the only sincere lovers of the Florentines were the English, which is as true today as it has ever been: in the rest of Italy the Tuscans are scarcely popular. The Romans and Neapolitans detest them and even dislike their accent which is considered uncouth, but the English have always had a fondness for the tough, terse population of the City of the Lily.

The lecture hall was packed with familiar faces. It was a very attentive audience, nodding with approval when I struck a sympathetic chord or made an obvious point. At moments I was distracted by a too ample bosom in the front row and a wall eye which was determined to hypnotize me. The more I tried to avoid it, the more that eye glared in my direction. To avert evil I made the horn sign and aimed my purple passages at the two hoary lions of local society, Carlo Placci and Arthur Spender. Not being an actor, I was soon carried away by my message.

As I mopped my brow I was greeted with a burst of applause. The two former directors of the Institute, Spender and Goad, expressed more appreciation than the actual director Francis Toye, who was jealous of his own Italian. 'One can see that you've been in China,' he remarked. Lina Waterfield, one of the founding members, limped up to me with a reproachful expression. 'You were too conciliatory, too partial,' she observed. 'You should have spoken of Italy's debt to us.' Though disconcerted, I believed that the friendly feelings I had kindled must do more good than harm.

The British Institute of Florence, the first of its kind, had been founded by a group of Anglo-Florentines in 1917 to promote intellectual relations between the two countries and provide a permanent meeting place for English and Italian scholars. At that time many peasants and workmen supposed that Germany was Italy's ally and an influential minority were stubbornly pro-German. The Socialists blamed England for dragging Italy into a senseless war and 'Down with the English' was plastered on public walls. Edward Hutton and Mrs Waterfield had been strenuous in defeating hostile propaganda. In 1923 the Institute obtained a Royal Charter, since when it had been steered through stormy weather by Harold Goad, whose sympathy with Fascism was notorious. He had published a book on the Corporate State which had gratified the Italian Government and, as he wrote in a concise history of the British Institute, 'the fact that the Director of the Institute had thus definitely shown that he understood the ideals and effects of New Italy was undoubtedly the factor that enabled it to survive the political crisis of 1935–36 when the Director was informed on more than one occasion by authoritative Italians that but for such proof of understanding the existence of a foreign Institute of the nation principally associated in the Italian mind with the policy of Sanctions would never have been tolerated'.

Many thought Goad should have resigned, but that would have meant the closure of the Institute. Since dictatorships tend to be unstable and subject to outside influences it seemed to me that his presence had been useful, for it had enabled Toye to step in and hold the fort for better days.

The Florentines were not in the habit of mincing their words. Those I knew joked openly about the Duce whose brain was said to be addled by over-indulgence in women, but foreign residents had to be careful. There were plenty of drawing-room spies who reported and misrepresented unfavourable comments. I had not come from England to carp, but to stress our common heritage, the ideals and values we had shared since Roman times.

After two days in Florence I proceeded to Rome, where Ian Greenlees was the British Council's leading representative, and he was supremely successful in that capacity. In spite of his youth he appeared a contemporary of Macaulay. He was Italophile to the backbone and no crisis could ruffle him: his calm was Olympian. As an Oxford undergraduate he had invited me to address the Sitwell Society which he had founded, but I was then in China. Now I was to lecture in Rome under his auspices and though the Sitwells were not my theme I felt assured of at least one benevolent listener.

To sit with Ian in the Caffè Greco and dine with him at Ranieri was to return to the Rome of Pio Nono: Fascism faded in his company. And to stroll from Piazza di Spagna to the Corso, through narrower streets to the Pantheon and on to the spacious splendour of Piazza Navona inhaling the warm air impregnated with whiffs of wine, of frying oil and ancient mustiness, or cooled by flashing fountains, was a luxury to the senses all the keener by contrast with frigid London. The threat against this nobility of human achievement gave it an added poignancy. The Romans I met did not appear to be conscious of this menace. The Duce was too astute, they said, and the country was not ready for war. Look at the new railway station, and the preparations for the international exhibition! Surely these were visible signs of the Duce's pacific intentions.

But one did not have to be psychic to scent an undercurrent of nervousness in the houses where I dined. Virginio Gayda, the Fascist mouthpiece who edited the *Giornale d'Italia*, breathed fire and fury at Ian Munro's, but he had been doing this so long that it ceased to have much impact. Recently he had mooted the advantages of an alliance between the three totalitarian Powers, Fascism, Nazism and Bolshevism, against 'the plutocratic democracies'. The bilious little man seemed on the verge of a stroke. Ian Munro's patience with him was exemplary. While dining with Sir Noel Charles, the British Minister, I heard that Ribbentrop was being fêted next door in the same palace. After dinner some of the neighbouring guests came over to join our party, attracted by the presence of Mrs Luce, the future Ambassador, then better known for the smartness of her satire, only equalled by the smartness of her clothes. Her icy radiance drew the Latins like moths, among them the susceptible Ciano, who was bored by Ribbentrop. What if Sir Noel and Ribbentrop should bump into each other on the stairs? The butlers and footmen on both sides of the palace overheard much private information which was often repeated to deaf ears. The Dutch Ambassador was to hear of the invasion of Holland in this way.

Giannalisa Feltrinelli took me to the poet Trilussa's studio which was full of rococo bits and pieces, a perfect setting for a ghost story. The elderly dandy recited scurrilous verses about the Fascist hierarchs and kept up a fusillade of topical quips throughout the evening. The three of us dined heartily at Alfredo's, a typically Roman repast of aromatic artichokes, spring lamb and impressionistic salad, washed down with wine of the Castelli, a wine that stimulates thirst rather than quenches it. Trilussa was inspired to fresh flights of fantasy by our hostess, a *maîtresse femme* who wore a monocle. Unfortunately the Roman dialect was less easy for me to follow than the old rhymester's gesticulations. In any other totalitarian State his indiscretion would have got him into trouble.

To see Ciano, Gayda and Trilussa in so short an interval was like seeing three specimens of different races – the flashy son-in-law who was already adopting the Duce's attitudes; the hysterical Party publicist like a provincial pettifogger; and the cynical survivor of old Roman *improvvisatori*.

My cup brimming over with pungent impressions, I had two more lectures to deliver in Naples and Palermo. Naples had never lost its spell on me. Generations of my ancestors had lived there as subjects of the Bourbons, which might help to explain a feeling of familiarity with the sights and sounds of a place where I had never spent much time. In 1940 Naples retained many characteristics of the Bourbon capital: the Vomero was still a maze of gardens and multi-coloured houses with flat roofs and winding terraces gay with irrepressible vegetation, fluttering laundry, and umbrella pines above walls of tufa, domes glinting in the sun like porcelain pineapples, balconies at every angle in blithe disarray, cactuses and palms among crumbling and oozing masonry. Posillipo sloped down to the sea in careless abandon. Except under the rain which seems sadder here than in other cities – the sea and the light are sufficiently liquid – Naples is singularly exhilarating. Even the changes since the war, appalling as they are, cannot damp the elation of a return to Parthenope. One hums for sheer delight at the first glimpse of its outline. Having run the gauntlet of roguish railway porters one can relax at an opera which never grows tedious.

No city bids one eat, drink and be merry in such caressing tones: Florence and Rome invite one, like Peking, to contemplation and serenity, but Naples quickens one's pulse with a delicious excitement, followed by a soothing languor. Here the war seemed farther away than ever, though Mussolini had arranged another meeting with Hitler on the Brenner.

Archibald Colquhoun, a fair young man with a ready smile and earnest eyes, rescued me from the chaos of the railway station. He had fallen in love with Italy south of Rome, and nobody could have been a more suitable Director of our Institute of Naples. He was to become the devoted biographer and translator of Manzoni: now his enthusiasm for Naples was akin to Stendhal's for Milan and he was well versed in its history and lore. This made him a delightful companion, and he had a painter's eye for details of the open-air life on the steep *salite*, the street vendors and their wares, the patches of pastel colour, the *acquaiolo* with his water jar and lemons, the dialogue of gestures instead of words, and the grimaces of singers in the restaurants along the waterfront. Jazz had not influenced the simple Neapolitan songs, like long-drawn sighs and rhythmical bursts of laughter, and the moon over Marechiaro still seemed to have risen from a virginal bed.

I was impressed by the perspicacity of Ian Greenlees in his choice of cultural assistants. While black shirts were officially turning brown, the English classes of our Institutes were thronged with students. Again my lecture was crowded to capacity and for the first and last time I was asked for my photograph by two young women, a contingency I had not foreseen. As my tour drew to an end I was struck by the total absence of hostility: the farther south the more cordial was my reception. I decided to stop in Naples on my way home and in the meantime revisited Baia, Miseno, Averno, Cumae and the Sybil's grotto, where the Greeks first settled in Italy and the Romans built luxurious villas, 'every emperor striving to surpass his predecessor's magnificence', as Josephus wrote. A few forlorn ruins were all that remained of the once glamorous Baia, now a shabby fishing village, yet the atmosphere sparkled with sensuous vibrations and it was easy to visualize what it had been.

Richard Wilson had painted the desolate lake which no bird would approach, known to poets as the entrance of the infernal regions, and Claude had evoked the bay in its Horatian splendour:

> Fair Baiae's shores, for tepid springs renowned,
> Where all the gay delights of life are found.

If no birds haunted Averno, there were no tourists either – not one in sight. But the *trattoria* at Miseno was loud with mandolines and the swallowing of heaped spaghetti *alle vongole*. Asking if we were German, a waiter exclaimed: 'But aren't we at war with England?' He was relieved to hear that this was not yet the case.

The few peasants who saluted us at the *Piscina Mirabile* might have been there since Nero's reign. Recollections of Suetonius cropped up, especially at the vast underground reservoir into which Nero intended to divert the warm springs of Baiae, and at the so-called tomb of Agrippina whom he had finally murdered

51

at Bacoli after several botched attempts with poison. A last look at the lone *Arco Felice* silhouetted against the azure sky, then back to the clamorous hive of the Toledo.

Recent books about Naples are unbalanced by insistence on its squalid aspects. As a reaction against the glossy postcard views this is comprehensible. Some of the noblest buildings rot away in forlorn back streets. Peer through a monumental portico and you may be staggered by a regal staircase leading through graceful arcades which are an architectural speciality of Naples.

The situation of Palermo in its 'golden shell' or fertile hollow is horizontal rather than vertical like Naples, and I rejoice to have seen it before it was battered by war and marred by concrete. The Marina still evoked the Orient. John Waterfield, the younger son of my Florentine friend Lina, had launched the British Institute here and he was already a popular figure in local society. Like me he had tried to join one of the services and found that he was not needed yet. Young, enterprising, handsome, happily married, he was to be killed by a bomb in Malta two years later on the first birthday of the son he had never seen. At this time he doubted if Italy would enter the war. As for the Sicilians, they wanted home rule and resented the interference of Rome in their affairs. I was asked rather gruffly for my passport at the hotel, but the clerk was wreathed in smiles when he saw that I was English.

After my lecture I was taken to a puppet show in a cellar-like room with an all-male audience, brigandish-looking workmen and little boys who broke into applause when a doughty deed was performed by a Christian hero and vociferated hoarsely when an episode stirred their emotions. There were battles between Normans and Saracens with much clashing of swords. The puppets were more crudely realistic than those of China, Java, or Bali, and they were manipulated against a canvas painted naïvely like the donkey carts. Evidently they kept the old legends alive. The performance lasted for hours, to most people's satisfaction. Daphne Waterfield was the only woman in the room but there was no rude comment or unseemly curiosity, and I was touched by the courtesy of an old man beside me who attempted to explain the plot. On the whole it seemed a more imaginative entertainment than the average film.

The mosaics of Monreale and the Cappella Palatina made me wish for the company of Robert Byron, but apart from these famous jewels there were aesthetic surprises scarcely noticed in the guide-books, such as the sculpture of Giacomo Serpotta, which are as in advance of their period as the frescoes of Domenico Tiepolo, and unique among eighteenth-century sculpture in Sicily. It is regrettable that his figures are modelled in stucco instead of a more durable material though he treated plaster with the delicacy of lace.

For me the strangest surprise was La Favorita, the villa built for Ferdinand I and IV of the Two Sicilies in 1799. According to William Rae Wilson, writing in 1835, 'the site was selected by Lord Nelson as one very suitable for their Majesties' residence when they were brought over to Sicily by him at the time of the revolution'. Its exterior is a conglomeration of neo-classical and chinoiserie styles. While the garden front has a semicircular portico with Doric columns, a pagoda-roofed turret surmounts the four storeys and a minaret leads to the first floor balcony – one of many with pseudo-Chinese railings once a-dangle with tinkling bells. The adjoining stables are shaped like a chinoiserie tent. The paintings on the façade have faded, but the interior is a quaint Pompeian pastiche of Chinese and Moorish designs. The dumb-waiter which sent dishes from the kitchen to the dining-room was pointed out with pride by the custodian, who explained that this enabled the king to gossip without being overheard by the servants, and 'Il Re Nasone loved bawdy jokes and a fine mound of flesh like la Hamilton' – whose portrait smirked on a wall.

A drive to the Villa Palagonia whose sculpted grotesques amazed Goethe and other eighteenth-century travellers was a disillusion, so pitiable was its state of decay. According to Brydone, writing in 1770, there were no less than six hundred statues lining the avenue and surrounding the outer court, 'notwithstanding which it may truly be said that he (the Prince of Palagonia) has not broke the second commandment, for of all that number there is not the likeness of anything in heaven above, in the earth beneath, or in the waters under the earth'. Brydone also relates that 'there is no kind of horn in the world that he has not collected; and his pleasure is to see them all flourishing upon the same head. The scandalous chronicle says that his wife has assisted him in making this collection, and that there are some of her placing as well as his. However this may be, she is at present within a few weeks of her time, and we have been told by several people of Palermo, that his sincere wish is that she may bring forth a monster.'

The interior was equally original, the ball-room ceiling glittering with mica, but in its actual dilapidation it evoked Poe's story *The Fall of the House of Usher*.

The old families of Palermo appeared to live like their patriarchal ancestors: the Princess of Trabia held a formal court of abbés who still took snuff, pallid ladies dressed in black, jaded gentlemen with pointed beards, a rubicund private chaplain, a learned librarian, an antiquated English governess of Jane Austenish gentility, and retainers who wore their liveries with a Catalan air. Social changes had been superficial: the same polysyllabic titles resounded. It was the atmosphere of Giuseppe Di Lampedusa's *Leopard*. Unfortunately I had no leisure to browse in the library which contained many rare tomes I longed to read. On a table I noticed the motto:

> *Triste la sorte dei libri prestati*
> *Spesso perduti, sempre danneggiati.*
> (Sad is the fate of books that are lent,
> Usually lost, always battered or bent).

At Mrs Whitaker's – the sister-in-law of Tina who had given me her book *Sicily and England* 'in memory of mutual links with the past' – I found the English clergyman sipping tea with a bevy of dames straight from the pages of *Pride and Prejudice*. Sicily had not penetrated this hermetic English sanctuary. As for the war, it might have been in the Crimea.

Since my applications for national service in England remained unanswered, I thought I might as well go to Florence till something suitable turned up: in the meantime I was at the disposal of the British Council. Cecil Sprigge had given me a letter to Benedetto Croce, the most eminent of living Neapolitans, who was invulnerable to Fascist shafts.

The great man received me in his library in Via Mariano Semmola, just off the beautiful Piazza Trinità Maggiore with its elaborate Guglia dell' Immacolata, in the heart of old Naples known as Spaccanapoli, corresponding to the *decumanus inferior* of the Greco-Roman city. The room exuded a pot-pourri of leather and vellum bindings and printer's ink, an odour which affects me like a mental aphrodisiac, with an itch to read books I should never read elsewhere. The silent witnesses along the shelves seemed to reproach me for neglect. Why, when I had so tenacious an attachment to books, such consuming curiosity about their contents, had I spent so little of my life in libraries?

The elderly philosopher, robust, thick-set, with heavy features almost ugly in themselves yet handsome in their total effect as an expression of ripe wisdom, seemed part of the massive table at which he sat like a monarch on his throne, and indeed he was monarch of all he surveyed in that library. The bulky torso was so rooted there that one could not conceive of his taking any exercise outside it. That he was no ascetic was apparent from his bulk: by contrast his hands were small. He leaned towards me with a hospitable smile: his eyes were those of a master of concentration.

Having little aptitude for philosophy, I felt abashed in the presence of this formidable thinker, but he put me at ease immediately. He knew more about my ancestors than I did. After one generation they had become Neapolitans, he remarked, how did I happen to be English? A curious case of atavism, I replied, but I often felt Neapolitan. He questioned me at length about China, Chiang Kai-shek and the Japanese, the vernacular movement, the theatre, and so forth, and I was astonished by the breadth of his interests. He was amused to hear that an English translation of his *Aesthetic* was in the library of Peking University, but I had to confess it was clearer to me in the original than in Douglas Ainslie's version.

In so far as I grasped Croce's theory of aesthetic activity I told him it was illustrated by Chinese painters, who formed a perfect mental image to capture the essence of the object perceived. When I was an undergraduate his theory had held the field as the most advanced. I could remember Professor J. A. Smith's summary of it: that there are no arts, there is only art – that the common distinction between the arts was philosophically non-existent. How sweeping yet how vague! And Professor Smith proceeded: 'What is art, the nature or essence or spirit of art? To this I reply categorically and unconditionally, "The beholding of what is individual", that and nothing less or more or other, that always and that everywhere.' Well, now I was beholding the embodiment of what was most individual in Italy. Croce smiled indulgently when I said so, no doubt in different words.

'You make me want to see China,' he said, 'but here I'm a fixture. I have to guard my library.'

'And the freedom of thought in the Corporate State,' I replied.

At one time his house had been pillaged by Fascist hooligans, but nobody could stop the avalanche of his writings, which were published with brick-coloured jackets by Laterza of Bari. When Croce's enemies threatened to use those jackets as bumf the Neapolitan publisher Ricciardi proposed: 'We must wire Laterza at once to have sandpaper covers made.'

Since Croce had denounced the First World War as suicidal mania I was anxious to hear what he thought of the present one. Not only did he regard it as a moral necessity, he declared it was Italy's only hope for salvation from Fascism. 'This isn't a mere matter of economic warfare. Mussolini is certain to drag us in and he will be beaten,' he prophesied. 'But the victorious Allies will be more generous than Hitler. And at last we'll get the poison out of our system.'

Behind the bastion of his library the philosopher spoke as a

56

representative of the Liberal tradition. I admired his courage, for even walls have ears. He had survived one earthquake in which he had lost both his parents and his only sister, and he had been buried for hours under rubble: his bones had been crushed but his spirit had been strengthened. There must have been intervals when he felt terribly alone in that silent library. Only his most loyal friends dared to visit him for he was anathema to the ruling authorities since he had drawn up an anti-Fascist manifesto in 1925. The ex-Minister of Public Education, who was also a Senator, was boycotted by the Fascist Press. Even in the serious reviews his name was seldom printed. The glaring omission drew attention to his eminence, which towered over his contemporaries. When a panegyric of his publisher Laterza appeared without mention of the philosopher who had made him famous, Laterza replied to its author: 'You remind me of Don Bosco, who in deference to his political convictions contrived to write a history of contemporary Italy without mentioning Cavour.'

Croce's influence as a reformer of Italian culture had gone underground for the nonce. Nobody else had raised so prodigious a monument to Neapolitan genius, and all who love Naples must consult his historical writings. The life of culture was his religion, his remedy for human ills.

As evening crept into the library I could hardly discern his features. He did not switch on the light and this seemed to me symbolical: the prophet of freedom was temporarily veiled in shadow. In complete darkness he accompanied me to the door: his voice was the only light. 'When you return to England,' he said, 'tell Sprigge that I am hoping for your victory.'

I stepped into the narrow street as one who had drunk too much wine and gazed up at the festive *Guglia* in the dim-lit square. That this *lingam*, far more flowery than those erected to Siva in India, should be dedicated to the Immaculate Virgin struck me as ironical to say the least, since it was raised at the instigation of the Jesuit Father Pepe – an innocent survival of the pagan emblem omnipresent at Pompeii. How gaily it glistened in the moonlight, a wreathed column of Neapolitan fecundity. Urchins were still scrambling around its base. One of them attached himself to me and pointed persistently at his mischievous mouth to hint that he was hungry. I tossed him a coin. He caught it deftly and ran away flourishing a banana in my direction with a Priapic grin.

Back in the teeming Toledo I joined Archie Colquhoun for a dinner of sea food. Again he had become a tireless boon companion. During the next few days we wandered through Capodimonte and the Floridiana which reflected the most genial qualities of the Bourbons, supped at rustic Marechiaro 'where even the fish make love when the moon rises' as Di Giacomo wrote, listened to the last Piedigrotta song-hits at the Trionfale (ex-Trianon), and laughed helplessly at one of Eduardo De Filippo's comedies. Every moment was enriched by the rediscovery of the Naples I remembered from my childhood, a recurrent *pizzicato* in my life, a plucking of heart-strings. The popular minstrel Ernesto Murolo had written a famous ballad '*Napule ca se ne va*' ('The Naples that is going'), little imagining how soon the dear familiar landmarks were to be wiped out. Even the simple treats he celebrated – Horatian pleasures shared by all classes of Neapolitans – have been commercialized. The cosy *tavernella* and the rustic *pergolatino* have been replaced by garish restaurants with neon lights.

Personally I hoped that Italy would keep out of the war. I could not believe that Fascism would be invigorated by an Allied victory. Though I sympathized with Croce I was sorry that he should prescribe so drastic a cure. For all Mussolini's bombast the peninsula was intensely vulnerable to air attack, and the destruction of so much historic beauty would mean an irreparable loss to civilization. Palaces, domes and *campanili*, I saw them in a nightmare toppling over in colossal bonfires. As soon as London was bombed there would be an outcry from the vandals who fancied themselves patriots for the bombing of Rome or Venice or Florence – reprisals like cutting off one's nose to spite one's face. Alas, rhetoric can be powerfully intoxicating and there were plenty of young Italians only too eager to be drawn into adventure for adventure's sake. Bored by the quiet life, it was easy to rouse them. D'Annunzio, Marinetti and Gentile, with their rebellious iconoclasm and glorification of 'Pure Act', had sown the dragon's seed.

The knowledge that I was a disappointment to my father proved a barrier to complete enjoyment of home life. I greatly admired his fine taste and intuitive flair for painting, sculpture and architecture; had I not been his son I am sure we would have been the best of friends. Unfortunately he expected my brother and me to live *in statu pupillari* under his permanent supervision and control. Sociable and gregarious, he had many more acquaintances than friends. Left to his own devices he grew restless and a prey to every kind of *Angst*, but he was seldom alone. My mother was the most angelic of companions and her sweetness of temper smoothed over the asperities – how trivial in retrospect! – that cropped up incessantly between us. No doubt she too would have wished me to get married and lead a different life, but far from reproaching me she encouraged me to be true to myself. I owe everything to her instinctive understanding.

Small and exquisitely pretty, with delicate hands and tiny feet, my mother was a perfectionist in every detail. Though she never dyed her silver-grey hair, she looked half her age owing to her natural agility and juvenile complexion. She was fastidious about her clothes but she was never ostentatious. More selective and critical of people than my father, in the absence of friends she took refuge in literature. She was an insatiable reader of historical memoirs and preferred her library to her drawing-room. Not that she was averse to witty company, but this had become scarce in Florence. Wit cannot thrive under a dictatorship.

Though prone to worry himself into sick headaches about minutiae, my father was unperturbed by the political situation. His antecedents were Neapolitan: most of his life had been spent in Italy, and his Italian friends assured him that nobody would dream of molesting him in the event of war, that they regarded him as a privileged compatriot. He allowed himself too easily to be convinced. Wishful thinking becomes blind faith when the wish is overpowering. Though my mother detested dictators and despised the folly of appeasing them, she succumbed to my father's fatalism.

There were no tourists to visit my father's art collection or take snapshots of the garden, but there were the same copious luncheons and tea-parties with the same alternation of hosts and guests, an assortment of Florentines by birth or adoption, or foreigners who had rented a villa or an apartment in one of the old palaces.

Dipping into Lady Blessington's *Idler in Italy* or any of the travel diaries written since the defeat of Napoleon, one is struck by the lack of change in this cosmopolitan community. Most of the Italian names are identical with those mentioned in the earliest chronicles. While the names of foreigners may differ, their characteristics are much the same. In 1824 Lady Blessington wrote: 'Madame la Marquise is a *bel esprit*, knows everybody and everything in Florence; can tell where the finest picture is to be seen, and the prettiest cap or bonnet is to be purchased; talks on all subjects, and well on all; in short is very lively and agreeable. Mr Francis Hare is here, and is as clever and entertaining as ever . . . Mr Strangways as chargé d'affaires, witnessed the solemnization of a marriage between an English young man of high family and a *soi-disant* widow of French extraction. This union has caused much surprise and, it is to be feared, may ultimately occasion much regret.'

Lively and knowledgeable marchesas and contessas still abounded; Francis Hare had been followed by Augustus and other Hares equally clever and entertaining; the gossip about marriages, divorces and affairs of the heart only differed in phraseology.

Fewer English writers and intellectuals had cared to stay on under the present regime, but Bernard Berenson still held a diminished court at I Tatti, the villa he had reconstructed below the wood of Vincigliata. This large-minded man of small stature was to become my mentor and I have never ceased to be grateful for his moral support when I was at my lowest ebb.

In spite of my father's exceptional taste as an art collector and creator of gardens, he was indifferent to literature and he rather looked down on writers. He did not want companionship but company and even then soon tired of the people he saw. A shifting kaleidoscope of strangers was what he preferred, the more ephemeral the better. So long as they had a steady flow of prattle combined with a pretty face and a certain modishness he was well satisfied. Every afternoon and many a morning was dedicated to stray callers with letters of introduction. These left little impression, but they seldom forgot to send others who levied the same toll. To the exasperation of my mother and the chef, he would often bring in people for 'pot-luck' and they would linger on while he took his siesta, waiting for a lift back to town. I wondered how he could endure this endless stream of time-wasters: evidently they served as incense to his self-esteem.

Since the outbreak of war the stream had dwindled. But the succession of substantial luncheons continued as in the days of good King Edward, whose friend Mrs Keppel was the leading hostess of the British colony. After perfunctory remarks about the phoney war, which seemed phonier than ever at this stage, the talk reverted to such *potins* as So-and-so's liaison with a chauffeur or the rumours of some Casanova's impotence – variations on the sempiternal themes. Though some of the dramatis personae had comical idiosyncrasies they were hardly more real than those of a drawing-room farce. Somerset Maugham had imprisoned them in the amber of *The Circle*.

Reggie Turner, better known as a loyal friend of Oscar Wilde than as a novelist, was a great loss to this society in which he used to twinkle like a fitful star. He had died in December, 1938, and perhaps it was as well that he did not live to see the war, for he was incurably Edwardian. What a difference he had made to those luncheons and teas: one forgot to eat while he spun his fantasies or merely blinked and listened with an expression which expressed so much that, as Max Beerbohm wrote, 'he would be eloquent even were he dumb'. Were his neighbour bosomy, he would roll his eyes and moisten his overripe lips; were she skinny, he would pull a long parson's face; were she young, his eyes would sparkle with schoolboy mischief. And his voice had a rich diapason, ranging from dry matter-of-fact to mellow prophetic.

His mimicry was hilarious but it defied definition. In the role of benevolent family friend, for instance, who is introduced with pride to the latest offspring, he picks up the infant, lifting it ever so lightly by the chin, and crack! the child's neck is broken. With mortified apologies he staggers off in despair. A year elapses and the family friend, forgiven for the tragic accident, is invited to visit the latest addition to the nursery. Still haunted by the previous accident and anxious to exculpate himself, he gazes tenderly at the tiny dribbler. 'I can't think how it happened,' he explains. 'I only did this!' He proceeds to lift the second infant and crack! another little neck is broken . . .

The comedy of Reggie's improvisations depended on his economy of gesture, the two hands gently raising the child, and the utter prostration of the reluctant murderer. Of course he had to be in the vein, but he was not critical of his audience. Often he excelled himself for the entertainment of the unworthy.

His rival Reggie Temple had survived him. He, too, was a friend of Max Beerbohm and had known Oscar Wilde: in his youth he had even played a minute role in *An Ideal Husband* – I fancy it was the Vicomte de Nanjac who says to Mrs Cheveley: 'Ah! you flatter me. You butter me, as they say here.' His Thespian ambition had been thwarted by his physical minuteness.

Spick-and-span and prim in manner, he winced at the other Reggie's name, for silly hostesses had confused them. Under his primness and neatness was an obsession with the macabre: he gloated on a Chamber of Horrors of his own creation. This penchant for brutal murders contrasted oddly with his daintiness.

To augment his modest income he painted little boxes with eighteenth-century *fêtes galantes*, which he lacquered and re-lacquered until they looked antique. Few Florentine drawing-rooms were without at least one of his boxes, and some found their way into shops where they were sold as genuine *vernis Martin*. Being an expert copyist, he was also commissioned to reproduce the missing panels of a predella when, as is often the case with Tuscan Primitives, these were scattered in different galleries.

Since Reggie Turner's death Reggie Temple was our last exponent of the naughty nineties and he played the part with unction. He was undoubtedly the model for 'dapper little Maltby – blond, bland, diminutive Maltby, with his monocle and his gardenia', in that story which Evelyn Waugh considered Max Beerbohm's best, *Hilary Maltby and Stephen Braxton*. But instead of Lucca, Reggie had settled in Florence, where he was pleasantly 'buttered' by a bevy of dowagers, who were titillated by the blood-curdling stories he told in his gentle voice. His manner was more demure than the other Reggie's but he was surprisingly informative about actresses like Marie Tempest and Mrs Patrick Campbell, above all about Eleonora Duse, with whom he had fallen in love. I presumed the infatuation was platonic for the Duse was well past her prime and Reggie was not even a simulacrum of Gabriele d'Annunzio – the mere comparison was ludicrous. Probably, as in Yeats's poem, he loved the pilgrim soul in her, and loved the sorrows of her changing face. Duse's naturalness and lack of make-up had bewitched him to such an extent that he followed her to America before her death in 1924. He surrounded himself with her signed photographs and spoke of her with bated breath. 'She was the last great actress,' he murmured with a wistful sigh. To tease him you had only to mention the Divine Sarah. 'A ridiculous *cabotine*,' he snorted. 'What they call ham, I believe, and a ham quite crawling with worms.' Which reminded him, had I read of the mutilated corpse that had been found . . .? And he went on to discuss the latest murder in an undertone slightly above a whisper. He cherished a theory that Reggie Turner had been poisoned by his

William Acton

Evelyn Waugh

servants. 'They said he died of cancer of the tongue but that was all my eye. The tongue was gradually destroyed by arsenic in his salad dressing, and he was a chain-smoker, which did not help. He had foolishly told them how much he was leaving them in his will.'

Over the tea-table Reggie Temple expanded more than others did over cocktails. Tea was his dominant meal: he seemed to live on buttered toast and nightmares.

The British colony had been on the wane since 1932 when sterling was worth only 62 instead of 92 lire to the pound. Florence had become too expensive for the retired gentlefolk of moderate means who used to fill the *pensions*. The tradition of country squires laying down English lawns and cultivating their *poderi* was rapidly declining. But one Lady Bountiful remained in residence.

Mrs George Keppel came and went with the seasons since she had bought L'Ombrellino, her villa on Bellosguardo, in 1925. The house was gloomy in spite of its splendid view, but Mrs Keppel brightened it with gay furniture and filled it with titled guests. Here none could compete with her glamour as a hostess.

All historians of King Edward's reign have paid tribute to her beneficent influence and remarkable discretion as his intimate friend. A large signed photograph of Queen Alexandra showed that she had been grateful to Alice Keppel for making the King so happy. To interest and amuse a blasé monarch for so many years – since 1898 – required exceptional gifts. A fine figure of a woman, as they used to say, more handsome than beautiful, she possessed enormous charm, which was not only due to her cleverness and vivacity but to her generous heart. Her kindnesses were innumerable and spontaneous. Altogether she was on a bigger scale than most of her sex: she could have impersonated Britannia in a *tableau vivant* and done that lady credit. One of the secrets of her success was that she could be amusing without malice; she never repeated a cruel witticism. Above all, she was not snobbish.

No snob could have won the confidence of the big bankers and

F

merchants who had surrounded King Edward since he was Prince of Wales. Most of these, like the King's financial adviser Sir Ernest Cassel, were of humble German–Jewish origin. They collected official honours with the same zest as they collected Old Masters, and they were sensitive to the racial prejudice of smart society. Like Balzac and the former King, Mrs Keppel was fascinated by the power of capitalism: for a worldling she was wildly romantic and she became more so with the passing of years.

In London she had been on parade, as it were, but in Florence she could lead, comparatively, the simple life. The food at L'Ombrellino was conspicuously more lavish when a Rothschild was being entertained, on the principle of 'unto every one that hath shall be given, and he shall have abundance'. Her butler was insatiable of tips, especially from the bridge-players: he had an intuitive knowledge of their winnings, and also knew that some of them depended on cards for pin money.

Colonel Keppel was well matched as to height and size, tall, with broad shoulders and a narrow waist, and one could picture him waltzing superbly to the strains of *The Merry Widow*. His nose was a touch too aquiline but he wore a bristling military moustache and looked every inch a colonel, with the hearty laugh that denotes a lack of humour. I remember how shocked he was to find my mother reading a book about Oscar Wilde. 'A frightful bounder, it made one puke to look at him,' he muttered. Fortunately Mrs Keppel had enough humour to spare. Did she ever remind him that he was descended from William III's minion who was created Earl of Albemarle for his *beaux yeux*?

The Colonel spent much of his leisure compiling booklets of contemporary dates for his sight-seeing guests. Naturally he acted as cicerone to the prettiest débutantes – 'such a little cutie', he said fondly of more than one. To a certain extent he shared his wife's aura. A rival guide once pointed him out to a group of inquisitive tourists as *'l'ultimo amante della regina Vittoria'* – Queen Victoria's last paramour.

One swallow makes not a spring, nor even two swallows, and

of the birds of a feather who entertained all the year round Marchesa Lulie Torrigiani was outstanding. An American by birth, her career had been unusual for a Florentine hostess. In her distant youth she was said to have been badly injured in a railway accident and to have sued the railway company for damages with success. Surgical treatment had produced miraculous results. One of her eyelids drooped and her face had been lifted, but one could not guess her age.

A chic little woman with a quizzical expression and a caustic tongue, her puckered face looked older than her figure which was trim and upright. Early in life she must have decided that risky stories are a substitute for sex appeal and she had a rich repertory at her command. One suspected that this had endeared her to Harry Dearbergh, her former husband, a tough old Englishman with a cockney accent and a bulldog manner. Together they had kept open house, gradually eliminating the dowdies and the dullards. Bridge tables, a copious buffet and a bar were sufficient to coax the supercilious who smiled at the crudities of their Amphitryon, for Dearbergh called a spade a bloody shovel. When he caught sight of one of his guests cramming his pockets with Havana cigars he said: 'Now you put those right back where you found them and keep one for yourself.'

An enthusiastic bridge-player, he became incensed if a male guest took leave too soon after dinner. 'Having got randy on my brandy, I suppose you're off to a whoreshop,' he barked. 'Go by all means and get yourself a nice dose of clap, but don't you dare show your mug in here again!' With ladies he was slightly more tolerant. 'I reckon she's having her monthlies,' he would say. He had the purple complexion and thick speech of a heavy drinker. Lulie had helped him to climb the social ladder and it must have been a difficult feat.

Lulie's dinners were as formal as her talk was loose – so loose that invalid officers convalescing from Gallipoli during the First World War, unaccustomed to such freedom of language among ladies, misinterpreted the morality of their hostess and her guests, who had a struggle to defend themselves from rape. In a comical description of dining with the Dearberghs, Max Beerbohm wrote that as he sat listening to his hostess's conversation, he felt he was having dinner in a cesspool. 'The well-trained English butler, noticing me grow paler and paler – and knowing by his experience of other débutants at his mistress's table, what was going to happen – placed beside my plate a large and priceless majolica basin. The first time I was sick into it I apologized elaborately to Mrs Dearbergh. She made very light of the matter. "You'll be worse," she said, "before you're better," and resumed the thread of her conversation.'

Not long after Dearbergh's demise incredible rumours about his widow were afloat. She was said to have grown deeply religious. Moreover she had become attached to a Knight of Malta, the aged patrician Marchese Carlo Torrigiani. After being converted to the Catholic faith she married the Marchese. To all appearances it was a love-match and the patriarchal bridegroom, who had been an austere widower for many years, was suddenly rejuvenated, chuckling like a cherub over Lulie's outrageous jokes. Norman Douglas's book of limericks was conspicuous in the drawing-room, but there was also a private chapel where the elect were bidden to Mass. The alternation of rosaries and salacious innuendo was Firbankian, but so savoury was the fare that the prudes smirked at Lulie's ribaldries, which could be cruel. On one occasion a retired diplomat who had been arrested for indecent behaviour in the Cascine was asked to turn round. 'I want to see if you wear a zipper behind,' said the Marchesa.

Lulie had no political convictions but her husband thought Mussolini had saved the country from Communism. Tactfully she steered him away from such irritating topics. The old Marchese once confided to me that his father had been a page to the last Grand Duke of Tuscany: 'I ought not to say so but we were all better off in those days.'

Nobody betrayed much interest in the war, and why should Mussolini risk losing the advantages he had gained? With few exceptions the ladies adored the dictator as a superman. They knew he was susceptible to their sex whereas Hitler was a mystery, perhaps a eunuch. As for the demonstrations of students against England and France, young bloods had to let off steam.

In this society, which lived for the exchange of gossip at gargantuan meals, I was tolerated as the son of my popular parents. Although I was no bridge-fiend I was useful at a pinch as an extra man. *Au fond*, these good people forgathered to reassure themselves that 'God's in his Heaven and all's right with the world'. But the most lavish hospitality grows tedious without the leaven of intellect.

Bernard Berenson's hospitality was of a finer grain. At I Tatti one invariably found guests who were attuned to contemporary modes of thought as well as to those of the ancients. Berenson himself resembled an Old Master, whether a Titian or an El Greco depended on his mood. Most art-critics are limited by the exigencies of their profession, but Berenson's mind ranged far beyond it. Fragile yet physically and mentally agile, he had the reputation of an intellectual despot. During my childhood I regarded him with awe: on my visits to Mrs Berenson, who loved organizing children's parties and games into which she flung herself with greater gusto than her guests, we were adjured to keep out of his way. Later on there was a breach between him and my father and they were not on speaking terms.

One evening when I was tired of ostriches with heads in the sand, Olga Loeser, the widow of my old friend Carlo who had also quarrelled with Berenson, took me up to I Tatti. What a relief, and what a refuge from the prevalent flippancy! I breathed more easily in this serene climate created not only by my host but by his wife Mary and his companion Nicky Mariano. Mrs Berenson had aged considerably since my brother and I had travelled with her from England during the First World War, but she was still monumental, an ardent feminist with strong masculine traits. That wartime journey was unforgettable, for Mrs Berenson had thrilled and amused us with ghost stories, games and ballads in which we joined lustily. To keep others out of our compartment we whooping-coughed and shouted, smeared our faces with rouge and pulled grimaces at the windows, so that we were left happily to ourselves.

Mrs Berenson had fierce prejudices which influenced her husband. Fortunately I enjoyed her good graces. The sweetness and tact of Nicky Mariano was to heal many a feud for which Mrs Berenson was responsible. At this time Mrs Berenson was ailing, but there was plenty of sparkle left in her and she revelled in the piquant stories she asked me to read to her, translated from the Chinese. It was strange and touching to see her lean heavily on her fragile mate and his tender solicitude while he guided her faltering steps along the corridor to the dining-room. One feared that her weight would capsize so light a craft. Yet he kept his balance, and one felt that he was the stronger in spite of his delicate build. 'Those goat-like little men are made of steel,' my father said.

B.B. (as he was known to his friends) welcomed me as a prodigal son and plunged me into a conversation about China, which he regretted not having visited. His knowledge of the Far East struck me as more profound than that of many who had lived there: he was an adroit questioner and his queries were probably more intelligent than my answers. He had studied Sanskrit at Harvard, where Denman Ross and his other cronies had an understanding then rare of Chinese art, to which a section of his library was devoted. He must have been the only man in Florence who had formed accurate judgements about the subject. Like Terence, he did not consider anything in humanity alien from himself. Discussing Arthur H. Smith's *Village Life in China*, he remarked: 'It might almost be a book about village life in Italy, there are so many analogies.'

As often happens with men of superior intellect who can listen as well as talk, B.B. elicited any latent brilliance from his interlocutor. Embryonic thoughts became crystallized; subconscious speculations rose to the surface in rational form. One enjoyed the momentary illusion of being his equal; one began to express the inexpressible. This was exhilarating as well as a sop to one's vanity.

B.B.'s health had never been florid and perhaps at seventy-five he was too morbidly aware of his advancing age. He had lived twice as intensely as most scholars. His dinners were not sumptuous yet they gave one the impression of banquets. This was due to the conversation which ranged from continent to continent, quickening one's perceptions and illuminating distant horizons. Vitality attracted him in others even when it was little more than physical, but the thin flame of his own vitality flickered with an intensity that owed nothing to any artificial stimulus, and he enjoyed an occasional whiff of Florentine gossip. His anti-Fascism had always been intransigent and this tended to isolate him from what he dubbed 'Florentine higlif'.

If B.B. was uncompromising, Mrs Berenson was more so, and her gibes at the Duce's activities were repeated in the wrong quarters. B.B. regarded her as a pure 'Angry Saxon'. Her brother Logan Pearsall Smith had settled in England and cultivated the purest English in his writings; her sister had married Bertrand Russell; but to my ear her voice was warmly and unmistakably American – an American of English stock and Quaker antecedents. Like my mother she had the faculty of pushing painful things aside. Not in the least perturbed by dismal prospects, she concentrated on the comic aspects of events. After forty years in Italy she still viewed most Italians as quaint foreigners.

Even B.B. could not believe that Mussolini would take part in Hitler's *Walpurgisnacht*. His younger Italian friends, Guglielmo Alberti, Arturo Loria, and Umberto Morra discussed the regime as freely as if they were in London, and their common-sense liberalism made one forget the confusion and fanaticism of the world outside. In other houses Mussolini was mentioned in hushed tones as Mr Smith or under some other sobriquet in dread of Ovra spies.

The serenity of I Tatti – apart from its sheltered situation on a Tuscan hillside – was due to B.B.'s good fortune in discovering ideal collaborators. Nicky Mariano assisted and protected him against encroachments and encumbrances; her sister Alda Anrep contributed more than her share as his librarian, which meant not

71

only the care of his books and photographs: like a dietician she had to produce the mental pabulum he required at a moment's notice. The library was B.B.'s real kitchen. There the gourmet became a glutton, and the only tempests were caused by the absence or loss of some necessary ingredient.

Nicky and Alda together saw that everything ran smoothly on silent wheels. Mrs Berenson left the tiresome details to them, and I doubt if B.B. ever approached a telephone. No scholar was more blessed in this respect. His modesty about his writings was almost embarrassing. Seeking the definition which expressed his thought most adequately and being multilingual, he found it in German, French or Italian when he could not find it in English. This added a tinge of pedantry to his prose, but he wrote as he talked and his meaning was sufficiently clear. Surely this is preferable to the jargon of many art historians. His signal virtue was that of a dowser: his divining rod bent over hidden springs. How many neglected subjects he recommends to the attention of his readers!

After labouring at his lists of attributions, his friends were his greatest solace, and only true friends came to visit him at this time when he was in bad odour with the hierarchy. Among the ladies I rejoiced to meet again were the Parisianized American expatriates Natalie Barney and Romaine Brooks. In spite of French confidence in the Maginot Line, Natalie had been frightened away from her temple of friendship in the Rue Jacob by the exodus of neighbours to Provence and the Spanish border. Romaine had bought a charming villa half in, half out of Florence where Natalie joined her – a retreat which seemed to offer *douceur de vivre* among cultured people like themselves.

Natalie belonged more to Paris than her friend Gertrude Stein who had introduced me to her. Unlike Gertrude, she was bilingual. Her dry French wit belonged more to the eighteenth than to the twentieth century and her Friday receptions in the Rue Jacob had been literary agapes. Remy de Gourmont's *Lettres à l'Amazone*, apart from her own writings, have given her a permanent niche in French literature. Ravaged with lupus,

Remy de Gourmont fell in love with this mercurial American who cared little for men, and she gave him her youthful affection – as much as it was in her nature to give – in return for his love. Hence she won fame as the 'Amazon' and as the Muse of the *Mercure de France*. She had also been the 'Loreley' of Renée Vivien, the Sapphic poetess. But except in her writings this high priestess of Lesbos with the ice-blue eyes maintained a strict reticence and many felt uncomfortable under her cold scrutiny. She was short yet stately, and her profile resembled that of Alfred de Vigny.

B.B. told me that she had aroused his ardour and hinted that this affection had been more than platonic. His letters to her hardly bear this out, though he ends one 'Yours as much as you will', and another 'I kiss your feet'. No doubt each appreciated the other's appreciation. As an expatriate American himself, albeit of Lithuanian origin, he descried in her 'the passionate pilgrim come from America home to beauty', which never failed to interest him.

Her friend Romaine Brooks, tall, athletic and intense, has related her extraordinary life in a biography of which only fragments have been published. Her rich mother had forced her to be the guardian of a dangerously demented brother until she rebelled and left home to become a painter, living on a pittance. Her portraits were somewhat etiolated but so were her models: in tone and style they reflect the Rostand-Maeterlinck period with a veneer of Art Nouveau. For a while she settled in Capri and married a queer Englishman who encouraged her to dress as a boy. The marriage had been short-lived but she spoke of it with detached amusement. More tolerant of males than Natalie, she had been an intimate friend of D'Annunzio, whom she understood better than most of the women he had dazzled, thanks to a sense of humour which the poet unexpectedly happened to share. She helped him out of his difficulties when he fled to France from his creditors, and she painted several striking portraits of him, one of which is in the Luxembourg. In her relations with D'Annunzio she was probably the more masculine of the two.

At I Tatti one's anxieties about the war were soothed by the discussion of things more permanent. My English acquaintances, even those in the diplomatic service, were so impressed by credible reports of Italy's unpreparedness and lack of equipment for the eight million men 'under arms' that they winked at the anti-British posters on the walls and the rabid articles in the daily Press. Carlo Placci, the most sought-after old bachelor in Florence, who enjoyed the reputation of being the confidant of prime ministers and ambassadors as well as royalty, a political opportunist but an Anglophil at heart, said to me in an imploring voice: 'If only you would give us *una piccola vittoria!* That is what we are all praying for.' Even a little victory might have tipped the scales in our favour at this moment.

The 'Musical May', which had become a Florentine institution, began with a gala performance of Rossini's *Semiramide* at the Comunale Theatre, all frilled and furbelowed for the occasion. The King and Queen of Italy were present and instead of the usual Fascist hymn the national anthem was played ostentatiously in their honour. As they entered the royal box, a bower of azaleas and roses, they were greeted with frantic applause. All wore spotless white shirts with full evening dress, and the ladies who had sacrificed their wedding rings to the Abyssinian campaign were arrayed in all their jewels. The loud and long applause was intended not only for the monarch, but also as a manifestation for peace. Let the King-Emperor step forward and express the popular will! But the little King looked pale and wan: an expression of anguish, almost of panic, quivered across his proud features at this unforeseen reception. He never smiled or relaxed from his puppet stiffness. He looked as if he longed to evaporate, to be anywhere but in that box emblazoned with the arms of Savoy. His Montenegrin spouse towered indignantly above him. They did not stay long enough to enjoy the opera. That ovation must have shattered their nerves.

After their premature jubilation the audience were disappointed. When the royal box was empty the opera was an anti-climax; even the singers lost their brio. One felt sorry to have witnessed such lack of spirit in a king christened Victor Emmanuel. A truly royal opportunity had been missed.

The conflicting rumours and wavering opinions about Italy's entry into the war had a numbing effect on me, and the war itself became blurred by the unreality of this 'Musical May'. My father would never have doubted an Allied victory but he seemed impervious to what was happening outside Florence. An old English lawyer called Copinger, who had been Vice-Chairman of the British Institute, advised him to 'stay put', as did his Italian cronies. So long as he was on the spot he might protect his property, and he fancied he could do so even as an enemy alien. According to Copinger, his age and long residence would be respected. He was determined to risk staying on and my mother was disinclined to repeat her journey to Switzerland without him.

My premonitions were sombre. When my kind friend Augusto Rosso, who had recently been Italian Ambassador in Russia, assured me that Italy was on the brink of declaring war, I decided to leave. Our garden had never looked lovelier and as I gazed at the familiar terraces with the peacocks spreading their fans by the fountain below I could not help wondering if I should see it again. Though everybody felt confident that Florence would be treated as an 'open city' no faith could be put in any promise of Hitler's. Friedrich Kriegbaum and his colleagues of the German Institute of Art History might attempt to protect works of art from depredation, but they were a mere handful against a horde of vandals. My house in Peking seemed safer than La Pietra.

Despondently I left for Paris, troubled about my parents, thinking of all the Italians who loathed the Axis Powers yet were obliged to do their patriotic duty. Paris was ominously tranquil for the month of May. As usual I sought distraction at the theatre. The two plays I saw were as remote as possible from actuality: Giraudoux's poetical *Ondine* with delicately ethereal scenery by Tchelitchev, and *Les Monstres Sacrés* by Cocteau, a drama already old-fashioned though it dealt with live characters.

the painter Sert's complex relations with his first wife, the dynamic Misia, and his second wife young Roussi Mdivani, who was cherished by both. Each play was performed with consummate artistry. As the heroine of *Les Monstres Sacrés* Yvonne de Bray was superb. She made the theatre seem the last refuge of civilized life.

5

The phoney period of the war was over when I reached London on May 8, 1940, and the growing accumulation of calamities has been recorded too often for me to add any spice of novelty. The two days of strenuous debate in the House of Commons stirred equally violent emotions outside it.

The few Members of Parliament I encountered felt it was high time for Chamberlain's Government to withdraw. When Hitler invaded Holland and Belgium and Winston Churchill became Prime Minister the war in Europe was launched in total earnest. Active participation in a tragedy may be a healthy cathartic, but for those who are bystanders without even a role in the chorus, there is only a sinking down into a solitary quicksand. A mechanical occupation was the best analgesic for the volunteer from abroad whose services were not yet wanted. Bliss was it then for politicians and bureaucrats to be alive, for they enjoyed the kudos of earthly divinities. Theirs was the type of intellect that could burgeon as never in peacetime.

I was employed in various incidental jobs such as lecturing about modern Italy to a hall full of W.R.N.S. for the British Council, and to this day I remember the hostility of those maids in uniform. Evidently they had expected another dreary denunciation of Mussolini's misdeeds: they did not wish to hear of his brave opponents. Because I spoke admiringly of Croce and Salvemini and reminded them that the Italians were essentially a peace-loving race I was almost spat upon. 'What about Abyssinia and Albania?' they shouted. They lumped all Italians together as 'Fascist wops'. I produced a detailed report of my recent tour, and Cyril Connolly asked me to write a 'Letter from Italy' for

Horizon, but Italy was in the war before this went to press. The weather grew finer as the news got worse: the parade of tulips in Regent's Park reminded one of the tulips in occupied Holland.

Cocteau once said that to make friends was more difficult than making love. This may be true of France: in England I experienced no such difficulty. Seldom have I known such sincere and spontaneous expressions of cordiality. The kindness of the English in time of trouble is only equal to their loyalty. Their casual manner of offering hospitality is as characteristic as their understatements. How I enjoyed 'not cricket' as applied to Hitler! They sensed the wretchedness I was careful to conceal as a person definitely displaced. In my day-dreams Florence had been superimposed on Peking: the sights and sounds of both cities blended in my imagination so that here and now was less vivid to me than elsewhere and otherwhile. My memories were in one place, my footsteps in another; and try as I might to realize London, I was never there altogether, so that this period of my life remains curiously vague.

More than ever I could sympathize with Dante in exile though I had no cause to complain of the bitterness of eating others' bread and the steepness of their stairs. My versatile and beautiful friend Lady Rosse offered me her attractive house in Eaton Terrace and this became my temporary dwelling. Michael, her husband, was in the Irish Guards, and she had taken her children to the country near Doncaster. Now and then they would join me, more often separately than together, bringing fresh flowers and high spirits with them, and their company livened my rather drab existence, since Emerald Cunard had reluctantly gone to America with her beloved Sir Thomas Beecham. Even when the bombing started, Michael or Anne would breeze in to cheer me.

The summer when France fell and Mussolini rushed in to share the spoils is best forgotten. I was cut off from news of my parents, and it was not till much later that I heard they had crossed the frontier into Switzerland after many vexations. One evening while my mother was entertaining a few friends a police official called on her and requested her to accompany him to the *Questura* – the police headquarters. He explained that it was only a matter of a trifling formality, something to do with her passport. Surprised and flustered, she told him that my father was out with the chauffeur. 'I'll escort you there and back,' said the police official, 'it won't take long.' Instead he drove her to a prison where in a flimsy summer dress without even a toothbrush she was immured among prostitutes and others of ill repute for the next three days and nights. Eventually her maid contrived to send her a bag containing the barest essentials, but she refused to undress or lie down in that noisome hole, nor would she eat the slops that were handed to her in a tin container. Maybe she dozed a little in her hard chair but she could not sleep. She always maintained that this sleeplessness had aged her, giving her the dark rings under her eyes she had never had till then, and that her anger had kept her blood on the boil, which had prevented her from catching cold in spite of her summer frock and the dank draughts. (At the time she was over seventy though she concealed it.)

No message reached her from outside except an insolent letter from a Fascist female, the wife of an art-critic, telling her she had only got what she deserved, she might have been treated much worse, with the slogan '*Il Duce ha sempre ragione*' ('The Leader is always right') appended to her florid signature. When my mother's maid telephoned a powerful friend for help, he snapped back at her: 'Don't you realize that we are at war and that Mrs Acton is an enemy alien?' This distinguished official had been a frequent guest in our house for a quarter of a century. Having married a rich but very plain American, he was known in Florence as 'Joseph sold for his brethren'. Perhaps this had embittered him, though he had been on excellent terms with my mother and other American residents.

My father had a similar experience, in his case aggravated by blackmail. He managed to bribe his way out. Corruption has its advantages and under Fascism it was rife. Having disbursed a considerable sum, he was escorted to the frontier by a party member. When the police attempted to stop him his escort merely showed his party badge, which allowed my father to totter to freedom in a state of nervous collapse.

It was a tremendous relief to know that my parents were safe in Vevey, for neither was robust and their age made them vulnerable to physical hardship. In Vevey they found many friends and fellow exiles.

Apart from the manner of her arrest, my mother was wounded by the stolid indifference of her Florentine familiars. From individuals she had dined and wined for the last thirty years she never received a word of sympathy. No doubt they were far too frightened. The only tokens of sympathy she received were an affectionate note from Princess Olga Koudacheff, a Russian *émigrée* who had lost all her property in the Revolution, and a bunch of roses from an old American pansy who collected lace. My mother declared she would never return to Florence, but for my father Florence was everything, his interests began and ended there. His collection and garden had been his life, and he was still there in spirit when these had been sequestrated. He bore no malice to his persecutors, who were mostly envious of his achievements, of his flair in spotting masterpieces that had escaped their attention. His anxiety about his treasured possessions was the worst torment he had to endure. Several of his Italian friends also hopped over into Switzerland when '*questa guerretta*', 'this little war' as they called it in June 1940, became inordinately prolonged. My mother would have nothing to do with them but my father thirsted for what news of Florence they could bring, and each snippet was another twist of the knife.

It was at this time that, lunching with Patrick Kinross, I met Paul Morand, the fashionable diplomatist-author whose novels conjure up the nineteen-twenties even more effectively than Michael Arlen's. He was connected with the French embassy and he had the reputation of an Anglophil. That he should be cast down by the fall of France was only natural: we were all aghast at that calamity which brought the Nazis so much nearer. But I

Lady Cunard

was shocked when he concluded that we were certain to make peace with Hitler over France's prostrate body.

'It is merely logical,' he remarked. 'You'll get the best of the bargain.'

'When have we ever been logical?' I protested. 'That we are addicted to compromise in peace-time is a truism: we have muddled along and been criminally complacent in the past. But in a war like this surrender is inconceivable, for a compromise would mean surrender. Hasn't Giraudoux said that even to think that defeat is possible is an act of treason?'

'Poor Giraudoux, what nonsense! Wait till they cross the Channel,' he replied.

I had not expected a man of Morand's intelligence to take this view of a perfidious Albion but it was shared by many clever Frenchmen. True, an old general of my acquaintance remarked: 'The fall of France will tighten our bonds with the Empire and we'll all fight better with our backs to the wall. I never trusted the Frogs.' He might have been a contemporary of the Iron Duke.

Perhaps few people realized how close we were to defeat that sombre summer. Among them I had friends in the Ministry of Information who could see no alternative. Arthur Waley, for instance, was profoundly despondent and I tried to distract him by drawing that red herring, China, across the lost Maginot line. When he contemplated defeat I talked about the Chinese theatre and put Pekingese records on the gramophone. Soon we became engrossed in legends of the White Snake Lady and Monkey Sun, whose exploits in *Hsi Yu Chi* he had begun to translate. I saw many Chinese friends in the meantime, the genial Ambassador Quo Tai-chi, the learned Liang Yuen-li and his wife, a paragon of Chinese femininity, the writer Hsiao Ch'ien, and others whose poise and pluck were exhilarating. Liang Yuen-li could sing difficult *lao-shêng* roles with the skill of a professional, and his wife prepared succulent Chinese dishes at their flat in Swiss Cottage: as her English was rudimentary her shopping expeditions were full of absurd adventures. Hsiao Ch'ien was my last link with literary China: he looked a mere boy yet his judgement was exceedingly mature. He was prolific of articles in English and Chinese, and it was a pleasure to collaborate with him.

These friends were all eager for me to promote their cause when the Japanese had installed Wang Ching-wei as head of a new Central Government at Nanking, and our Ambassador Sir Robert Craigie and the American Ambassador Joseph C. Grew appeared to be out-bowing each other in courtesies at a Japanese tea ceremony.

Under the threat of invasion few of us spared a thought for distant China, the Burma Road, or such trifles as the settlement of the Tientsin dispute – less trifling for those who were swelter-ing in the British Concession. China and her millions might have been on another planet. The Japanese had switched their tele-scope towards South-East Asia which their confederate Hitler might claim for his dominion. While we faced Germany alone it was obvious that war with Japan should be avoided, since we had no positive assurance of American aid. The Burma Road was closed during the rainy season when traffic was reduced, but the moral effect of this on my Chinese friends was discouraging. When Armageddon started, these friends could sympathize with our predicament.

The small house I occupied in Eaton Terrace rocked and trembled while fires blazed around it and bombs exploded on every side. Had the bursting of the intellectual bonds in our progressive era released only this new surge of demoniac destruc-tion? How philosophically the Londoners adapted themselves to this daily and nightly terror! And I pondered, like many others, on how air-raids could unify a vast population. Some could sleep through the raids above ground, others felt safer in crowded underground shelters. When I was not fire-watching I sat reading *The Thousand and One Nights* – how different from these deafening cacophonies! A good night's rest was the rarest of luxuries. The word 'blitz' passed into our language and afflicted our ears as incessantly as the violence it represented.

My brother, who was fearless, was often drawn as by a magnet towards the spectacle of destruction. One particularly loud night he called on me while I was reading about the youth who could not escape an appointment with Death in Baghdad, a beautiful story which is often plagiarized. 'Come and see the docks on fire,' he proposed. The vast expanse of reddened sky, like a prolonged sunset in the east instead of the west, could be glimpsed from Eaton Square. We walked in the direction of the catastrophe. And I thought of the words in the Book of Revelation: 'Woe to the inhabiters of the earth and of the sea! for the devil is come down unto you, having great wrath, because he knoweth that he hath but a short time.'

When we reached the Thames embankment the sky suggested a rehearsal for the Last Judgement, with dragons breathing fire and smoke and brimstone. Fascinated by the blaze, my brother decided to walk on but after a while, overwhelmed with a feeling of hopeless impotence, I crawled wearily home through the deserted streets. It was a scene to surfeit a pyromaniac. Gorki would have exulted in it. I remembered his description of a whiskered man in a panama hat brandishing his stick and shouting Hurrah! while he dodged the falling beams of a burning house till the firemen dragged him away still cheering wildly. The panama hat dropped among the smouldering débris and flared up merrily in an orange flame. That Nero was a pyromaniac has never been proved in spite of the legend that he set Rome on fire. It is probable, however, that the spectacle appealed to his temperament even if he did not fiddle during the week it lasted. For me the fire in a chimney grate on a winter's evening sufficed. So long as it was tamed, its blessings were greater than its curses. Maybe this was in Cocteau's mind when he was asked: 'If your house was burning and you could take one thing, what would it be?' And, Prometheus-like, he replied: 'I'd take the fire.'

The air-raids had gathered intensity when John Sutro, who remained my most steadfast friend since we were at Oxford, announced his engagement to a girl I had never met nor heard of, who had been living in Paris. One must be prepared for surprises when friends become engaged: usually these are disagreeable. Behold a slim shy girl more French than English, who looked as if she had just been let out of a convent. Her voice evoked Colette's Claudine and she moved with the natural grace of a Persian cat. It seemed she had been lost in London until she had found John, who had taken her shivering to his warm heart. She was a little scared of his Oxford coevals and a little perplexed by his flights into fantasy, for John could be an inspired comedian, but there was an inward harmony between them which fostered mutual tolerance and understanding. Her nostalgia for Paris was contagious, and our first meeting was a happy surprise which is constantly refreshed.

In retrospect it is extraordinary how social life persisted between and during air-raids and how we kept up the pretence that life was normal. Fire-bombs were scattered near Eaton Terrace and some dropped in the small garden behind my dwelling, but my buckets of sand were inadequate, the bombs blazed stubbornly on. Shane Leslie turned up with some A.R.P. colleagues to extinguish them and soon we were chatting about our friends in Florence, Ruby Melville who had married the fencing champion Aldo Nadi, and others with whom I had fox-trotted at Rajola's in the 'twenties, while a crescendo of bigger bombs exploded – could it be at Victoria Station or in Sloan Square? The kitchen was the liveliest part of the house, for the jolly Irish cook entertained the visiting firemen and their laughter and song were a festive counter-point to the percussion outside.

Some people recall this as a happy period – victims of dull routine or opponents of private property. Parlour revolutionaries are callous until they are hit, but as every class shared the same risk their arguments lost their punch. One lived more dangerously and there were happy moments. I still had opportunities to escape from my nostalgic self with boon companions. John Lehmann would pop in to discuss some new project for *New Writing*; Cecil Beaton would brave the blitz for a quiet dinner; and my brother would call with some transcendental Hindu.

Tall, sanguine, glittering eyed; poet, editor, critic and man of the world, half American yet robustly European, John Lehmann formulated his opinions like a full-blooded orator. We agreed about so many people and subjects that he could finish my sentences for me and often did. As greedy for life as for literature, he was one of the very few to rise above nationality and keep alive the spacious tradition of the Republic of Letters – the only form of republicanism I cherish – in the pages of *New Writing*. Without thought of profit or glory, he never rested from his editorial activities, and I was proud to contribute to this exceptional publication which counteracted the confusion of tongues. John never rested but he never seemed weary. I would suffocate among the piles of manuscript he devoured daily, scrupulously sifting the grain from the chaff, never wholly rejecting when he discerned a spark of promise. He was unconsciously a literary instructor seeking disciples who had not been tainted by academic reading, and who spoke the idiom of English fields and woods and waters. This gave *New Writing* a rare freshness and actuality. He found contributors if not disciples, and they were as pleasant to read as to meet. I was still a provincial, so to speak, and he introduced me to writers of a younger generation whose work had not reached Peking. I should have liked to know these better, but I had hardly met one before he was whisked away to rejoin his ship or regiment or squadron. Nearly all were dispersed and not a few were killed.

Though the smell of beer is abhorrent to me, John would beguile me into pubs where poets and painters forgathered in a haze of tobacco, like Turkish baths in the deeper fog of the black-out. Jammed together at the bar, shouting to be heard above the hubbub, gulping pints more thirstily as closing time drew near, self-consciousness evaporated and class barriers collapsed. Chance acquaintances struck up like tinder became intimate friendships, tongues loosed by liquor, hands clasping, addresses scribbled on bits of paper. Perhaps I was not sufficiently English in manner and appearance, for the only friend I made there was with an R.A.F. pilot who quoted Baudelaire's words: '*Il faut être toujours ivre.*' He had literary sensibility combined with coltish charm, but he insisted on chewing glass. Grinding it between his teeth with a daredevil grin, he cut his tongue as he spat out the sharp fragments – a disquieting foible which I tried in vain to discourage. In other respects he seemed rational, if more anxious than most of us to live hectically in the moment, comprehensible in a pilot. He took the trouble to write to me between missions, and his letters were poems in prose. Alas, he was killed before I knew him better.

Only the eccentrics were drawn to me in pubs, for some reason I was not able to fathom. And in every pub I entered there was Nina Hamnett, once a talented artist whose sloppy bohemianism wrecked her, pleading for another little drink. Again she would remind one that she was a colonel's daughter, that the roystering chanties she sang had inspired Auric to compose *Les Matelots*; Hemingway, Cocteau, the *Boeuf sur le Toit*, Roger Fry and Osbert Sitwell, whose *People's Album of London Statues* she had illustrated, were among the names she dropped between hiccups, as if to convince herself that she had been in Arcady.

The literati of my age, most of whom had become civil servants *pro tem.*, were more likely to be met at the Gargoyle, a dinner and dance-club with paintings by Matisse on the walls. There Brian Howard created some of his typical scenes, as when he went up to some officers just back from Dunkirk and twitted them with: 'You haven't done too well, have you, my dears. Dunkirky-worky!'

Though Brian and I had been friends at Eton we had drifted farther and farther apart, he in Germany and I in China, and now we only met in groups of grumblers. He had not changed much except that his mannerisms were more accentuated: he flaunted the same air of nonchalant ease, the same elaborate charm which was apt to turn vicious after a number of drinks. Masochistically he almost begged to be knocked down. Among the cronies with whom he drank and argued for hours many were parlour pinks, who talked as if nothing could be worse than the freedom they enjoyed to damn the Government and the old order that had given them that freedom. The most vindictive of these was Guy Burgess, later to win notoriety as one of the 'Missing Diplomats', though nobody could have been less diplomatic. Brian confided to me that his equipment was gargantuan – 'What is known as a whopper, my dear,' – which might account for his success in certain ambiguous quarters.

Apparently members of the Secret Service enjoyed a special licence to misbehave: there was always some hidden motive as an excuse. Brian spoke of working for M.I.5 as if he had joined some very exclusive club. He had begun to look at me with pitying condescension as one of the doomed. There was an obvious current of sympathy between Burgess and Brian, who fulminated against *rentiers* and Money Men in his latest role, but at bottom he remained a hedonist and a snob. He had a heart, however, and the helpless misery he had witnessed during the fall of France had provoked a new spurt of literary activity. If only he could concentrate, Brian might yet surprise us with a masterpiece. Sitting in the Gargoyle or the Café Royal, he could still impose himself by his superior command of language. While others hemmed and hawed he spoke with precision.

Save in the company of John Lehmann who always, I noticed, kept one eye on his watch, I seldom enjoyed excursions among the intelligentsia. When the news was depressing they depressed me more. Many of the writers who had been excited to frenzy by the Spanish civil war were now pacifists and defeatists when they were not Communists. It was as if the images of war they had scattered in the thirties had already become threadbare clichés, and the present conflict was a futile anti-climax.

Brian Howard and Guy Burgess seemed epitomes of this muddled intelligentsia, for in spite of their alleged Marxism they were schizophrenic, guilty about belonging to the so-called ruling class and divided about Russia, to whose imperialism they were blind while ranting against ours. At least Brian, like Robert Byron, had been consistently anti-Nazi during the appeasement period.

Though I was inclined to agree with Pascal's thought – '*Tout le malheur des hommes vient de ne savoir pas se tenir en repos dans une chambre*' – it was difficult to sit still in a room when the bombs were exploding. Moreover I was afraid of fossilizing in a Chinese rut. To hear the opinions of other writers should make one's mind more flexible, but most of the civilian specimens I met were devitalizing.

As the prophecies of futurism were fulfilled in the First World War, the prophecies of surrealism were fulfilled in the Second. The surrealist effects of Dali and Buñuel were stage-managed in London by the German bombers and photographed with artistic insight by Cecil Beaton, who spent many a relaxed evening with me after a gruelling day with his camera in hospitals and among the ruins. Under a lackadaisical manner he was a determined dynamo and a stalwart patriot. His seriousness was held in reserve. Together we shared the humours of many an odd situation.

Ironically it was during the height of the blitz that some Chinese short stories translated by Lee Yi-hsieh and myself were published by the Golden Cockerel Press. Considering the period it was a unique production, an exquisite note of defiance to pessimists and Philistines. Owen Rutter persuaded Eric Gill to illustrate it, and these were his last drawings before he died. It was some solace to hear that he had enjoyed the task, and that these seventeenth-century stories had distracted him from his fatal illness. With Mrs Le Gros Clark, the elegant Muse of the Golden Cockerel, Owen Rutter and I went down to Pigotts, near High Wycombe, to visit Gill's widow and son-in-law Denis Tegetmeier, who was engraving the drawings on copper. It was the coldest of December days but their selfless devotion to art kept me warm. The atmosphere of Pigotts reminded me of William Morris though it was austere under wartime restrictions. The book, entitled *Glue and Lacquer* from an old Chinese metaphor for sexual intercourse, was immediately sold out on publication and it has become a 'collector's item'. Though caviar to the general, it was republished in a popular edition by John Lehmann after the war. *Peonies and Ponies*, a light novel about the foreign community of the Peking I had known, was published in 1941, and perhaps because it offered release from tension it enjoyed a favourable reception. I also contributed a survey of the Chinese theatre to Phyllis Hartnoll's encyclopaedic *Oxford Companion to the Theatre* and spent several months in Blackpool teaching English to the Polish airmen quartered there.

The Polish pilots were obsessed with one idea, to bomb the hated enemy, and they chafed under what they considered an intolerable delay until they were allowed to do so. They had been through hell on earth and in consequence it was difficult to make them appreciate the value of military discipline; even in the course of training they were likely to play truant in order to have a crack at the Germans. They were not easy to teach, but the scanty English they picked up seemed adequate for practical purposes. On the whole they were handsome specimens, endowed with a superfluity of virile energy, and they wrought havoc among the Lancashire lasses unaccustomed to such dazzling directness. Language was no barrier when they could be so eloquent in other ways and so generous with bottles of scent. Even if Blackpool did not produce another Chopin or Mickiewicz as a result of their intercourse, one hoped it would produce a more romantic breed. Devout Catholics, their fervour at Mass was impressive, and they sang with a depth of emotion rare in Rome itself.

Maybe I was presumptuous, but I could not be satisfied with this occupation. Like my Polish pupils, I longed for an activity in which my talents could find an outlet. Explaining grammar to indifferent pilots infected me with their own restlessness. Older men, professional teachers, could have done it better. Was this a life? I gazed at the empty sea, the empty promenade. No, this was sheer stagnation, though I tried to comfort myself with the recollection of James Joyce teaching English in the Berlitz school of Trieste, dreaming of the Dublin he had never left in spirit as I dreamt of Peking.

It was with a resounding 'Hallelujah' that I finally heard of my acceptance for the R.A.F. in May, 1941. After a three weeks' preparatory course at Loughborough, more physical than mental, with more barrack square drill than instruction in Air Force matters, extremely effective as a slimming cure, I had an interview at the Air Ministry which filled me with hope. Culture, accurate observation and psychological insight – Squadron Leader Patrick Guimaraens possessed these qualities to a singular degree. Had it been in his power I should have flown to China forthwith.

What would I do when I got there? Absurd as it may sound in retrospect, I had a sense of vocation that was almost mystical: I could almost compare my experience to Joan of Arc's voices. In my case the voices urged me to Chungking as, if even in a humble capacity, I could clear the air of suspicion and mistrust that seemed to clog our relations with the Chinese. In China I was certain to justify myself in the struggle against the *samurai*. And the R.A.F. would enable me to reach my goal.

In the meantime I was to be posted to several bomber stations and a fighter station to acquire as much knowledge as I could digest. To leap from a sedentary life into a world of Homeric heroes, *mutatis mutandis*, was a form of self-renewal which I welcomed. Since we were all at war was it not preferable to be present 'at the focus where the greatest number of vital forces unite in their purest energy?' And couldn't it be said of the R.A.F. that its spirit burned with a 'hard, gemlike flame'?

6

How many gallant friends of mine look back to the war as the period when they felt most intensely alive. John Verney, for instance, a gifted writer and painter who experienced appalling hardships in the Abruzzi after escaping from a P.O.W. camp, has declared 'almost everything in my life that has really mattered goes back somehow to the war'. I wish I could say the same of my own experience, except that at times the nearness of death made one more conscious of being alive and sharpened one's appetite for beauty. The war jolted me out of my ego but it did not increase my self-confidence. If I gained anything it was humility and tolerance of people who would have bored or repelled me in civilian life, but I lost rather more than I gained. In most of us, as Sainte-Beuve remarked, there is a poet who died young – a poet we survive. The mere fact of war suffocated the poet in me. It taught me how to wait when I did not have much to wait for, but it never impelled me to write. For me art is the highest truth and I have always lived more intensely through works of art. And art is silenced by mechanized modern warfare. Now I felt with de Vigny: *'Seul le silence est grand, tout le reste est faiblesse.'* Yeats has expressed a similar sentiment in his lines *On being asked for a War Poem*:

> 'I think it better that in times like these
> A poet's mouth be silent . . .'

Unfortunately the one diary I kept to record my early apprenticeship in the R.A.F. was flung to the fishes when the S.S. *Llangibby Castle* seemed ready to sink somewhere between Ireland and the Azores. As an Intelligence officer I was ordered to destroy my papers, so that after a quarter of a century I can only remember sporadic incidents, a few names among the many I met during those months of extraordinary tension and elation. Those months are now telescoped into a jerky confusing film.

Each R.A.F. station I stayed at was a school of systematic destruction: all human resources were devoted to that end, and since war is inhuman this was the most logical technique. There every kind of courage was to be found as well as that which is due to good health and high spirits.

I was posted first to No. 2 Group and when I reached Horsham St Faith a party was in full swing. A successful mission was being celebrated and it seemed an auspicious beginning. My arrivals invariably coincided with some festivity. Next day I was initiated into the mysteries of the Ops Room by Flight Lieutenant Brooks, known as Brooky, the first of a series of Intelligence officers who were kindly mentors to novices like me. The pilots and their crews depended on most precise preliminary briefing to pin-point the targets they were to destroy. These briefings contained the raw material of an epic. They ended with a prophetic summary of weather conditions. One had to brace oneself against the thought of the dangers ahead of the pilots, navigators, wireless operators, flight mechanics and air-gunners who listened so calmly to the decrees of fate. Such dangers could only be relished by a very small minority. Perhaps they were mitigated by an absorption in technical detail and by the assurance, even the thrill, of mastery over complex matter.

Considering the frequency of operations, I was amazed at the even temper of those who took part in them. Unusual stamina was needed to overcome the fatigue of those long frigid journeys through the night; co-ordination must be perfect, reactions instantaneous. Inevitably some would fail to return, and one never knew which of the young men one had supped with would be among them. I watched their take-off with a leaden heart. Their self-control was god-like. I remember interrogating a bomber crew, one member of which had been struck by a bullet just under one eye. He answered my questions patiently and drank a cup of tea, though I urged him to see the medico at once. 'I'd like an aspirin,' was all he said before he wandered off to have his wound dressed.

My admiration for these fellows amounted to hero-worship. It made me feel butter-fingered but I hope I contributed to their amusement. Laughter irrigated our relationship though I never became proficient in their patois. While rather self-consciously I might ask: 'What's the latest gen?' or say with a shrug 'Duff gen!' I could never exclaim 'Wizard show!' or 'It's a piece of cake!' without acute embarrassment. In spite of their apparent sang-froid, I realized that their blood was warmer than most people's: if they were utterly fearless they would not be so intelligent. They faced danger with open eyes and they loved life. Those who were married were handicapped as they could hardly help worrying about their wives and children. Some wives harassed their husbands by telephone and tried to find out the target for tonight. One who lived in the neighbourhood was deeply resentful of her husband's flying ability. 'I wish to Heaven he'd get out of this racket,' she told me candidly. The strain of night operations was quite sufficient without this extra needle to his nerves. He looked more haggard than the bachelors. Flying did not seem to harmonize with domesticity.

For a bomber station the atmosphere of Horsham St Faith was remarkably cheerful. The pastoral surroundings and the jocular conversations of the mess provided a background lull to the activities of my comrades. Having returned from barrages of flak over the Ruhr and been tossed about in sheets of bursting metal, they knew that they would have to repeat the same voyage again and again, yet they drank their tea and answered technical questions with cool aplomb. They had been above the clouds yet their heads were clear, without trace of inner tumult. They were 'giving Jerry a bad time,' tit for tat.

'Big show' followed 'big show' and I learned my first lessons about their organization and fulfilment. As I had never been a pilot my rank seemed a misnomer, but if 'penguins' were scorned by flying men it never came to my notice. I was touched by the courtesy and confidence of those heroes with whom I jested and sang, more actor than Acton. The landscape had that rural charm one associates with the Norwich school of painters, lush meadows and cosy hamlets with Norman churches whose sleepy stillness contrasted with the Blenheims thundering overhead.

In the mess I enjoyed a sensation of anonymity until I was hailed by the voice of my perennially youthful friend Oliver Messel, who invited me to visit his camouflage base near Norwich. His mastery of stage design was being applied to the disguise of gun emplacements and other military objectives. For once camouflage had become artistic as well as imaginative. Hangars and gun batteries became pointillist paintings or tapestries woven with chameleon colours, a pleasure to the eye. Not only branches of trees and netting and splotches worthy of the Fauves but Victorian monuments, lych-gates, and other constructions of deceptive ingenuity were designed like Oliver's theatrical scenery. His masterpiece of camouflage was the famous Lady of Fakenham. This simulated a huge eighteenth-century Baroque statue of a female moulded in papier maché, and was erected at the strategic crossroads entering the town from the east. It was so designed that if the invaders appeared the statue would split in half, and as her legs parted a subtly concealed cannon would fire at the approaching enemy.

I regretted that my brother was not employed in the same field. He had been drafted into the Pioneer Corps in spite of his poor health. Though he looked robust he had never entirely recovered from an accident as an undergraduate at Oxford when he had fallen from a third floor window. Luckily he had landed in a plot of grass and broken no bones, as he was limp with excess of liquor at the time, but he was taken unconscious to hospital where he suffered from internal injuries. In the Pioneer Corps his gifts were wasted.

From Horsham St Faith I proceeded to Grantham where I studied aerial photographs; thence to Coningsby in Lincolnshire, where I arrived for a briefing of crews who were to bomb Hanover. I took part in their interrogation at four in the morning, and again I marvelled at the resilience of these boys

94

after their protracted ordeal. Cologne, Frankfurt, Brest, Lorient – the targets varied but there was always the same barrage of flak to be surmounted. Our sorrow was wordless for those who failed to return: morale had to be maintained.

The temperamental contrasts between bomber and fighter pilots were most evident at Tangmere, which played a decisive role in the Battle of Britain. But this is a part of history chronicled by expert eye-witnesses and I am not so foolish as to compete with them. The individuality of these pilots was even expressed in their appearance, which would have shocked the button and boot polishing martinets of Loughborough, for they went about in the travesty of a uniform with squashed caps and scarves and unorthodox footgear, nearly all of them aces who snapped their fingers at 'bullshit' and joked about 'dicing with death'. The most flamboyant ace I met at Tangmere was Wing-Commander Bader, the legless pilot whose exploits were already legendary, whose courage and tenacity were dauntless despite so serious a handicap. It was said that he even danced and played tennis, but I only saw him in the mess, a modern musketeer who enhanced the joie de vivre of any company. Here Intelligence officers had to chase their elusive quarry, for sorties against the enemy were sudden and innumerable.

Unfortunately my right knee was broken while I was taken up up in a Beaufighter: in order to see better I had stood beside the pilot when I should have been sitting and during a steep turn both legs seemed to part from my trunk with a painful crack and I fell in a heap into the escape hatch. At first I was moved to the sick bay but I was so horrified at the sight of those suffering from burns that I begged leave to stay in my room. For a while I was laid up in plaster, dreading that my career in the R.A.F. might be cut short. Thinking of Wing-Commander Bader, I was determined to make light of the maddening accident. My amiable comrades kept me in touch with events. When a party was in progress they would bring me drinks and feed me with the latest 'gen'. Their parties were the noisiest I have heard but alas, I could only imagine the saturnalia below me.

As soon as I could limp about I was sent for a refresher course in Chinese at the School of Oriental Studies for, like any other language, it had rusted from lack of practice. The broken knee still wobbles when I try to run – a souvenir of a sunny afternoon over the Channel with a fighter pilot in hilarious mood.

In September I heard that Robert Byron had probably been drowned on his way to Egypt as a 'Special Correspondent' and this was eventually confirmed. His boat had been torpedoed. It was a heavy loss to his friends as well as to literature, for in a sense he was everybody's uncle, always generous with sound advice though this might be given like a punch on the nose. Christopher Sykes has portrayed him with perceptive sympathy in his admirable *Four Studies in Loyalty*.

Despising Eton masters and Oxford dons with one or two exceptions, he was mainly self-taught and, like George Moore in this respect, he was constantly elated by some fresh discovery. With what pleasure and surprise I listened to his raptures over Cimabue on his first visit to Florence! Cimabue opened a new road for him which led to Byzantium. From Byzantium he was diverted to Persia and the origins of Islamic art, and he wrote so bracingly about his aesthetic discoveries that the reader is tempted to follow in his footsteps. But his enthusiasm was matched by his invective. He damned as often as he blessed, but he blessed with wholehearted fervour.

Though he could seldom discern merit outside his chosen field, he was entirely free from pedantry. Like Evelyn Waugh, he exaggerated his insularity, yet he was responsive to Asiatic ways of thought. He had none of the distinctive traits of the man of letters. His high spirits and his readiness for adventure were akin to those of the fighter pilots at Tangmere, but his pugnacity concealed a Victorian earnestness. He was convinced that he had a mission as he grew older. At first this was 'to further in any way the new sense of "European Consciousness" that is gradually coming into being'. Latterly he had flung himself into the campaign to preserve Georgian architecture, but exasperation got the better of him. Hitler had turned him, as Christopher Sykes wrote, into a 'violent prophet of approaching doom', and it was in this role I had seen him last in Swan Walk. He had never looked healthy, and he had grown puffy and jowly with pale blue red-rimmed eyes. He strained his energies to the point of exhaustion, but his recuperation was sudden: he dropped into a deathlike slumber from which he rose and shook himself, more zestful than before. Pugnacity becomes a patriotic virtue in wartime but Robert's made unnecessary enemies. Evelyn Waugh, who had also been one of his cronies, was antagonized by the violence of his opinions and talked as if he might become a public menace. To borrow an epithet of Max Beerbohm's, Robert delivered his opinions hot and strong, as from the spout of a kettle boiling over.

Robert's exasperation had been lashed to frenzy by our pre-war complacency. He proudly described himself as a warmonger. He had watched the junketings of the storm troopers at Nuremberg with appalled fascination. Always he prefaced his narrative with 'If you'd *seen* them!' and he made you see them. During his short intense life he had moved in many circles distributing salutary shocks, but his most vital quality is seldom present in his literary creations. Creations they were, laboriously wrought from the hasty notes on his impressions. He worked hard to obtain an effect of spontaneity. *The Station* and *The Road to Oxiana* are permeated with his personality and we must be content with these.

So often had I seen him fall asleep that I expected him to wake up somewhere and float back to us. While the news of his loss was not confirmed I attempted to console his mother. She replied that she had given up hope since he had visited her in a dream and told her that he had been drowned. His image remains clearer to me than that of most vanished comrades, and it was particularly clear when I seemed to be on the verge of sharing his fate.

In the meantime I had to dismiss Italy from my mind and concentrate my thoughts on China. What a joy to re-enter a liberated Peking! Chungking was my immediate goal and that was very different. There the fine flower of Chinese civilization was still alive, but it was wilting for lack of sustenance. Since the fall of France, Malaya, Burma and the East Indies were all in danger. That Singapore should be attacked seemed inevitable, but who could have foreseen the attack on Pearl Harbor?

At last I was posted overseas and packed my tropical kit with a few carefully chosen books in a tin trunk clearly marked with my name and number. There was no trace of the trunk when I reached West Kirby camp near Liverpool and all my efforts to recover it were unavailing. Thefts on British railways were more frequent than I had imagined: R. H. Dundas, who had been Senior Censor at Christ Church while I was an undergraduate, told me that his accumulated notes for a lifetime of lectures had been stolen from him the same way. They had probably been thrown into a rubbish heap. 'I would gladly see that thief rot in Hell,' he muttered. My own loss was nothing to his.

The sooty bleakness and devastation of Liverpool were soul-destroying, the cold was gripping, and I had no desire to join the New Year revellers who shared my hut. I had to draw heavily on my store of patience until we embarked on January 7th and even then five shivering days were to pass before we sailed. Every day the jovial stewards hinted hopefully that we might sail tomorrow. Our ship, the *Llangibby Castle*, was about twelve years old: it seemed infinitely older. We were hardly on board before the electricity failed and it was rumoured we were already on auxiliary generators. The self-starter of the diesel engines was also reputed to be out of order. Though the lights were restored they continued to fluctuate. Like most troopships the *Llangibby* was packed beyond capacity: her speed was fifteen knots, probably the slowest in our convoy. I was fortunate in sharing a small cabin on A deck with an easy-going Rotarian type who had been in Japan and Korea. There were not enough chairs in the lounge but as there was a piano and invariably someone to strum it many of us stood there or at the bar, which was so well stocked that at least we kept warm with liquor. As the days dragged by we realized that the ship was undergoing some essential repairs. A dense fog delayed us further.

We were fogbound until we sailed at dawn on January 12th with an icy headwind blowing, escorted by a purposeful destroyer. There was an impromptu boat drill in the afternoon and we were to carry our life-belts and sleep fully dressed until further notice. So boisterous was the sea that the majority were sick. A loquacious old steward, who seemed permanently tipsy and whistled like a blackbird as he served our meals, remarked: 'We're one of them holy rollers.' Perhaps this was a sort of insurance.

Soon after eight in the morning of January 16th a tremendous explosion was followed by a blinding flash: the whole ship reeled and shuddered to a standstill. We had been torpedoed. Soon we learned that the stern, the rudder and steering gear had been shattered and the question remained, would we sink? Ordered to boat stations on the sloping deck, I hurriedly destroyed my documents and in my great-coat and life-belt I tried to keep my balance with a small dispatch case. Uncertain as to whether we should have to abandon the ship, we remained scanning the horizon for another torpedo, or for the submarine to surface and shell us. No sea ever looked angrier: the waves were like cataracts: the rest of the convoy had vanished. For several hours we drifted in circles, bespattered by salt spray. The life-boats could only have held a minority and I could not conceive myself wrestling with such formidable billows. But the prodigious swell had saved us. Suddenly I had a dark vision of tapering wings, as of a monstrous bird of prey. A Focke-Wulf Condor dived out of the clouds to deliver the *coup de grâce*, and we scrambled for cover. Either our guns drove it off, or its pilot decided that we were done for. The bombs fell wide of the mark but the machine-guns claimed some thirty casualties – I never knew the exact number.

After this lightning incident there was another endless wait on the slanting slippery deck. There was not the slightest panic, just gloomy resignation. Numb with cold and damp with spray, I was surprised by my own detachment. Would one really relive one's whole life in the moment of drowning? I thought of Robert Byron and hoped he did not have to endure a long-drawn agony.

And I remembered a phrase in Jules Renard's diary: 'The smell of a putrefied shell-fish is enough to accuse the whole sea.'

A friendly destroyer hove into sight with sealed orders for our Captain. This somewhat relieved our tension. We began to feel less forlorn. The sailors waved and cheered and we cheered back, hoarse greetings full of hope. The sealed orders delivered, or rather flung at us, the destroyer sped swiftly away, presumably to join the vanished convoy. Again we were left to our crippled devices, expecting more Focke-Wulf Condors to return. It must have been our longest day.

Eventually a Dutch tug-boat arrived and we were towed like a broken-down car – whither we knew not but we were still mercifully afloat. A pocket Chinese dictionary helped to soothe my nerves in the dim saloon where we sat silently huddled, our tin hats and life-belts beside us. Gradually our numbness thawed, we were invaded by drowsiness.

I had realized from the start that the voyage would be long and tedious but at least I was on my way towards China, which had become the symbol of everything from which I had been severed. This misadventure had been a cruel setback: it would take an age to reach any harbour in our actual plight. In the meantime the Dutch tug dragged us across the choppy ocean. Thanks to the helpful Hollander we zigzagged into the sun and made good speed.

Part of the lounge was converted into a temporary hospital for the wounded. Most of my time was spent on deck watching for submarines. As officer of the guard from one to eight o'clock in the morning, I went round talking to the sentries as cheerily as I could. There was a rumour of our possible internment in the Azores when this was known to be our destination.

Four days later we reached Horta-Faial, whose multi-coloured buildings in the brilliant sunshine seemed to be cut out of cardboard for a doll's house. Though tantalizingly near we were not allowed to land and there were no facilities for communication, which worried those who longed to write home. The débris aft had to be cleared, and the stern was so damaged that this seemed an insuperable task in the fortnight allotted to us in neutral waters. The worst casualties were removed the same afternoon. One stalwart old seaman was hoisted overboard on a stretcher more dead than alive. He grinned gallantly and made the V sign, but it was plain that he dreaded the prospect of dying abroad.

Towards evening Faial was cosily illuminated, whiffs of aromatic soil were wafted by the breeze. While repairs were under way we sat between Faial and Pico, a volcanic island rising to 7,713 feet with a luxurious vegetation and a few scattered houses – how beguiling from our battered vessel! Here and there a baroque belfry reminiscent of the Sorrentine peninsula inspired in one a feeling of trust and gratitude. Fruit already scarce in England, such as oranges, lemons and bananas, was peddled in little boats that bobbed beneath us.

Next day, a Sunday, a thanksgiving service was held with collective emotion. The Captain made a stirring speech amid cheers he richly deserved, for we all admired this heart of oak, who lived up to one's ideal of the indomitable English sailor. André Malraux has said that 'a man becomes truly Man only when in quest of what is most exalted in him', and I think this applies to sailors even more than to airmen: both stand for 'a victory over the human situation', but the sea in the long run requires greater endurance and forces a man to meditate in solitude on destiny and what is eternal. The best sailors are natural sages.

After dinner there was a sing-song to raise our spirits. The chorus of male voices had a nostalgic ring, like those in Puccini's *Fanciulla del West*. We were visited by the Portuguese police, who placed pickets on board, good-natured rustics who brought bottles of the sweet local wine in exchange for cigarettes. Trifling incidents were welcome distractions: the arrival of a Clipper bound for America; the Free French sloop of a mine-sweeping patrol christened *La Moqueuse* – what English sloop would be given such a name? On board 'The She-Mocker' we could see the flashing smiles of Negroes, the gay, almost feminine laundry hanging up to dry, and we could hear the light concertina tunes of *bals musettes* evocative of the rue de Lappe. A cargo boat arrived with coal. Three coffins were buried at sea from a cable ship. Then a great treat was offered, since all of us longed to tread solid earth again.

Four days after our arrival the Captain announced, amid frantic cheers, that shore leave would be granted to sixty men and officers at a time. But there was a hitch: perhaps an invasion was feared, for when the first batch set out their landing was opposed by the Portuguese authorities. A machine-gun was trained on them from a tower, so they had to content themselves with boat races round the ship. We were informed that Horta-Faial had no food or accommodation for 1,200 men, and the promised shore leave was cancelled. Day after day we watched the sun rising over one island and setting over the other and gazed at those tempting green declivities while our ruined stern was being repaired with concrete. No doubt we were spied through the German consul's telescope.

To thank our reluctant hosts a party was given on board for the military governor and his associates. They brought their wives and children dressed up in their Sunday best and we toasted – whom were we to toast, Carmona or Salazar? – vague about their relative status, we raised our glasses to both, and they drank to our King and Queen. They expressed polite regret that we could not land: though their sympathies were with us they had to observe neutrality. A few senior officers were invited to a party on a small Portuguese cruiser, the *Douro*, and I was included as an interpreter though my Portuguese was as sketchy as their English. We exchanged platitudes in French and the twittering amiability of the dark little ladies who replenished our glasses with syrupy wines and offered us honeyed cakes was a substitute for conversation. This brief interlude of feminine society had a magical effect on my fellow officers: they danced to a gramophone in a blissful trance. The mere touch of soft arms and delicate hands, the cooing of gentle voices, transported them to Elysium after their dreary duties.

Games, exercises, 'housy-housy', sing-songs – all manner of pastimes were devised to keep the troops and aircraftmen amused in claustrophobic conditions, cooped up in a narrow space with no hot meals and a scanty ration of tea. Since we were threatened with a food shortage our victuals were restricted. I arranged classes in French and Italian though I was handicapped for want of textbooks. A local priest came on board to hear confessions but he said he was not authorized to serve Mass. I urged him in vain to consider our predicament: was it right to abandon us to our own resources when we were in a chronic state of insecurity? No, all he could do was to hear our confessions. He eyed me severely as if I had much on my conscience, but I suspect he was only hiding his dismay. My fellow Catholics were mostly rough diamonds from Glasgow whose language was almost as incomprehensible to me as Portuguese. As I had to guess the meaning of their simplest remarks I wondered how he could cope. Shrugging my shoulders I left him to it but I was not edified by his negative attitude.

At last our two weeks' interlude was over. It would have required months to make us self-sufficient. Three of our wounded passengers were brought back on board. The tug-boat *Thames* from Rotterdam returned to chaperon us and it was rumoured that we should proceed to Freetown or Bermuda. Lame duck though we were, we served as a useful decoy. Enemy submarines were waiting for us outside Horta and at least seven of these were reputed to have been sunk in the brisk battle that followed our departure. Five days later when we approached Gibraltar we counted nineteen British destroyers in our vicinity. Our last night on H.M.T. *Llangibby Castle* was the noisiest. One could hardly blame the troops for getting drunk and I slept fitfully through their caterwauling.

Next morning our passengers were squeezed into other troopships. With a small R.A.F. group I embarked on the Polish ship *Stefan Batory*, formerly of the Gdynia-American line. Overcrowded though she was, it was like stepping into the Ritz from a suburban boarding-house. I was smacking my lips at the pleasant change of cuisine when I was called to deal with a complaint about it from the sergeants' mess. Off I trotted to investigate the cause, for we all had the same bill of fare. Pointing at the borsch which I had swallowed with relish, one sergeant barked indignantly: 'Just look at that, sir. It's stuff we wouldn't give to pigs at home.'

Perhaps the beetroot colouring had repelled him. I assured him that though it was Russian it was considered a delicacy in expensive London restaurants but he looked incredulous. 'Well, all I can say is that none of us here can stomach it,' he replied with disgust. 'And there's that phoney stuff they call chicken. It doesn't look or taste like chicken to me. More like rabbit in fancy dress. Anyhow chicken's no meat for a hungry man on the job.' 'Why, it's chicken Pojarsky. I wouldn't mind a second helping.' 'You're pulling my leg, sir.' 'Indeed I'm not. Tell me what you would prefer and I'll try to obtain it for you.' 'If we can't have mutton we'll be satisfied with bully. And boiled greens with spuds instead of this greasy mess' – pointing to some aubergines with grated cheese. 'I can promise you the bully and potatoes,' I said, 'but don't blame me if they get monotonous.' 'As long as we get good helpings we're not particular,' said the sergeant with a grin.

Musing on the dullness of the average English palate, I wondered if the American synonym for excellent derived from our bully beef. I received no further complaints.

New Writing was often to break the ice with fellow passengers, opening conversations which in some cases led to friendship. Now that it was issued as a 'Penguin' I saw it in unexpected places, as on the deck of this troopship, in the hands of a rugged young officer of the 9th Nigerian Regiment whose broad-brimmed hat gave him the air of an American frontiersman. The ruggedness proved superficial, a military veneer over a sensitive Oxford graduate who had joined the Nigerian Civil Service not long before the war. Though Oxford had been changing rapidly, many of the dons I had known still enlivened its society and their figures rose before us as we talked on the bustling deck. As Hector Jelf had been at Exeter we had such friends in common as Nevill Coghill and Professor Dawkins. We could picture the former producing Shakespeare on board the *Batory*, but the Professor of Byzantine Archaeology and Modern Greek was more difficult to imagine though he had served as a Lieutenant-Commander, R.N., in the last war, a versatile exponent of Oxford eccentricity with his staccato voice and movements and his marmalade moustache. While we lounged at the rails in the muggy heat I recalled his anecdotes of Baron Corvo, who had characteristically maltreated him in return for his generosity. Though I never shared the Corvo cult, his admiration for Norman Douglas and Ronald Firbank had been a congenial bond. The echo of his shrill cackle cheered me as I gazed at the desolate sea. Knowing little about Nigeria I urged Hector Jelf to write about it, for at this time of comparative isolation I felt sure that John Lehmann would welcome some stories of that remote country and its influence on the civil servants employed there. But our few conversations were invariably interrupted by summons to play bridge in the suffocating lounge. He reappeared beside me in the dusk, and though neither of us spoke I was aware that he had much to say as he puffed at his cigarette with a muffled sigh. There was the same silent harmony that old acquaintances feel at each new encounter. He had much to say but no time to say it in and we were separated by our various duties. Almost before I knew it vast distances prevented our friendship from maturing. The lights of Freetown glimmered as through a vellum lampshade pricked out with a winding pattern of convolvulus.

With a small group from the *Llangibby Castle* I disembarked, but only to climb on board a depot ship, the S.S. *Manela*. Feeling like a packhorse, I sweated up the companion-ladder, girdled with webbing and piled with equipment, gas-mask, tin helmet and dispatch-case, after searching for my luggage like needles in the haystack of the broiling hold. Here was frustration materialized, the atmosphere of Sartre's *Huis Clos*, except that we were cooped up with pleasanter companions. We all suffered from prickly heat and moved in a sort of daze, watching the terns and gulls swoop vertically from the sky for fish, or the submarine-spotting Sunderlands brushing the water with their tails down, or a sunbaked village shimmering in the distance. We saw the passing of a powerful convoy in which we could distinguish the *Monarch of Bermuda*, the *Strathaird* and the *Volendam*, which added to our sense of being the lost tribe of Israel. The pseudo-Tudor lounge was a comic anachronism in this torrid climate. The winding and unwinding of mosquito nets about our bunks made us feel like the cocoons of silkworms enmeshed in ignorance of our destination. 'We may hear something in a day or two,' was repeated hopefully when we were inoculated against yellow fever.

When we were supposedly immune to infection a launch took us to the shore, then past corrugated tin shacks and clumps of sick vegetation a lorry drove us to Lumley Beach for a swim. The sea was coolly caressing after the hot sand but jelly-fish pullulated and one young man cried out that his John Thomas had been stung. As he was rather obstreperous we hoped this would calm him down. 'If my missus were here she'd give me hell,' he said. The local fishermen beat an incessant tattoo on their boats to beguile their inquisitive prey, but the gulls seemed more efficient.

We sailed again on March 7th, this time on a Norwegian vessel, the *Bergens Fjord*, but we were still uncertain of our destination. Rather than stifle with three others in the blacked-out cabinette I preferred to doss down on the upper deck, congested as it was with some three thousand troops on board. Half my time was spent censoring letters and during the leisure between boat drills most of my fellow passengers had let their pens run away with them. Oblivious of security regulations, all the details of the *Llangibby Castle*'s torpedoing were fully described and had to be deleted. The general tone of these letters was resolutely cheerful: any extra space was monopolized by crosses for kisses. There were quizzes in the lounge and sing-songs in the black-out. The favourite songs were 'South of the Border', 'She'll be coming round the mountain', and 'Home on the Range': I have not heard them since but they evoke the troopship more clearly than anything else. The sergeants provided us with a vaudeville entertainment of professional quality, including an eccentric dancer, a crooner, a performer on the guitar, and a duplicate of George Formby who sang a ditty appropriate to the body-bestrewn decks of the *Bergens Fjord* – 'My little stick of Blackpool rock'. They gave one the agreeable sensation that the Music Hall of the nineties was still going strong.

Within ten days we reached Cape Town, whose citizens covered us with kindness. I think every man on board was invited to some private house and shown the sights. For the passengers of the *Llangibby* it was a taste of Nirvana. After long abstinence from wine the local vintages were as nectar, and the local fruit was most grateful to the palate. Judging by the letters I had to censor many of our troops had become engaged to Cape Town girls during the three days we berthed there, and even more wished to emigrate to South Africa.

❧ 7 ❧

Our voyage continued for another three weeks till we landed at
Port Tewfik, Suez. To all appearances I should now be bogged
down in Egypt. Farewell to the Burma Road I had hoped to cross!
In a camp near the Bitter Lakes I wrote applications and filled in
forms, supped on bully and drank tea from a beer bottle. The
days were hot, the nights under canvas were chilly, and I was
given more letters to censor. A trip to Cairo by lorry was a
welcome distraction. By chance I ran into Romney Summers,
perhaps the only undergraduate who had a private house instead
of lodgings when we were at Oxford. There, surrounded by his
collection of old English glass, he had received his friends in
princely style after a day at the races, which he substituted for
lectures. He maintained the same hospitable tradition at Gezira,
and I could not but smile at the contrast between his commodious
apartment and my tent at Kasfareet. He took me to the Mousky
and the hooded lanes where spices, dyes and scents were concocted
and sold, and I was tempted by woven silks and Turkish silver
until with a jolt I remembered my situation. What should I do
with such gewgaws if I went to China or even, as seemed likely, if
I were sent to the desert? So back to my tent, whose single luxury
was more elusive, the indescribable and unpaintable glory of
shifting colour in the sea of desert sand. It was a prospect with a
sinister power in its silence. For those enervated by the discords
of urban traffic this vast emptiness was a healing balm, and it was
a place to make one aware of one's insignificance. Gladly would I
banish our meddling politicians to the Sahara: their shadows may
lengthen at dawn but at midday they will shrink to small bipeds
of dubious identity.

The multitude of flies was our greatest curse: the bare torsos of riggers and fitters servicing aircraft were as covered with them as if they wore bodices of jet black sequins. Fly-whisks only seemed to allure the pests, which appeared in swarms from nowhere after sunrise. Gloster Gladiators were sitting on the runways of Almaza: these biplane fighters were highly manoeuvrable, but they were becoming obsolete on account of their lack of speed. When I was resigned to becoming obsolete for the same reason, a postagram informed me that I was to proceed to India. At last China was in sight.

Having risen from my tent at four in the morning after a sleepless night, I took off at 7.45 as one of twenty-eight passengers on a Sunderland flying boat. It was April 29, 1942, over three months since I had left England, and this was the most beautiful part of the journey, refreshed by orange juice near Jerusalem and a good night's rest at Habbanya, thence via Basra and Bahrein to Karachi. We left the Sunderland at Gwalior, where our most distinguished passenger, the Maharajah of Dewas, was loaded with necklaces of flowers and escorted to the massive castle which dominated the dried-up plain – a great cliff of yellow sandstone crowned with ornate battlements. A few bullocks, all skin and bone, were tottering about the parched landscape and I wondered where the Maharajah's flowers had come from. When the Venetian traveller Manucci was here in the seventeenth century crystal springs irrigated gardens of cypress and jasmine like the Alcazar of Seville, but of these I could see no vestige. In clotted heat I caught a train to New Delhi.

I could not have arrived at a more chaotic season. Our small air force in Burma had been decimated; our troops and thousands of civilian refugees were escaping through the jungles and mountains, an agonizing trek of six hundred miles, and the rains were soon expected. Half the Chinese forces had retreated to their own country, the rest were following General Stilwell to India. Small wonder that I was eyed askance when I reported to P Staff. What the devil was I doing here and what did I think I could do?

The mere sight of me seemed to irritate the only rude officers I met in the R.A.F. In the circumstances I could hardly blame them. They were harassed and the weather was oppressively hot. But the heat of Delhi, which was dry, was tolerable compared to the steamy heat of Calcutta.

Posted to Bengal Command at Barrackpore, near Calcutta, I shared the duties of a delightful group of Intelligence officers, sifting, collecting and filing reports, arranging maps, spending long hours at inaudible telephones, and interviewing stray military visitors from China. While I tried to make myself useful I was aware that others could have done my job quite as well if not better, and I continued to hope that with patience and persistence I would reach Chungking. But as the weeks dragged by and the monsoon bogged everything down, this hope began to fade. As we know now, General Wavell envisaged the risk of losing India altogether. Fortunately the Japanese advance was halted by the strenuous resistance of our air force in Ceylon when Colombo was heavily raided in April, but the Japanese had gained control of the Bay of Bengal and our aircraft were greatly outnumbered. General Alexander was guarding India's eastern frontier and Kalewa and Imphal were his advance posts. The aircraft of Bengal Command were mainly employed on errands of mercy, dropping stores and medical supplies and evacuating the wounded.

Calcutta was our chief link with China and I met many Chinese there who candidly admitted that they had lost faith in us since the collapse of Singapore. As General Wavell had said at the time, we had less than twenty light bombers to meet an attack which had cost us three important warships and nearly 100,000 tons of merchant shipping while over two hundred heavy bombers attacked one town in Germany. Our pilots in Bengal could not help envying their opposite numbers at home, and even in North Africa, who enjoyed the thrills and the glamour of heroic action. The pilots who flew over the jungle in poor visibility and cantankerous weather, and those who crossed 'the hump' into China, had none of the satisfaction of our strategic bombers and fighter escorts whose missions were clear and decisive.

Since the Battle of Britain, America was left to negotiate with Japan while we concentrated on the defeat of Germany. Our Foreign Office had little time for Chinese problems and the International Settlement of Shanghai had to fend for itself until Japanese troops marched into it on December 8, 1941. I wished we could enjoy closer co-operation with American Intelligence. Apart from General Stilwell even junior American officers were such expert linguists that theirs – Aldrich's and Rattay's – were the most practical manuals to the Chinese vernacular. General Chennault's confidential memoranda contained the most trustworthy information. Chinese reports tended to fanciful extravagance. Their Ministry of Information in Calcutta issued a weekly bulletin which contained eloquent items about the Burma Road, the air service from Calcutta to Chungking, Madame Chiang's transatlantic tour of the U.S.A., and the 'Lone Battalion' heroes of Shanghai, eighty-eight of whom, unarmed, killed their Japanese guards and escaped to northern Anhwei, 'where they were warmly welcomed by the people. They are now on their way to the war-time capital, where they will be assigned to fight the Japanese on more equal terms.' I scanned these with little profit. A fair sample of the 'News Brevities from Chungking' ran under the heading 'Hair-clippers in Sinkiang': 'Following repeated trials, the repair workshop of the Sinkiang Printing Company of Tihwa (Urumchi) has succeeded in manufacturing a hair-clipper which compares very favourably with imported clippers. At present the workshop is producing only eight pairs of such hair-clippers a week, but production is being stepped up so that in addition to meeting the local demand some clippers can be marketed in other cities and provinces.'

I felt sure that I could collect news brevities of greater import on the spot. But as time went by I began to realize that there must be some serious hitch. I met many Chinese who contrived to look exquisitely cool and unperturbed. During the last five years they had become inured to disaster and war was accepted as a normal course of life. One Chinese pilot said he could not understand my mania for Chungking. 'There is such a nice Chinatown here in Calcutta,' he said, 'and the Chung Wah restaurant is better and cheaper than any we have in Chungking. I am always glad to return here: it is like peacetime.' But I was in no mood to appreciate these advantages. He invited me to the Chinese South Physical Culture Club on Chandney Chowk Street and introduced me to some of his compatriots who played and sang the melodies I had not heard since leaving Peking. On the other hand I also saw refugees from Hong Kong and Burma who had barely survived their escape.

Of the innumerable accounts I heard of the thousands, mostly women and children, who were trapped in the hills of North Burma by monsoon floods and had to lead 'Robinson Crusoe' lives for three miserable months, I was haunted by that of a fragile girl of Anglo-Chinese stock. Her ivory skin was almost transparent over the childish bones. She had left Moulmein with her parents in December, travelling through Prome, Mandalay, Maymyo to Myitkina, where her father fell dangerously ill. Unable to move, he urged his daughter to start hiking. Her mother stayed behind to look after him.

Though she had been told that the rest of the journey would only take a week, it took over four months. The first lap was comparatively easy, for she joined a troop of fifty evacuees, the road was not too bad, food was obtainable and she got an occasional lift. But soon the road dwindled to a track which was turned into a bog by the incessant rain, and they could only travel a few miles a day. Food became scarce and there was little to buy from the Kachin villages through which they passed. The party split into groups to forage for victuals and every evening when they met again a few were missing, either lost or attacked by dacoits or overcome by fever.

Another couple of girls from Moulmein, sisters aged twenty and eighteen, tried to nurse the fever-stricken: they had charming voices and they sang to keep up their courage. These had been joined by four Tommies. Though they were suffering from malaria, the soldiers helped them through the most difficult part of the journey, the ill-famed Seven Streams where many of their companions were drowned. The girls swam naked across the swollen currents and the soldiers followed with their haversacks, containing their scanty clothes and supplies. There were many halts, sometimes of several days, on account of the prevalent fever. Some died of it and were buried in graves one foot deep. The sisters said prayers for the dying. Those who could still walk trudged on through the grim swamp of the Hukong valley. Eventually they reached a large camp where they had their first solid meal for a week. Next day the soldiers who had accompanied them collapsed: three died and the fourth was far too weak to move. The sick decided to stay near medical supplies rather than struggle on through the jungle.

The girls joined a group of thirteen women and children led by a Bengali who claimed to be a doctor. Among them was a boy of fourteen whose parents had died on the road. Twice the party was assaulted and robbed by hill bandits. Leeches fastened on their bare legs as they sank into the mud and they had no matches to burn them off. The Bengali 'doctor' became a sadistic tyrant. He beat the women with a swagger-cane if they did not jump in obedience to his orders. If they fainted with fatigue he shouted at them: 'You bitches are holding me back.' And he would thrash them until they got up. He monopolized the rations collected from dumps supplied by our food-dropping aircraft and he compelled the weaker women to submit to him by threats of starvation. The more spirited girls resisted. When he threatened the Anglo-Chinese girl with one of his six revolvers she said: 'Go on then, try it!' But he lost his nerve. However, she got even less to eat for her temerity.

The track grew worse and they had to slither on their bellies through lakes of mud. More often they had to stop from weakness and exhaustion: even so they managed to cover between seven and ten miles every day. The farther they tramped the more corpses and skeletons they passed and the 'doctor' robbed them of clothes and whatever money he could find. For a whole month they were detained by floods at a camp of bamboo huts containing five hundred refugees, half of whom died of meningitis within a fortnight. When the water subsided enough to let them continue their trek the girls found Kachin porters to carry them. They were so famished and feverish that they could scarcely remember the last lap of their journey. When they reached the ration dumps at a border camp they were barely alive. The rations were mostly tinned meat which gave them dysentery, after which they were found unconscious on the track by a rescue party organized by some Assam tea planters. Thanks to these good Samaritans, who had been the first to help hundreds of refugees from Burma, they were carried into India on pack horses. At last they had medical attention, nourishment, and the comfort of clean beds. The Bengali 'doctor's' reputation had preceded him and he was arrested when he reached the India–Assam border. £30,000 worth of rupees had been stuffed in his knapsack, of which £7,500 belonged to the fourteen-year-old boy who had lost his Punjabi parents.

Others corroborated these stories. The ordeal of these refugees struck me as far more gruesome than that of our European fugitives. So much for Rousseau's notion of primitive goodness and the noble savage.

Calcutta derives its name from the shrine of Kali, 'the Black One', a gorgon-headed goddess dripping with the blood of which she is insatiable, adorned with a necklace of skulls. She sends famine and pestilence, and in former days human heads wreathed with flowers were offered at her altar whenever a famine raged. Goats were sacrificed instead of human beings when I visited her loathsome temple.

In spite, or perhaps because of, her destructive tendencies, Kali was once a *prima ballerina*, and she is said to have made a triumphal tour of India challenging famous dancers to compete with her. Naturally she won – until she competed with her husband Siva. In order to defeat her Siva 'raised his leg vertically above his head, a position which Kali's womanly modesty forbade her to copy' – an episode often portrayed in Indian sculpture. Whereupon Kali retired to her temple in a tantrum. That so frightful a virago should have been so demure was curious, but the monsters of history and legend are often bashful. No doubt Hitler was a pattern of primness.

Kali apart, Calcutta used to have an English veneer but this had begun to crack. Its palatial buildings were peeling, sun-parched and mildewed: here and there a house with an eighteenth century portico was crumbling among bamboo shanties and teeming vegetation, grandiose anachronisms awaiting the brush of John Piper. Government House, an imitation of Kedleston Hall, was the most imposing in its garden of well-kept lawns and trees. The domed central building was approached by a double flight of steps, and the four wings connected by galleries were ingeniously ventilated. From either side the impression was of a semi-circle with Ionic columns and a central porch, and similar columns silhouetted the wings.

In Thomas and William Daniell's *Picturesque Voyage to India* (1810), which shows the former capital in its prime, we read that the buildings were 'covered with *chunaur*, a species of stucco possessing the delicacy and lustre of marble'. Through spacious streets 'the chariot often comes in contact with the palankeen; and the phaeton is seen lightly rolling before the litter-like hackney, a covered cart slowly drawn by bullocks, and appro-priated to the service of secluded females. Amidst the pro-miscuous concourse of people and equipages stalks a tall meagre crane, nicknamed the adjutant, which performs the useful office of scavenger and is perfectly familiar with the inhabitants. This bird is remarkable for the slowness of its movements, and often stands on some roof, dropping its head with ludicrous solemnity, and looking as abstracted as a fakir at his devotions. The river presents a scene of almost equal animation and variety.'

Fear of Japanese raids had driven ships away from the Hooghli, but the traffic on Chowringhee was still promiscuous with honking lorries, pattering rickshaws, lumbering bullock carts, and curious cabs with louvred shutters. Dazed cattle had the right of way and I was all but lynched for colliding with a cow. Rotting garbage overflowed from tins and besmeared the pavements. Enormous rats proliferated. The stark skeleton of a holy man with a chain round his genitals stepped superciliously through the crowd and a dhoti-clad Bengali held an umbrella over his head when it started to rain. The holy man's expression struck me as more self-conscious than aloof. But the adjutant crane seemed to have been ousted by an army of carrion crows. These were the chief scavengers and I was often entertained by their impudence, as when one of them filched a slice of papaya from my plate at breakfast.

John Irwin, who was A.D.C. to the Governor, afforded me occasional glimpses of the local intelligentsia as well as of the grandiose interior of Government House. Through John, who resembled one of the Knights of the Grail as depicted by Burne-Jones, I met several Indian writers who could forget their political grievances to discuss poetry and painting with eloquence and acumen. They spoke as if reciting Swinburne and it was a pleasure to listen to their lilting voices. With Bishnu Dey, Buddhadeva Bose, Datta, Chakravarty and Suhrawady I was able to forget the drudgery of Barrackpore, for as such I came to regard my duties when China faded farther into the distance and the monsoon hampered aerial activity. Messages were often bungled by Indian employees, the secrephone which 'scrambled' reports was often out of order, and the clammy humidity addled one's efforts to interpret questionable figures; a prisoner had been taken with the wreckage of a Japanese aircraft near Cox's Bazaar; the Wing Commander was in 'a flap'; the electric fan had stopped working. My senior officers were so secretive that I seldom knew what was happening: I was never invited to any conference. Having to guess from scrappy reports in telegraphese and hunt for missing fragments of a jigsaw puzzle, how often I wished that 'Intelligence' could be pooled, as I believe it was among our American allies.

I had the unpleasant feeling that I was not trusted. Then by chance I came across a file emanating from an embassy official which opened my eyes to the harsh reality. This was not only a gross libel on my character: it was a plain statement that I was not *persona grata* and that I was by no means to be allowed to proceed to China. The most sinister implications hovered between the lines. I could only thank Heaven that this scrap of paper had not kept me out of the R.A.F. So this was why I was being detained at Barrackpore. In my rage I consulted a lawyer, but there was no way to seek redress. The scrap of paper was unsigned but it was official and it was secret – a foul blow beneath the belt. I was defenceless. I could see myself nailed in Calcutta till the end of the war.

Friends in R.A.F. Public Relations sympathized with my predicament, and I promptly applied for a transfer. After all, I was a writer of sorts and there was plenty for me to do in that line. Public Relations in India had been launched by the dynamic Brigadier Jehu and he needed fresh recruits. Wing Commander Falk hoisted me out of the Slough of Despond. The signal about my posting was held up for three weeks – I suspected out of malice – but I was released in October with a railway warrant for Delhi.

Thenceforth I felt happier as a liaison officer with the Press and the other services. Albeit a mere 'penguin', I was exhilarated by contact with our pilots. Their pride in their prowess and their frequent disregard of danger, often coupled with gaiety, set them with poets above the rest of mankind. The R.A.F. introduced me to a world so different from any I had known that I longed to be as much part of it as my circumstances permitted. At Barrackpore I was so cut off from the mainstream that I felt a bureaucrat, ashamed to be doing so little, though one could not make bricks without straw. Our weakness in the Far Eastern air was still deplorable and this undoubtedly had a bad effect on morale. I had heard far more grumbling in Bengal than in battered England.

Delhi was invigorating after Calcutta and my new assignment enabled me to meet a number of international journalists, whose freedom from cant and independence of mind were refreshing.

Gordon Waterfield, whom I had known in Florence and later at Oxford, was Reuter's representative. Having written *What happened to France*, an incisive account of his experiences with the French army, I presumed he would write *What happened to India*, for he was threading his way through the maze of Indian politics at a time when Congressites were attacking British officers and our war effort was being obstructed by myopic nationalists. Personally I could not blame the Indians for wanting to rule their own country but they had chosen the wrong time to agitate since we were protecting them as well as ourselves against a fanatically feudal foe. The blimps of Poona with their sahib complex had done us a grave disservice, for many of us loved Indian culture and sympathized with their ideals.

Wen Yüan-ning, who had originally invited me to lecture at Peking National University, was also in Delhi as an ambassador-at-large and I was astonished at the transformation in his physique. He who had always been so delicate, living on a strict diet and walking with a stoop, had become robust, almost athletic. He had written to me in the previous June: 'I was in Hong Kong when the Japanese attacked the place, and I was still there when it was given up to the tender mercies of the enemy. I hid for slightly a month after Hong Kong capitulated. I could not leave the place until I had seen my family who were cut off from me after Kowloon surrendered, and I left them without a cent in the house and without rice or food of any kind, on the day that Kowloon was lost. At that time I was in Hong Kong Island. Almost a month after the fighting was over I saw my wife; fortunately she and my children were all right, and my house was intact. As the enemy was after my blood my wife thought it unwise for the family to leave with me so, dressed as a workman with beard and moustache and hair unkempt, and with nothing except what I had on my person, I walked with over a hundred coolies across the Kowloon border. Most of the workmen who went with me were robbed of everything they had. But I was lucky: I did not lose a single thing. I walked for seven days, covering about twenty-five miles per day, and going without food for two days and without water for one day. I had to sleep in any old place: once I slept in a place covered with cow dung and I did not know it till the following morning, so tired I was. But at long last I arrived in Free China, not without excitement. The Japs were attacking Waichow on the very day I arrived there. Fortunately there happened to be a boat waiting – it was the last boat. I got into it and we sailed that same evening. The next day Waichow fell to the enemy. Ten of my party who did not leave with me were killed. We were packed like sardines in the small boat, not enough room even to sit down. After travelling nine weary days on that little boat in the East River I got to Lao-lung, just in time to pass my Chinese New Year in peace and quiet in Free China. I was ill, but I was so happy that I could not lie in bed. I ate and drank and enjoyed myself. But always at the back of my mind was the thought of my family in Kowloon. I trusted to luck and the devil that they would be all right: that was all I could do, hoping against hope that I would later on find ways and means of getting them out. After five days at Lao-lung waiting for transportation to Shao-kwan, I left by motor through some of the wildest country I have ever seen. It was bitterly cold and I had little on me. I had fever. The whole countryside was covered with frost. Two days by motor brought me to Shao-kwan, where I remained for a month, the first week of which was spent in hospital. I spent the rest of my time trying to find people to undertake the risky job of getting my family out of Kowloon. On March 3rd one man volunteered to go to Kowloon to contact my family and to carry a letter from me to my wife. On March 5th I left Shao-kwan by rail to Kweilin. There I rested a bit. I took the trip to Yang-shao and saw some of the loveliest scenery in the world. Then I flew by plane to Chungking, and here I have been since. I can't go anywhere until I have got my family out of the enemy's clutches. So far I have not succeeded. But I have heard that they are safe, except that their health has not been good. One after the other they have been ill, due no doubt to insufficient food and exposure to the heat, as they have to go out marketing and waiting in long queues for rice in the broiling hot sun. But I am not without hope that soon they will be able to join me, and then I shall be the happiest man alive.'

Wen's family had been restored to him and indeed he was far happier than when I had seen him in Peking. His ironical sense of humour enabled him to relish the contrasts between the English and Indian officials with whom he associated. Among the Indian leaders he was forcibly impressed by Mohammed Ali Jinnah who had received him seated on a lofty swing, a convenient way (he explained) of clearing one's head and keeping cool. Mr Jinnah invited Wen to sit beside him and together they swung to and fro till Wen began to feel queasy. By contrast with the gentle Hindus whose talk trailed off into metaphysical abstractions the Muslim leader seemed a human hawk, very brisk and dictatorial.

Metaphysical abstractions predominated at Adyar, the cradle of theosophy near Madras, which I visited with Wen. Annie Besant had long been the heroine of a novel I hoped to write, and I was not disappointed in what I saw of her spiritual headquarters: the mammoth banyan tree beneath which congregations were held, the various shrines and the limpid pool, the religious library where the works of the high priestesses held places of honour.

Wen presented me with one of the Adyar publications called *Thought Forms*, by Annie Besant and C. W. Leadbeater. The general principles underlying these thought-forms were: 1: Quality of thought determines colour. 2: Nature of thought determines form. 3: Definiteness of thought determines clearness of outline. A key to the meanings of colours was printed as a frontispiece and it was interesting to compare these with the symbolism of Chinese theatrical make-up. Red indicated anger, of course; black, hatred and malice; deep heavy grey, depression, while pale grey was associated with fear and grey-green with deceit; brownish green with jealousy. Most of these might be guessed by a tyro: pure pale rose marked 'that absolutely unselfish love which is possible only to high natures', and the various shades of yellow – memories of Beardsley's *Yellow Book*? – denoted intellect or intellectual gratification. The colours and shapes were minutely defined: a yellow snake-like squiggle indicated 'the intention to know and to understand'. A theosophical lecturer had seen many of these forms projecting towards him from his audience, especially when questions were asked. If the questions were idle or frivolous, the colour ceased to be yellow but resembled that of decaying meat.

I had never enjoyed this experience, perhaps because I was not a theosophist. Anger was like scarlet fireworks or a pointed stiletto, and according to the text 'the lurid flash from dark clouds (as depicted) was taken from the aura of a rough and partially intoxicated man in the East End of London as he struck down a woman'. Greed was depicted in muddy green with claw-like antennae 'frequently to be seen converging upon a woman who wears a new dress or bonnet, or some specially attractive article of jewellery', and people in front of shop windows might often be observed 'thus protruding astral cravings through the glass'.

The thought-forms became increasingly complex and lurid, ending with a Chagall-like representation of Wagner's music: 'a vast bell-shaped erection fully nine hundred feet in height, and but little less in diameter at the bottom, floating in the air above the church out of which it has arisen.' Since 1901, when the book was published, many a modernistic painter would seem to have borrowed freely from its contents – the images of Paul Klee, Miró, and even the Walt Disney of *Fantasia* were here in embryo. Somebody ought to bring it up to date, if only as a provocative pastime. Evidently Annie Besant and Dr Leadbeater did not suspect that under the guise of 'a striking moral lesson to every reader, making him realize the nature and power of his thoughts, acting as a stimulus to the noble, a curb on the base', they were really playing a sophisticated parlour game.

On my way to Ceylon I stopped at Madura, the religious capital of the south where Siva had chosen the great temple as his residence. Its finest parts were built by Tirumala Nayak who reigned for thirty-six years and was almost contemporary with Louis XIV. Being more attuned to the taste of Louis XIV, I could only admire the details which the guide-books deplored. Their naïve sensuality, the curves so tenderly carved, were a paean in stone to creation – a creation run riot, however, like the jungle. There was too much of the inspissated jungle in this architecture, so that the tired eye longed for the austerity of blank space. Remove a few of these writhing figures and place them against a white-washed wall, and their sculptural qualities would be enhanced. But the technical skill of these artists so in love with their labour, or so dedicated to Siva that they could not leave a square inch unchiselled, was more impressive than the perforated blocks in vogue today. When such fervour of invention, as of inspired bees, existed in India – for the gopurams or gate pyramids resembled magnified honeycombs combined with the structures of termites – it seemed regrettable that a Le Corbusier should be commissioned to design the new government buildings.

The rest of my short leave I spent in Kandy, which I should have enjoyed more had I not been to Bali. Buddha's tooth, whether genuine or false, deserved a loftier temple for its palate, but the dancers I was lucky to see there whirled with a frenzied animation not easily forgotten, and their head-dresses and silver ornaments were superb. Every imaginable plant of the tropics flourished in the Peradeniya gardens, whose avenue of palms like immense inverted mops was more strange than beautiful.

In Colombo we were all on the friendliest terms with the local Press. Lecturing, broadcasting, writing for R.A.F. publications, visiting remote air-stations, arranging special flights for enthusiastic reporters and providing them with 'stories', we really did something to quicken the tempo we found there. We could not rule out the possibility that the Japanese might return to attack us.

Since Edgar Snow's *Red Star over China* was available in a cheap edition it had been widely read by soldiers and airmen, who swallowed this glorified account of Chinese Communist aims and achievements so credulously that I had much ado to defend Generalissimo Chiang against their Snowbound prejudices. Mindful of the Generalissimo's merits before he was forced to fight the Japanese, when Jardine Matheson were extending their ramifications and Sir Victor Sassoon emigrated, bag and baggage, from Bombay to Shanghai, I supported a losing cause. According to rumours from Chungking, the Kuomintang showed signs of senility, of fatalism, of *sauve qui peut*, and the Generalissimo was creaking at the joints. He lacked the essential gifts of the demagogue and his wife was too autocratic. The Communist partisans had been disciplined in adversity and united by a simple ideology. In Chou En-lai they had an advocate of genius who exerted a powerful influence on the most unlikely people. The Soongs and the Wangs were merely smart business men in comparison, able organizers in time of peace but unimaginative in time of war, too attached to material interests. More and more intellectuals were drawn to the Communist camp. But the Chinese in Ceylon were capitalists to the core, industrious small traders with a respect for their ancestors.

I had few opportunities to know the Sinhalese, but their gentleness of manner and feature was engaging. Astrology ruled their existence. Often while passing through the suburbs of Colombo I heard the sound of mysterious drumming, which reminded me that magical ceremonies filled the quiet background with excitement – ceremonies to counteract unlucky omens in a horoscope, since nearly everybody had a horoscope cast soon after birth. I was never able to attend a so-called *bali* ceremony, but the Kandyan dancers were a sufficient compensation, prancing ecstatically among the flames of torches which they rubbed over their chests and thrust into their mouths to the crescendo rhythm of drums. Jingling in every limb, as it were, relaxing and straining, straining and relaxing, faster and ever faster, the muscles of his chest and arms rippling, his golden head-dress glinting, to the sharp and ever more violent pattern of sound, Guneya Yadessa surpassed the other dancers I saw, who flashed before me like birds of paradise.

Rainstorms were frequent, but I was fully occupied with journalists, airmen and photographers, with trips from Ratmalana to the Beauforts of Minneriya, to Koggala and to China Bay, where I visited a Dutch squadron of Catalinas, the *Marine Luchtvardienst in Het Oosten*, and wrote a long article about the pilots and crews, many of whom had fled from Java and Sumatra. Those from Sumatra were skilled artisans who made their own lathes and drilling machines, and special platforms for working on wings and engines. One of them even made a resonant violin. As eighty-four of them had escaped from Java on a single Catalina, which sounded an impossible feat, we arranged to have eighty-four lined up beside one for a group photograph. Often after take-off we had to return on account of impossible weather. The climate did not agree with my colleagues and I did not feel too frisky after a bout of dengue fever, but I was so fascinated by the variety of people I met, not to speak of the animals, birds and flowers, that I never considered my health.

Conventional people in unconventional situations and exotic surroundings have always interested me. On the whole my fellow officers were conventional. Though flying brings out unusual qualities, very few were able or inclined to express their emotions in words. Saint-Exupéry was a meteoric exception. Old Etonians were so rare that it was a surprise to come across one as a corporal who specialized in aircraft recognition. Having published a satire against O.C.T.U.s, he had been debarred from a commission, but he was quite content in his present capacity. Late one evening he called on me with a singular request. He had brought and bought a Sinhalese girl from a remote village – yes, he had paid her parents for her in hard cash, but he could find no suitable accommodation for her in Colombo. Could I procure a room for her in my hotel? She was deliciously primitive and very young, a true child of nature who spoke no word of English.

The hotel was like an assembly station packed with officers and civil servants and I could imagine their reaction to the entry of this juvenile concubine. Even if I offered her my room I doubted if the hotel management would allow her to remain. Surely awkward questions would lead to indiscreet answers. How my friend solved the problem I never discovered. Apparently the girl ran back to the jungle.

My shaving mirror assured me that I was not the wreck I felt I was. I moved like a somnambulist dreaming that he was awake even when I lectured to the Rotary Club and the Y.M.C.A. of Colombo. We cannot picture ourselves as others see us, but I was as amused as Squadron Leader Dickson, the convivial Scot whose office I shared, when he showed me a letter of sincere condolence for having to bear with so dismal an associate. Dickie and I cracked many a joke with Norman Fisher, Oswald Henry, Duke Wright, and other bright journalists. Assisted by Sergeants Butt Reed and Dowd, and Pilot Officer Penfold, our indomitable photographer, we were a happy family, and I think we did something to bridge a boring gap. If the war in the Far East was not exactly 'news', we helped to make it so. Since the heavy Japanese raids on Colombo and Trincomalee in April, Ceylon had been strengthened and the attitude of her people towards the war was less lethargic. Our relatively small air force under Air Vice-Marshal Dalbiac had repelled the assailants. Had we been caught defenceless they might have attempted an invasion. They had inflicted enormous losses on our shipping.

Since my pleasant association with Squadron Leader Dickson, Butt Reed, the editors of the leading Ceylon newspapers both named Stewart, and Walter Duncan at Barrackpore, I retain a strong predilection for Scots in general. Considering their native clime they were wonderfully adaptable, and they struck me as excellent ambassadors of goodwill. Our R.A.F. boys took an intelligent interest in their tropical surroundings. They had hobbies; they kept animal pets – one L.A.C. was inseparable from his mongoose; and they made friends wherever they went, being free from any tincture of racial prejudice. And I am sure that, like me, they left with fragrant memories and an appreciation of a culture very different from their own.

✤ 8 ✤

The fantastic heat, quite apart from the war, played havoc with my memory, and waves of oblivion swept over me with the sweat that rippled down my spine. My duties took me back to Calcutta and Delhi, flying to and fro in Beechcroft biplanes or a de Havilland 'Rapide' which conjured a temporary coolness. Only two incidents of my last visit to Calcutta remain fairly clear: a meeting with the painter Jamini Roy and a consultation with an astrologer.

Thanks mainly to Rabindranath Tagore, Bengal was considered the cultural vanguard of India and the arts and sciences were said to flourish at Shantiniketan, 'the abode of peace', a school founded by the poet in the country some ninety miles from Calcutta. But what I was shown of the paintings produced there seemed rather more craft than art – graceful enough but lacking the life-force of the master whose personality still dominated the place.

The élite of Calcutta assured me that there was one outstanding Bengali painter who possessed this life-force. Even as Tagore had written in English, this artist, Jamini Roy, had produced landscapes in European style, and I was shown several in the manner of various French Impressionists whose work he could have only seen in reproduction since he had never been to Europe. These made one wonder if Whistler could be right in his contention that there is no such thing as nationality in art. Here was an elderly Bengali painting the olives of Provence and the apple-trees of Normandy in a remote lane of North Calcutta. As an experiment in virtuosity it was surprising. *Très ressemblant*, as Cocteau said when the waiter lifted the dish-cover. But Jamini

126

Roy came to realize that it would not do: this was not his native medium. Maybe under the influence of Tagore he turned his back on this alien style as not true to himself. He took to painting figures and scenes of Hindu mythology in a style purely Indian, adapting the crude religious pictures popular with temple pilgrims to bold yet sophisticated compositions, using bright primary colours in gouache and tempera. Of these I bought several examples: gay groups of dancing apsaras with Ajanta curves and patterns borrowed from the ephemeral designs in sandal paste on floors and walls at Hindu festivities corresponding to our Christmas decorations; a mischievous white cat with a crayfish in its chops; a puppet horse ready to prance at a magician's bidding.

The artist lived in a modest house with scanty furniture. A kindly old soul in a loose dhoti with a shawl on his shoulders, he worked at a low wooden stool surrounded by earthenware pots of colour like the notes of a xylophone. Placidly content he seemed in his world of simple patterns. Though not a Christian he was depicting the Last Supper, evidently derived from a Byzantine source he had seen in a reproduction. As he knew little English we could not converse, but he managed to convey a belief in the unity of human values.

Chungking continued to retain the attraction of a promised goal and I still hoped to reach it. The journalists I encountered were puzzled by this perverse enthusiasm for Free China and one of them, an Indian, said: 'Why don't you consult an astrologer? I know an excellent one. He will tell you what to expect.' On the spur of the moment he took me to a shrivelled Bengali who could not have known the slightest thing about me, and he obligingly acted as my interpreter.

The soothsayer cast my horoscope and all the facts he told me about my past were correct. In the near future he predicted a severe illness and a long journey. 'East or West?' I asked him. My mind was on China so he could not have read my thoughts, for he answered: 'West. After your illness you will return to England in several months' time.' Though disappointed I did not

127

take this prediction too seriously. I realized there was something wrong with me for I had frequent attacks of violent nausea. I said nothing about these and tried to conduct myself normally. But after a bumpy flight through a rainstorm and a crash landing I had to admit defeat: I felt thoroughly whacked. In the end I had to have a kidney removed. My surgeon was a splendid Irishman appropriately called Colonel Carver, and I am indebted to him for prolonging my life.

The military hospital at Dehra Dun was worthy of a documentary film directed by Robert Flaherty. While the jackals were howling in the distance, before dawn a so-called bihishty, pronounced 'beasty', clattered into our ward with cups and a can to distribute sweet soupy tea. Lights were switched on while the cocks were still crowing, and yawning orderlies went round taking temperatures and interrupting dreams. Mosquito nets were removed from rickety bamboo poles which converted each bed into a miniature tent. The crows started gabbling around seven. Throughout the routine of the day there was a façade of general bonhomie which disintegrated after dark. Then sighs and groans were audible, incoherent muttered phrases, whistling breath and grinding of teeth. One was aware of sleepless eyes peering through the penumbra of the ward, seeking a loved face or a friend. Only the night seemed real, for then each patient forgot his self-disciplined role and relapsed into his aching self. Sometimes there was a desperate call for the sweeper from one of the 'dizzy' boys – those who also suffered from amoebic dysentery – but most of my fellow patients had broken limbs and lay with legs suspended, weights dangling from their feet, *Tib* and *Fib* pencilled on the plaster a shade whiter than their faces. There was one harrowing case of a youth who had been blinded: both his arms were paralysed, yet when there was no nurse about he would try to leave his bed and collapse on the floor with a bewildered grin. 'He seems to have got an awful packet,' remarked my neighbour. I thought he were better dead, for his mind had been unhinged by his accident. At night he became hysterically turbulent. No, I should never want to live in such a condition, yet perhaps – how can one tell? There again he was falling out of bed, yelling – one could not understand what.

'They generally give 'em a shot of something but it doesn't seem to work,' my neighbour muttered with typical understatement.

From broken sentences one could piece together the loneliness and strain of fighting for months in the jungle. The wounded from Burma were still haunted by ominous sounds in the night, the snapping of twigs or the rustle of leaves that might signify a prowling tiger or a murderous Japanese. Where nature appeared most wonderful it was most cruel. It was enough to turn men against nature 'in the raw' and make them prefer prefabricated houses. A great many were afflicted with sprue, for which there was then no cure except a sea voyage.

My recovery was slow. At one moment I appeared to be dying: my wound had turned septic. In those pre-penicillin days M and B tablets were the leading antibiotic: they seemed to increase in size, to flavour the food I could hardly swallow, to hover above my bed like bloated balloons. Father Clancy, the Irish padre, gave me Extreme Unction, after which I began to feel better. I drew encouragement from his comment when he closed his missal: 'So that is that!'

For once I was not tempted to read, but I thought of a thousand stories I should write. Some of the ideas that came to me seemed so original and important that I did not bother to make a note of them. Who was likely to forget, as it were, that he had to cash a big cheque? Lulled by this comfortable feeling, I watched the minah birds and squirrels, one of which ran away with my soap. And when I found paper and pencil the idea which had seemed most vital escaped me, and I belaboured my memory in vain. It never returned and I have never written my masterpiece. If I had had a dictaphone, I wonder if those prolific ideas would have stood the test of analysis. Possibly they were ideas of ideas, illusions, eidolons begotten of a high temperature. I regret them nevertheless.

Of my parents in Switzerland I heard nothing. I had no news

of my brother in the Pioneer Corps, of what was happening in Italy since Mussolini had fallen. During this phase the most trifling incidents seemed fraught with symbolic significance. A beautiful moth, for instance, fluttered in and clung to my sheet, and I believed it had come as a messenger from a distant friend. It appeared to be gazing at me, conveying the message of greeting with the quiver of its powdered wings. And I remembered Chuang Tzǔ's dream that he was a butterfly, and his uncertainty as to whether he was then a man dreaming he was a butterfly, or whether he was now a butterfly dreaming he was a man. I never felt less 'a simple separate person'.

New neighbours created a little diversion, especially a Sikh pilot who resembled a bearded woman with large lustrous eyes and long sleek hair which he oiled and coiled with fastidious deliberation before he adjusted his turban. He was more demonstrative than the other patients, who seldom flinched when their wounds were dressed and maintained a stoical reserve. His groans were disturbingly dramatic. But he was as merry as a grig when his wife visited him, a sari-draped nymph who walked like an empress and talked like a parrot. More distressing was a fever-stricken captain. Maybe there was some method in his madness, for when we were inspected by a pompous general he bellowed at him: 'Are you a man or a mouse?'

I used to think of Walt Whitman and his tonic effect on the sick and wounded of the American Civil War. Few mystics exude such an ozone of optimism. The nurses had their favourites but I was not among them. Many became engaged to their patients. I am sorry to say that the prettiest passed me by. No doubt my middle-aged aspect was forbidding. Perhaps it would have depressed Walt Whitman.

However, another good grey poet came to see me with a letter of introduction from Wen Yüan-ning. His name was Hamid Ali and he had been assistant governor of Sindh province. Very upright, he sat beside me in his neat black coat, a formal Indian gentleman of the old school. For courtesy that school is pre-eminent. He had distinguished aquiline features, wise sympathetic eyes, and a pleasant voice with a perfect English accent. We should learn from such Indians how to articulate, for most of us swallow half our words as if we were ashamed of them. Hamid Ali was a master of many languages and his knowledge of poetry extended to Dante and Petrarch, but he confessed that of all the poetry he had read the Persian seemed richest in music as in content. Unfortunately no translation could render justice to Hafiz and Firdousi, and FitzGerald's version of Omar Khayyám's *Rubaiyat* was but a pretty paraphrase. Hamid Ali quoted passages to stress the musical rhymes which made me despair of translation.

Talking of melody and rhythm, which I could appreciate though ignorant of the language, I mentioned how much I enjoyed Indian music, especially the *Rāgs* I had heard in Delhi and Calcutta. 'And you come from Italy. How surprising!' he remarked. 'Our music is the antithesis of Italian opera. It is all restraint: gaiety and sadness mingle, and there is gratification of an intellectual kind, very quiet and reposeful. Rossini and Verdi excite the emotions – I think of the overture to *William Tell* and the march in *Aida* which must arouse patriotic sentiment in the Italians. Our music is different: it leads us towards abstraction.' And he went on to explain that there were special *Rāgs* for special hours of the day or seasons of the year. 'You can tell whether it is morning or evening, summer or winter, when you listen to them. My wife is an expert player of the *vina*, the oldest of Indian instruments. You must come and hear her as soon as you are well.'

It was a long time since I had been lifted beyond practical concerns to exchange ideas in serious conversation and I was grateful to Wen for this timely introduction. Hamid Ali set my mind moving again in its natural direction, away from this backwash of war, from this total upheaval of my being.

Great was my joy when I could walk, after more than two months in bed. A Sicilian prisoner who was also a patient in the hospital had refused to eat and I was asked to persuade him to do so. The poor fellow was depressed to the point of suicide, with nobody to talk to and only semi-literate. Though a native of

Agrigento, he had never heard of his compatriot Pirandello. He lay churning his private misfortunes, and though he was as well treated as any of us, he was full of dark suspicion and distrust. He was convinced that one of the nurses had insulted him. 'She turns her thumb down whenever she sees me,' he complained. 'And they feed me with meat, always meat. I am not accustomed to meat. If they would only give me *pasta* and baked beans . . .'

The nurse explained that her gesture had meant to convey the question, was he feeling very low? No insult had been intended. We promised him some spaghetti, though I warned him that they did not know how to cook it. And he smiled for the first time when he showed me his plate, with a small helping of macaroni minced fine and served with marmalade. However, he appreciated the goodwill behind the cook's effort, and he began to improve with the assistance of baked beans. I visited him daily and urged him to learn English. The few words he picked up he would memorize and repeat to me, and together we made up sentences rather like his minced macaroni. I left him in a less morose mood and I hope he returned to Agrigento without animosity against us.

While convalescing in Mussoorie, the Victorian hill station north of Dehra Dun, I was invited to stay in Hamid Ali's house. Although it was November, his garden was full of mauve salvias and Himalayan dahlias, with a jutting lion-shaped rock and a sweeping view over the valley which vaguely recalled that of the Arno, and everything tasted better in consequence, soup with a flavour of aromatic herbs, curried meat balls with fluffy rice, guava and luscious pears and creamy walnuts. Ghee was the sole ingredient I failed to appreciate, for it reminded me ever so faintly of castor oil.

Hamid Ali's wife, the Begum, was an ardent feminist, and she shared her husband's enthusiasm for popular education. That this could involve penalties of tedium was proved by the incursion of a large Indian family who expostulated with my hosts for hours because they had not supported the application of their grandfather to continue teaching geography in a local school. The teacher was well over the age of retirement but his family were indignant, tearful and imploring since his application had been rejected. Then there was a female missionary doctor who asked me if I knew Louis Bromfield. Having spent many years in Baroda, she described his book *The Rains Came* as a monstrous libel on the ruling family. 'Such adorable people!' she exclaimed. 'That Bromfield deserves to be horse-whipped.' *Mother India* she dismissed as outrageous sensationalism. I was tempted to give her Norman Douglas's riposte, *What about Europe?*, but on second thoughts I refrained, for this pamphlet might have shocked her for other reasons. Uncle Norman had as little respect for Western civilization as Miss Mayo for Oriental, and his sense of fun was definitely not a lady missionary's. Where was he now? I had heard of him last in Portugal. He would have been happier here, watching the peaks of the Himalayas in the sunset . . .

After dinner the Begum would regale us with music on the *vina*. I may not have understood all its subtlety, but it set my mind wandering to those marble courts illustrated by Rajput artists. It was evening music: the fingers caressed the strings with the delicacy of whispering leaves, lingering now and then to listen to their meditative reverberation. At night I could sleep again, undisturbed by moans, groans, jackals, and a clattering bihishti at six o'clock in the morning. Buckets of water were brought in for my bath behind a glass partition. 'We do not consider it hygienic to sit soaking in a tub,' my host explained. 'Fresh water should continue to flow over the body to carry the pollution away.'

My host let me browse in his polyglot library, where there was a mummified vulture which a friend had sent him from Egypt. This struck me as a peculiar gift. The Begum told me that she always consulted her sister before buying a precious stone, for if it were genuine it would throb and glitter in her hand, while imitations remained still and dull as pebbles. From her I picked up many scraps of recondite information.

After this convalescent interlude I returned to Dehra Dun to be X-rayed, the result of which was that I was 'recommended for repatriation'. The medical officer fancied I should be pleased. 'You're in luck,' he said with a smile. 'What wouldn't I give to be in your shoes!' But I felt cheated and defeated, as one who had lost the race through twisting an ankle. To return to England now would be a mortifying check to my wishes and ambitions.

With a desperate spurt of energy I tried to postpone my departure, and succeeded in doing so for three months, during which I contrived to see some of the monuments so often described and photographed. Not having visited Persia, I was able to admire them without any *arrière pensée*, especially the tombs of the Mogul rulers of Delhi. Unlike our tombs, these are pleasure pavilions in gardens kept green by channels of running water, with roses to bloom by day and jasmine by night, and trees full of blossom or fruit or singing birds. You could picnic there without irreverence. Some consider this concern for sepulchral magnificence morbid, but surely it is comforting to contemplate that 'peace which passeth understanding'.

The princes who designed these tombs were not able to enjoy them as much as posterity. Humayun returned to Delhi after sixteen years of exile and died as a result of falling down some steps. It was his widow who built the mausoleum in 1565, grandest and best preserved of the many tombs near Delhi. The octagonal mass of white marble and pink sandstone soars from a high square plinth and is crowned by a dome with a crescent. Formerly the pavilions around the dome were used by students of Arabic. From its parapet you may see the other tombs and the bare white breasts of mosques.

The celebrated Qutb Minar remains a subject of controversy: too high for the minaret of a mosque, it was probably a pillar of victory. Struck by lightning and shaken by earthquakes, it has been carefully restored since its erection in 1220. No doubt it is a remarkable feat of engineering for its period, but few (certainly not I) would agree with Sir James Fergusson that it is superior to Giotto's Campanile in poetry of design and finish of detail. The design is rigidly geometrical, the carved scrolls repeating verses from the Koran can hardly compare with the bas-reliefs of the

Florentine bell-tower. On the other hand the Red Palace or Fort is very fine indeed, though we should read the account of François Bernier, who was court physician to the Emperor Aurangzeb, to imagine its former splendour. An inscription running round the cornice of the private Hall of Audience in letters of gold on a ground of white marble says: 'If there is a paradise on earth it is this, it is this, it is this.' But it has lost its ceiling of silver foliage inlaid with gold, its priceless peacock throne, and its judgement seat of crystal, in front of which three jets of clear water were continually kept playing.

The whirling of flocks of pigeons reminded me of Peking. Obedient to the shrill calls of their keepers, who threw grain into the air, they would fold their wings and nose-dive on to a roof. In London we were subjected to another sort of nose-diving pigeon.

My last days in Delhi were brightened by meetings with old friends, Laurence Sickman on his way to China, John Keswick on his way back, Simon Elwes, who was painting official portraits in the Viceroy's House, where a spacious studio had been allotted to him. A Gurkha who had won the V.C. was his present model and I fancy he painted a whole gallery of heroes. I forget if Brigadier Wingate was among them: he had already instilled a new spirit into the forces fighting the Japanese in the jungle and all who met him were impressed by his genius as a leader of irregulars. To the bored journalists in this area he was a godsend. The Viceroy, Field Marshal Wavell, was less sensational. A great soldier but a man of few words, it was said that he had the gift of silence in a dozen languages. He loved good literature and his eloquence was reserved for the pen. Austere amid the pomp of his environment, he was surrounded by suave and sprightly A.D.C.'s who helped to conjure up the atmosphere of a court. To Peter Coats and Billy Henderson in particular I was indebted for a peep at this fugitive glamour. Both were dilettanti of taste, with whom an exchange of ideas was possible.

Limited by my duties, I had not seen enough of the real India to write about it. Unlike Phileas Fogg, that phlegmatic member of the Reform Club whose circumambulation of the globe in eighty days was chronicled by Jules Verne, I had found no Hindu bride, but I had found friends old and new too numerous to mention.

My return voyage was uneventful. No alcohol was permitted on the ship, where it would have been an invaluable asset, and my meals were rendered more indigestible by the company of a sour clergyman with Communist sympathies which he aired on all occasions, presumably for my benefit – a wicked way of being good, I thought. Fortunately there were some jolly nuns on board with whom it was almost a voluptuous pleasure to recite the rosary.

9

I returned to London with the buzz-bombs, but the atmosphere was more buoyant than when I left in 1942. We all felt that victory was nearer. London in May was frigid after India, but the intervals between my duties were filled with warm reunions. First with Lady Cunard, who had followed Sir Thomas Beecham to America and returned to London alone with what is commonly called a broken heart. Few of those who listened to her scintillating persiflage could imagine how deeply she had been wounded by Sir Thomas's estrangement. She had devoted the best part of her life to him and to the promotion of his ambition. Gallant soul that she was, she dominated her grief.

She had transformed a couple of rooms at the Dorchester with elaborate furniture and the pictures George Moore had left her by Monet, Manet, Berthe Morisot, Guillaumin and Mary Cassatt — shimmering vibrations of a halcyon period. Though she could not entertain on the scale of Grosvenor Square, she received the same unpredictable assortment of politicians and poets, diplomatists and dukes — how responsive to the touch of her wand! Her spontaneity and her freedom from clichés never ceased to dazzle me. Fearless of bombs as if they were mosquitoes and detesting the war, she behaved as if it did not exist. 'War's so vulgar,' she declared. But most of her guests were involved in it and they came to her for relief and recreation. Duff Cooper would breeze in from Algiers and Randolph Churchill from Yugoslavia to enjoy the stimulus of her conversation, from which the tedious and prosaic were excluded. The news, the latest news, was exchanged like the clicking of castanets between Flamenco dancers. When the Allied armies were about to land on the north coast of France Gaston Palewski's ebullience at dinner with Emerald told me more than the newspapers. At the branch of the Air Ministry where we sorted out Japanese aircraft puzzles I felt as far from the war as in a laboratory – until the building I worked in was destroyed by a bomb overnight. But from Palewski's high spirits one perceived that General de Gaulle was winning his way, in spite of President Roosevelt's antipathy which he was never to forgive.

The first V-1 raid was very close to the Dorchester: as far as Emerald was concerned it might have been a wasp. I visited her next day and she asked me why the most civilized American soldiers in London were sergeants or corporals. 'The generals I have met are hardly civilized,' she said, 'and I should hate to spend an evening in their company. But it does seem strange that the nicest young Americans one meets are not even officers.' Apart from one naval lieutenant, George Dix, who had charming manners, there was Rory Cameron, the bibliophile son of the beautiful Lady Kenmare, and the mysterious Stuart Preston. Known simply as The Sergeant, since he held that rank in the U.S. army, Stuart Preston was here, there and everywhere, society's latest darling. 'I wish you'd explain him to me,' said Emerald. 'I can't make out what he does in the army. He is too cultured and well-informed for a sergeant, yet he never says anything memorable.'

'That is asking too much of him,' I protested. 'Do I ever say anything memorable?'

'Of course you do. Everybody quotes you. You never disappoint.'

It seemed to me that I was a looker-on and a listener-in at Emerald's parties, and that at most I contributed to the general conversation. 'After all,' I said, 'Stuart is a Henry James American collecting impressions and opinions. He may be overawed by some of your guests.'

'Nonsense. You must tell him to say something memorable. Otherwise he will find he has been dropped.'

My comparison with the young American in Henry James's

novels led to a discussion of that author whom Norman Douglas had described as 'a feline and gelatinous New Englander'. Emerald conceded that he had a genius for suggesting evil but she had no patience with his later style. She went on to praise Balzac and again I wondered at the variety of her reading, the acuteness of her judgements, and her retentive memory. She read while others slept, but she also thought, and her thoughts were fresh and personal like George Moore's.

My task among blue-prints of the Japanese air force was too academic for my taste and I was glad to be attached to the SHAEF Press Censorship Unit in Bloomsbury. Since the landings in Normandy we were snowed under with communiqués, announcements, reports and articles, all in a hurry for instant release, with journalists prowling impatiently outside the door. We censors were regarded as pedantic spoilsports by those whose hunt after scoops made them myopic in matters of security. It was amazing how much 'off the record' information they tried to smuggle through during the peak-hours of our activities. At night I was haunted by the dread of having overlooked the number of a group or the name of an Air Marshal which should have been omitted.

Arthur Waley worked in the Oriental section of the same building, translating and interpreting Japanese documents from which he extracted considerable fun. We met for meals in a small Italian restaurant round the corner where drinkable Chianti was still obtainable, though the meat was usually horse-flesh. 'I rather enjoy its sweetish flavour,' he averred.

With Arthur there were no conventional preambles about health or weather. He went straight to the subject that interested him at the moment. 'Has Hsiao Ch'ien sent you his story in *Life and Letters*?' or 'Did you subscribe to *Man in India*? I should like to see the folk-song number.'

Completely detached from the hurly-burly in Malet Street, he could concentrate on the most arduous translation with an absorption which nobody and nothing could disturb. There were days, as he wrote in *Blitz Poem*, when

each sound and sight
On some blank shoal of inward feeling
*Lies new and separate and bright**

Arthur's shoals of inward feeling could only be reached through some form of poetry or music – for the time being through Buddhist legends of which I had seen versions in the Chinese theatre.

After finishing the superb translation of *Hsi Yu Chi* entitled *Monkey*, which he dedicated to Beryl de Zoete and myself, he invented an additional chapter so true to the style of the original that even a Chinese scholar might be hoodwinked by it. Into this he had introduced episodes and images – such as the river-people, subjects of the Dragon King, who resembled men but were unable to speak, 'moving their lips silently, like fishes in a bowl' – which tempted one to believe in metempsychosis. He could have produced a credible counterfeit of a Chinese novel as easily as he composed Japanese *hokku*. I urged him to take Pai Shih, the White Snake Lady, as his next theme, a legend connected with Thunder Peak Pagoda on the Western Lake of Hangchow. Though an 'evil spirit' the White Snake had been a devoted wife, and her husband was, like most of us, a willing victim. Mei Lan-fang was so bewitching in the role that one sympathized with the Snake Lady when she was defeated by the superior magic of the Buddhist 'Master of the Ocean of Law'. 'Sins of the flesh are a very serious matter and cannot be overlooked,' he declared. Turning her into her original shape, he popped her into an alms-bowl which he carried to Thunder Peak Temple, where she was eventually buried under a pagoda. In the play *Chin Shan Ssŭ* he hurled a 'spirit-catching urn' at the lovely transgressor. As usual in old Chinese stories, the supernatural was blended with the realistic in a matter-of-fact way. Keats's treatment of the Lamia theme was very different, but his bald philosopher Apollonius was a counterpart of the Buddhist monk. Not long after our conversation about the Snake Lady, Arthur produced a charming version entitled *Mrs White*.*

* Published in *Horizon*, August 1946.

140

Indian folk poetry interested him on account of its analogies with the Confucian folk-songs he had translated, and he was an enthusiastic admirer of Verrier Elwin's *Songs of the Forest* and *The Baiga*. Beryl de Zoete was even more excited about the Baigas because their songs accompanied their dances. The Baiga riddles made her gurgle with delight, for instance: 'The tiger roars in the ant's hole' – a gun; 'A frog drinks the water of two tanks' – a child at the breast; 'It falls from on high. Pick it up and lick its buttocks' – a wild mango. When I compared them to surrealistic crossword puzzles she was annoyed. 'How so?' she objected, 'You must give us an example.' 'A ball-bearing mouse-trap in six letters – a tom cat,' I replied.

Arthur Waley was indifferent to what he ate, unlike Norman Douglas, whom I met again at this time. I had not seen him since 1936 when he had got into trouble over a little girl. A precocious lass, she loved lipstick and liqueurs as well as Norman's company. Norman indulged her juvenile caprices and her parents raised no objection to her friendship with such a generous old gentleman. Her father was a waiter in a humble *trattoria* where Norman once took me to dine. With his usual forethought he had ordered the meal in advance so that it compared favourably with more popular restaurants, but I noticed that he supplied the wine himself since the waiter had warned him that the *vino nostrale* was watered.

It is useful to keep on good terms with waiters, as I tried in vain to convince Evelyn Waugh, who had an unreasonable phobia against the profession. My uncle Guy Mitchell was much gratified when the head waiter of a famous London restaurant advised him against ordering lobster which was not fresh. The same waiter confided to him apropos a regular client who invariably made a fuss about meat: 'So we take it back to the kitchen, stamp on it, kick it around and spit on it for luck, then serve it up to him with an extra pinch of salt, and he goes and eats it without another word.' My uncle was amused but he was also rather shocked. He never entered that restaurant again.

When I dined with Norman his little friend was not with us,

but the sight of him strolling through the streets, a *Toscano* between his lips and the girl pattering beside him, was noted by the Fascist authorities at a time when the English were in bad odour. To such hostile observers it seemed a plain case of abduction of a minor. The girl's father, moreover, had been reported for rude remarks about Mussolini. Norman was advised by his lawyer to make himself scarce. 'At my ripe age I can prove that I'm impotent,' he snapped.

'They will accuse you of acts contrary to decency,' the lawyer replied, 'and heaven knows what else. They are after your blood.'

'The sons of bitches. But I tell you I'm ready to swear . . .'

'Not a bit of use. Don't you look at the newspapers?' Impervious, Norman strolled on with the laughter-loving child to a café and proceeded to cram her with chocolate éclairs, wiping her chin when the cream overflowed – an old-fashioned *genre* picture for the Royal Academy.

Later on he was called to the telephone by a young official in the Fascist administration who had an English wife. 'How long will it take you to get to the frontier?' he was asked.

'About eight hours I imagine.'

'We have received a telegram concerning you from Rome. I'm afraid the matter is urgent. Within eight hours we shall be forced to take action.'

Grateful for the hint, Norman had to bolt across the border. He remained at Venice till he escaped to Portugal in 1941. Torn from his Latin moorings Norman was very miserable: he looked pinched and old until he had swallowed the right amount of whisky. He told me that the last three years had been the unhappiest of his life: only the hope of returning to Italy kept him going. Literature? He could read little except *The Times*. As for writing, what was there to write about with the whole world going to blazes? 'Life must be lived, not endured,' he repeated. 'Now all we can do is to endure it.'

The company of a few cronies, the exploration of restaurants for a palatable dish instead of the prevalent Spam or ersatz sausages, the hunt after fresh eggs, beguiled his nostalgic boredom. He took the buzz-bombs in his stride, but the urgency of food and drink loomed out of all proportion, it seemed, to other matters. Although he complained of feeling 'squimpy' now and then – his expression for dizziness – he seldom had the solace of feeling 'swimpish' – his expression for a mild hangover. For a stalwart of seventy-six who had taxed his constitution more than most of us this preoccupation struck me as a healthy sign. He still held it of supreme importance 'to pasture the inner man'.

Having drawn my ration of drink I invited him to share it. The sparkle returned to his eyes and the colour to his cheeks as he polished off half a bottle of whisky over his random reminiscences. Our mutual friend Pino Orioli had died in Portugal but Norman was curt to the point of callousness when I asked for details. Evidently they had quarrelled since Pino had inherited a legacy from Reggie Turner. 'Too much booze,' said Norman. 'He came to a sticky end.' Remembering them as boon companions whom Osbert Sitwell had aptly compared to Volpone and Mosca, I was distressed. Pino had been a perfect foil for Norman; he had published his later writings, and they had apartments in the same house on the Lungarno. But Norman let the subject drop with an angry grimace. Whatever the rift between them, it still rankled. I suspected that Pino had been alienated from him by Reggie's legacy; possibly he had feared that Norman would squander it.

'I was on my beam ends in Lisbon,' said Norman. 'It was Neil Hogg who saved me.'

In London he was cherished by an appreciative circle, and he spoke of Nancy Cunard, Faith Mackenzie and Viva King with genuine affection. I had invited Nancy to join us for dinner. Already the bombs were crashing. 'Another lively night,' he muttered. However, the Ritz Grill was quiet. Nancy sprang towards us in her usual breathless manner, embraced us fervently amid sighs and exclamations, and leaned forward on her multiple bracelets to give vent to her frustrations. She who might have added lustre to the B.B.C. or the Ministry of Information was drudging in a Free French organization, transcribing enemy broadcasts from Vichy, yet she hoped this would lead to something more congenial.

'Pure waste,' said Norman. 'Masochism,' *sotto voce*. Nancy pecked at her chicken absentmindedly but she enjoyed the wine which won Norman's approval, a Pouilly then rather scarce. I could not help thinking of her mother at the Dorchester, the pathos of their irreparable feud. As if she read my thoughts, she asked in a mocking tone: 'And how's her Ladyship?'

'Why don't you call on her? I'm sure she could find you something more suitable than your present job.'

'I have no wish to see her. I just wondered what she was up to.'

'Smiling through the Blitz very gallantly. Like yourself.'

'Surrounded by the same gang, the same dismal grind, I suppose. I'm freer with the Free French. At least they're real people.'

Her expression became hard and hostile: from their pencilled shadows her eyes glinted like jewel jade. While she thought she was mimicking her mother's voice her own voice and idiom were almost identical, a staccato hovering over a phrase and a sudden drift elsewhere. Perhaps she could not forgive the basic resemblance. Norman was tucking in like a boy at a school treat. He pronounced the broiled kidneys he had ordered 'scrumptious'. Then he fell asleep, his head nodding over the table. Nancy talked on unperturbed, except by the fate of her house in France. Would she find it standing? After all her ideological wanderings she missed her books, her printing press, her African sculpture . . .

The explosions were louder and nearer, yet we had much ado to wake Norman. He rubbed his eyes and blinked. 'A bit squiffy I fear,' he apologized. Having to be on duty at ten, I reluctantly left Nancy in charge of him amid an intensified cacophony of crashes. A taxi was found: it was amazing that taxis were still about during raids. The elderly drivers were as plucky as Commandos. Norman was remarkably tough, I mused, but in spite of her brittle bird-like bones Nancy was a match for him. She saw more good in humanity than Norman, who was candidly misanthropic. 'Consider well your neighbour, what an imbecile he is,' as he wrote, and he had developed a thick hide in self-protection. But his Scotch sense of humour saved him from turning sour and there were vestiges of German romanticism under the skin.

Many a farcical incident of our sojourn at the same hotel in 1930 Paris arose before my mind's eye — that string of wet handkerchiefs across his bedroom when he received me in his shirt-sleeves. Obviously he had been doing his own laundry. 'Just been tossing myself off, my de-aw,' he explained. 'One must keep in practice. Besides it gives one an appetite. Where shall we dine? I've a motherly craving for *kebab* . . .'

Now I was forty and he was seventy-six. Chamfort's dictum recurred to me: '*Qui n'est pas misanthrope à quarante ans n'a jamais aimé les hommes.*' I had loved plenty of people and I was not a misanthrope yet. Though they often disappointed me they never filled me with savage indignation. Curiosity always got the better of me. Arthur Waley translated a fine parable from Mencius about a mountain covered with beautiful trees which people cut down until it became quite bare. As with this desolate mountain, 'so too in every man . . . there assuredly were once feelings of decency and kindness; and if these good feelings are no longer there, it is that they have been tampered with, hewn down with axe and bill'. I had found a kernel of kindness in many rascals though I never liked people *en masse*, and the word democratic had been debased by the totalitarians. 'He who would do good to another,' wrote Blake, 'must do it in Minute Particulars. General Good is the plea of the scoundrel, hypocrite and flatterer.' Too sweepingly dogmatic perhaps, but the General Gooders are more so: they are certainly more intolerant. And intolerance is the breeder of crime.

It was with a rapture of relief that I read 'All Florence in Allied Hands' on August 11th, though in fact only the centre of the city had been liberated. The Germans had withdrawn to the outskirts after blowing up all the bridges save the Ponte Vecchio, either side of which was piled with Cyclopean rubble. The city was still in danger of destruction. I was soon to glean further details from Eric Linklater, who had visited my home and assured me that it was safe, servants and all, occupied by decent British officers. He had even visited the castle of Montegufoni, the property of Osbert Sitwell, where masterpieces from the Uffizi and Pitti galleries and various Tuscan churches and museums had been stored. Previously the German occupants, paratroopers and S.S. groups, had used Ghirlandaio's 'Adoration of the Magi' as a table-top. When the temporary curator of the Uffizi implored them to remove their bottles and glasses they had stabbed it with a knife. Luckily this had only pierced the sky. The pictures deposited in other country houses fared worse. The corridors of Montegufoni had been used as latrines. Linklater's account of the havoc he has witnessed have been supplemented by Frederick Hartt in *Florentine Art under Fire* and by Sir Osbert Sitwell. Never since Savonarola's 'bonfire of vanities' had so precious a heritage been in such danger from human vandalism.

Florence is apt to be scorching in mid-August, when the Arno is usually reduced to a muddy trickle. It was easy to conceive the misery of the population with hardly any water or food and with no electricity, since the water mains, gas and light, had been destroyed with meticulous thoroughness. Mercifully my parents had remained in Vevey. That the second cradle of European culture after Athens should have been subjected to such horrors in our age filled me with a sense of universal failure, as if scientific progress had strengthened the powers of evil. The jewelled compactness of Florence made it more vulnerable than most cities, and the vision of Brunelleschi's dome under fire often flickered between me and the communiqué I had to censor about the landings in the South of France.

A tragic bombing mistake occurred at this time and the journalists rushed to report it like hungry jackals, causing a 'flap'. Obliged to dam this foul flood of material after a sleepless night, I failed to pass on a doubtful item to my military colleagues and was solemnly reprimanded. It was hard to see the wood for the trees and I was caught off my guard, ambushed as it were, by secret snipers. My R.A.F. colleagues realized the unusually heavy pressure produced by that 'flap', of which I had borne the brunt. Badly stung, I redoubled my scrutiny. What a vile jargon they scribbled, or perhaps dictated, like messages in some disreputable code! Often I turned to Gibbon and Voltaire for a tonic.

'Advance 15 miles beyond Paris. Rhône Valley entered. Avignon taken,' I read. I followed the movements of vast armies on scraps of mottled paper. Then to my joy I heard I was to be sent to Paris.

Early on October 5th I flew to Orly, almost a shambles under sheets of rain. The suburban streets had a deserted air. Here were the modest buildings Utrillo had painted, the mellow bakeries and corner-house cafés neither handsome nor picturesque, but cosily reassuring and harmonious in spite of comical discords, as empty as picture postcards. Half the houses were shuttered and closed. Few people were visible and these were pedalling bicycles. The bicycles increased as we drove into Paris, more grey than gay, but little scarred by the recent occupation. The women cyclists wore overwhelming hats as a protest, I was told, against recent sumptuary laws, and their shoes had wooden soles. From the Champs Elysées to the Place de la Concorde I rejoiced to see that none of that elegant symmetry had been deranged. Great was the thrill of glimpsing the tree-lined avenues, of sniffing the familiar exhalations of the Paris métro. Externally Paris had changed far less than London during these tragic years. Externally . . . What of the heart?

Climbing the formal staircase of the Hotel Scribe which was crowded with uniforms, I reported my arrival. This was our Seine Base Sector. I was allotted to room 108, spacious but sparsely furnished with desks and chairs retrieved from the Germans. SHAEF was settling in. With the exception of two Frenchmen, the younger of whom had fought with the Resistance and looked half-starved, the elder a slick and *mondain* captain in a spotless uniform, my fellow officers were American. I could not have wished for pleasanter companions, conscientious, unruffled, eager, humorous and civil, and they mellowed like wine on acquaintance. For the majority this was their first visit to

'Gay Paree', and they looked about them with the freshness and frankness of young explorers. Few of them happened to be French linguists, however, so that I was often borrowed as an interpreter when I was not censoring the material of war correspondents. I was even asked to translate some curious love-letters.

We were conveniently billeted at the neighbouring Hotel Chatham whose bar supplied copious champagne and cognac also retrieved from the Germans. It contained a piano which enhanced sociability, for we had one or two skilled exponents of the tuneful jazz of the thirties, the carefree lyrics of Gershwin, Kern, and Cole Porter. Hearing Gershwin's *American in Paris*, I was struck by the dismal contrast between then and now. In that coldest of winters only alcohol imparted a temporary illusion of warmth, for our rooms were unheated and baths were rationed to once a week.

Having spent the previous winter in Delhi, the cold seemed arctic. But the cooks of the Chatham wrought prodigies in making our imported victuals taste Parisian. Though coffee and peanut butter were served with meals and our bread was not the incomparably crusty and comely staff of life whose mere scent evokes French civilization – one must know France to appreciate the full significance of *La femme du boulanger* –it was amazing how chicken à la king could be transformed, how at last potatoes, in England so drab that they deserve the name of spuds, became crisp or creamy, and the compote of fruit made one forget that it was canned. Those cooks deserved medals for maintaining their high standard with unpromising material. They also helped to keep the chill out of our bones.

We were allowed to invite one guest a week – or was it two? – for dinner, and I was touched by the pathos of some of the ladies my comrades brought in. *Grisettes* they would have been called in the last century. Those who could afford to procured their provisions on the black market, but so scanty was food that these girls filled their bags with bread and whatever was transferable from our bill of fare.

'I'm afraid of this fellow,' one confided to me. 'With Americans you can't tell what they want to do. They prowl after you in the street like panthers and offer you chewing gum as a *gage d'amour*. In truth it is disconcerting. This one looks gentle, but you never can tell with Americans. Some of them get wild. He invited me to dinner though I am not acquainted with him: we never met before this evening in fact. I think I can trust him to behave. Am I mistaken? Forgive my *franchise* but I have a large family, I have to work for a living. I feel I can confide in you, Monsieur. You speak my language.'

'Say, what is this all about?' asked her host with vague suspicion.

'You should get her to teach you French,' I replied. 'She likes the look of you but she's rather shy.'

'Shy!' he guffawed. 'Why she propositioned me in the street. And it's a long time since I've had a piece of ass. I can hardly wait.'

As I saw her again in the same company I deduced that neither had been disappointed.

'I hear she is teaching you French,' I remarked to her swain.

'You've said it,' he replied with a complacent wink. He was, I discovered, of Turkish ancestry. The mixed origins of my American colleagues, each so different in physique and mentality, made them all the more interesting. But in most cases their French was limited to: *'Voulez-vous coucher avec moi?'* which, after all, was not a bad beginning. The best idiom is often learnt in bed.

On my first night in liberated Paris I sallied forth after dinner in spite of the rain and almost danced with elation along the rue de la Paix to the Place Vendôme, then up towards the Seine. Though they were dark and deserted I could flood-light the streets with my imagination. The Egyptian obelisk, the fountains of the Place de la Concorde, and Perronet's bridge over the river glistened in the velvety penumbra. I wandered on to the Institut and then to Notre-Dame: I must have walked miles with my memories.

Our Supreme Headquarters was at Versailles where I drove in

a lorry next morning. Here the business of winning the war was conducted in its final stages. The Cour Royale had become a Cour Démocratique, which was at least better than a Cour Totalitaire. Having dispatched such formalities as signing-in with the Camp Commandant, A.E.A.F., I sauntered through the gardens of Le Nôtre. The vast ponds and fountains were dry, the stately trees had turned yellow and russet in the melancholy haze of autumn, and falling leaves had begun to carpet the walks and avenues. It had become *'le vieux parc solitaire et glacé'* of Verlaine's *Colloque Sentimental*, but the great palace was overrun with scurrying G.I.'s. Though the destruction of bridges beyond Paris had helped our invasion it had disorganized communications and SHAEF controlled the only efficient transport, which was by air.

General de Gaulle's Government had been installed yet President Roosevelt withheld recognition while appointing an Ambassador to France, an absurd situation. Our own Ambassador, Duff Cooper, had been in Paris since mid-September, and though he had always been a stalwart supporter the General would not receive him since he had to act in concert with his American *confrère*. The State Department procrastinated until October 23rd and the event was celebrated with a dreary dinner. 'It should have been a gala evening,' remarked Duff Cooper, 'but gala is not a word included in the vocabulary of General de Gaulle.'

Our Ambassador's task was not eased by the prickly susceptibilities of those who were 'making history'. The great were grating on each other's nerves with consequences that affect us deplorably even today. Duff Cooper understood and loved the French to such an extent that he had come to resemble their national emblem. Short and stocky with combative eyes under an intellectual forehead, he suggested a battling turkey-cock, feathers bristling. His wife, Lady Diana, was renowned as a beauty in the classical tradition of Lady de Grey and Lily Langtry whose photograph was reproduced in every other magazine. Other ladies graced our Embassy in Paris, but none have done so with a nobler disdain for the pettiness of protocol.

There was embarrassing friction between the Free French who had lived in exile and those who had never left their native shores since 1940. Lady Diana disregarded this where apolitical figures were concerned, and she was criticized by the Resistance puritans for receiving some who had had to earn a living under the German occupation. History repeated itself as when the Bourbons returned from exile. To the diehards all those who had not emigrated were suspect.

Impatient of Philistine bores, Lady Diana was an Ambassadress of international culture. She filled the Embassy with wits and beauties, poets, painters and musicians. Louise de Vilmorin, Édouard and Denise Bourdet, Cocteau, Poulenc, Georges and Nora Auric, Henri Sauguet, Christian Bérard and Boris Kochno were among those who added lustre to her receptions. Since Louise de Vilmorin's last husband, Count Palffy, was an Austro-Hungarian, it was said that she had hopped straight from the German to the British Embassy. Cocteau had blotted his copybook with the diehards by praising Arno Breker, a pupil of Maillol and Despiau whose sculpture happened to be admired by Hitler. But art is above nationality, or should be. There are many brands of patriotism and that which could be used as a bludgeon against private bugbears had come to the fore at this season of liberation. Probably Dr Johnson had this in mind when he observed that 'patriotism is the last refuge of the scoundrel'. Many a skilled actor and dancer, such as Sacha Guitry and Serge Lifar, was under a cloud because he could not resist German flattery, and a French publisher told me that Cocteau had been too susceptible to their blandishments: *il buvait du lait*. Uncertain of himself during the liberation, he asked his friends who had been in the Resistance: 'But why didn't you ask me to join you?'

At the Hotel Scribe there were three conferences daily for the benefit of war correspondents accredited to SHAEF, when a staff officer reviewed the military situation on a platform before a blown-up map. Questions were asked which often betrayed a shameful ignorance of geography and the lecturer was sometimes heckled as if he were a slippery politician juggling with the facts. After these conferences the correspondents submitted their copy to us for censorship. Though they drew the same P.X. rations as we did the majority were chronic chain-smokers and they resorted to the exorbitant black market in desperation. When our cigarette rations were cut short their despondency was so acute that, as one of them complained to me, it would take him hours of cerebration to formulate a message he would normally type in a few ticks. It was like Flaubert's struggle for the *mot juste* – if only they could write like Flaubert!

Martha Gellhorn's were the best written and most vivid of the articles submitted to me, though this was some time later. I thought they compared favourably with the writings of her husband Ernest Hemingway, upon whom she must have exerted a wholesome influence. She was a very acute observer.

Among the later correspondents who sought me out at the Chatham was George Orwell, who usually joined me for meals when he was in Paris. Though my senior by a couple of years he said he remembered me from Eton, and I vaguely remembered him as a stork-like figure, prematurely adult, fluttering about the school yard in his black gown. I had never identified Blair K.S. with the author of *Down and Out in Paris and London* but I knew he was a friend of Cyril Connolly. I was perhaps even less typically Etonian than Orwell but I was wearing an officer's uniform and it struck me as ironical that Eton, of which he disapproved on principle, should have brought us together in this strange mess. I should not have been surprised had he cut me, but he was as amiable as he could be in his dry frustrated manner. I was impressed by his mournful dignity. Evidently he had a great need to unburden himself, for he told me about the death of his wife and his anxiety about a baby they had adopted, since he was left alone and defenceless without experience of infant welfare. He also mentioned his lung trouble as if it were something to be ashamed of. There was ample cause for the gloom that was deeply engraved on his features. Yet gradually the gloom dissolved as I prompted him to reminisce about his life in Burma, and his sad earnest eyes lit up with pleasure when he spoke of the sweetness of Burmese women and I joked about the cheroots they were reputed to roll on their thighs. But for his nagging 'social conscience' I suspected he might have found happiness there. He was more enthusiastic about the beauties of Morocco, and this cadaverous ascetic whom one scarcely connected with fleshly gratification admitted that he had seldom tasted such bliss as with certain Moroccan girls, whose complete naturalness and grace and candid sensuality he described in language so simple and direct that one could visualize their slender flanks and small pointed breasts, and almost sniff the odour of spices that clung to their satiny skins. A description worthy of Gide, I mused, and equally sincere.

Was he egging me on to confess my own Oriental diversions? No: I doubt if he regarded me as more than an attentive listener. He wished to evoke happier moments in the midst of his present distress. He looked like a soul in pain in spite of his puzzling moustache, but he was more complex, more ingrown than a Latin intellectual suffering from similar sorrows. Gide also had a Puritan strain but Orwell's was more robust. But for the grace of God his voice might have been that of some Kipling hero: it belonged to the Indian Civil Service from which he had sprung. Different as we were, I was touched by his spontaneous bursts of confidence. He admired Gissing, but it was the Gissing of *Demos* rather than of *By the Ionian Sea*, which I preferred. Altogether he kindled my sympathy, and he must have found me agreeable to seek my company. But I never saw him again, and I fear his politics would have prevented our friendship from maturing. That he retained an open mind on fundamentals was proved by the courage and honesty of his *Animal Farm*.

My American colleagues found their bearings pretty soon. Shortly after my arrival a party persuaded me to accompany them to a musical evening at Raymond Duncan's 'Akademia' in the rue de Seine. Raymond was the brother of the famous Isadora, whose inspiration as a dancer was largely derived from her study of Greek vases in the Louvre. During my childhood I had seen her in the streets of Florence with her lover Gordon Craig: once seen, never forgotten, for she floated rather than walked, a moving statue of liberty. How she and her brother discovered Greece – how they knelt down and kissed the soil, half mad with joy – how they wished to build a temple on the way to Hymettus and doffed their degenerate modern garments for the tunic and chlamys and peplum of ancient Hellas – is related in her rapturous autobiography. Raymond haunted the Acropolis, searching for the footprints of the goats which had pastured there a thousand years before it was built. He even claimed to have found them. Henceforth he never abandoned his Grecian garb and what he imagined to be the Grecian way of life. He wove and taught others to weave Grecian textiles at a classical loom. He remained a vegetarian and a drinker of goat's milk. He also remained a Californian of Scotch and Irish descent.

In his skinny bare legs and sandals, a fillet on his hoary head, he was among the first to greet the American troops with a flourish of the Stars and Stripes before the U.S. Embassy when they marched into Paris, and he welcomed those who cared to visit his Akademia, hoping to convert them to the life of Plato's Republic. My companions, including my friend and publisher John Cullen who has refreshed my memory of this and other Parisian occasions, were met by two sandalled figures in homespun togas, who presented each with a flock of wool and asked them to spin it as the evening wore on. I managed to avoid this corvée but they, somewhat abashed, sat down and pecked at their distaffs in awkward conversation with 'the artists of Paris', who had, according to the printed invitation, been mustered to entertain us. A Latvian dame, dressed more as the abbess of a convent than as a priestess of Pallas Athene, officiated as Raymond's hostess. Doubtless it was she who ran the soup kitchen on the ground floor where I noticed a group of dilapidated people. Perhaps these were the academicians.

One buxom body in her late fifties was introduced as Mademoiselle Dupin of the Opera: she might once have been a member of the chorus. Others were retired teachers of elocution, actors and musicians pathetically past their prime. I imagine they came here to be fed on a communal basis since Raymond Duncan could hardly afford such extensive charity.

The rooms were sombre in spite of the handwoven rugs and fabrics which hung on the walls. Our host remarked that he had brought them from Attica and delivered a lecture on the purity of their design. Pointing out some bronze tripods, he explained that they were models of the altar at Delphi where the priestess sat uttering her oracles. 'These were given as prizes at the Pythian games,' he said. 'Sublimely simple the Greeks, they just had everything and more. Three feet or legs – what genius of invention when we poor humans have only two! – and so uniquely balanced that you can push them around and they refuse to fall. See here!' He gave one push: it tottered but soon recovered its equilibrium. One of my friends proceeded to push another tripod and it crashed to the floor. I felt embarrassed, but our host pretended not to notice. The paintings in one room had been executed by himself. These represented naked women with pendulous breasts in various stages of pregnancy, the very nega-tion of Greek art, but I could not offend old Duncan by saying so.

The largest room contained a stage with a piano. With much simpering and maidenly hesitation the *prima donna* obliged us with a medley of unmelodious songs, but neither she nor the other singers ever struck the same note as the piano. Raymond Duncan followed with some sailors' chanties in a cracked and tremulous voice, accompanying himself on a lyre that sounded like a banjo. His grey eyes flashed with the fire of lumber camps as he sang about 'Jenny Lee upon my knee' and beat time to the rig-a-dig refrain, winding up with a selection of his own doggerel verses. All this contrasted oddly with his Grecian togs. Finally a paunchy little Frenchman – he too had been 'an illustrious artist of the Opera' – proceeded to bellow the *Marseillaise* with a barrage of rolling r's. Sweat streamed from his forehead and I feared he would burst a blood-vessel as he struck the attitude of Rouget de Lisle in Isidore Pils's hackneyed picture. For the time being he felt he was interpreting liberty, equality and fraternity all at once.

We applauded with perfunctory politeness. There were tears in the women's eyes. In spite of his absurdity, that Parisian Pickwick in the frayed frock coat had thrilled their national pride, as if the liberation of France was here and now in Raymond Duncan's Akademia.

Not to be outdone, an even paunchier American lieutenant wrapped himself in a toga and bellowed 'The Star-spangled Banner' and I was induced to contribute the Chinese National Anthem and *Ch'i-lai*! Though unfamiliar to the audience — perhaps for that very reason — there were clamours of *Encore*. John Cullen assured me that I was the success of the evening, but one such evening was enough for me.

The impression grew upon me that France was intensely creative after her chloroformed slumber. Paris was still the centre of modern painting, but all the arts were treated with respect and discussed with youthful animation. In that respect the lights were coming back to the *Ville Lumière*. The painters of 1904 who belonged to what Cocteau called the heroic epoch were still exhibiting at the *Salon d'Automne*: one forgot their age until one saw Cartier-Bresson's photographs of them. Perhaps because they were so typically French in their subtle sense of colour and design, their vitality of texture and their avoidance of abstractions, I preferred the paintings of Bonnard and Vuillard, true heirs of the great Impressionists. The Surrealists were painful plodders in comparison.

An entire room was dedicated to Picasso, whose canvases had been hung in higgledy-piggledy haste. Without frames they looked unfinished, even when such features as eyes and noses were multiplied. Since obstreperous students had tried to damage them they had the honour of being guarded by police. Explaining this ever-present risk to me, one gendarme remarked: 'Luckily he's not French!' Misia Sert told me that she had burst into tears at this exhibition so unworthy of the painter she had always admired. Touched by her tears, a guard said to console her: 'Cheer up, Madam, don't upset yourself. What would you do if, like me, you had to stay here all day long?'

156

The fresh word Existentialism swam into my ken and a galaxy of names new to me. Sartre, Camus, de Beauvoir proved that French writers had been stimulated by persecution. Aragon and Éluard were to poetry what Matisse and Picasso were to painting, and they had gathered strength from their dangers and difficulties under the occupation. Their poems were no longer gymnastics in imagery: less complex and esoteric, more lyrical and dramatic, they reached a higher degree of eloquence. Sartre's influence was at its apogee. Clandestine literature had flourished but so had the theatre, for the enemy had failed to detect the subversive content of such plays as *Les Mouches* and *Caligula*. The play that impressed me most was Sartre's *Huis-Clos*, which was so well acted that when the characters complained of the stifling heat of the apartment where they were condemned to torment each other for eternity one forgot how bitterly cold the theatre was. One of the protagonists wore a low-necked evening dress: absorption in her role had evidently kept her from catching pneumonia on that draughty stage. Sartre had created a credible, perhaps too rational nightmare, but it struck me personally as Cocteau expunged of poetry. Poetry pervaded the French films I was able to see, sequences of splendid photographs remote from commonplace realism: all these owed much to Cocteau.

Claudel's long and tortuous *Le Soulier de Satin* was performed in the grand manner with lavish elaboration at the Comédie Française. The packed audience followed it entranced, none more so than the venerable author who sat applauding it frantically in the front row. We had nothing of the kind in England. Such a production was inconceivable on the contemporary stage in London.

157

❧ 10 ❧

Everything seemed ripe for a lasting *Entente Cordiale* when Churchill visited Paris on November 11th. As I was on duty that day I could not watch the grand military parade from General de Gaulle's headquarters to the Arc de Triomphe, but I saw the crowd even on the housetops and heard the prolonged cheers that greeted our Prime Minister and found myself involved in the embracing and the pumping of hands. The sun for once decided to bless the occasion. So collective was the euphoria that the war might have been over and won. Presumably the German army was exhausted, and Hitler was reputed to have gone mad. It was expected that the Ruhr would soon be reached. But the weather was not in our favour and there were serious setbacks. The Germans were preparing in secret for their final push. Our staggered advance was not easy to explain to the impatient war correspondents.

Churchill's arrival overshadowed Cecil Beaton's, but for me it was equally delightful to find my old friend in Paris. He had succeeded where I had failed in getting into China and he had brought back vivid records of his journey. His impressions confirmed my gloomiest prognostications. He thought it as well that I had not gone to Chungking: it would have only discouraged me. Under a languid manner he was a penetrating observer, and he was quick to catch fleeting ideas and adapt them to his purpose, to discern beauty where others failed to see it. 'The artist is he whose taste runs ahead of his talent,' wrote Jules Renard, and this applied to Cecil. Though he had tamed his restless sensibility by systematic work, like a true artist he was seldom satisfied with results. I enjoyed his astringent criticism.

Compared with him I was a Rip Van Winkle, and he was generous in introducing me to friends I had missed through settling in Peking. First among these was Christian Bérard – Bébé to his intimates – who in a special Parisian way had become an arbiter of taste. He was the Gavarni of his period and everything he did was signed with his style, an elegant calligraphy derived more from Pompeiian frescoes than from the Picasso he revered. The style has been popularized by imitators, but the difference between his work and theirs is as that between chalk and cheese. His admirers were wont to complain that he had prostituted his talent by surrender to the chic, but he did not surrender to it, he reformed it. Compare his designs for theatre and ballet, fashion and book illustration with those of Erté in the 1920's, and their superiority is evident. His more serious work was founded on a study of Degas.

Even now that beards have grown ubiquitous, Bébé Bérard's would claim attention. After the first shiver of repulsion I grew conscious of his highly individual charm. Pink and pudgy with melodramatic eyes, clad in soft velveteens and so strongly scented that you smelled his approach before seeing him, he suggested a bearded lady at a fair. His fingers were so grubby that one suspected the scent was a substitute for soap. He had an endearing waddle and his whole being yearned for sympathy. Women realized this and they beamed when he kissed them on both cheeks: he was their privileged pet.

Boris Kochno, who shared his existence, had made himself indispensable to Diaghilev during the last years of that supreme impresario's life, and when Diaghilev died in Venice he had a violent scuffle with Lifar beside the prostrate corpse. A small dark wiry Russian, his coal-black eyes had a feverish glow which seemed to dominate the tender Bébé. His *charme slave* was faintly macabre.

Their apartment near the Odéon was a hodge-podge of evocative associations. Whether by accident or design, Bébé's beard was perceptible on most of its contents, apart from which I noticed a black wooden horse of the Empire period and an unfinished portrait by Degas: the top hat, black frock coat and pearl-grey trousers were meticulously painted but the features were as lost as in a faded daguerreotype. A wheezing white poodle occupied the sofa, and one felt it had never been taken out for a run. Everything was spotted or stained like Bébé's fingers and clothes. It was as if an indefinable air of corruption had crept into a frigid nursery. Though the stove was unlit a faint whiff of opium wafted an illusion of the tropics.

Denise Bourdet and Marie-Louise Bousquet appeared – Minerva and the Fée Carabosse. Young dancers tiptoed in to catch a glimpse of Bébé's designs for a new ballet. Polite questions were asked about mutual friends in England. 'Was it true that Lord Berners had bought his dog a diamond necklace?' Their ideas about England were conventionally exotic. Somebody told me, for instance, about our bombing of the Longchamps race course. The R.A.F. swept over just as the first race was starting and bombed both the Renault works near by and an ack-ack battery in the middle of the course. Everyone was covered with dust but the secretary of the Jockey Club ordered racing to proceed. In the paddock nobody could understand the bombing, which contradicted their notions of fair play. 'But the English are sportsmen. They knew that the first race at Longchamps starts at 2.10. Why should they have chosen this moment . . .' etc. The secretary of the Jockey Club, who happened to be my interlocutor's father, tried to explain that air raids were not planned by a committee headed by the Earl of Derby.

Coming from the war news at the Scribe, I felt like a diver who discovers a garden of sea anemones and flowering coral inhabited by mermaids and mermen. A slim youth in khaki battle-dress walked in as I was about to leave. 'Do stay a minute,' said Bébé, introducing me to the juvenile French lieutenant with pardonable exaggeration as one who was almost Chinese. The lieutenant, he explained, was a parachutist who had fought gloriously with the Free French as soon as he had escaped from school. 'And now,' muttered Marie-Louise Bousquet, 'he has parachuted plumb into the Faubourg Saint-Germain.' He looked too young for his uniform, a sort of shy gazelle, self-conscious and disconcerted by the compliments he was paid by his exuberant elders. 'If only General de Gaulle had his looks!' a lady sighed. 'And his brother is even handsomer.' His figure was incongruous in this aquarium. Evidently he was seeking adventures of the mind which the army had denied him. Always in immaculate battle-dress, he grew younger and more ethereal every time I met him, usually with the spectral Misia Sert, who was old enough to be his grandmother. (Her portrait by Renoir is now in the National Gallery.)

A nephew of the jeweller Lacloche, his American mother had sent him and his brother to school in the United States, but the boys had played truant to join Admiral Muselier in the Atlantic islands of St Pierre and Miquelon. The Parisian milieu into which they had fallen completed their education. Both were patriotic idealists but their ideals became confused and obfus-cated among the cynical epicureans who welcomed them as heroes and tempted them with drugs.

At first François envisaged himself as the leader of a Gaullist youth movement, but in order to lead you must find followers and his were on the average over sixty. He was bored by his coevals. One of his ambitions was to parachute on to Mount Everest. I was fascinated by his imaginative daydreams, so full of gladness, innocence and colour, and I was flattered by his con-fidence. We discussed future journeys to the Orient which, alas, never materialized. He had a life-enhancing presence. But his parachuting days were over. He had graduated from the life of motion to that of sensation, and he soon became a fashionable worldling. Somewhere Jean Cocteau must have portrayed his features among the Adonises of the period.

Cocteau pretended to scorn the worldly: 'So-and-so would never produce anything, he was *mondain*!' Yet he was irrepressibly sociable and I saw much of him at this time. The most generous as well as the most intoxicating of talkers, he never stinted him-self whatever the company. He dramatized his experiences in dazzling cataracts of words. Possibly, as Gertrude Stein said, he 'talked too much to write anything that would live', but posterity may not agree.

A Parisian sparrow of genius, he was a poet in whatever he did, and he had so many strings to his lyre that he could play on each of them singly or together with consummate art. All his novels, plays, films, ballets and drawings were emanations of his poetry, of a personality as diverse, chameleon-like, prismatic, acrobatic, pyrotechnical, as that of the symbolic Harlequin to whom he was compared by those who envied his capacity for self-rejuvenation. Conscious of the label attached to him, he protested that he did not care for Harlequin except in the paintings of Cézanne and Picasso. Harlequin wore a black mask and a costume of many colours. 'After denying the cock's crow he goes into hiding. He is a cock of the night.' On the other hand he liked the genuine cock who said 'Cocteau' twice and lived on his own farm. To an American he explained that his name was the plural of cocktail in French.

Though quintessentially French – he could not have belonged to any other country – he was allured by the China that has ceased to exist and he professed to see me as an Oriental sage in disguise. His magnetism in incongruous surroundings was most evident when he dined with me at the Officers' Club where he was the cynosure of the feminine guests. Several of these young women came boldly up to our table and begged for his autograph. In that quasi-military setting this slight testimony to his fame seemed to gratify him, for he not only signed menus for them but accompanied the signature with a flourish of linear drawing à la Picasso. As my publisher friend would have said: 'il buvait du lait.' For so subjective an artist he was modest: he could not help wanting to please. I suspect it was this innate modesty and receptivity to fresh ideas that made him impervious to the arrows of his detractors, many of whom, like Claude Mauriac and Maurice Sachs, had formerly sat at his feet.

During dinner I was the spectator of a masterly performance. He evoked the German occupation so vividly that one saw and heard it all, the tramp tramp tramp of the triumphant enemy marching like superbly drilled automata down the silent Champs Elysées, the windows shuttered in mourning, the rare bystanders pale and dazed with tears in their eyes; and then the gathering cloud of universal dread, of being arrested in the middle of the night, of being denounced or tortured or sent to a labour camp; the tentacular spies, the octopus grip of the Gestapo – above all of the Gestapo. After the first shock of bewilderment there had been a lull: the conduct of the German soldiers had been 'correct', the propaganda of the Old Marshal had been plausible, France was indeed exhausted and Hitler seemed certain to win. But without free speech the people felt suffocated and any protest led to savage reprisals.

Of course many a blond young Siegfried had been petted by a *parvenu* society and Jean mentioned several well-known hostesses who had taken German lovers. *L'odeur de blé des blonds* had its dangerous attraction to which, he confessed with a smile, he was not totally immune. Jean Genet had written a prodigious novel on the theme. As I had never heard of this author he sketched him for me in a contrapuntal digression, then returning to the German occupation he told me about the blinding of his friend Jean Desbordes, whose puerile volume *J'adore* he had helped to launch. It was a Greek tragedy translated into colloquial French: the fact that Desbordes was handsome sharpened the sadistic lust of his torturers. The cruelty of the Gestapo had infected their French collaborators, and now there was a danger of this spreading among the FFI boys still hunting for scalps.

There was no denying that Cocteau was theatrical. The originality of his conversation was that he saw everyday things in dramatic terms. 'With us,' he wrote, 'there is a house, a lamp, a bowl of soup, a fire, wine and pipes at the back of every work of art.' But his pipes were of opium and they served him as a magic flute to transform an ordinary still life and make it dance like the toys in *La Boutique Fantasque*. Opium had grown scarcer in wartime and the confirmed addicts had to be satisfied with dross. Maybe this was the cause of the migraines and skin irritation that tormented him. He was being treated with acupuncture by an old sinologue whose needles afforded him some relief, but when he was not talking he had the haggard expression of a suffering child. 'My health is wretched,' he said. 'Work is the only cure. I forget my ailments while I'm writing.'

His small apartment in the Rue de Montpensier was as packed with evocative odds and ends as Christian Bérard's – masks, portfolios, a blackboard with memoranda chalked up like astrological symbols, a lithograph of a horse by Delacroix – a rendezvous of the anomalous and unexpected. Since he had recommended Jean Genet to me as a great writer who was also a great moralist I had procured his poem *Le condamné à mort* (printed in Fresnes prison) and *Notre-Dame-des-Fleurs*, whose morality escaped me but whose style impressed me, as that of a Mephistophelian Chateaubriand. When I met him at Cocteau's his formal manner and suave diction were at variance with his forbidding appearance. Even if I had not read his writings, his shifty eyes above a boxer's nose in a small tight skull with close-cropped hair would have disconcerted me. Small wonder that convicts and their ethos had been the chief inspiration of such a type, but I thought he had romanticized them through his pederastic vision. He had told Cocteau that it was not enough for an author to watch his heroes live and pity them: 'We should take their sins upon ourselves and suffer the consequences.' And he looked as if he felt responsible for his characters. Of all the writers Cocteau had sponsored he was the most perverse. One would not care to encounter him in the black-out. Yet he discoursed with acumen on a recent exhibition of paintings, and his enthusiasm for the landscapes of Monet was akin to George Moore's. He greatly admired Sisley and he even had a good word for a landscape by Churchill which had been included in the same show. Stap my vitals, thought I, what would our Prime Minister say of *Notre-Dame-des-Fleurs*?

Was it pure coincidence that so many of Cocteau's friends were named Jean? He was so neatly dressed that he gave the impression of a dandy, but he remarked that he could never keep any clothes: his shirts, neckties, sweaters, even his trousers, were

constantly vanishing. Whereas other writers barricaded themselves like Evelyn Waugh behind a notice 'No admittance on
business', or with a posse of secretaries to guard them against
intrusion, Cocteau seemed always accessible, Richelieu 0680. He
spoke of writing, however, as a sacrificial act of self-dedication.
The writer should sit at his desk and sweat it out, filling page
after page, deaf to telephone calls and blind to *pneumatiques*, per-
severing like an ox. Perhaps this was a fallow interval and he
needed a new audience to test his ideas and exercise his virtuosity.

In mid-December the German Panzers collected by Rundstedt
made their supreme effort to break through the Ardennes.
Military historians have described this formidable struggle when
the Allied High Command was caught by surprise. So terrible
was the weather that it was assumed that the Germans would
remain on the defensive. After torrential rains and flooded rivers
came heavy snow and ice: the setting of the battle was suitably
Wagnerian. Many soldiers on both sides were frozen to death.
Rumours of the evacuation of Strasbourg, which had been
liberated in late November, sent a wave of depression through
Paris, too swiftly following the previous euphoria. Our gloomiest
correspondents prophesied that we would be swept back into the
Channel. 'And I just don't see another landing in Normandy
after that,' one added, 'not yet for a long while.'

The heroic resistance of the American G.I.s at Bastogne and
St Vith defeated Hitler's last attempt to win a breathing space
for Germany. Eisenhower showed his discrimination in calling
on Montgomery during the crucial crisis. For a week or more
SHAEF had difficulty in explaining conditions that were chaotic.
Germans disguised in American uniforms with American mark-
ings on captured tanks and trucks had added to the confusion as
well as a barrage of flying bombs. Shortly before Christmas a
number of German parachutists wearing American uniforms
were caught because of their lack of dog-tags in the neighbourhood
of Paris, and a curfew was imposed from 8 p.m. to 6 a.m. It was an
anxious Christmas for all of us, but when the German offensive

failed, we began to see the end. The conquest of Germany had only been delayed by this disastrous offensive.

We censors were kept very busy. Evidently I had a reputation for cutting red tape, for several correspondents came to me with messages which had to be redrafted for security reasons. Among these I was delighted to see Christopher Sykes, who had parachuted into the Vosges to support the Maquis at the end of August. He has left a poignant record of his experiences with the Maquisards in *Four Studies in Loyalty*.

Christopher had more recently been in Eastern France to discover the fate of men from Airborne Corps who had been lost in operations in Lorraine. With one exception all of them had been murdered by the Gestapo, and he had to report this dreadful news by telegram to Headquarters in England. His message dispatched, we talked of other matters. For a writer he had been in a singular position to observe a microcosm of the essential France triumphant over calamity; and he had returned from the Vosges with a deep respect for the enduring solidity of the French character. I thought it would interest him to meet Gertrude Stein, who had spent the last years with her inseparable companion Alice Toklas in rustic seclusion near Culoz, since her own views on nearly every subject were amusingly unpredictable.

He has reminded me that I asked him to dine at Maxim's, which had been re-opened as 'The British Empire Club'. The number of guests was limited by rule as at the Chatham but the food was comparatively luxurious in the circumstances. Since my memory of the occasion is telescoped with so many others he has kindly allowed me to quote his personal impression.

'There was only one other guest, Marie-Laure de Noailles, whom I had not seen since some years before the war. We had what I can only call an evening of violent interest, because we all had so much to talk about since 1939. Thinking about it after, as I often have, I am reminded of Pierre's dinner with Natasha and her family after the campaign of 1812, as described in *War and Peace*, with the difference that none of us burst into tears or wished to do so. It was a very gay evening, and a very moving occasion too. At the end of dinner Harold and Marie-Laure declared that we "must" go and see Gertrude Stein. I think both of them had seen her in Paris recently before this. I knew her hardly at all, having only once met her, not very rewardingly, in London with Bertie and Diane Abdy two or three years before the war.

'So off we went to her house on the Left Bank. I remember that it was a very stormy evening with thunder which was building up into a *tutti crescendo*.

'Miss Stein was alone with Miss Toklas. She seemed glad to see us and Miss Toklas brought in coffee and brandy. There started a conversation between Marie-Laure and Miss Stein about Pétain and de Gaulle, but I remember it being good-humoured, in spite of the tenseness of the difference of opinion, and Gertrude Stein showed an agreeable common-sense view of the whole subject. She was like a good old American Mom, and I thought what a nice old party she was.

'Then she turned to me and I quickly received a different impression. She dimly remembered me and I gave her news of Bertie and Diane. She made affectionate inquiries about them, but I noticed a severe look on her face, defiantly directed at me. Suddenly she spoke in a new loud harsh tone. She wanted to know what the English thought they were doing. I was not very satisfying on the subject, having had no notice of the question, and my feeble remarks seemed to rouse her to deliver a long-pondered onslaught on Great Britain, the Empire, Winston Churchill and other prominent British features. She said that men would always want to fight each other and America was going to fight for things that mattered. She extolled Russia and loudly declared that America and Russia were modern, and their purpose was to smash up unmodern peoples, notably ourselves.

'Marie-Laure was quietly dissenting from these views but with no effect. The old lady roared on, getting louder and louder, till she was in a fever of indignation. I found this hysterical anglophobia altogether too much and I told her she was talking Rot.

"What's that?" she exclaimed. My remark had coincided

with an absolutely colossal clap of thunder, and several more succeeded to it. Remembering her deafness I now positively shouted that she was talking Rot, and I got the message across, over the thunder which continued ceaseless with an uninterrupted flickering of lightning.

'Miss Stein glared at me like a tigress, then turned to Marie-Laure and began talking about something else. Miss Toklas immediately leaped to my side and plied me with coffee and brandy and questions. I wondered if I had gone too far in accusing this famous old lady of talking Rot, though Rot was what she had undoubtedly been talking. Miss Toklas told me how very glad Miss Stein was to have made my acquaintance again, but I suspected her of empty politeness. I was wrong. She had the most polished intuition imaginable.

'It was by now growing late and Miss Stein showed us some new pictures she had acquired. As we were looking round I saw Harold talking to her evidently about me. I fixed my eyes on the famous Picasso portrait which I had never seen before, and Miss Toklas came up and again said that she could see that Miss Stein liked me and hoped I would call again. I could not help being reminded of Boswell meeting Johnson in the bookshop.

'The thunder and lightning diminished and we left. I was so fascinated by this encounter that I took Miss Toklas at her word and called again with a French friend, Jacques Jay. It was a beautiful spring evening in 1945. There was no thunder and lightning. Miss Stein had a few guests. She was quite charming and we had a long, grave conversation. I really felt I loved her. I never saw her again.

'I am left with two questions to which I do not know the answer. Was she one of those people of battling temperament who take a liking to someone who stands up to the bullying and enjoys the battle? Or did Harold Acton say something which melted that fierce heart? And if so, what?'

My answer is, a bit of both. Gertrude Stein enjoyed a skirmish but she was usually surrounded by Yes-sayers who dared not contradict her. Often she indulged in argument for argument's sake. Modernity was her religion: one must be absolutely Modern, as Rimbaud had written; and she harboured a notion that Great Britain suffered from hardening of the arteries. During her absence from Paris she had become even more ingrown. Surely her theory of Modernity conflicted with her stout defence of the Old Marshal, but she maintained that Pétain was a modern realist and de Gaulle an old-fashioned chauvinist. As she loved to quiz and astonish I never took her opinions quite seriously though there was often a grain of sense in the most paradoxical. 'We are not serious because we are serious,' as she used to say. She had imagined that Christopher was a hidebound British officer, and I enlightened her about his chivalrous exploits and his genuine literary gifts.

Christopher has related another incident of that evening in his *Four Studies in Loyalty*. Among the pictures she showed us was a self-portrait by Riba-Rovira who had been imprisoned in a concentration camp. He had preserved his sanity by imagining a picture and how he would paint it in every detail, stroke by stroke, but when he was liberated he found he could not transfer to canvas the picture he had completed in his imagination. He painted the self-portrait instead and, as Christopher remarked, it had a Grecoesque spirituality.

Marie-Laure de Noailles, herself a painter and poet of distinction as well as a liberal patron of the contemporary arts, had previously taken me to see Picasso in the Rue des Grands-Augustins. An unshaven Spaniard like one of Goya's picadors scrutinized us suspiciously before leading us up the winding stairs of his mansion. A voluble group was discoursing around the Master who listened, nodded, and said little, but looked at everyone with the alert black piercing eyes that have been photographed so often – eyes so much younger and more vivacious than his other features carved out of very hard boxwood. His white hair emphasized his youthfulness. How sturdy he was, how nimble in his movements, earthy and engagingly pleased with his earthiness. His glances darted round the studio like humanized Leica lenses.

169

The principal talkers were Georges Hugnet, Henri Sauguet and the statuesque Dora Maar, soon joined by Cocteau, who outtalked them all, and I realized that Picasso's influence on writers was even stronger than his influence on painters. Cocteau's words took wing and soared in a stratosphere of metaphysical rapture as the Master leaped about, half ballet-dancer, half weight-lifter, bringing up canvas after canvas, shifting them from stacks against the wall for us to see. French is the language of superlatives and these were never exhausted. Perhaps Picasso had heard too many in his lifetime but he looked as happy as a successful conjurer.

A small Bacchanalian scene kindled comparisons with Poussin but it was more erratically erotic. A large picture of a supine woman with a guitar player beside her was clearly a cubist version of Titian's recumbent Venus in the Uffizi and I marvelled at the ecstatic murmurs it evoked, as of children round a blazing Christmas Tree. 'I must have it, I must have it!' cried Marie-Laure, 'I'll give you my Rubens in exchange' – referring to the resplendent Adam and Eve in her collection. But Picasso did not want her masterpiece and he told her so rather bluntly. He preferred his own masterpiece. He switched his glance to each of us in turn with a twinkle that might be described as mischievous were it not so genial. Then he peered at his cubist Venus and I could swear he had his tongue in his cheek. At that moment the man interested me more than his work. The others quivered with an emotion which might have been aesthetic. Their comments had more sentiment than sense. 'She moves, she moves! Don't you see, the sofa is really a swing? I have never seen a picture before which actually sways towards you rhythmically to and fro.' 'The guitar is twanging. C'est Vénus toute entière à sa proie attachée listening to Canto Flamenco,' and so forth. They had succumbed to a spell to which I was immune, for I continued to see the Titian it was derived from.

Four small canvases depicting views of the Pont-Neuf were disarming for their simple similitude. When compliments about these were forthcoming Picasso shrugged them off with: 'Those were done by Kasbek.' Kasbek was his Afghan hound, or rather the walking skeleton of a hound, the metempsychosis of some rickety Harlequin he had painted in his Montmartre days, so mangily melancholy that I gave him a pat as if to say 'Cheer up!' 'Better not touch him,' Picasso said. 'He has the itch.'

The paintings he liked least were attributed to Kasbek. A set of hybrid still lifes followed, of which a skull beside a pot excited Cocteau. Pompeii reappeared in a series of drawings in flowing chiaroscuro, most of which represented the sleeping beauty theme in reverse, for the prostrate nude male was contemplated by a seated female in classical drapery. 'My war work,' the Master explained. 'I did them during the German occupation.'

The drawings were curiously static and serene: nothing could have been more remote from his famous 'Guernica'. No doubt Picasso had his escapist moods. He remarked that he usually worked at night by electricity. The studio on the top floor under heavy wooden rafters was exceedingly chilly. With a chuckle of merriment he showed us a book on degenerate art containing re-productions of his least controversial productions. On the walls I noticed a bright bouquet of flowers by Matisse: a child in bed under a red and yellow quilt with an old crone in a chair by Vuillard; and a typical Modigliani. 'My personal collection,' said the Master. I envied him the Vuillard, which had the quiet harmony of a Fauré string quartet.

Bruised by the cold, we adjourned for a hearty luncheon at a Catalan *bistro* nearby where the Master was treated with becoming reverence. Though he let others do the talking he radiated content-ment in a detached way special to celebrities. Dora Maar was a soothing presence, Marie-Laure an eloquent Muse. The Master purred. Gertrude Stein's name cropped up during the meal. She and Alice Toklas had just returned from exile in a taxi bearing her most cherished possession, Picasso's portrait of her painted in 1906 – together with her white poodle Basket and a large store of edible provisions.

'Let's all go and see her,' said the Master. So there was a grand reunion with everyone talking at once in the Rue Christine.

Picasso hugged Gertrude like a beloved bolster. '*Et mon portrait?*' he asked with a sudden note of anxiety, as if it were a lucky talisman. How often had he raised that question since it had been painted? It was there waiting for him and he examined it minutely. 'Ah, it is finer than I had dreamt,' he said, embracing her again.

If only as a publicity agent Gertrude had brought him luck. Her brother Leo, who was as repetitive as he was deaf – there was a strong family likeness – had often told me that when he had bought the early Picassos 'she pretended to have discovered' Gertrude had been furious with him for buying such daubs. Be that as it may, she had revised her first impression. Her article on Picasso in *Camera Work* (August 1912) begins: 'One whom some were certainly following was one who was completely charming.' After repeating this sentence with minor variations she proceeds: 'Some were certainly following and were certain that the one they were then following was one bringing out of himself then something that was coming to be a heavy thing, a solid thing and a complete thing.' The theme of 'something had been coming out of him' alternates with 'This one had always been working' – yet 'He was not ever completely working'. The longest sentence in the article attempts to summarize his achievement: 'This one was always having something that was coming out of this one that was a solid thing, a charming thing, a lovely thing, a perplexing thing, a disconcerting thing, an interesting thing, a disturbing thing, a repellent thing, a very pretty thing.' Later, in her best known and most lucid *Autobiography of Alice B. Toklas*, she paid him the supreme compliment of bracketing him with herself as a 'first class genius'.

It was amusing to watch the geniuses together. Both were rugged and squarely built; both had short hair and might have been taken for Aztec Mexicans; but whereas Picasso was muscularly mobile Gertrude was dumpily static. Though fifteen years had passed since I had seen her and Alice Toklas I could detect little change except that Gertrude had become more aggressively American in idiom and the use of slang, which seemed odd considering that she had been an expatriate most of her life. We had many friends in common and I saw her often. If one respected her colossal ego she could be warmly sympathetic. Her attempt to revitalize language was chiefly remarkable for its pertinacity, but only a fraction of her sense of fun percolates into her writings. Here and there a phrase arrests one's attention, such as 'Civilization begins with a rose', but how many pages of stuttering repetition must be negotiated in order to find a gem of this quality!

In *Composition as Explanation* she wrote: 'For a very long time everybody refuses and then almost without a pause almost everybody accepts.' Almost everybody had accepted Picasso as a painter, but I fear that Gertrude Stein's 'continuous present' is already a thing of the past. Her *Three Lives* had influenced writers of Hemingway's generation.

Having complete faith in herself, she had some to spare for others. Her memory was retentive and she praised my long-forgotten fantasy *Cornelian*. I might still become a good writer, she observed: I had plenty to say and could say it well if I forgot all about English literature and remembered that I was half-American. 'Your next book,' she added, 'must be a book of memoirs.' Eventually I took her advice. While she discoursed with much humour and sense in a placid voice Alice attended to domestic details, acted as interpreter and tactful go-between. Hemingway has hinted that Alice had a vicious side, but I never saw her other than gentle and devoted to Gertrude, whom she cosseted with creamy cakes.

I invited them to lunch with me at the Chatham and the Officers Club and in each place they created a sensation. John Cullen, who was often in the company of a pretty French girl — 'they are pretty like orchids, not like primroses,' he remarked of the women of Paris — was shocked by the extreme dowdiness of this elderly couple. Gertrude's billowing skirt was not low enough to hide a pair of woollen gaiters which fell about her ankles, and Alice, tiny and hunched beside her with a hooked nose and light moustache, reminded John of the maiden ladies who fusted at Bath or Cheltenham, Gertrude insisted on bringing her poodle Basket, which made them even more conspicuous among women who resembled sleek mannequins. But Gertrude carried herself with the assurance of a Cleopatra. John was soon won over by their conversation and remarked: 'I can see that I shall be calling Miss Stein *"chère maîtresse"* next time I see her.' When he mentioned that Hemingway was in Paris, Alice Toklas speaking for both of them as usual, said the only thing they liked about him was his good looks when they first knew him at the age of twenty-four. They thought he had become hopelessly commercialized. 'But the *career*,' he once said to them. It was always 'the career' . . .

My American colleagues at the Chatham were thrilled to meet her and in a very short time she was distributing autographs in her sloping scrawl. This was my second guest who was asked for an autograph in public. The third was Norman Douglas in a Capri restaurant. 'Certainly not,' he snapped. 'Unless they're prepared to pay me a fee. Never heard of such cheek. They'll be forging my signature next. I've seen that happen before.' Had he been asked personally he might have obliged them, but they had sent the request by a waiter he disliked. For Gertrude the request was an outward and visible sign of her celebrity. Considering that she seldom went out except to take Basket for a walk, her intimate knowledge of other people's lives was astonishing: she excelled in the analysis of human relationships, yet her pen-portraits of Cocteau, Edith Sitwell and other friends, contain no trace of her psychological insight. The repetition of 'Needs be needs be needs be near' conveys little of Cocteau whereas in conversation there was some truth in her remark that he prided himself on being eternally thirty.

An assiduous crony of hers was Thomas Whittemore, the Bostonian professor so comically sketched by Evelyn Waugh in *Remote People*. Although Berenson and many scholars deemed him a pious fraud, he had been responsible for the restoration of the Byzantine mosaics at Hagia Sophia and other mosques in Istanbul and had founded a Byzantine Institute in Paris which he had come to reopen. Under the Occupation it had become a shambles, he said, and he complained that the Ritz Hotel, where he was staying, was positively Siberian, and he kept running into that awful cad Hemingway (a fellow Ritzonian but not a Bostonian) who gave him the cold shivers. Recollecting the dire discomfort of his trip to the Abyssinian monastery of Debra Lebanos with Evelyn Waugh, I had to smile.

The professor was almost as enthusiastic about Gertrude as about Byzantium and his flattery warmed the cockles of her heart. His articulation was painfully deliberate, but there was an ironical gleam in his eye which belied his solemnity. He told me that he had started cleaning the mosaics of Hagia Sophia with very fine dental instruments: 'I scraped them like ivory teeth with marvellous results.' Whatever his shortcomings, he deserved credit for this achievement. He gave me to understand that it had largely been due to his friendship with Mustafa Kemal, whom he had been able to influence in many constructive ways.

I doubt if the G.I.s who flocked to visit Gertrude had perused her writings. For them she was one of the living monuments of Paris, and they were attracted to this elderly frump as if she were a glamorous film-star. She must have felt like one when she posed for their cameras in front of the Stars and Stripes. She also felt fiercely democratic. This intellectual *vivandière*, as Natalie Barney called her, showed them her pictures, watched their reactions, encouraged any signs of independence, and scolded those who were fixed in their ideas. They sat on the floor and looked up to her with ravenous reverence while she spoke on a wide variety of subjects in a vigorous monotone, reducing them to speechlessness. I often wondered if and how she would influence their lives when they returned to the United States. Once I heard her explain to them that in her opinion all modern painting was based on what Cézanne had failed to do, instead of on what he had nearly succeeded in doing. To show what he could not achieve had become Cézanne's obsession and that of his followers, who had originated a system of camouflage which had developed into an art in peace and in war. Her argument was ingenious, but somewhat abstruse for the ingenuous, who listened open-mouthed, an occasional tongue displacing a gob of chewing gum.

When they were not calling on Gertrude and Picasso they were lining up for Chanel 5, the only scent in constant demand for transatlantic sweethearts.

In the absence of Natalie Barney, whose French was classically fluent, Gertrude Stein was queen of the expatriates, but one seldom heard French in her company though she spoke it fluently with a strong American accent. To be in Paris without conversing in the language seemed a regrettable limitation. Much as I enjoyed my visits to her, my happiest hours in Paris were spent with Marie-Laure de Noailles, who was as representative of her period, the nineteen-thirties, as Madame du Deffand was of the first half of the eighteenth century. A versatile artist who wrote and painted as a musician, for *La Tour de Babel* and *Les Iles Invisibles* are as musical in prose as her rustling foliage and clouds with the heads of cherubim in paint – clouds that burst into song – her name was linked with such classics of the avant-garde as Cocteau's *Le sang d'un poète* and Buñuel-Dali's *L'âge d'or*, apart from the composers she had sponsored. She did not conduct anything so formal as a salon but she welcomed her friends in one of the few grand mansions kept up in proper style. The most diverse paintings ranging from Cranach to Picasso looked at home on her walls; there was a Burne-Jones above the staircase and a stupendous Adam and Eve by Rubens dominated the drawing-room where I heard so much fine music and stimulating talk, but if I had been offered my choice of pictures I should have chosen her Goyas, which vied with his best portraits in the Prado. To live with great works of art can be daunting, but being a creative person with a vision of her own, Marie-Laure advanced like a galleon in full sail. Tall and imposing with the features of George Sand, only the violence of her emotions could daunt her. When a tipsy Flying Officer whirled her into a dance at the Officers Club John Cullen remarked aptly that it was like a Victorian picture of Dignity and Impudence.

176

Musicians prevailed at her receptions and I have seldom encountered a dull one. Poulenc, Auric and Sauguet were as spirited and witty as their compositions. So subtly feline was Sauguet that one might guess he was the author of *La Chatte*: his mockery of the average musical hostess, for instance, of whom one specimen exclaimed in a stentorian voice: 'If I wasn't in my own house, I would leave,' kept one in fits of laughter. He had recently composed *Les Forains*, whose success had put him in an excellent humour. Puns were as popular as in Florence and Peking and Poulenc had invented many. For an enigmatic singer with a commonplace name he proposed the *sobriquet* Irma Frodite. Cocteau's poems were full of puns such as *un os* (a bone), *une noce* (a wedding feast) in *Clair-obscur*. This was in the tradition of Victor Hugo – 'a madman who fancied himself Victor Hugo', as Cocteau epitomized him. No Frenchman could escape the lure of that lord of language.

Marie-Laure's circle of friends was closely knit and I had the sensation of picking my way through invisible spider-webs until they became accustomed to me. Their jokes were as allusive as their conversation, and some knowledge of their background was needed to seize their full import. They revelled in each other's idiosyncrasies but their curiosity seldom extended beyond their private frontier. Their flair for the fantastic appealed to me strongly after my routine at the Scribe.

Among those whose originality was most apparent at a glance were Isabelle de la Moussaye, a young woman of such spun glass refinement of mind and feature that others looked coarse beside her, and Olivier Larronde, a poet who looked no older than fifteen. If orchids could write novels they would write like Isabelle: hers were published at an unfavourable time in small editions but they deserve to be revived. She was convinced that she had proved the identity of the Man in the Iron Mask, and that he was the Duc de Beaufort. As she was gifted with second sight I was ready to believe her though she tended to mythicize her own existence. She told me that she had quarrelled with her husband's family because they were pro-Vichy but her two small sons, aged six and eight, were as pro-English as herself and had set off on their bicycles with the intention of getting to England. About two hundred miles from Brest the boys were stopped and sent home. Her mother was the ultra-fashionable Daisy Fellowes, a feminine dictator of impenetrable hardness, and there was no love lost between them, any more than there was between Emerald and Nancy Cunard with whom I discerned a parallel. Both Isabelle and Nancy were animated flowers in revolt against the hot-house of their girlhood, but there the comparison ended for Isabelle had but one profile whereas Nancy had several. I was a little in love with both. But Nancy was in love with a dozen lost causes and Isabelle with the Man in the Iron Mask.

Oliver Larronde also suffered from an overpowering mother, a fanatical spiritualist who employed him as a medium at her séances and kept him short of money when he ceased to oblige her in conjuring ectoplasm. He recited his ornate verses, much influenced by Maurice Scève, in a voice that had not been broken by puberty, with the naturalness of a child who is asked to sing for his elders. I tried to translate some of them but the charm of their language was so specifically French that my efforts were daunted. They contained many references to roses, of all flowers the most exploited by poets throughout the ages, yet these were still fresh, the dew sparkled on their petals. And since his evocation of snow-flakes has probably melted into oblivion I cannot resist quoting these delicately diaphanous lines:

> Danse sur du papier comme les Japonais,
> Neige – trépignez, d'ange, d'âne, petits pieds,
> Petits pieds japonais, pieds de la neige, n'ai-
> Je pas le droit de vous baiser, pieds en papier.

Larronde might have been the reincarnation of some sixteenth-century poet. His precocity was formidable, his spontaneity disarming. He wore his shabby clothes with a jaunty bravado, and a long scarf wound about his threadbare jacket was his substitute for an overcoat in that icy winter. Eventually his poems were published by Gallimard but since drugs had become his chief pabulum he died prematurely.

There was a sprinkling of decorative young editors and reviewers with names like Henri Hell, and while these clustered round Cocteau the young women surrounded Paul Valéry, whose face time had worn to a fastidious mask but whose utterance was the least distinct of any, for he talked as if he had a hot potato in his mouth. If he made any imperishable remark I missed it, though I strained my ears to hear the poet's words. He basked in the adoration of the nymphs who sat at his feet. As I had a jeep at my disposal I offered him a lift which he accepted eagerly. *'Tiens, c'est mon premier jeep,'* he said, *'il fallait décrire cela.'* I recalled his *Colloque* for two flutes, dedicated to Poulenc who had also been present, and he told me that of all composers Poulenc was the finest interpreter of poetry since Debussy.

How Marie-Laure succeeded in writing between constant telephone calls, her hectic social life, her demanding dog Diego, and her two cats Ernest Trismégiste and Prince Michka, was a secret I never solved, yet at this time she produced a fine translation of Edith Sitwell's *Green Song* to which she asked me to contribute a brief introduction. Edith wrote to me: 'I feel it to be a magnificent translation, and I *could* not be more delighted. For some reason my actual vocabulary seems to translate admirably into French, and so do the themes.'

In spite of my enduring admiration for Edith's poetry which I tried to express and assess intelligibly for French readers who had never heard of her, she was displeased because I mentioned that she had been influenced by the Russian Ballet. I still believe this to be true of her earlier poems. All the significant artists of her period and mine had fallen under the spell of the master magician Diaghilev, to whom Osbert Sitwell has paid tribute in his autobiographical masterpiece. Moreover Edith was indignant about French ignorance of modern English literature as evinced by an English number of the French review *Fontaine*. 'It is an absolute disgrace – a laughing-stock,' she wrote, 'and I am afraid it will do the greatest harm to English literature in France . . .

'I have never seen greater insolence than that extended to poor Charles Morgan, who had generously given them something. I hope you will do your uttermost to convince the French that x and y had no right to speak for English literature at all.' In a postscript she added: 'It is a *scandal* Arthur (Waley) is not even mentioned. He is one of the two great writers I refer to in the letter enclosed' – a longer and more specific complaint to Marie-Laure, who had no connection with *Fontaine*.

The dismal truth was that France had been even more isolated during the German occupation than we had been in England. Apart from a few students and professors of English, most cultured Frenchmen were absorbed in their own literature, the best of which had been clandestine: they had little interest in ours. John Lehmann, Cyril Connolly, and the Free French were our go-betweens with the literature on the other side of the embattled Channel. Since they were published in London, perhaps we read Aragon and Vercors with greater appreciation than they deserved, but we read them with frustrated love for the French people and with an Oliver Twist's hunger for more. All my friends in London were clamouring for the most recent French publications and wrote to me for news of the French theatre and film productions. With rare exceptions this interest was not reciprocated. Marie-Laure was one of the exceptions.

I I

At last on May 7th we heard that the unconditional surrender of Germany had been signed at Rheims, but it was not announced officially till the next day when sirens sounded the last All Clear and all the church bells rang in an explosion of joy. The celebrations were passionate yet orderly. In a foaming, cheering crowd I surged along the Place de la Concorde to the Arc de Triomphe, oblivious of myself in the mass intoxication. In spite of my intense relief I did not feel wide awake: half of me could not believe that the war had ended. While the Japanese fought on there was still more suffering than one could bear to contemplate, but at least in Europe the good cause had triumphed. Like most of my fellows I longed for a life of my own. For those of us – the great majority outside the politico-diplomatic stratosphere – the war had been a disintegrating parenthesis. And now, as Churchill wrote, 'new perils loomed and glared upon the torn and harassed world'.

Roosevelt had shown excessive tenderness for 'Uncle Joe's' sensibilities, yet when 'Uncle Joe' had had a free choice between Hitler and the Allies he had chosen Hitler, with whom he divided Poland. Attacked by his Nazi confederate, he had been forced to fight back. Now he was liquidating Hitler's enemies in Poland, gobbling up the Balkans, and trying to swallow Austria and Trieste as well. The prospects were not reassuring. Already the fruits of victory had a bitter taste.

SHAEF would soon be dissolved, and until that happened I remained in Paris with less to do. I looked on with delight at the recovery of the fine arts, at the return of gaiety even if it was superficial. Art had again become the great stimulus to life – to me the greatest of all. The reopening of the Louvre with a provisional exhibition of some eighty masterpieces was the first exciting step towards recovery. The Victory of Samothrace had never looked so supremely victorious though an American G.I. was heard to exclaim: 'I guess it's had another of those bombs!'

Though my feelings about the Louvre were ambivalent, since Napoleon had set the precedent for the systematic plunder of works of art which Hitler hoped to emulate in a so-called Führermuseum at Linz, I have always been won over by the magnitude of Denon's achievement, which provided an impetus for the foundation of other public galleries. But I still think the two ceiling paintings by Veronese should be restored to the Doge's Palace where they belong as an integral part of the decoration.

Roland Petit and Boris Kochno revived the ballet with more talent than funds at their disposal; Roger Desormières conducted a concert in memory of Diaghilev which revived *Petrouchka*, *Parade* and *Le Tricorne*: and Poulenc gave a prodigious solo performance of Apollinaire's *Les Mamelles de Tirésias* which he had set to scintillating music. Of *Les Forains*, the most poignant of Roland Petit's ballets, I have written elsewhere: it epitomized the pathos of the travelling showman's existence and seemed to symbolize the public's indifference to art. The trudging weary rhythm of Sauguet's music as the vaudeville troupe packs up and moves on is haunted with the fatality of failure.

In June when I flew to London on leave the General Election was the predominant topic. At dinner with Lady Cunard, Lord Margesson and the other guests were sure of a Conservative victory: Churchill's name was flourished as a banner by those who had opposed him during the pre-war years. The most jovially optimistic of my friends was Mrs George Keppel, who was empress of the Ritz at this period. Wherever she pitched her tent she appeared to rule. She created her own aura of grandeur in the suitably Edwardian lounge, far more regal than poor King Zog and Queen Geraldine of Albania, who had taken refuge in the same caravanserai. Traditionally better informed than anyone else – and when the fact failed her she would embellish it with plausible fancy – she divulged the latest Florentine news. 'We shall soon be meeting in Doney's,' she assured me with that smile which had captivated kings. 'All our old friends are waiting to welcome us. Neither my house nor yours has suffered any damage but they won't be habitable till the troops clear out. We'll have to get Lulie Torrigiani to put us up.'

Her daughter Violet Trefusis, who had inherited her strain of fantasy, was impatient to return to France where she owned a pretty château near Provins. The château, she alleged, had been discovered by her while motoring with Marcel Proust, who had left his cork-lined bedroom for this excursion. 'It is worthy of my hero Saint-Loup,' he had observed. And by a curious coincidence it happened to be called Saint-Loup. For her as for other expatriates London had become claustrophobic.

Violet was more fortunate than Nancy Cunard, whose house at Chapelle-Réanville had been looted and wrecked under the eyes of the complacent mayor. She had raked through the shambles for days to recover a few broken odds and ends. The African sculpture she valued so highly had fed the kitchen stove.

In Heywood Hill's bookshop which she had converted into a salon for the exchange of literary gossip, Nancy Mitford was also pining for Paris. Already she had hitched her wagon to the star of General de Gaulle. For her this was a lucky star, but I must not anticipate. From the *succès d'estime* of her exuberant early novels she was to reach the summit of profitable popularity. In the meantime she charmed all who dropped in to browse among the keepsake almanacs, engravings, books and mechanical toys with which Heywood created a Tales of Hoffmann atmosphere. Old colonels and young subalterns forgot to have their hair cut at Trumper's next door, beguiled by the siren tones of the Mitford voice, for all the Mitford sisters shared the same cooing intonation and a silvery peal of laughter that banished care. Under the pretext of buying a book more than one colonel and subaltern sought a few words with Nancy, and would purchase a musical monkey under a glass dome or a bust of the Prince Consort in order to prolong so sweet a pleasure.

Knowing that her heart was lost to the Free French, I consoled myself by seeing her as a sister. Our friendship was founded as much on the same wave-length of humour as on a sympathy akin to consanguinity. But all the Mitfords exerted a fascination purely English, clear-eyed, rose-petalled, instantaneous, which no caprice could shiver: on the contrary, the forthright independence of their outlook added a piquancy to our relationship. No political difference could alter my affection for the radiant Diana. Tom had been as dear to me as a brother, and dearer still he must have been to the gods, for he died of wounds in Burma in the plenitude of his youth and promise. In him – to paraphrase Nietzsche – power had become gracious and stepped down into visibility to delight less gifted mortals. His death cast a shadow over my last days in Paris. Even now when I listen to Bach's fugues his spirit is near me, encouraging me to enjoy and give enjoyment.

In August I flew to Wiesbaden just after the first atomic bomb had exploded on Hiroshima. In spite of the Japanese tendency to collective suicide, their rejection of the ultimatum to surrender and contempt of the millions of warning leaflets dropped on twenty-three cities, it was plain that their barbaric oligarchy was doomed to defeat. Since their attack on Pearl Harbor it was nonsense to talk of their chivalry. Itagaki refused to surrender in Malaya: for him and his like war was a heroic game. The scientists taught them a lesson; but has it been learnt? When some 40,000 are killed by a momentary flash it is a monstrous imbecility to consider war. But atomic weapons dwarf imagination and imbeciles abound. When Dr Jacob Bronowski proposed that the bombed area of Nagasaki be preserved and that all future conferences on disarmament, 'and on other issues which weigh the fate of nations', be held in situ, his official colleagues pointed out to him that delegates would be uncomfortable in Nagasaki. Personally I am in favour of his proposal. Not in commodious hotels but in an ocean of rubble should statesmen discuss the problems that trouble the rest of humanity.

Heavy rain made the dank desolation of Germany more desolate. Yet Wiesbaden had suffered less damage than the other bombed cities I glimpsed. The remains of our unit were installed partly in the battered Landeshaus and partly in the Grüner Wald Hotel. One of my most disagreeable tasks was to evict tenants from the flats to be used as our billets. They wept, they protested, they refused to budge till they were compelled to by tough G.I.s. The war was over as far as they were concerned: they were stunned and horrified to be evicted from their homes at such short notice. They had to leave most of their furniture behind, but they removed all they possibly could in bags and baskets. Tense and quivering with hatred, cursing and shaking gnarled fists at us, they stumbled up and down steep musty staircases with baskets of potatoes, preserved fruit, a few books – what were the works of Schiller and Goethe doing there? – and such valued possessions as cuckoo clocks. Many of them congregated forlornly in a modern Gothic church while we took over their lodgings. I occupied a flat without a bath, swarming with cockroaches, and I had brought no sheets. Having caught cold in the rain I slept none too well. The vast stretches of rocky emptiness, the craters of shattered concrete and skeletons of buildings I had seen made me marvel at the Spartan endurance of the German people. In courage and fortitude they were certainly our peers. Their slavish obedience to a Hitler remained an enigma. Had not one of their great philosophers defined rebellion as superiority in the slave?

After Paris the pervading grimness, the hatred and bleak despair of the population filled me with despondency. But my American colleagues appeared to welcome the change of scene. Their cheerfulness and good nature were impervious to the blanket of hostility, to the ugliness of the flats where they were billeted, each drearier than the last. In all my life I had never seen such hideous furniture, such distressingly stupid pictures hanging on walls. The dwellings of Tuscan peasants were patrician in comparison. The cooking is best forgotten, but even that pleased my affable colleagues. Though fraternization with Germans was forbidden they were all eager to fraternize. A night club run by 12th Army Group in a gloomy dance hall made an effort to create some distraction, but all the feminine dancers were in uniform and there was a natural craving for partners in less masculine attire.

A small area of the U.S.A. was transported into this great grim mortuary by a performance of Thornton Wilder's play *Our Town*, with Raymond Massey in the role of the Stage Manager who conjures the non-existent scenery and comments on the activities of Grover's Corners. In *Yank*, the army weekly, there were photographs of American towns – captioned 'a look back home since you went away' – whose main streets must have resembled Grover's Corners. The life 'back home' evoked with quiet humour and pathos by seemingly simple means in a language which everybody could understand had a visible effect on the soldiers who had fought with such courage, and many an eye was moist. No audience could have been more appreciative, and I wished Thornton Wilder had been present.

Excursions to Mainz, Bingen, Coblenz and Nassau, were enough to surfeit anyone with ruins. The Rhine was crammed with sunken barges inhabited by flocks of screaming gulls. Once we picnicked near the fort of Ehrenbreitstein above Coblenz which affords a fine panorama of the junction of the Rhine and Moselle, pale jade and milky coffee. The French commandant protested against our intrusion. Acting as interpreter, I had much ado to calm his dudgeon. We were harmless tourists, I explained, and since the war was over surely we might be allowed to enjoy the view. Very grudgingly he accepted a cigarette, muttering that it was not at all *en règle*.

After seeing the total devastation of Frankfurt – abstract sculpture of twisted steel on a colossal scale among mountains of rubble already choked with weeds – I was glad to avoid Berlin. How the population contrived to exist there astonished me, yet those we encountered appeared fairly neat and clean as like ants they dragged or wheeled boxes and bundles through the few streets that had been cleared of debris. The men were mostly maimed; the women stared straight ahead as in a trance; the chubby children begged for chewing gum. What a superhuman faith in Hitler when hardly any building was intact! The grandeur of Roman ruins had been sublimated by Piranesi and Hubert Robert, but there was no grandeur in this chaos of crumpled concrete. This was the real waste land.

The G.I.s were singing to the tune of *Lili Marlene*: 'Oh Mr Truman, when can we go home?' While air- and sea-borne squadrons were occupying the Tokyo area the harping on 'Home sweet home' became more insistent. Since the death of Tom Mitford in Burma I was grieved to hear that my promising young cousin Gaylord Dillingham, had been shot down over Tokyo. To be killed at the culmination of war seemed the cruellest of ironies.

In September I left my American buddies to join Air Information Unit, B.A.F.O., at Minden, which might have been in England. The hotel we occupied on the Market Square was called Victoria and it was full of sociable war correspondents, including the famous Richard Dimbleby of the B.B.C. and Cooper of *The Times*. When the electricity failed, as it often did, Dimbleby played nostalgic English ballads on the piano. Most of our stomachs had been turned by the sights we had seen but in English fashion we avoided unpalatable topics. Gentility and heartiness reigned. But soon I was called to Brussels to deal with a summary of evidence against an airman accused of purloining service petrol. The young man was engaged to a flaxen Belgian, whom I had to cross-examine together with various members of her family. These defended him with such eloquent tributes to his character that I gave him the benefit of the doubt. If he had driven out of his way to visit his sweetheart, the petrol consumed had been infinitesimal compared to the frequent waste I had witnessed on airfields.

In my spare time I visited my father's old friend Adolphe Stoclet, who had one of the finest private art collections in

Europe. This contained at least thirteen Italian Romanesque panel paintings of superb quality, including the gemlike Crucifix which now hangs in the London National Gallery. My father possessed a Crucifix by the same painter, usually known as the Master of St Francis, a North Umbrian working in the thirteenth century. The Stoclet collection had been stored elsewhere for safety and only part of it had returned to his Brussels mansion, a surprising Art Nouveau building, but how splendid and varied in range even that part was, whether of Cambodian sculpture or Limoges enamel. Each object reflected the discrimination of an original connoisseur whose taste revolted against realism. Stoclet was an outstanding example of a vanishing species, for hardly any modern collector has his impeccable sense of quality even if he could afford to indulge it when prices have become so exorbitant. Though his once vigorous frame was crippled with arthritis Monsieur Stoclet told me that he did not consider it worth while to obey doctor's orders about diet. 'I suffer so much anyhow that a slice of foie-gras or a glass of brandy could make no difference except to enhance my enjoyment of the moment, and at least that is something positive.' He was a *grand amateur* in the highest tradition. His smallest medal was perfect of its kind. He eschewed compromise with the second best.

On returning to Minden I received the news that my brother had died in Ferrara. Recently he had written to me after years of silence: he had been to Florence and seen our house and garden, where a few servants and the old head gardener, who had stayed on through the war, had given him a touching welcome, loading him with fruit and flowers. He was overjoyed to find the property unscathed. Everything had enchanted him, the friendly population, the climate, the food and wine: it was a comforting climax to those miserable years in the Pioneer Corps. He knew that my mother was reluctant to return but he was anxious that she should do so since he argued that it was a sort of defeatism to let oneself be uprooted permanently by the war. My father required no persuasion: outside Florence he felt lost. His heart was with the garden he had created, with the collection he had gradually formed since his youth, to which everything else was subsidiary. In some respects William resembled him, in his nervous vitality and impulsive sociability, in his pictorial talent and taste for decoration. But his health had never been robust and he had neglected it, relying on stimulants when he felt exhausted. He had been found unconscious in his bath and I never discovered the cause: it was too late for an autopsy. He must have succumbed to the strain of his existence in the Pioneer Corps, for which he was totally unfitted. He had the qualities of his defects, of a nature far more generous than mine.

While my parents were in Switzerland and I was in Germany my mother's old maid arranged for him to be buried in Florence. After his last cheerful letter which had seemed to promise a new lease of life the news of his death, which reached me by telephone three weeks later, was all the more shocking a blow. He would have been an inestimable support to my ageing parents as well as to me. He had always been their favourite, and I was aware that I could never be a substitute in their affections or in any other way.

My mother was inconsolable. Never demonstrative or confidential, she could not bear to see anybody. She shut herself up in her hotel room, completely prostrated. Whether she returned to Florence or not had ceased to matter now. Suddenly deprived of the being most precious to her, it was as if all her light had gone out. The future spread grey before her. Now she had only my father to live for. Fortunately in spite of his growing infirmities and his tendency to fret he still had a great zest for life. My brother's death drew them together and made her more pliable to his will. It would be an exaggeration to say that I was left out in the cold, but that was how I felt. I was no real comfort to either of them though I tried to be.

To return to Peking, as I had originally intended, was out of the question now. My parents were in their seventies, my father's strength was ebbing, and they would need whatever support I could give them. I applied for compassionate leave to visit them but I was told that the Swiss Government required me to fill in certain forms and that even then it would take a month or more to obtain a visa. My commanding officer could not give me more than three days' leave because I was due to be demobilized in October.

There was much wearisome waiting before I was demobilized at Uxbridge, and a crawling train journey through France as far as Bologna, where I obtained a lift in a lorry full of military prisoners, lusty rapscallions who had been too reckless on the rampage. No doubt the wine of Italy had over-excited them. I was impressed by their decent behaviour and politeness. Dishevelled, dusty, hungry and tired, I felt rather like a prisoner myself when I was dropped at the front door of La Pietra.

The long avenue of cypresses was tinted with evening gold; the tawny Baroque façade with its familiar green shutters was all aglow in the sunset. In the crepuscular hall the fountain was trickling to the goldfish – the only sound except my footsteps on the marble floor. The dimly lit drawing-room was hushed – like a silent chapel after the bumping of the lorry on the battered road from Bologna which had set up a throbbing in my ears. Wrapped in a rug, my mother was lying on a sofa with her eyes closed and I was almost afraid to disturb her. I was alarmed by her pallor, the sorrow of her expression when she saw me. She could not smile; she could not pretend to look pleased, for she was still too deeply upset and her recent drive by motor from Switzerland had unnerved her. I realized that she could not bear to speak of my brother, and what a vast difference it would have made if he had returned in my stead. In avoiding the subject foremost in our minds our conversation was unnatural and awkward. My father took me aside and questioned me about William's death but I knew less than he. The old maid who had seen him had found him terribly changed: she could not describe it, his complexion had been mottled, his manner incoherent and vague, unlike his former self. 'Era tutto cambiato,' was all she could say, and she was sure that his appearance would have given my mother a shock. But with medical care and his innate stamina his life might have been prolonged. My father still talked as if I should have been responsible for his welfare.

I had written to my parents regularly since the beginning of the war but my style had been cramped by conditions: I could not relate my more exciting experiences and many of my letters from India had gone astray. After five years of absence I had a mixed accumulation of incidents on the tip of my tongue, impressions still churning inside me all ready to be poured out, but I soon realized that what I had to tell interested them less than the second-hand rumours of the war they had heard in Switzerland. I seemed to be talking as a stranger to indifferent strangers, but we were all benumbed by our loss.

Thanks to his manifold activities, my father could be more easily distracted. Apart from certain gaps in his private collection most of the contents of his other five villas (Sassetti, Colletta, Natalia, Emilia and Ulivi, all of which had been sumptuously furnished with the overflow of antiques he could never stop buying), had been dispersed: some had been stored miles away in the country, others had been appropriated by Fascist tenants when the estate had been sequestrated, and for some reason the finest tapestry furniture had been sent to Brescia. To trace and retrieve these one by one, restore the broken pieces and torn canvases, check the inventories and calculate the total damage, was an occupation which engrossed him for the next few years. Day in, day out, he discussed his claims with lawyers and anti-quarians, and with the aid of photographs sent agents in search of the missing objects he prized most. Villa Natalia, named after the Queen of Serbia who had lived there, had been pretty well wrecked by its conversion into a military hospital; the other villas had been occupied by S.S. troops who behaved as in Maupassant's stories of the Franco-Prussian war, splintering lacquer commodes and inlaid chests of drawers, splitting the marble tops and breaking the legs of fine console tables, and using the pictures as targets for pistol practice; or by Fascist officials who had helped themselves liberally to the objects which had caught their fancy and cut down the trees for firewood. Roofs, gutters, windows, doors, statues and trees in the garden, had suffered from shell-fire and exploding mines in the adjoining *podere*.

All this property was on or near the strategic old road crossing the Futa pass to Bologna, and it was a wonder to me that the main buildings were intact and that so much had survived when the Arno had lost its bridges. I had seen such wide areas of destruction that I considered we had been lucky. But my father, for whom every antique he had owned had its personality, could only lament his losses, which mounted as he pored over his inventories and wandered through the rooms that had been desecrated. The damage preyed upon his mind and he became incensed when I urged him to count his blessings, since none of the Tuscan Primitives, the cream of his collection, had been removed. While I sympathized with his distress I believed that this stubborn obsession served him as a mental stimulant as well as an outlet for his nervous energy. I offered to help him but he did not want any help, except in the drafting of letters and applications. Suspicious and secretive, he would never take me entirely into his confidence. For hours he remained closeted with dealers I did not trust. Their gossip entertained him but I was aware of their covert hostility to me as an obstacle to their schemes. Owing to temporary restrictions money was scarce, and the dealers were always trying to cajole him into selling this or that for sums which seemed high at the actual rate of exchange. Sometimes the temptation was overpowering, and more than one picture and statue fell into their eager clutches.

Our excellent head gardener Mariano Ambrosiewicz lived with his family on the premises: being of Polish origin he had been arrested but later released since he had married an Italian and spent his whole life at La Pietra. His subordinates had gone, so apart from the *pomario* which served as a fruit and vegetable orchard, the garden had been uncared for. Many of the box hedges and golden yews had withered and a magnificent cedar had evidently been cut down for firewood – I could not believe that this noble tree had perished because the peacocks had roosted

Villa la Pietra: the Southern terrace

Villa La Pietra: the cypress drive from upper terrace

in it; as for the peacocks, they had been killed and eaten. For all their beauty they were said to bring bad luck. Several of the garden statues had been chipped and castrated by the occupying troops, perhaps by puritans who disapproved of their nudity or fetishists who wanted a phallic memento, but I fear they were common vandals; the limbs of others had been carried away by shells.

Though it had been bruised and abandoned, the garden had assumed a patina as of antique bronze, as if it had been standing on the hillside since the seventeenth century, when in fact it had been laid out not by Cardinal Capponi but by my father during my own lifetime. This was the background of my boyhood and we had grown up together, except for a few clumps of cypresses and ilexes of venerable age. The stone arches, benches, colonnades and balustrades were weather-stained and mossy; weeds burst through the cracks and forced their way through the pebble-patterned stairways; the stone vases were empty, the gates were coated with rust. Had I undergone a similar transformation? I almost felt I had when my father remarked upon my baldness. Certainly I looked older than my age. I could not see the villa and garden again with the innocent eyes of my youth but thoughts and emotions long dormant came drifting back, as when the terraces were lit up by fire-flies in June, the midsummer shrillness of the cicadas, the high-pitched voices of peasants singing *stornelli* in the fields below, the air so deceptively crystalline that beyond the shimmering olives of the *podere* you felt you could stretch out your hand and touch the Duomo. This background meant even more to me than the people associated with it. Of all panoramas it was this of the towers and cupolas in the valley framed between vineyards and the never distant hills which gave me that little stab now and then, as Vernon Lee used to say, that overpowering sense that 'This was Italy'. And whatever degree of constraint embarrassed me with my parents evaporated when I stood and gazed at this familiar view. To its potent harmony I felt I owed the vein of poetry in my nature which has never been adequately expressed.

The farmers of our *podere* had fared better than the townsfolk for they had reaped exceptional profit from the sale of eggs, milk, oil, wine, pigs, rabbits, fruit and vegetables when provisions had grown scarce, though the Germans had made a clean sweep of the hens and cattle before retiring. When the shelling became intense half the district had taken refuge in our cellars. *'Che paura!'* — what a fright! they repeated with the gloating satisfaction of people who had escaped with their skins. Two or three paratroopers had been shot dead near the empty garage, for of course my father's two Fiats had been stolen. But such anecdotes, with which I was surfeited, had a sickening monotony now that the war was over, and they were related as if I had been basking in a tranquil Eden remote from such calamities.

To justify my existence during this difficult period of reconstruction I hoped to find employment through the British Council which had sent me to Italy in 1940, but every available post had been filled. Francis Toye, who used to remark complacently, raising his square jowl and rolling his eyes the while, that he was often complimented on his resemblance to the *Duce*, had returned to the Palazzo Antinori as Director of the British Institute after spending the war years in Brazil. Ronald Bottrall and Roger Hinks, who had represented British culture in Sweden, were installed by the British Council in Rome, where Ian Greenlees had done such admirable spadework until 1940. Those who had been 'on active service' were evidently at a discount.

Bottrall had been hailed as a poetic genius at Cambridge by Dr Leavis, who had given rise to the expression 'pure Bottrall' as a synonym for all that was best and brightest in modern poesy. But his precocious talent had apparently been diverted into bureaucratic channels and the teaching of English, and he wore his responsibilities with a heavy air. I found his enunciation almost incomprehensible. His assistant Roger Hinks was more suave but he had already conceived a prejudice against Rome. His erstwhile patroness, the imperious Mrs Arthur Strong, who had been Assistant Director of the British School of Archaeology, had died there in 1943, and with her had vanished any lingering enthusiasm for Roman sculpture, which he used to contend was superior to the Greek. A frustrating curatorship of the Elgin marbles, which he was blamed for having scrubbed at Duveen's behest, had led him by reaction towards Merovingian art – nay, any other branch of art but Graeco-Roman. Wayward and paradoxical, his predilections were Nordic and he still hankered after the less inhibited society of Stockholm.

Suddenly Caravaggio had captured his attention and he proposed to devote a study to that turbulent genius. I was disappointed when the book appeared about ten years later for, during the labour of its composition, his academic discretion had got the better of his romantic theories. Rabidly anti-Catholic, it was the crude irreverence of Caravaggio's painting that appealed to him primarily, his portrayal of a drowned prostitute for the death of the Blessed Virgin, as well as his frequent brawls and frenzied escapades. No doubt Caravaggio like Cellini was bisexual, but his Bacchus, his musicians, the languid-eyed adolescent with the basket of fruit, the sinuous torso of his *Amore Vincitore*, the doting Narcissus, the juvenile St John the Baptist in the Doria Gallery, besides details in the 'Call to St Matthew' and other characteristic works, denote a deeper interest in the male than in the female form, and his female models have the faces of boys. Roger Hinks cherished a theory that his 'David with the head of Goliath' portrayed the lad he loved dangling Caravaggio's agonized head – a symbol of what the artist had been made to suffer – and he quoted Manilli and Bellori to support it. Manilli referred to the David as *'il suo Caravaggino'*, which might also signify the painter's son.

Not being much addicted to stark naturalism, I cared less for the Caravaggios than for many other paintings in the Villa Borghese, which in October 1945 was a repository of masterpieces including several from other collections, exhibited in the caressing Roman light. Like other art historians who specialize in a single painter or school, Roger Hinks passed over Titian and Raphael to scrutinize his latest protégé. Pausing before the

Narcissus, I ventured to point out his resemblance to the angel swooping towards St Matthew in San Luigi de' Francesi, but Roger retorted that the picture's attribution to Caravaggio was doubtful. 'None of the leading authorities have accepted it,' he snapped. Nobody could purse his lips so effectively, as of an old-fashioned butler announcing: 'Her Ladyship is not at home.' 'What about Longhi? Personally I trust his knowledge of the Seicento.' Roger shrugged his shoulders in disdain. Later I was amused to find the 'Narcissus' in his list of Caravaggio's works.

With Roger Hinks as with certain other English critics of his generation I was disconcerted by an air of supercilious arrogance as if they and only they understood the picture under discussion. Unfortunately the type persists, and it has taught me to pay more attention to the comments of the ingenuous and unassuming who simply use their eyes instead of quoting from textbooks.

The war had done less than subsequent developments to mar the many Romes within Rome, Classical, early Christian, Medieval, Renaissance and Baroque, which showed their facets like jewels through the mellow light of autumn. My friends of the British Council were hospitable but evasive: I was reminded of Jules Renard's reflection that a man whose meal you pay for is a man half tamed. Perhaps I would lecture for them when things became more settled? My advent was embarrassingly premature. However, this fleeting visit to Rome gave me deeper satisfaction than any visit since, so happy was I to rediscover the details of its grandeur, to renew acquaintance with Bernini and Borromini, to realize amid the squalor of modern accretions the continuity of Rome's visual rhetoric. In full view of the colonnade of St Peter's the gibes of agnostics seemed flippant. What was the value of archaeology unless it helped you to understand the link between the classical and Christian worlds? At least Mrs Arthur Strong had understood this though such writings of hers as *Apotheosis and the After Life* may be superseded. Her passion for Rome had blinded her to Mussolini's errors and she had seen him as the reviver of Rome's ancient glory. German guns were booming outside the city when she died. She was one of the last to carry on the tradition of the great lady who was also a scholar and an international hostess.

What spirited dames those old Roman hostesses were, the nonagenarian Miss Kemp and Princess Caetani, determined to promote the avant-garde in literature and the arts until her last gasp. Equally forceful but more retiring was Tina Whitaker, née Scalia, aged eighty-six, whose *Sicily and England* evokes the Italian exiles during the Risorgimento. As with many octogenarians, she recalled her youth with amazing accuracy. She had known my grandfather Roger and his brother Harold after whom I was named, Neapolitans by birth who had gone to England to claim their rights as British subjects after the fall of the Bourbons. Oddly enough she described them as far more Neapolitan in appearance and speech than their naval brothers who had remained in Italy. Their sister Donna Laura Minghetti was completely international: her second husband was the Prime Minister who had been devoted to Cavour; her daughter by her first husband, the Sicilian Prince Camporeale, had married Prince von Bülow, the German chancellor who had twice been ambassador to Rome. Musing on the contrast between Minghetti and Bülow and their successors, I walked to the Monti Parioli where Mrs Whitaker lived with a daughter who seemed little younger than herself but was treated as a child. A copious tea was prepared to refresh our conversation. My hostess was tall and upright, an exotic blend of Sicilian and Victorian English, to whom the Bourbons of Naples were wicked bogies. All round us were relics of her Risorgimento ancestors whose exploits thrilled her with actuality as she talked. Lord Palmerston and Lord John Russell were still her heroes. 'And I think Churchill can hold a candle to them,' she added. 'Where have you hidden the sugar-tongs, Delia? Ah, when I think of all that Italy owes to those giant statesmen . . . But I'm afraid one is in a minority when one is getting on to ninety, and the youngsters have forgotten. The Fascists doctored the history books. Well, I'm glad that chapter's over. When Prince Castelcicala trumped up a false charge against my uncle Luigi Scalia, Lord Palmerston cut the Neapolitan envoy dead. He stood by his principles.' Of Crispi, Panizzi, Quintino Sella, Sir James Lacaita, she had a rich fund of anecdotes, not invariably to their credit.

To touch the pulse of the distant past and hear its reverberating echoes has always been a luxury to me, and I enjoyed it in particular with Tina Whitaker. The conspirators who had helped to mould United Italy were more vivid in her talk than in her book *Sicily and England,* which I tried in vain to get republished.

I could not but regret that the British Council had no use for me at this recuperative period. Mrs Whitaker reminded me of my lecture in 1940. 'You ought to repeat it,' she said. 'It would do more good now than then. If I were your age I'd lecture about Sicily and England. Lord William Bentinck is a splendid subject.'

My views on the latter would have shocked her, but I agreed that a review of our relations when we had been the friends of Italy in adversity might not be unseasonable.

Empty handed I returned to Florence. The destruction of so many fine buildings at Terni and Viterbo was heart-rending; all the cities I passed on the road had gaping wounds, but the spectacle of Rome had been more than a spiritual consolation.

❧ 12 ❧

Mindful of Gertrude Stein's suggestion – she repeated even her suggestions – I sat down to write my memoirs, but I should never have done so without the encouragement of my R.A.F. comrade John Cullen, who had returned to the firm of Methuen and had later married the winsome Micheline whom he had met while we were working for SHAEF in Paris. Except for the scholarly botanist Patrick Synge, he was one of the few colleagues with whom I could talk literature, French as well as English – discussions that were as shining lights in a pool of darkness – and I could not have wished for a more sympathetic publisher.

Gradually my mother braced herself to meet the old friends who came to call on her. This helped to break the ice that had settled over her sorrow. She appeared much younger than her visitors, many of whom were struggling against the ravages of age, but their gossip was a salutary distraction as she seldom left the house except to walk in the garden. In a mood of tranquil renunciation she sat in the same high-backed chair in the drawing-room poring over the newspapers, a volume of recent history within reach. She became such a voracious reader that she regarded most visitors as a tiresome interruption. Nearly all of them were widows who had been unhappily married but were even unhappier in their widowed state. Love affairs were still the chief topics that concerned them – who went to bed with whom – apart from their aches and pains, doctors and domestics. They were slightly apprehensive of me and eyed me as a sort of freak. 'What is he writing now?' I heard them ask perfunctorily. 'Something terribly highbrow, I suppose.'

Misfortune had dogged Princess Koudacheff since the Russian

Revolution. Bit by bit she had had to sell her heirlooms and she lived in dignified poverty with a daughter who had not known the glamour of the *ancien régime*. Her one recreation was to weep over a sentimental novel. 'It does me good to cry,' she said, and her eyes were always ready to brim with tears. Her life had been tragic but she was plucky and she wore her woes with distinction. When she did laugh it was a musical exaltation of laughter, perhaps because this happened so seldom. Whenever she had to sell anything it was a drug in the market. Though an Orthodox Christian she throve on oriental superstitions. Unburdened of yesterday's mishap she became more buoyant, her Russian accent gained momentum. But I tended to sink in her company and I must have become invisible for she treated me as if I were not there.

Another frequent visitor was the widow of an ambassador who claimed precedence over the widows of other ambassadors. As Florence was full of retired diplomatists and their wives who were accorded the same honours as if they were *en poste* this caused anxiety to punctilious hostesses. If they considered themselves *mal placées* at dinner we never heard the end of it and their voices were shrill enough to shake the chandeliers. The neurotic pessimism of certain other guests was so extreme as to be farcical. My mother called them her *oiseaux de malheur*, or harbingers of woe. One's whole outlook brightened after their departure.

Marchesa Lulie Torrigiani was a swan by contrast but she was too tough a bird for my mother's taste. Enriched by her last widowhood, she continued to entertain in regal style, supported by a butler who combined courtly manners with flashes of amazing impudence. Not only did he preside over her household in town and country with resourceful ingenuity, procuring unseasonable delicacies and arranging masses of flowers, but one suspected that he also arranged her parties and vetoed the guests he disliked. His table decorations would have won prizes at a flower show. He received one at the door with polite inquiries about one's state of health. Tall, willowy and aquiline, he might well have been, as Lulie alleged, the natural son of a duke. He doted on duchesses and treated them with a familiarity that made them chuckle. 'Beware of this Strega, Your Royal Highness,' he warned one, 'it might go to your beautiful head!' And when she dropped a shoe he knelt down to adjust it, murmuring with an affected sigh: 'How many gentlemen would envy me this moment!'

After Mass in her private chapel Lulie's guests would assemble for a gargantuan luncheon. The vast drawing-room of the palace on Piazza de' Mozzi was heated like a conservatory and heavily scented with tuberoses. Centenarian parrots waddled purposefully along the floor as if they owned it. During luncheon I felt a stab in one foot: with its razor-sharp beak a macaw had ripped a triangle out of the shoe. 'That bird isn't usually so friendly,' remarked my hostess as I surveyed the damage. 'Your feet must smell delicious.' Mighty pleased with itself, the macaw went back to its perch.

Evidently Lulie was resolved to squander as much of her last husband's estate as she could lay her hands on – to the delight of all Florentine society except her in-laws, who looked on at her increasing extravagance in impotent anguish. One of them complained to me that she was selling the family silver and historical portraits, 'all for the butler's benefit', he added with a wry face. At this period of post-war depression no other hostess could afford to keep open house with such flamboyant generosity. Lulie ate little herself but she enjoyed vicariously the appetites of her guests. When such dainties were still scarce she offered them caviar, foie-gras, lobsters and white truffles as well as tonic laughter. She had extracted more fun than sorrow from life, and she had certainly made her last two husbands happy. As she preferred card-games to any form of literature she must have liked me for my own sake. She also liked Berenson's company, and when he told her how much he enjoyed her visits she replied: 'But you don't know how amusing I could be in bed.' She was then eighty-five or eighty-six, a few years older than B.B. Though she had never been a beauty she had improved with age. As B.B. remarked, she was still good to look at, for she had kept her trim figure, dressed in pastel shades that suited her, and her eyes still sparkled as she told her naughty stories. She had as many of these as veteran actors have roles. One of her mildest concerned two policemen on the prowl for indecent behaviour in a public park. Hiding behind a bush, they heard a feminine voice implore: 'Oh, do let me take a last look before you put it in!' Leaping forth to catch a couple in 'flagrant delight', they found two old women burying a cat.

Another concerned a girl whose charm was mitigated by lack of eyebrows. A plastic surgeon grafted dog's hair to remedy this defect, and the result was successful except that she could not help raising her new eyebrows when she passed a lamp-post.

I was unable to compete with her stories, most of which went into one ear and came out of the other. Once, however, when the conversation became too physiological, I mentioned the lady who asked the keeper of a zoo to which sex a huge hippopotamus belonged. 'Madam,' he replied in the style of Dr Johnson, 'that is a question which could only interest another hippopotamus.' Lulie did not approve of this retort.

She had travelled far, in every sense, from the Cambridge, Massachusetts, of the 1870s. B.B. epitomized her as 'amoral, heartless, fond of her playfellows while playing, but not longer'. I considered her more superficial than heartless, like many of her Edwardian coevals. When she died a Florentine lamented: 'Alas, those delectable dinners! Now where are we to spend our Sunday evenings?' It was a poignant epitaph.

What I missed in Florence was the company of younger friends. On the average the people I consorted with were well over seventy with fixed habits and opinions, dowagers with hardened carapaces but seldom a fresh idea.

The oldest resident whose mental agility continued to stimulate me was Berenson. But I Tatti was a long walking distance from La Pietra. Petrol was still scarce and it was not easy to borrow a car to reach him. Whenever he could he was kind enough to send for me. Nobody I had known ever blossomed into so productive an old age. He had kept his own legend warm and had focused the light of a many-sided intelligence on his rich experience of life. The war had given him an opportunity to gaze inward, to read books outside his chosen field and ponder in the enforced seclusion of his retreat.

The last humanist, as Cecchi called him, had entered upon the last, perhaps the richest phase of his exceptional career. His diary often records his dissatisfaction with himself, but what genuine artist or scholar was ever self-satisfied, especially one with a Faustian thirst for knowledge? His wife had faded out after a long illness, but his inseparable companion Nicky Mariano introduced a greater variety into his social existence and patched up old feuds, so that he was surrounded by more Italians. These replaced Mrs Berenson's Bloomsbury connections – her daughter had married a Strachey – whose priggishness had been wont to irritate him. They knew how to argue and disagree without causing offence, and in spite of their disparity of age they shared his revulsion against the irrational. For lighter conversation there was a bevy of solicitous ladies. His routine remained as rigid as before, but once he stepped out of his library he was ready for verbal recreation.

We had not met for five years – some of the most baneful in history – but his mental vigour was unabated, his presence more imposing. In 1940 his circle had shrunk to a small anti-Fascist group: now he was lionized, photographed and 'written up' as an international celebrity. Not a day went by without his receiving some form of homage, if only a box of American marshmallows. I Tatti was invaded by Allied officers and journalists: B.B. held the centre of the stage without blinking under the limelight. The table of his sitting-room was piled with an assortment of erudite reviews and as I glanced at them he walked in with a light step and greeted his guests in several languages. After five minutes, as if we had met yesterday instead of five years ago, he was plying me with questions about mutual friends in London and Paris. His comparative isolation under the exchange of artillery fire in the grilling heat of last August had not impaired his curiosity. He was anxious to regain the ground lost during that dire emergency and he was elated by his survival and that of I Tatti. Thanks to their perfect knowledge of German, Nicky Mariano and her sister Alda Anrep had managed to keep the wolves at bay. For the third time in their lives Alda and her husband lost a home, since their picturesque apartment on the Arno, where several of B.B.'s pictures had been stored for safety, had been blown up with the bridges. Their cheerfulness in the circumstances contrasted with my father's gloom.

Life was keenly relished at I Tatti where time was regulated so that the utmost pleasure and instruction could be drawn from every minute. In that atmosphere one felt impelled to work, for everybody was gathering honey. Sometimes I wished that B.B. were less omnivorous: he would discourse on military strategy when one would have preferred him to expound his aesthetic theories. His communion with beauty was forty years older than mine, more intimate, concentrated and intense. During our country walks he would stop to admire a tree or a passing cloud with the rapture of a young discoverer. More and more he felt that painters had barely skimmed the surface of nature, that the contemplation and investigation of nature from which art is born were in their infancy. There was always more to be seen, grasped, absorbed and understood in a landscape, especially in a Tuscan landscape. The road to Vincigliata above I Tatti was almost identical with the one depicted in Benozzo Gozzoli's winding procession of the Three Kings: here were the same rows of cypresses and spruce pines sprouting from rubbly hillocks and delicate ridges, reminding one that the ancient Tuscans knew the lie of the land. B.B.'s reverence for nature was akin to that of the Chinese poets and painters of yore: it is becoming scarce in our urbanized world.

The vagaries of art historians had always fascinated me and I was guilty of goading him on to indiscretions about Langton Douglas, Mason Perkins, Richard Offner, and rivals with whom he had crossed swords in the past. Though his attitude towards them had mellowed he was excruciatingly funny about them. Perkins, a pathological miser who refused to heat his house and starved his wife, was perhaps the most original. Langton Douglas, the son of a bishop, was a full-blooded Renaissance character, the antithesis of Perkins. Roger Fry could still move B.B. to indignation owing to his bygone transactions with Pierpont Morgan. 'He pretended to scorn money but he saw that he was paid through the nose for his attributions. One of those ethereal hypocrites,' he said. 'But what a superb lecturer!' I interposed. 'He inherited rhetoric from his Quaker ancestors. The gift of the gab. But it had very little meaning. Our Italian friends do it better. Roberto Papi for instance.' Though he had made his peace with Offner, he remarked: 'What repels me about him is his perpetual sneer.' And Offner said precisely the same about B.B. Of his pupil Kenneth Clark B.B. used to say: 'He would have been equally successful as a Prime Minister or an Archbishop of Canterbury.'

Until his premature death – for when a man is getting on to a hundred his death is premature – B.B. was an illuminating beacon in my existence. Through him I met the Florentine friends I value most and whenever we meet our thoughts return to the Sage of Settignano.

At home I did not feel as welcome as at I Tatti. My father resented my writing as an unprofitable hobby, 'scribble, scribble, scribble.' His mercenary cronies set him against me and though we did not quarrel openly I suffered from frequent pinpricks since his longing for grandchildren had been frustrated. Yet I could not visualize him as a contented grandfather, for he had never been suited to the role of family man: few art collectors are. Children are a menace to fine furniture and there is invariably something the matter with them.

My mother maintained her gentle aloofness but she was aware that the atmosphere was somewhat strained. Should I leave or should I stay? Peking was a powerful magnet and there was still a chance of recovering my possessions there, yet Florence was in my bones and I was extremely devoted to my mother. Osbert Sitwell said I should stay. He had been harassed by similar problems and his arguments were so cogent that I took his advice. But it was not easy to overcome the sense of inadequacy that sapped my natural *joie de vivre*. Was I not living in an earthly Paradise? Yes, my environment was beautiful and I owed it to my father's cult of artistic perfection. Art experts and connoisseurs came up to the villa as before the war and they were ecstatic with admiration: 'What taste! what flair! what genius!' By modern standards most of his treasures had been stupendous bargains for he had not paid anything like the prices they would fetch today. He never stopped buying but he bought with discrimination. Usually he made up his mind at first sight, as when he bought the whole Alexander collection during the First World War, keeping the pictures he wanted and weeding out the rest.

Francis Alexander had been an American painter who settled in Florence for the sake of his daughter's health. After a while he became an ardent collector of old pictures and furniture. 'What's the use of painting,' he remarked to his friend Thomas Ball, 'when I can buy a better picture for a dollar and a half, than I can paint myself?' According to Ball, 'he spent most of his time repairing and touching up old paintings which he delighted to hunt up in every out-of-the-way corner. They (Alexander, his wife and daughter) were living . . . opposite the Strozzi Palace and every morning there would be an array of 'old masters' in various stages of dilapidation, strung along in front of the palace, their owners watching intently the house opposite, for Mr Alexander to appear at the window, when, if he saw anything promising he would descend and examine it.' Like Ruskin he loved the Tuscan Primitives, whose art was then unpopular and incomprehensible to the majority. His daughter Francesca, a saintly spinster, collected folk stories in prose and verse which she illustrated. Ruskin was so charmed by these when he saw them in 1882 that he published them with enthusiastic comments under the title *Roadside Songs of Tuscany*. This brought her fame, and her friendship helped to cheer Ruskin's sad old age. In a lecture on her drawings he went so far as to say: 'Since Leonardo da Vinci's flower studies we can recall no drawings of the herb of the field equal to Francesca's for strength and delicacy, for truth, and the reverence that comes of truth; though she has, perhaps, somewhat to learn in expressing human form.'

Neither she nor her mother would step into an automobile or use electric light, only candles and an oil lamp. They said simply: 'Electricity is of the devil. God made the lightning but man has no right to use it for his own purposes.' Mrs Alexander died in 1916 at the age of one hundred and two, and Francesca lingered on for another eighteen months, till the age of eighty-two. Many of the pictures 'repaired and touched up' by Francis Alexander were almost restored to their pristine condition by my father, but the majority were in a fair state of preservation. Central heating is now their worst enemy.

Occasionally my father would take an object on approval and after considering it in every light and from every angle return it to the dealer. I remember a glazed terracotta figure attributed to Luca della Robbia: it was exquisite but a little too perfect in form and feature, too streamlined in technique. The more he examined it, the more suspicious he became about its origin. Very like Luca at a glance, yet something seemed wrong. Reluctantly he decided it must be a brilliant fake. I have met this figure since in a museum and I am sure that he was right.

With Charles Loeser he had exchanged an equestrian statuette by Rustici for a thirteenth-century Madonna and Child which glowed with new life after careful restoration, so much so that Loeser wanted it back. It is now attributed to that rare painter Coppo di Marcovaldo.

Ultimately everything at home revolved round the collection, of which the garden was an open-air extension. Whatever plans my father had for their future were never discussed with me. That he had plans which he discussed with others could not be doubted. 'Why don't you move into one of the villettas (the smaller houses next door)?' he once suggested. 'The Ulivi, for instance, where Faust wrote so many books.' (Our genial tenant

Faust had produced popular novels of the American Wild West under the pseudonym Max Brand.) The prospect did not appeal to me. Rather than that I would move to some other city, to Naples or to Paris. Those seven years in Peking, followed by the five years of the war, had turned me into an outsider though I was the son of the house, born and bred at La Pietra. One thing I knew instinctively, that my father's longing for grandchildren was chiefly due to a desire to ensure the preservation of his collection. He could not endure the thought of its dispersal. He did not realize that I, of all people, was most likely to carry out his wish as far as possible, that by nature and inclination I was best qualified to do so. He did not really know me. That I had embarked on a book of memoirs exasperated him. 'Who do you expect to read it?' he exclaimed.

Writing my memoirs made me live more in the past than in the present and considering the dreariness of this post-war period I was thus enabled to lead a double life. The present was a period of reconstruction, recuperation, convalescence. My parents were busy setting their house in order. For them indeed it was a dismal change from the Florence of international sociability they had shared for half a century. The Fascist sequestrators had broken every lock inside the villa, so that if they did not help themselves to the contents of cupboards they made it easy for others to do so. Before escaping to Switzerland my mother had scrupulously packed most of her private papers and possessions in heavy trunks; others, neatly tied in bundles, were arranged in cupboards with written lists of contents. These had all been ransacked and turned topsy-turvy. A great many were missing, especially the scrolls and silks I had brought back from my Far Eastern travels, for I was almost as acquisitive as my father on a more modest scale.

During the next five years or more austerity was imposed on England with a masochistic complacency which contrasted ironically with the unabashed hedonism of Italy. Italian acquaintances chaffed me about this. 'We lost the war but at least we have plenty to eat,' said one. 'When I go to England I suffer

Villa La Pietra: the upper parterre

Villa La Pietra: the lower parterre

from hunger-pangs.' I could not reply that we were a more spiritual people since there was a certain self-righteousness about our asceticism: queuing up had become a national habit. Many friends from England were unable to do justice to our copious Florentine fare, to the *pasta* and *risotto* served at the average meal. When Fitzroy Maclean visited his parents on the Lungarno he remarked that his stomach had shrunk, but I noticed that others were ready to risk indigestion and enjoy 'unbuttoned ease'.

Having grown up in Florence, its churches and palaces, pictures and statues were familiar to me, but my English friends often helped me to discover facets of it anew for myself. Their fresh impressions mingled with my old ones and enhanced my appreciation and insight into what I had taken for granted. I was less familiar with Rome, where I joined Michael and Anne Rosse in the February of 1948. They are the most loyal of the friends I have known since Eton days, and they had been my hosts in London during the blitz. I would join them even in Timbuktu, but Rome was preferable. Michael was related to Prince Filippo Doria, whose English traits were much more pronounced than his Italian. He had been persecuted and even exiled by Mussolini because he had refused to hand over a percentage of Italian Red Cross funds to the Fascist party. Moreover, since he had private access to the King of Italy, he had warned him in advance of Mussolini's intention of entering the war as Hitler's ally, and this had been bruited abroad. His moral integrity was transparent: among the Roman aristocracy he was surely the only saint. While rowing at Oxford he had suffered a spinal injury and his wife told me that he was never free from pain. Tall and fair with a stoop, he lived with patriarchal simplicity in his enormous palace. The Princess and his tall, fair daughter Orietta were addicted to charitable works: embarrassingly modest and unassuming, they seemed oppressed by the magnificence of their surroundings. The palace contained an overwhelming number of fine paintings, but they were poorly lighted and arranged like postage stamps. The reception rooms were hung with Flemish tapestries and upholstered in Spanish leather, a little too grand to be comfortable, but a few choice masterpieces had been moved into them, such as Velazquez's incomparable portrait of Innocent X. The magnificent Gallery of Mirrors designed by Valvassori in the 1730's, with *trompe l'oeil* motifs and panels portraying The Fall of the Giants, The Labours of Hercules and allegories of the Four Continents, retained its original furniture upholstered in Genoese velvet, and there was a more intimate mirror room of the same period with children's games depicted above the doors and allegories of the Four Elements on the ceiling. The formal grandeur of Papal Rome was crystallized in these apartments and one felt improperly dressed.

In spite of his lameness, Prince Doria was a tireless cicerone: without coat or hat he took us on a rapid tour of the palaces in his neighbourhood, since when no day went by without the enjoyment of astonishing harmonies of space and perspective. Aristotle's dictum that 'beauty lies in bigness of style and in construction' had been applied to Rome above other cities, for mere bigness in construction without style is boring even if it is not ugly. Michael Rosse, who took infinite pains to preserve Georgian architecture in Britain, was thoroughly equipped to appreciate the buildings we saw, and Anne often noticed some subtle detail that escaped us. Relatively small in size, Sant' Andrea al Quirinale appealed to us more than the larger Baroque churches as a pure composition realized by Bernini *in toto* instead of being an addition to a more ancient structure. Here the bigness of style, the high altar bathed in amber light, the soaring dome reminiscent of the Pantheon, sweetened by sportive cherubs and angels fluttering round the lantern, the rich marbles like fossilized velvet, seemed to justify Aristotle's definition of beauty. No fellow sight-seers or worshippers were visible and we had the church all to ourselves. The eighteen-year-old Polish Saint Stanislas Kostka, who was buried in one of the side chapels, said: 'I was not born for the good things of this world; what my heart desires are the good things of eternity.' In this church we are offered both.

Before the war Rome had been almost provincial, without any concentration of industry or commerce, but now it was fast becoming a metropolis. One of the noisiest if not the noisiest of cities — but this had been so even in the time of Martial, who complained that a poor man could not think or sleep there owing to the pandemonium — the Romans were proud of this proof of its vitality, for it was growing into a capital of the film industry, invaded by actors of every nationality. This efflorescence of creative directors, scenario writers and technicians after the feeble productions of the Fascist era, had made Hollywood look to its laurels. Rossellini and De Sica had obtained sensational results on a comparatively meagre budget.

After the First World War American writers and artists had emigrated to Paris: now they pitched upon Rome. According to Stendhal, the climate was enough to gladden anybody, but this was not the reason: one of them explained to me that it was the facility of finding taxis, and very little of Rome can be seen from a taxi. Classical and Romantic Rome was no more to them than a picturesque background. Tennessee Williams, Frederic Prokosch and Gore Vidal created a bohemian annexe to the American Academy, where Laurance and Isabel Roberts created a cultural annexe to the American Embassy.

The muted voice of Laurance Roberts — he spoke in a barely audible whisper — was more persuasive than the voices of his colleagues, and such was its effect on me that I, too, found myself murmuring as in church when we met. Under his aegis the Roman Academy became an international rendezvous for artists and intellectuals. Among the writers Tennessee Williams, whose dramas palpitate with storm and stress, seemed the mildest of self-effacing individuals. A pudgy, taciturn, moustached little man without any obvious distinction, he wandered as a lost soul among the guests he assembled in an apartment which might have been in New York, for it contained nothing suggestive of Rome. Prokosch, whose writings, *genre génie*, fell short of his perfervid imagination, had the dark good looks of an advertiser for razor blades, but I was told he was a tennis champion. Gore

Vidal, the youngest in age, aggressively handsome in a clean-limbed sophomore style, had success written all over him. He was piqued that I had not yet read his *City and the Pillar*, which he informed me was a pioneer among homosexual novels, but it had not yet been published in England and few novels came my way. His candour was engaging but he was slightly on the defensive, as if he anticipated an attack on his writings or his virtue. Perhaps because I am diffident about my own work, I appreciate writers who are quite sure of themselves.

Tennessee Williams struck me as excessively diffident, but this might have been a mask for self-assurance. He had known poverty and struggle in New Orleans which had inspired his early work. Rome only inspired *The Roman Spring of Mrs Stone*, the grim story of too many frustrated women past their prime who fall under the sway of the primitive pagan Priapus. What a change had occurred since Henry Adams wrote that 'American art, like the American language and American education, was as far as possible sexless!' Tennessee Williams was obsessed with sexual frustration and its deviations but at least he treated it in a poetical manner. His Rome was limited to the Via Veneto and to the fringe, if not the reality, of Fellini's *Dolce Vita*. Neither he nor any of the group I met with him spoke Italian, yet he had a typically Neapolitan protégé who could speak no English. The youth looked unutterably bored by this society but he brightened as soon as he could unbosom himself. 'I am hoping that Mr Williams will take me to America,' he told me. 'I have relatives there, a married uncle who is a hairdresser, and I would do anything to join him. America is the land of my dreams. I have no future here. But none of Mr Williams's friends give me much encouragement. They chatter among themselves as if I was not there. They drink strong liquors and I do not drink. Sometimes I lose patience. They can be generous, but it is all impersonal. I suppose they are the same with everybody. You are the first *galantuomo* who has spoken to me this evening.'

I did not think he would be happier in New York, but he was

convinced he would make his fortune there. Finally he said: 'Let's go out for a *passeggiata*. It would be nice to spend the evening together – away from these *scucciatori*.'

'I'm afraid my host would take offence if I left his party with you.'

The young man laughed. 'Well, I really can't stand this a minute longer. If you can extricate yourself you will find me at Rosati's.' He slipped out.

Mr Williams had been observing our colloquy from a quiet corner and he came over to ask me with a faint flash of curiosity what we had been discussing. I told him as tactfully as I could that his young protégé felt neglected: after all he was a fish out of water among so many strangers who could not or would not make any effort to communicate with him. He rubbed his chin and said nothing, a little perplexed. There was something innocently childish about his expression. Evidently he was not aware that Pierino wanted to be taken to America, and I have wondered since whether he took him there, for that was my last meeting with Tennessee Williams, though I have seen most of his plays.

This trifling episode illustrated the casual yet condescending attitude of certain foreigners towards the young Italians they cultivated on account of their Latin charm without any interest in their character, aspirations or desires. I was tempted to write a story about it, but it would have read like a pastiche of Tennessee Williams.

Few of the Anglo-Saxons who frequented the Via Veneto had any feeling for the *genius loci* so potent in the writings of Hawthorne, Henry James, W. W. Story, Vernon Lee, and other antecedents who saw Rome as 'the aesthetic antidote to the ugliness of the rest of the world'. *Mrs Stone* was a twentieth-century phenomenon. Tennessee Williams attempted to idealize her at the expense of Italian gigolos, as if she too were seeking an aesthetic antidote.

I have known several 'Mrs Stones' in Florence as well as in Capri and the South of France: Tangier pullulates with them.

The one who killed herself in Capri was a hard-drinking grand-mother who had been married many times, but apparently none of her rich husbands had given her satisfaction. The local boys were eager enough to enjoy her hospitality and virile enough to make her forget her wrinkles, and how she twinkled through those wrinkles after the last nightcap! *La nuit tous les chats sont gris*, as the French say. She wanted to be adored for her own sake and this was too much to expect of unsophisticated southerners, most of whom had a teen-age sweetheart. Her tragedy was that she could not feel her age. As soon as she was forced to feel it she committed suicide. One could not blame the penurious youths who had pandered to her illusions. If one asked who took advantage of whom, they were quits.

The sad story of the Florentine 'Mrs Stone' resembled Maugham's *Up at the Villa*. Pretty and slim in middle age, she had befriended a half-Jewish boy maimed by polio whose parents had been exterminated in a concentration camp. For this pathetic waif she was a visiting angel from Eldorado. He fell desperately in love with her and she was too good-natured to resist his infatuation, unconscious of the risk involved. He had never had a chance of meeting such a woman and the physical act meant more to him than to her. All the while her deepest affections had been engaged elsewhere – to a married man in America. When he obtained a divorce she decided to return to him. Her crippled lover was shattered when she broke the news as her conscience dictated. Demented, he crept into her bedroom while she was taking her afternoon siesta: first he shot her dead, then he shot himself.

Few if any of her friends had been aware of this liaison and she had been immensely popular. Her funeral was crowded with mourners – all those I had seen at her farewell party a few days previously when she had received their congratulations on her new engagement with the happiest of smiles. The owner of the palace she had lived in was importuned with letters from people who wanted to buy the antique bed in which she had been murdered, including the bloodstained sheets. This true story and its various aspects, the contrasting ages, conditions and attitudes of its protagonists, were more dramatic than Tennessee Williams's novelette and in my opinion more interesting. An article in *Esquire* was entitled 'Latins are lousy lovers', but this did not diminish a steady demand for them, especially from American women.

❧ 13 ❧

Ever since the war I seem to have lost my sense of time: in some places it dragged, in others it galloped too fast for me to catch up with: certain days were like months, certain months were like days. The process of writing often slowed me down so that time vanished altogether. Having finished my memoirs in 1946 I felt free to lecture and travel, and until I embarked on my history of the Bourbons of Naples I gave many lectures and travelled widely not only in Italy but also in America.

My American uncle Guy Mitchell, a paragon of generosity with a strong family feeling unusual in a bachelor who disliked children, had long besought me to change my nationality. Having shaken the dust of Europe from his shoes, he urged me to do the same. After spending half a lifetime in Paris, Florence and London, he had come to regard those years as wasted. Only America was dynamic and modern: why linger in mouldering Europe? Moreover blood was thicker than water, he argued: my closest relations except my father, a 'freak' Englishman who had never lived in England, were all American. He offered me a house and much else besides if I became an American citizen, and on the surface his offer was tempting. But my education made me feel English and the war had strengthened this sentiment. My loyalties were divided, however, and there were occasions when I felt Italian. My roots were in Florence and I was over forty, but at home I had little independence and I feared falling into a rut.

My previous visits to the United States had been sporadic and I wished to find out if, as my uncle insisted, I was in fact more American than English. Unlike the chameleon, with Americans I turned English, with English American, and I resented animadversions on either from either. But my most valued experiences had been aesthetic and I still hoped to remodel them in a suitable form. Could this be done if I transplanted myself?

It was my benevolent uncle Guy who had enabled me to visit China, a debt I could never repay. I owed it to him to try an experiment which might give me a new direction. It is so much easier to sit back and enjoy beauty and in Florence, surrounded by masterpieces, one is apt to ask oneself: why bother to compete? Contemplation and criticism engross one. The climate is relaxing. Unless one becomes involved in past history – a permanent attraction – the available subject-matter is limited. America seemed overpowering in comparison, the freshest of pastures for an inquiring and impressionable mind, but I doubted if I could change the whole tenor of my life there as in China.

My uncle was also anxious to see my mother, who had not visited America since the slump in the thirties. Though she had slowly recovered from the shock of my brother's death, her existence had been drearier than my father's since he was fully occupied with restoring his property, with his garden and collection, and she was indifferent to the society which kept him amused. I was convinced that a visit to her brother, among old friends and relations, would cheer and refresh her. We decided to fly to Chicago since all the ships were packed. Unfortunately a strike delayed every stage of our journey, and while we were detained in Rome my father became increasingly nervous. He was opposed to my mother's departure by air and he entreated me to dissuade her from taking such a risk. The prolonged strike added to his forebodings. He telephoned me constantly: 'If anything happens you will be responsible. Remember your mother's age. Her life is in your hands.' But she was younger for her age than I was for mine and though she had qualms about leaving him even for a month or two, she had an adventurous spirit. Owing to the strike we were held up at Shannon airport and had to spend a couple of cold nights at Tipperary – a long, long way from Chicago. We could have made the journey by ship in the same time. But these inconveniences were soon forgotten in the warmth of her reception on arrival. For years she had not dined out: now her friends rivalled each other in hospitality and rekindled her appetite with her favourite American dishes.

Very few of the private houses she had known were left standing on Lake Shore Drive where my grandmother had lived: the castellated Potter Palmer mansion and the Gothic Crane mansion were dwarfed by the blocks of modern apartments. The pseudo-medieval Water Tower which had survived the disastrous fire of 1871 resembled a forgotten stage property among the recent constructions which form an imperious skyline against Lake Michigan, more sea than lake.

Many of my mother's old friends were already commemorated in public monuments such as the Clarence Buckingham fountain and in the Chicago Art Institute, which testified not only to the social responsibility but also to the original taste of Chicagoan collectors, who were buying the paintings of French Impressionists before these were appreciated in their native land. The Birch-Bartlett collection, for instance, was the first great cluster of modern European painters in any American gallery, and it was admirably displayed. 'Chicago was the first expression of American thought as a unity,' wrote Henry Adams when he visited the Exposition of 1893, and Chicagoans were proud of being pioneers in many fields. 'We were buying Manets and Monets cheap when New Yorkers were paying top prices for Romneys and Hoppners,' said Chauncey McCormick, who was President of the Board of Trustees of the Art Institute, a position he held with panache. He also told me that the French Government had tried in vain to buy back Seurat's masterpiece, *Sunday Afternoon on the Island of La Grande Jatte*. When a distinguished French visitor asked him: 'How can you possibly afford to buy all these marvellous Impressionist paintings?' he replied: 'We do not buy them; we inherit them from our grandmothers.' Mrs McCormick's father, Charles Deering, having owned a castle in Spain, had formed a collection of Spanish paintings which also enriched the Institute.

A loan exhibition of old English masters served as a reminder that the French Impressionists owed something to Constable and Turner. When Sir Kenneth Clark proposed that these might be shown in New York as their first port of call on the way to Chicago, Mr McCormick told him bluntly: 'In that case we are not interested.' My Chicago friends despised New York and tended to avoid it. Their chauvinism reminded me of the Florentine *campanilisti*. But the capriciousness of a climate which might vary more than thirty degrees in twenty-four hours, drove many to more temperate zones for several months of the year.

Theodore Dreiser and other realists have portrayed the grim aspect of Chicago, but this was none of my concern. What fascinated me in a city renowned for its tough individualism was the genuine quest of beauty, the desire to embellish Chicago and help less privileged fellow-citizens to appreciate art. The fire of 1871, when two thirds of the buildings were of wood, had served as a stimulus to architecture; so had the World's Columbian Exposition of 1893. Frank Lloyd Wright had worked there for twenty years, but some of his best buildings had inevitably been demolished. Nowhere was the cult of modernity more emphatic, and the only danger I discerned was a too general eagerness to admire anything stridently novel. While this would have delighted Gertrude Stein, I asked myself if she would have chosen to settle in Chicago instead of Paris. I am sure that even she could be satiated with novelty. Experimentalists of the avant-garde usually prefer to live in some crumbling old village.

Each visit to the Art Institute suggested that painting was extremely popular in Chicago: the stalls of picture-books, catalogues and reproductions were as thronged as the cafeteria. Whole classes of boys and girls raced from room to room with camp-stools to listen to a teacher expounding the virtues of Cézanne's *Basket of Apples* or El Greco's *Assumption of the Virgin* which had been presented to the gallery in 1906. Stepping into this world of colour and imagination from the bewildering babel of the neighbouring Loop was always an exhilarating experience. To find Giovanni de Paolo's *Scenes from the Life of St John the*

Baptist, so quintessentially Sienese, was perhaps even more surprising: how far this series of delicate panels had travelled from *quattrocento* Siena, six to Chicago, two to Munster, one to Tours, and one to New York, while four similar panels are in London's National Gallery, and these have retained their brilliance and narrative intensity.

My mother's generation had paid annual visits to Europe till the war had kept them at home, and after the exchange of reminiscences and family gossip, she had to realize that their paths were so divergent that they had little left in common. The men spent all day in their offices and seldom appeared before dinner, and my mother had no liking for hen parties. But hen parties predominated, and even the ladies who were not punctilious social workers had a sense of mission which my mother could not share. She grew reconciled to the thought of her future in Florence, to what Henry James described as 'a way of life that is not afraid of a little isolation and tolerably quiet days'.

Left alone in Chicago, I began to feel solitary, for though I had a large acquaintance and relationship these were all absorbed in some branch of business activity and I could find no boon companion with similar interests. The Art Institute became my club; but until Laurence Sickman appeared I had nobody to confide in. Though he had not yet been appointed director of the Kansas City Gallery he had built up its collection of Chinese art since he had gone to Peking from Harvard. His understanding of Chinese aesthetic values was unique and he was able to communicate it to others. I can only compare the delight of his companionship with that of mountaineering minus the fatigue, for we seemed to climb peak after peak and from every summit there was a grander view of other summits with fertile valleys in between. To look at any scroll or artifact with him was to breathe a purer air. And a large proportion of the scrolls we examined depicted mountain panoramas, painted as only the Chinese could paint them, range after soaring range, vast, bold, abrupt, often misty and cloud-capped, suggesting dizzy heights and depths and boundless space beyond. Nothing seemed too far away for the eye to follow: fresh worlds appeared beyond gorgeous pageants of cloud. Minute passing figures reduced man to insignificance.

No non-Chinese, and not many Chinese connoisseurs, had Larry Sickman's unerring sense of style, form, quality, in Chinese painting – apart from ceramics and the various crafts. Perhaps because I had known him in Peking, I enjoyed the illusion of being there still when I visited him in Kansas City. The Oriental section of the Nelson Gallery, which had cost a mere fraction of the European section, was the best arranged I had seen. Larry had been mainly responsible for the choice of its contents, from the smallest jade pendant of the Chou Dynasty to the rhythmical relief of an Empress and her attendants from Lung-mên in Honan, about A.D. 522, a tapestry in limestone which had to be fitted together from fragments like a jigsaw puzzle by Larry himself. Being so young a gallery, first opened in December, 1933, the curators had learned from others' mistakes. The lighting, cleverly concealed, was soft and natural, and the Chou bronzes and T'ang ceramics were grouped against fine-grained woods on suitably proportioned pedestals. The painted hand-scrolls, some from the ex-Emperor P'u Yi's collection, were of superlative quality, and I spent many a quiet hour in admiration of Ch'ên Tao-fu's *Life and Death of the Lotus* and a range of mountains attributed to Hsü Tao-ning. Larry allowed me to unfold many others which were not on display: he was a perfect Chinese host of the good old days that are now condemned as wicked.

The Nelson Gallery and Atkins Museum was situated in a restful park of twenty acres and my host lived near by with his mother, whose passion for Peking kept her youthful. She had stayed on there alone till the outbreak of war and she kept in touch with all her old Pekingese friends and followed their vicissitudes with the keenest concern. It was almost as if she lost a son when her faithful servant Hui Jung, a handsome Manchu, was kidnapped and shot by the Japanese. Looking at Chinese objects by day and talking of our Chinese memories by night made us relive that extraordinary period which had left an indefinable yet indelible influence on each of us.

After a month in Chicago I felt I had been there much longer, and from the medley of first impressions I concluded, like Osbert Sitwell, that the difference between Europe and America is as great as that between Europe and China. Had I been younger I might have adapted myself to this difference. American hospitality is justly proverbial, and my family friends went out of their way to entertain me. As a writer I was unknown, since only one of my books, a juvenile novel, had been published in New York. I had no success story to tell, where nothing succeeded like success. However, I was courteously accepted at my face value since I had nothing more remarkable to show. This saved me from being asked what I thought of the American Woman and other stereotyped questions, for I met more women than men. Had I been asked, I should have paraphrased Henry Adams's statement that 'the American woman of the nineteenth century was much better company than the American man'. Within my limited experience the women were polished works of art magnificently eager for life. It was still true that 'wealth valued social position and classical education as highly as either of these valued wealth, and the women still tended to keep the scales even'.

Though my uncle was a loyal Chicagoan, he preferred the climate of California. He had one house in Los Angeles, not yet afflicted with the smog that was to descend on it later, and he built himself another in the comparatively virginal Cherry Valley. Here he imagined that, like Aldous Huxley, Christopher Isherwood, Gerald Heard, and other English writers who had settled in California, I should find every incentive to write with pleasure and profit, stimulated by the propinquity and golden opportunities of Hollywood. He loved the cinema and was amused by its back-stage gossip, whereas I was only an intermittent addict, usually when I was tired or had nothing better to do. A mediocre play performed by enthusiastic amateurs interested me more than the average film. Even today, in spite of sensational progress in technique, I do not consider that the medium has been adequately exploited as a form of art, and the exorbitant sums spent on film productions seem monstrously out of proportion to the results.

Edward Eberle, a genial Californian who lived with my uncle and kept a flourishing antique shop in Hollywood, was an indefatigable guide to that ever-spreading suburbia. Some of the film stars were his clients and he told me enough about them to induce nausea. One felt sorry for the agents who had to build up their 'public images'. Celebrity was too heady a potion for the majority. Those who did not take to the bottle fell a prey to some psycho-analyst or joined some new-fangled sect. Consequently it was the haven of every type of quack, and I doubt if any novelist has done it justice. Here was fantasy waiting for a robuster Ronald Firbank. Carl Van Vechten had reproduced its aroma, but as Norman Douglas remarked, he wrote like an upholsterer. Perhaps Christopher Isherwood will do it, for there is a seamy side to this fantasy – the pathos of innumerable failures, the sudden meteors that have fizzled out in obscurity, the village belles and beaux who had relied on an attractive physique to become box-office stars overnight. Some had been extras, but most of them had never reached the silver screen. Still they clung to their dreams of auditions and contracts, of Paramount and MGM, and prostituted themselves for the sake of the role which was to win them an Oscar. The cleverest of the failures became interior decorators. Hispano-Mexican influence prevailed and the modest villas which had cost as much to build as palaces in Italy seemed as wide open as the 'nice guy grins' of the convivial Californians: none of them looked private.

The super-civilized Huntington Library was as much a memorial to Lord Duveen as to the railway magnate who had married his widowed aunt Arabella and bought Gainsborough's *Blue Boy*. Here aristocratic portraits of the English eighteenth century were displayed in Duveen condition, a little brighter than when they had left the painter's studio. They made me feel I had been gorging on strawberries and cream with too much sugar.

Outside the library in the Californian sunshine, I caught sight of two familiar figures who in spite of their modern attire seemed

223

to belong more to the eighteenth century than the pictures I had examined: Evelyn Waugh, rubicund as a master mariner in mufti, and Simon Elwes, the suave portrait painter I had seen last in New Delhi. Since then Simon had been paralysed by some Oriental bacillus, but owing to his courage and sterling constitution he had recovered sufficiently to walk with the aid of a stick and he had trained himself to paint with his left hand. No nonsense about open-necked shirts; they were dressed as for the Eton and Harrow match at Lord's.

Evelyn and his shy little wife were staying at the extravagant Bel Air Hotel as the guests of MGM, who wanted to film *Brideshead Revisited*. Wisely he had reserved the right of veto, and he exercised it when the script failed to satisfy him. An artist first and foremost, he would not compound with mammon like Simon Lent in his story *Excursion in Reality*, who was summoned by a film tycoon to write the dialogue for a production of *Hamlet* in modern speech. Let the film experts have a go at it, he said, the place was teeming with them. In the meantime his witty eyes, slightly astonished under his raised eyebrows, registered every detail of the terrain and his ears, more fallible, recorded the peculiarities of local speech. He had been fascinated by a posh cemetery called Forest Lawn, he told me; his eyes shone as he described it. 'You must see it,' he said, 'it is a Tivoli garden for the dead.' But I preferred the beauty parade of Santa Monica. Having seen the tombs of the Ming Emperors and those of the Kings of Delhi as well as the grotesque mausoleums of Genoa, even Evelyn's enthusiasm failed to lure me to Forest Lawn. It sounded a shade perverse and I was puzzled. But I could understand it when *The Loved One* appeared, for it had inspired him to write a masterpiece. There is so much of Evelyn's brand of humour in this tale that it stands in relation to his *oeuvre* as *Un Coeur Simple* to Flaubert's. Evelyn was little versed in French literature, so it must have been a coincidence that a parrot held the same place in Mrs Joyboy's affections as in good Félicité's. Hollywood's revenge was to turn the novel into an atrocious film.

After the food restrictions in England the cuisine of the Bel Air Hotel was lavish but Evelyn had plenty to find fault with. He was a gourmet of honest English delicacies which are seldom available in the restaurants of hotels. Here the cooking was meretriciously international. Evelyn turned it over on his fork with an expression I knew well, the colour rising together with his eyebrows. Peremptorily he summoned the head waiter. 'Send for some fresh asparagus. This stuff is tinned and absolutely tasteless.' The head waiter apologized that fresh asparagus was out of season. 'Nonsense, I've seen bundles of it in the market.' Evelyn refused to be fobbed off with the second best of anything and the imp in him enjoyed these little tiffs. 'In a place like this they should know better than to serve tinned fodder,' he grumbled.

The waiter looked as uncomfortable as I felt under Evelyn's stare. His arrow having hit the mark, Evelyn recovered his joviality as he described his Hollywood adventures. Adaptability was not among his traits and I confess that his intransigence amused me. He was as censorious of certain American habits as Frances Trollope. He objected to the food, to the showers in bathrooms, to the chewing of gum, to the habit of smoking at meals (women were the worst offenders since they believed that cigarettes between courses prevented them from getting fat), to the volubility of taxi-drivers, and so forth. 'How I wish the beasts would stop talking to one,' he moaned. 'I tell them to shut up but they will go on and on. One is totally defenceless. It's an outrage to be charged for such boredom.' When a hostess expostulated with him for handing round the cakes at a party held in his honour he replied: 'It will save me from having to talk.'

Though I agreed with a few of his strictures – smoking through meals is an insult to good cooking and dulls the palate for any decent wine – I extolled the little neck clams, soft-shell crabs, Maine lobsters, T-bone steaks, avocado pears, lima beans, sweet corn, and other indigenous dishes. As for the taxi-drivers, I had been charmed by one in Chicago who remarked: 'Gee, I wish I had heard that concert!' after Horowitz had been playing at the

Symphony Hall. He had proceeded to explain with that naïve effusiveness which always went to my heart, that he was an alumnus of Chicago University who took turns with his brother to drive a taxi; that he was majoring in literature but that he actually preferred painting. 'My ambition is to paint like Picasso,' he confided.

Evelyn listened with a frown of mock disapproval. 'The trouble with you is that you're really a Yank,' he observed.

Surely he would have also been touched by the aspirations, howsoever misguided, of this young taxi-driver, but he maintained that I should have discouraged his gratuitous avowal. There was always an element of chaff in his comments. He was obviously enjoying the strangeness of the Hollywood scene, though he disliked the cinema. 'After driving tractors and growing turnips, it's a nice holiday for Laura,' he remarked.

Romantically English and attached to hierarchical traditions, he feared that the Socialists would soon render England uninhabitable. He considered emigrating to Ireland if he could discover a Georgian house there suitable to a budding family, but I was none too sure that he would tolerate the Irish brogue any better than the Californian, though the rigidity of Irish Catholicism might appeal to the Victorian side of his nature. He had become defiantly Victorian in the Bel Air Hotel and I relished the incongruity. He pretended to dread the appearance of my *Memoirs*. 'This is probably the last time I shall speak to you,' he said with a flicker of his juvenile truculence when I mentioned that I had written about our friendship at Oxford. Evidently he anticipated some shaft of malice, though he was the last person I should have wished to offend. When the book appeared he wrote me a characteristically generous letter and our friendship remained unshaken till his death in 1966. Under his crusty cuirass there was always the acute sensitiveness of a fastidious artist. Financially he could only gain by coming to terms with MGM, but he refused any compromise with mediocrity even if *Brideshead Revisited* were converted into a visual Rolls-Royce. I admired his integrity.

Los Angeles and its purlieus offered rich pabulum to the satirist. Since nearly everyone possessed a motor car, hardly anyone walked except in the shopping district. Were one so intrepid as to stroll, I was warned that one might be arrested for loitering with some sinister intent. The park was full of pitfalls. I regarded this as a tiresome restriction, for it is chiefly by walking that one can get the measure of a city.

> 'What is this life if, full of care,
> We have no time to stand and stare?'

One could seldom stand and stare in Los Angeles, though there was plenty to see and taste in the Farmer's Market, where I lunched on a salad of avocado pears and watched cakes being decorated with rococo patterns, and the *flâneurs* in flowery shirts cruised lackadaisically among enormous lilies as if they were trying to compete with them; and there was no lack of evening entertainment, either at the Turnabout Theatre, where the Yale Puppeteers and Elsa Lanchester were performing, at the Flamingo, where female impersonators warbled 'He's ma man of war' and other salacious ditties – how tip-toe dainty they were compared to the dames in the audience! – or at the Philharmonic Auditorium, where Markova, Dolin and Eglevsky were twirling in the de Basil Ballet. But with due respect to my uncle and the amiable people I encountered, I felt I should soon wither in such a place, and I could understand why its residents hankered after strange gods. Comfort rather than beauty seemed to be their criterion and the most brilliant intellects were scientific, which might explain why Aldous Huxley felt at home there.

Like Walter Pater and Sacheverell Sitwell but without their grace of style, I have a tendency to let my mind wander through time, to transport myself to Medicean Florence and Norman Sicily and seventeenth-century Versailles, and to analyse the quality, the personality of bygone periods and phases of culture. Apart from the wonders of the Californian desert, the wild fauna and flora, there was no dearth of curious flavours, but they failed to stir my emotions. At its best the architecture was a foretaste of Colonial Mexico.

To Mexico I was drawn for several reasons. First because it was reputedly the most dynamic of Latin American countries and I longed for a draught of Latinity; secondly because my ears had been filled with reports of its artistic renascence. In order to be appreciated the Mexican mural painters, with Diego Rivera in the van, had to be seen in their native light, and the names of Giotto and Piero della Francesca were freely quoted in comparison. Moreover certain elements of Aztec architecture, sculpture and jade carving seemed to have something in common with those of ancient China, and I wondered if an enclave of primitive China were to be discovered among the Mayas. There was also the lure of Mexican Baroque, that hybrid of Spanish and Indian craftsmanship: was it really as astonishing as the photographs I had seen? And my friend Geoffrey Gilmour had offered me a house in Cuernavaca, where I hoped to marshal my thoughts after a surfeit of sight-seeing.

Dreaming of enigmatic masks of jade and obsidian and aventurine quartz superior to those I had seen in the British Museum, and of mighty pyramids and Churrigueresque cathedrals, I flew to Mexico City. After reading Madame Calderon de la Barca's *Life in Mexico* and more recent accounts of the country which had been an inspiration to so many writers, I was all keyed up for enjoyment. But either my liver was out of order or some demon of perversity began to vex me upon my arrival, for I failed to respond to the genius of the place with my usual sympathy. That genius was an interbreeding of Aztec and Iberian, of mules and motor-cars, of steel and glass and cement. The capital was in a fitful fever of modernization but I was none too confident that the skyscrapers shooting up would not sink like the old palaces into the spongy soil which had formerly been a lake. The remains of the colonial period had a decadent grandeur as distinct from the sheer bulk of Aztec ruins lately restored. And it was the pyramids and the power they symbolized that appealed to the national pride of the mixed population.

Though it had absorbed certain elements of the Aztec theocracy, the Catholic Church was blamed for collaboration with the detested Conquistadors.

While one deplored the iconoclasm of some early missionaries, the human sacrifices and barbarities of Aztec superstition were enough to sicken the most callous of sixteenth-century Spaniards, and they were overlooked by the eulogists of Aztec culture. Bernal Diaz and the Franciscan Father Bernardino de Sahagun have left ample descriptions of the costumes and ornaments they found in New Spain. Brilliant as the decorations for a Diaghilev ballet, even they involved physical discomfort, if not pain. Children's foreheads were deformed by the pressure of small boards clapped on them from birth; lips, noses and ears were perforated: it was a distinction to have the septum of the nose pierced since it was equivalent to a medal for valour. The filing and chipping of teeth was practised as in Africa and incisors were inlaid with discs of jadeite, obsidian and pyrites. Lip-plugs were worn by the bravest warriors: according to Father de Sahagun, 'large discs in the lower lip, with four other discs arranged about it in a cross-shape, often representing small dogs, sometimes lizards, or two little squares of metal' – others were of 'oystershell cut into the form of an eagle'. The tubes of hard stone with bright feathers inserted between the nostrils must have hampered articulation. According to Bishop Landa, who was responsible for the bonfire of Maya manuscripts at Merida, the Maya admired cross-eyes so much that they hung trinkets from the foreheads of babies to induce a permanent squint. These details of bygone fashion are less trivial than they sound, for they illustrate the old adages that one must suffer to be beautiful and that beauty is in the eye of the beholder.

The Mexicans *en masse* are not a cheerful mixture of races – I doubt if they ever were. They have their moments of exaltation: under the influence of liquor their violence can be homicidal. In the taverns of Tenampo where I had gone to hear the *mariaches* – popular songs strummed and bellowed by groups of mestizo voices – the drunks were always ready to run amok with knives.

Inscrutable masks were suddenly distorted with passion, as if some atavistic fury were lusting for blood. The masks resembled those in the museum even in their grimaces, more frightful than comic.

Without understanding their symbolism it is not easy to appreciate sculpture whose elaboration is too dense to achieve the dignity of art as distinguished from meticulous craftsmanship. But the same sort of elaboration was applied to their Christian buildings where at least it had the charm of rococo design. What I could see in the dark, overcrowded museum reminded me of the excesses of Hindu carvings, of that *horror vacui* which is pleasant enough in a pastrycook but that in a sculptor denotes mental vacuity. The stone stelae were chiefly of anthropological interest: originally they were daubed in gaudy colours. I preferred them 'penny-plain'. Those who rhapsodize over these bas-reliefs forget the more sophisticated carvings of Egypt and Mesopotamia. Their purity of line is undeniable, especially where costumes and feathers are reproduced. The skull was a favourite motif and whatever it had of grace and beauty was, as Pater would have said, of a somewhat mortified kind. Which recalled his dictum: 'A museum is seldom a cheerful place – oftenest it induces the feeling that nothing could ever have been young.'

Leaving the museum for the great pyramid to the sun god which many of these objects adorned, one could conceive the vertigo of victims who had to climb its craggy steps before submitting to the sacrificial knife. I felt dizzy myself as I climbed its slope, rising from the dreary plain of Teotihuacan. Horrible place! yet the tourists raved about it, thrilled by the lurid travelogues which described the fanatical sadism before the Spanish conquest.

Diego Rivera was careful to exclude such barbaric rites in his frescoes of *The History of the Aztecs* – travesties of history not nearly so well painted as they are reputed to be. For once I agreed with D. H. Lawrence: 'They are like vulgar abuse, not art at all.'

Rivera's work was an amalgam of styles too provincial to create a furore on this side of the Atlantic, but in Mexico he was considered a genius even by those who disapproved of his politics. He combined Communism with dogmatic nationalism and both served as profitable publicity. His experimental modernism belonged to his student days in Paris where Apollinaire observed that he was 'by no means negligible'. When he returned to Mexico he dropped cubism for pseudo-primitivism and propagandist expressionism. An indomitable mestizo Falstaff, he proceeded to fresco the walls that brought him fame. Those in Mexico City were as packed with figures as the Aztec monuments were with reptiles – how remote from the noble Chinese dragon! (Whatever kinship I had hoped to find between ancient Chinese ritual objects and those of ancient Mexico had soon been dissolved.) In the Cortés palace in Cuernavaca, now converted into government offices, Rivera again depicted the brutality of Spanish domination. The scenes are like illustrations to a child's story book and are therefore comprehensible to the illiterate. The figures have no weight, no 'tactile values' or gradations of shade: they are like paper silhouettes and the types are conventional. However, they are more pleasing in colour and design than his other frescoes, and they contain occasional felicities of composition.

Woe betide anyone who, like me, thought Rivera overestimated, for his name was as sacrosanct as Picasso's in Paris. It was invariably linked with Orozco and Siqueiros who, despite divergences of style and outlook, were united in their aim to appeal to the masses, to teach history, or their own version of it, to the uneducated peons.

A retrospective exhibition of Orozco's work at the Palace of Fine Arts struck one like a hurricane of misguided energy. In his youth he had come under the influence of the fiery Doctor Atl, a leader of the 'Back to Mexico' movement in revolt against artistic servility to Europe. Doctor Atl painted – none too well – muscular Titans and volcanoes in eruption: a devotee of the primitive forces of nature, he chose to settle on Popocatépetl. During the revolution he had preached his cultural crusade from the pulpits of derelict churches and launched his paper *The*

Vanguard in Orizaba. But even his vehement proselytes concluded that revolutionary chaos was not favourable to their artistic development. The excesses of bandit-soldiery, the massacres of Zapatistas by Carranzistas, the subdivision of political factions, subterranean intrigues and mutual exterminations were rather more stimulating from a safe distance.

In 1917 Rivera was in Europe, Orozco went to the United States and Siqueiros followed suit. By 1922 their prospects improved, since José Vasconcelos, the Minister of Education, appealed to all artists and intellectuals to collaborate with him. The painters rushed home to seize their opportunity. They formed a syndicate with Siqueiros as secretary general, who issued a manifesto to 'the soldiers, workers and intellectuals not serving the bourgeoisie'. Art was to be socialized; bourgeois individualism destroyed; easel-painting and other forms of art begotten of ultra-intellectual and aristocratic cliques were to be repudiated, and so forth.

The manifesto also insisted upon the importance of 'content' – the sum of ideas and emotions expressed in a work of art – which would lead directly to formless anecdotal painting and the photographic document. To put an end to 'bourgeois individualism', Siqueiros, upon whom Doctor Atl's mantle had descended, persuaded groups to collaborate on a single fresco, each contributing his share according to his talents and following a preconceived plan. The members of the syndicate had decided not to sign their paintings, a resolution that quickly melted away.

As interpreters of the past the mural painters were ardently pro-Aztec and anti-Conquistador. One is reminded of the Celtic Revival in Ireland: Cortés, like Cromwell, might have lived yesterday, and he was caricatured as a villainous-looking hunchback. But the Aztec Revival was pictorial rather than literary. Appropriately, two of its chief exponents, Juan O'Gorman and Pablo O'Higgins, were of Irish origin. One of O'Gorman's most ambitious frescoes covers the vast wall of the public library in Patzcuaro, Michoacan, and it is crammed from top to bottom with historical and legendary anecdotes. A pamphlet has been published explaining the personages portrayed. These are arranged under forty-seven headings, a compendium more erudite than artistic.

Siqueiros, the most turbulent of the 'big triumvirate' and a character more credible in fiction than in reality – (Widow Trotsky accused him of murdering her husband) – had dissipated so much energy in revolutionary antics that his achievement fell below its potential. Its immediate effect of power was undeniable. His pictures bore such titles as *The Sob, Anguish, Loneliness, Call to Arms, Echo of a Scream, Sunrise of Mexico* – the latter a squat Aztec woman nursing oilwells in her capacious lap. But the merely arresting never arrests for long. In the long run so much sobbing and gesticulation grow wearisome, and one suspects that his rhetoric is mechanical. I could not share American enthusiasm for his 'Duco technique' – Duco enamel applied with a spray-gun upon plyboard – the result of which was a poster-like harshness of colour. It was said to last for ever. What of it? Is not the work of, say, Fra Angelico still as fresh as when it was painted?

But there were other artists less famous to whose work I was introduced by Ines Amor, an enterprising lady who managed a gallery of modern art in Mexico City. Fortunately these reacted against the violence of the veteran crusaders without losing their native virtues. On the contrary, Rufino Tamayo, a Zapotec Indian, still clung to his Oaxacan roots. The colours and designs of his native pottery seemed to glow in his canvases and a pre-Colombian dignity distinguished most of his work. A Mexican *Fauve*, he had already won a museum reputation in New York. Ines Amor regretted his absence, but even as an expatriate he would remain as Mexican as James Joyce remained Irish.

The painters I met interested me more than other Mexicans. Each had an individual talent, allegorical, fantastic, or folkloristic. Some were voluble, some reserved, but because I am usually drawn to painters rather than writers I conversed with them easily in Italo-Spanish. Most of them had served their apprenticeship in some other profession. The affable Chavez Morado had spent his

233

youth in factories and fruit plantations, but he could not help drawing and his fellow-workers had been his models. A chance encounter with the engraver Leopoldo Mendez, who had noticed his sketches and woodcuts at an open air show, led to his appointment as professor of the Elementary Arts Department of the Ministry of Public Education, since when he had divided his time between teaching, painting and illustrating books. Although a realist, he believed that fantasy added emphasis to reality. He was also a satirist in the tradition of Guadalupe Posada, the more vigorous draughtsman of a much older generation. His landscapes were as quiet in tone as early Corots. 'People paint Mexico as if it were a blazing Christmas tree,' he remarked. 'The landscape of the central plateau is stark and rugged, its colouring delicate and evanescent. The cactus itself is a pale, smoky plant, not emerald green.'

Few painters have conveyed more intimately the peculiar quality of Mexican street scenes, the old tram rumbling along the homely track beside the Baroque façade, the full moon on a posturing statue wasting its rhetoric on rows of shuttered windows, a crazy roof-sign in process of construction opposite, the ubiquitous dawdlers, the ice-cream vendor leaning against his swan-shaped barrow by a white adobe wall while a boy on a balcony gazes wistfully towards him. Avoiding the obvious, he captures the *genius loci*, and it is not easy to describe exactly how he does it: perhaps it boils down to a subtle selection of essentials.

Guillermo Meza, a self-educated Tlaxcalan Indian, was one of the most prolific of the younger painters – he was then under thirty. As a child he worked in his father's tailor shop, studied drawing at a night school, and earned pittances by retouching photographs and carrying loads in the market. He drew whenever he had the chance, with any material that came to hand. Sometimes he dreamt of becoming a musician, and music entered into the texture of his work. He told me that no composer had stirred him as much as Stravinsky and, after Stravinsky, Mozart. Some of his best drawings were inspired by ballet, impressions of rhythmic movement in which the nerves and sinews of the body coagulate into stalactites and crystals; some were treated like ancient bronzes excavated from volcanic soil, with gaping holes in their flanks, as if to stress that they were but graceful shells.

On the strength of his drawings Rivera recommended him to Ines Amor, who bought him painting materials and urged him to devote himself exclusively to art. Two years later his first exhibition enjoyed an encouraging success. The poetry of earth in him was strong: in his picture *The Cornfield* a sun-blackened skeleton clad in the white cotton of the Mexican peon strides between waves of corn sloping down from a rocky hill. A twisted tree is hunched behind him, tremulous and dark; the clouds above are billowing in the breeze like the skeleton's clothes. It is an evocation of life and death in the Mexican afternoon, with Nature indifferent to the *memento mori*, and to the dead animal rotting in an adjacent pool.

Melancholy and voluptuousness were mingled in Meza's painting. In some there was a morbid streak – I recall an elemental wolf-boy howling into the wilderness. Yet as a person Meza was the reverse of morbid: he enjoyed carpentry and dissecting radios, and his first purchase after a successful show of his work was a microscope.

What often strikes the foreigner as morbidity is a Mexican idiosyncrasy, a constant awareness of death and an attitude towards it compounded of humour and horror. One found it in bakeries, where skull-shaped cakes were sold for All Souls' Day, and at the confectioner's, where sugar skulls competed with edible crossbones and skeletons. To suck skulls like fruit drops was therefore an experience common to children, and one fraught with festive rather than gloomy associations. The Mexican joked about death and sent pictures of skeletons to his friends without any malicious intention. Hundreds of hectic skeletons make merry in Posada's engravings and his series of *Calaveras* are his liveliest productions.

Chavez Morado painted a group of soldiers in peaked

sombreros shooting at a skeleton; Juan Soriano a dead little girl laid out on a flowery bier and a serio-comic wake; and Manuel Rodriguez Lozano, a painter of reveries in moonlight tones, has celebrated death in sixteen panels for Don Francisco Iturbe's residence, wherein the horizontal lines symbolize death 'in contrast with the vertical life'.

🎝 14 🎝

'A joyful sunny land' according to the travel posters, Mexico has been so copiously described that I need only record a few personal impressions. There was no lack of sun but I seldom found it joyful. Ronald Firbank's title for one of his most popular novels, *Sorrow in Sunlight*, applied to it more aptly. Perhaps I was mistaken to visit it alone: it is a country to be shared with a blithe companion of lusty constitution. I should not prescribe it for the delicate.

The dwelling so kindly placed at my disposal by Geoffrey Gilmour in Cuernavaca was entered by an inconspicuous door on Netzahualcoyotl, near a Franciscan church like a massive fort dating from the Spanish conquest. The airy rooms opened on to a veranda framing a view of undulating hills, flamboyant vegetation, and Popocatépetl soaring beyond, its summit invariably veiled in mist. Already it was summer weather in early March.

The real proprietor, Eduardo de Rendon, was a cultured Spaniard who had lost his estates in Yucatan during the revolution. He wore the *ancien régime* like a black rosette: regretting his affluent youth, he was profoundly pessimistic about the future. For the last fifteen years he had not left Cuernavaca and his pessimism infected me like an insidious disease. He let me browse in his library, but I was saturated in literature about Mexico. Dry facts apart, the archaeologists and academic pundits had added little to what the creative artists had divined intuitively: they lacked the necessary vision, imagination, and descriptive power. D. H. Lawrence, Graham Greene, Malcolm Lowry, each had expressed his perceptions with artistry, and had they investigated archaic pottery or maize-cultivation, they would have excelled the pundits.

Cuernavaca was a place for idling. I had hoped to correct the proofs of my memoirs but they failed to arrive. The foreign residents who vegetated in adobe de luxe villas did not know what to do with themselves outside their swimming pools. Englishmen who had bolted from the war with smuggled ingots and makeshift lovers, failed artists who had taken to marijuana and tequila in boredom or despair, characters without character who mooched about the shady, shoddy plaza where a rudimentary band wheezed operatic extracts of an evening, the young men padding round the bandstand in one direction while the young women fluttered past them in another, the boldest exchanging messages with eyes – the atmosphere was musical comedy provincial. But I was still simmering with nervous energy: it seemed a pity to stagnate when I might be exploring new ranges of knowledge and sensation or simply seeing new sights. At this point two sprightly American ladies came to my assistance, Mrs Moats and her daughter Alice Leone.

Mrs Moats belonged to the union of international hostesses and she had long queened it over the amorphous society of Mexico City. She was a picaresque novelist *manquée* with a rich fund of information about the country and its rulers past and present, a perennial fount of highly seasoned gossip, but in her eagerness to amuse and amaze she was often tempted to kick over the traces between fact and fantasy. I had met her in my teens at St Moritz, where her film-star quality had caused a flutter among the middle-aged cosmopolitans of the Palace Hotel. At Hanselmann's she seemed as exotic as the quetzal. Her fair young daughter Alice Leone had been one of my playmates. Since then she had graduated in freelance journalism and had published at least one book entitled *No Nice Girl Swears*, though her own language was sufficiently startling. Her escapades in Russia and occupied France during the war had been hair-raising. In her mother's presence, however, she was slightly subdued; so was I.

Throughout her conversation one became aware that Mrs

Moats envisaged a society that had all but vanished during the war. She did not realize to what an extent Europe had changed, and that even in conservative Spain very few were able to cultivate the gilded vanities. Her social ambitions yearned for wider scope, but there she was stuck in Mexico which she had squeezed, as it were, like an orange. Her husband, a hard-bitten breadwinner with a dry sense of humour, looked on and listened to her improvisations with an admiration in which I detected a benevolent irony. She reminded me of the heroine of a comedy by Turgenev, the wife of a provincial official who pines for the splendours of the capital and coquets with a superannuated big-wig in order to get there. In spite of her frustration, apparent in her comments on distant rivals, I felt that like certain Fabians and the devotees of Marx, she enjoyed her hallucinations of an idealized society. She was an assiduous student of Elsa Maxwell. Weekending in Cuernavaca, she followed the week-end activities of the Duke and Duchess of Windsor and discussed them as if they were golfing round the corner. The remaining owners of *haciendas* were a feeble substitute: most of them had been impoverished. Those who owned property in Mexico City were still prosperous but their parsimony was proverbial. In Paris they might make a splash but at home they counted their small change. Carlos de Beistegui was their typical representative in Europe.

Mrs Moats took me to a *hacienda* near Puebla which gave me an idea of what the others must have been in the reign of Don Porfirio. This Hacienda de Dolores was efficiently run by its owner Mike Diaz Barriga, a country squire of the old school, a fine horseman and breeder of thoroughbreds more Spanish than Mexican whose retainers were patently devoted to him. Unfortunately there was an epidemic of foot and mouth disease and he was compelled to kill off his prize cattle. Roast beef abounded at his hospitable board. We supped on thick chocolate and sugary cakes to a chorus of lowing cows, and I was reminded of similar collations described by Madame Calderon a century ago.

Puebla struck me as pretty rather than beautiful, for its buildings depended on the gleam of coloured tiles more than on elegant structure. Domes and façades were encrusted with glazed patterns which glimmered in the sun, and several suns of orange tiles glittered on the dome of the Cathedral, whose twin towers were also inlaid with red and yellow mosaics. Here the variations of tile arrangements appeared to be endless, majolica and delft and chinoiserie applied to rococo with hints of Ispahan. Angels are said to have chosen the site where Puebla was founded by Spanish colonists, and it was a religious centre till the monks and nuns were expelled in 1857. That it ever had sixty churches was hard to believe. Those that survive are spectacular, in especial the Rosary Chapel of Santo Domingo, whose interior is of a giddy polychrome elaboration that strains one's vision and vocabulary. Yet it is not unique for Mexico: Guanajuato, Taxco and Tepoztlan offer interiors equally dazzling in their inspissated excess. Churrigueresque *retablos* upon which the Indian craftsmen let their fancy run riot, piling profuse Pelion on profuser Ossa – only Sacheverell Sitwell can render poetic justice to what a Mexican described as this 'glittering ornamental dissipation'. Much of the detail was closer to confectionery than to sculpture: the curlicues of garlands and twisted columns were livelier than the statues they surrounded. Most of the paintings were murky imitations of Murillo.

Perhaps it was a symptom of middle age that after the first gasp of wonder, as when the curtain rises on a sumptuous production of *Aida*, I soon wearied of the coiling over-emphasis inherited from the Aztec *horror vacui*, though it takes one's breath away in the midst of a desolate landscape. I preferred Morelia to the other towns I visited because it was soberly Spanish by contrast. The long but narrow Lake Patzcuaro with its flat-bottomed sailing boats had a tranquil charm but its fish were inferior to their reputation. The misnamed 'chillis' and peppery condiments conceal the basic insipidity of Mexican fare. Madame Calderon relates that a Mexican friend promised to send her 'a box of mosquitoes' eggs, of which tortillas are made, which are considered a great delicacy. Considering mosquitoes as small winged cannibals, I was rather shocked at the idea, but they pretend that these which are from the Laguna, are a superior race of creatures which do not sting. In fact the Spanish historians mention that the Indians used to eat bread made of the eggs which the fly called *agayacatl* laid on the rushes of the lakes, and which they (the Spaniards) found very palatable.'

Since my residence in China I have been reasonably free from dietary prejudice, but my palate rebelled against *moles* and other vaunted delicacies of the Mexican cuisine, which stung the mouth like mosquitoes even if these were not among their ingredients.

At Morelia I sat through a small-scale bull-fight, when several urchins leapt into the ring to prove their prowess in finishing off the wounded beasts. Let Hemingway, Picasso, and other super-men eulogize this sport. Evidently I have the instincts of what they would call a cissy. For me the picturesqueness of the scene was no compensation for its cruelty.

On Maundy Thursday I drove to the crumbling village of Tzintzuntzan on Lake Patzcuaro to watch a dramatization of the scenes leading to Our Lord's Crucifixion enacted on the atrium before the church. Arriving at four in the afternoon, I waited for hours while an Indian Judas and Indians masquerading as Roman soldiers ran about collecting coins, and the vendors of repulsive refreshments drove a brisk trade. The performance, which did not get going till dusk, was of a kindergarten crudity remote from any spirit of reverence, but the mummers appeared to be enjoying their indulgence in horseplay. A polite young priest who showed me the church and museum shrugged his shoulders apologetically, as if to say: 'One has to make concessions.' He assured me that it was not worth my while staying till the bitter end. The church contained an 'Entombment of Christ' attributed to Titian. Philip II of Spain was said to have presented it to the local convent of San Francisco and though vast sums had been offered for it the devout Indians of Tzintzuntzan refused to part with their treasure or allow it to be photographed. It was spoken of as 'one of the most important paintings in the world'. The composition was dimly Ribera-esque: it was probably Spanish. Certainly it bore no relation to the Titian whose works we know.

On Good Friday a realistic image of the Mater Dolorosa was borne through the streets of Morelia in procession by a bevy of mourning matrons who were annoyed by the tourists with cameras who tried to photograph them. Wherever I went I met tourists with cameras and I am told they have become more numerous since then. In Mexico it was easy to detach oneself but in Yucatan it was more difficult, and all of them were eager to relate the story of their lives. 'This country's lousy with archaeologists,' remarked one of them, but none were visible during the ten days I spent at Chichen Itza and Uxmal. The highest claims for Maya art and architecture, for their skill in mathematics and astronomy, were made in their publications, and it was dinned into my ears that the Maya calendar was far more accurate than that in use today.

Thanks to intelligent restoration, the scattered remains of Chichen Itza were almost as impressive as Angkor. Lack of metal tools and ignorance of the true arch made building twice as laborious, for all the material was quarried and dressed with stone implements. Walls had to be thick to resist the outward thrust of the false arch and support the heavy roof, yet most of them had been torn apart by tropical vegetation or had collapsed through the decay of wooden lintels. Comparing old photographs with the actual reconstructions, one could gauge the accomplishment of the restorers. The main buildings had evocative titles such as the House of Tigers, the House of Warriors, the House of Mysterious Writing, the Castle, and our guide regaled us with lurid accounts of sacrifices to the god of spring and fertility. The victim was painted a heavenly blue and wore a gorgeous head-dress of plumes. After being cut open in the temple his corpse was hurled down the steps and skinned like a rabbit. A naked priest wore the skin as a vestment and proceeded to dance before an edified congregation.

At the sacred *cenote*, a pool some sixty feet deep, other victims were sacrificed to the rain god, and of course these were said to have been virgins chosen for their beauty. Precious offerings were also thrown into it and an enterprising American consul called Thompson had succeeded in fishing some of these out, a variety of bracelets, rings, beads, masks, cups and saucers, as well as bones which were proved to belong to dames of a certain age. Even if one knew nothing about these functions, the pool had a haunting atmosphere of evil. Featureless but reclining, the figure of the rain god might have been carved by Mr Henry Moore.

The huge ball-court had its sinister aspect too, for the game had been part of a ceremony connected with the sun and the loser was condemned to death. Thither I wandered after dining at Mayaland Lodge. Wagging his tail in a friendly manner, a spotted mongrel attached himself to me. He belonged to a boy who was piping a primitive tune with an effect as melancholy as the flute in *Tristan and Isolde*. The boy told me not to fear: he was the guardian of the court, which was about three hundred feet long. Leading me by the hand as if I were in danger of stumbling, he showed me the temples at either end, explaining the ball-game in comprehensible Spanish. Theoretically he preferred modern football but he had no chance of playing it. His was a lonely life but he was resolutely cheerful. The ruins and the strangers who visited them were his chief distraction. His ancestors must have lingered on when the Itzas abandoned this country ages ago, for he had the salient features depicted in their sculpture: a squat figure with a sloping forehead, hooked nose and full lips, his almond eyes were perfectly crossed so that he would have been considered handsome by the standards of ancient Maya. His white cotton clothes were remarkably clean. He invited me to his family hut which was slung with hammocks but contained little furniture: turkeys and chickens had the run of the floor. Bidding me rest on a hammock, he offered me Coca-Cola with a ceremonious air and would not hear of payment. I was much taken with his gentle courtesy: he was nearly twenty but he looked about fourteen. After the guided

243

tours of Chichen Itza it was agreeable to visit the more spectacular ruins in his company, and the absence of any mercenary motive was refreshing. In my limited cognizance of Mexico such people were rare. Not that I blamed those who hoped to turn an honest penny at my expense: the trouble was that they were so often dishonest. I lost various articles during my Mexican wanderings and since I was travelling light, mostly by air, these losses were hard to replace off the beaten track. No doubt I had been spoiled by the respect for property I had experienced in the Far East. Foolishly I had entrusted a batch of stamped letters to the head porter of my hotel in Merida. The man looked reliable, and I could not picture him licking off the stamps. Yet none of those letters, written in tropical heat without air-conditioning, reached its destination. Since then I have been so scrupulous in posting letters myself that many friends laugh at this mania.

The henequen plantations which produced the sisal hemp were like a choppy grey sea along the road to Chichen Itza and the landscape became a scrubby wilderness as one approached the ruins. Small wonder the Itzas abandoned this low tableland of rocky crust, devoid of flowery meadows and shady groves. Mayaland Lodge was a cultivated oasis. My room was a thatched hut with a porch facing a rudimentary garden, which was tended by a Chinese gardener. Though he came from Hainan he understood a few words of Mandarin and he was delighted to exchange them with me. Old and wizened, he had a youthful smile when I told him: 'Here you have raised a phoenix from a hen's nest.' 'Too complimentary, too complimentary!' he muttered in familiar tones, and he pointed with pride to some miniature plants which enlivened that stony soil. Older in appearance than the gardener, with prickly grey scales, a pendulous dewlap and shrewd little eyes, an iguana nearly six feet long sat pondering on my porch. It had a prehistoric air, as if it had survived Olmec, Maya, Toltec and Aztec civilizations, but it did not look edible, though the gardener assured me: '*Hao chih*' – 'it is good to eat'. Its flesh had a flavour of chicken, he said, but I was not tempted to sample it. The creature did not mind my presence but it was camera-shy, for when a tourist attempted to photograph it, away it scuttled with a flick of its whiplike tail.

Mexico City was cooler and I made solitary excursions in the neighbourhood, last but not least to the sanctuary of the Virgin of Guadalupe, the most popular shrine in the country. At all times it was thronged with Indians from distant provinces who knelt there for hours holding tapers that dripped on their offerings. They made esoteric signs of the Cross and some crawled on the pavement licking the dust in abject humility. I felt uncomfortably like a Peeping Tom. Their rapture contrasted strangely with the merry-go-round and fun fair outside where hideous drinks and victuals were on sale at canvas-covered booths, together with rosaries, medals, sacred images and other gaudy mementoes arranged like fruit, and men were shooting at clay pigeons. Children were reciting shrill prayers before the image printed miraculously on the Indian Juan Diego's cloak about a decade after the Spanish conquest. According to the painter Cabrera, it was in a medium completely unknown and betrayed no trace of brush-strokes. To my eye it resembled gouache. Our Lady clasps no Blessed Child as in European pictures, which had caused some authorities to identify Her with the Aztec goddess of earth and corn whose temple had stood where Juan Diego had his visions. Three times the Virgin had appeared to him, bidding him tell the bishop that she wished a church to be built there. The bishop remained incredulous until the messenger could produce a proof. The Virgin then told Diego to gather flowers on a barren hill, where he was amazed to find white roses in full bloom. These he folded in his cloak, and when he presented them to the bishop an image of the Virgin was discovered on it. The roses were of a Castilian plant never seen in Mexico. A chapel was duly built for the miraculous image and the present basilica in Baroque style was completed in 1836.

An anthology of Mexican miracles would fill many a tome. Another image of the Virgin was found floating in the water by an Aztec chieftain when the capital was flooded in 1580, and the church of Our Lady of the Angels was built over the adobe chapel containing its replica. The image was damaged by a later flood, excepting the face and hands – another miracle. But the Virgin of Guadalupe, as patron saint of Mexico, takes precedence. Being partial to miracles I often forget that unbelievers are apt to scoff. I have a tendency to discern them everywhere, and I am vexed by those who, surrounded by every kind of miracle, stubbornly close their eyes and deny their existence.

One last excursion and I was sated. The Baroque shrine of El Señor de Chalma, a crucifix which appeared in a cave where an Aztec deity had been worshipped, was not mentioned in the guide-books but I had heard that Indian pilgrims danced in ecstasy before it, and that the site was more authentically indigenous than others of comparable sanctity. No great distance from Mexico City as the crow flies, it was a day's journey by jogging bus and mule over rough roads and a narrow mountainous track. The buses were overcrowded with pungent pilgrims: four hours in one bus, three hours in another, jolted to a jelly, and then two hours by mule on a wooden saddle that flayed my behind, and I came to a straggling village and a canyon with a sombre church. Many Indians travelled on foot, their women-folk burdened with babies and baggage; others crawled part of the way on their knees. The situation was wildly romantic and the atrium before the church was thronged with families camping there like gipsies. Some were already dancing to a slow and clumsy rhythm; others were swilling *pulque* and munching tortillas. As dusk deepened the canyon was lit up by hundreds of oil lamps flickering like fireflies. Genuflexions alternated with conviviality. Here even more than at Guadalupe, I was conscious of eavesdropping as vows were fulfilled or blessings were invoked with exaggerated demonstrations of piety. The worshippers swayed together in a trance out of time and out of mind, a scene curious in its throbbing intensity. Rather dazed, I withdrew, feeling totally alien from this multitude.

As there was no inn I spent the night among other pilgrims on the dirt floor of a large adobe hut, wrapped in a *petate* or rug. A small lamp before an image of the Virgin provided the only light.

When I woke I was covered with fleabites. But I must have slept soundly for the bag I had been careful to lock and used as a pillow had been slit open, and my wallet, watch and fountain-pen had been removed with some other necessities.

My host seemed sincerely perturbed since his other guests had gone and of course he had seen nothing suspicious. He had an honest peasant face and I was sure he was not the culprit. No police were on duty among the horde of pilgrims but eventually I found an officer to whom I explained my plight. His expression was magnificently blank. He was sorry he could do nothing about it. As a foreigner I had been unwise to come here unescorted. He advised me to consult a *sacerdote* of the sanctuary.

The priest, a swarthy *mestizo*, was strolling with his breviary apart from the crowd. He listened impassively to my stammered tale of woe. Surely I could walk back to Mexico City like other good souls? The journey by bus and mule had been sufficiently tiring. Harassed and aching after a night on the hard floor, and very hungry, I appealed for a loan which I promised to repay a hundredfold. Never had I been obliged to beg before, but the priest was accustomed to beggars. His jet eyes scrutinized me none too kindly, and he relented so far as to lend me fifteen *pesos*, which allowed me to return by mule and bus, leaving me with twenty *centavos* for some *pulque* to quench my thirst at Ohuila, the bus-stop. That draught of *pulque* revived me. Fermented juice of the agave, its flavour was musty but after prolonged abstinence it affected me like champagne.

No, it had not been worth the fatigue. My attempts to learn something of the manners and customs of the Mexican people, either Indians or *mestizos*, had involved too much discomfort without any aesthetic compensation I could have gained equally from books and museums. Aztec artefacts displayed in the museums were as representative as any I had seen in their place of origin and in most cases photographs flattered them. The prototypes of the finest churches existed on the Iberian peninsula: the Mexicans had merely gilded the lily. The Aztec pyramids and temples reminded me too often of war memorials. Malevolent spirits hovered round their angularities. For Americans seeking an indigenous past as a substitute for 'Westernism' this art had greater significance than for Europeans whose sense of beauty is still influenced – or was till yesterday – by ancient Hellas. The relics of Latin civilization in Mexico were wearing as thin as the relics of the Aztecs. The dominant language and politer customs remained Spanish, but scores of churches and convents had been converted into schools, offices, and warehouses. Catholic altars and Aztec stones were being reduced to the same level of disestablishment. Time did not have the same value as in the United States. In elucidation of this the editor of a Mexican weekly remarked: 'Good news is like good wine: it improves with age. It is always better to hold news over for a week. If it is true, we shall get more facts; and if it proves to be false, why should we print it?' It was restful to see nobody in a hurry, but when I was in a hurry it was rather enervating, especially in restaurants and railway stations. Patience struck me as the crowning virtue of the Mexicans.

I had begun to think more about time on the plane to New Orleans, where I expected to meet some cousins who had invited me to stay with them. Arriving late at Houston, Texas, I was delayed by a suspicious virago at the customs who rummaged through the contents of my bags, peeping into shirts and shorts with more than feminine curiosity, so that I missed my connection and had to spend the night in a frowzy hotel. Some club or masonic lodge had been celebrating, for the corridors were infested with elderly drunks in false noses and ludicrous hats being helped to bed by hefty black attendants. Owing to the female customs officer's upheaval I had an arduous search for my toothbrush before retiring. I was dozing off when I heard a rap at my door. Drowsily I fumbled for the light-switch while the rapping continued. 'Say, mister, would you like a couple of nice girls?' the night porter asked me. 'I'd prefer a kinkajou,' I answered. 'Leave me alone. I'm sleepy.'

Our take-off next morning was further delayed by a senile Mexican who had lost his pearl tie-pin. He created such a fuss about it that I wondered how he would have behaved in my predicament at Chalma. My first good meal in many months – good even by Parisian standards – was enjoyed to the last mouthful in New Orleans. Soft shell crab and fresh trout from Lake Pontchartrain delicately broiled in butter, crisp French bread with Brie, accompanied by cool dry Chablis – ah, this was the acme of succulence after Mexican *moles* and *frijoles*. In spite of the steamy heat I ate with relish. At that moment New Orleans provided just the right note of Latinity I was looking for. Though most of the old French quarter had been destroyed by fire, a few trellised balconies on sophisticated houses remained like 1830 settings for the Opéra Comique.

My hearty appetite surprised my cousin Rothwell and his wife, Mary, who was suffering from slight concussion as the result of a plane accident but felt all the better for a round of gin slings. After a leisurely luncheon we drove to their house near Covington on the edge of a bayou. The trees were festooned with Spanish moss like cobwebs of monstrous spiders dangling over the sluggish water, where rotting logs might be sleeping alligators. Iridescent in the late afternoon, the bayou seemed the liquefaction of decadence. Queer squawking birds cruised about lazily in the clammy air, frogs croaked among the reeds, mastodonic beetles swarmed. It was a hypnotic scene, a film that was over-exposed. The low-lying timbered house had recently been flooded and it oozed an aromatic dampness: the window netting was thick with moths and clustering insects. 'Pure Poe!' I exclaimed.

I had the sensation of floating on an antiquated barge and I wondered what had induced my cousins, a couple still young, to settle in this isolated district. They had the charm of carefree people who let nothing disturb them. Their gaiety from morning to night was enviable. Everything tickled their mirth, especially the gramophone record of a song called 'Open the door, Richard', which they played again and again. The abdominal voice of a Negress repeating 'Open that door and let me in!' reduced them to fits of helpless laughter. The weather was tropically sticky and at intervals throughout the day they would dive into the pool. Theirs was truly a relaxed existence. Rothwell possessed a tung-tree plantation in one of the few regions of the United States where these Chinese trees could flourish. Apart from gathering the nuts, which produced an oil for varnishing woodwork used mainly on aircraft, the plantation required a minimum of care. Driving for miles on dirt roads over swamp to Nut Ridge Farm in Mississippi, I felt at the back of beyond.

Unlike most Americans, Rothwell and Mary were self-sufficient and indifferent to society. If they invited neighbours for drinks it was entirely for my sake. The neighbours, who lived twenty or thirty miles away, were mostly of French extraction and hankered after France. I spent more time with them than with my hosts. Owing to her concussion Mary had to rest a good deal and Rothwell kept her company: they were considerate in leaving me to read and write without interruption except from thunderstorms, which made a prodigious noise. One evening I attended a performance of *Richard III* by the seminarists of St Joseph's Benedictine Abbey. The scenery and costumes were designed with ingenious economy by Father Gregory de Witt, who had also painted a fresco of the Last Supper in the refectory, and the actors recited their roles with Elizabethan gusto. While we were enjoying the beauty of the language, a terrible stench invaded the hall. A skunk was protesting against Shakespeare. The audience dispersed and when I returned to the bayou near Covington I heard the gramophone still playing 'Open the door, Richard', as if to ventilate that hall.

Flashes of summer lightning made the moss-dripping trees resemble rows of gibbets. The owls were hooting like amorous cats. The grass was full of creeping, crawling creatures one sensed without seeing. Black magic was in the air. Surely witches were abroad. But inside the house my cousins were laughing over gin slings, such a happy couple, overflowing with good nature! This was like a Victorian interlude before returning to the twentieth-century.

Chicago and New York were no cooler than New Orleans. In a

temperature averaging ninety degrees I tried to peddle my writing to American publishers and I was forced to realize that I was a nonentity from their point of view. They invited me to their clubs to discuss the popularity of other English writers now quite forgotten.

Even in mid-July I found old acquaintances in New York, but they were not typical New Yorkers. Alan Priest, the curator of Chinese art at the Metropolitan Museum (which Berenson dubbed the Necropolitan), was a Bostonian who liked to visualize himself as a Chinese mandarin. 'Only Bostonians can understand Bostonians and thoroughly sympathize with the inconsequences of the Boston mind,' as Henry Adams wrote. In Peking Priest used to wear priestly Chinese robes. As he had a crimson face with russet hair *en brosse* the effect was striking. He was one of the very few non-Chinese who could warble *K'un-ch'ü* in falsetto with little fat Fu, the Manchu mentor of many language students. At the Metropolitan Museum he had long been an institution, but I could see that he inspired terror in his colleagues. When I called on him there he seemed out of humour, for he gave his waste-paper basket a fierce kick before greeting me in a tone to which I was not accustomed. Did he suspect that I had come to beg a favour, another loose Englishman looking for a job? What was I doing in New York? His suspicions allayed, he showed me the Chinese exhibits. They were less interesting than those in Kansas City and their arrangement was certainly inferior. Several of the archaic bronzes from Tuan Fang's famous collection had proved to be fakes and had been consigned to the basement. Since Tuan Fang had been accused of abusing his position as viceroy to obtain these treasures and had been beheaded during the revolution – I had seen a photograph of his head on a table surrounded by them – this seemed a cruel irony.

Alan Priest was an organizer rather than a scholar, and he had developed a technique for coping with opulent old ladies which won my admiration. He quizzed and bullied them and they adored it. The rich dames bequeathed their heirlooms to the museum for love of Alan. They saw him as a Lo-han, though nobody could have been less Chinese in outlook and manner. The Chinese of my generation believed that to lose one's temper was to shorten one's span of life. Alan lost his temper frequently, and he enjoyed doing so. His talent for organization was such that he had piloted a party of prominent American hostesses to the Buddhist temples of Wu T'ai Shan in the hills of northern Shansi at a time when roving bandits were still at large – an excursion which inspired Allan Marquand to write his novel *Ming Yellow*. No bandits attacked the society pilgrims: if they had, they would probably have been vanquished, for American hostesses are indomitable. Orange or grapefruit juice and cereals were provided for copious breakfasts together with a choice of Chesterfields or Lucky Strikes, and everything proceeded without a hitch as if it was an excursion in the Adirondacks.

In Peking Alan Priest had rented a dreamy house on the moat by the Forbidden City where he played non-stop records of *Pelléas and Mélisande*, an opera of which he never wearied, and the music seemed to float up from the water lilies below the veranda. There he served cocktails among sumptuous Chinese brocades and embroideries – *k'o-ssǔ* of dragons and phoenixes, birds and flowers, clouds and waves, in fine silk and gold thread – the superior precursors of those produced in Europe. He understood textiles better than human beings.

That incident with the paper basket made me ponder. It warned me to keep my distance. I might be welcome as a fleeting visitor, but would I have been so as an American resident? There was a surfeit of politics in the museum world. Had not Henry Adams, a classical scion of Boston, declared that 'politics, as a practice, whatever its professions, had always been the systematic organization of hatreds, and Massachusetts politics had been as harsh as the climate. The chief charm of New England was harshness and contrasts and extremes of sensibility – a cold that froze the blood, and a heat that boiled it – so that the pleasure of hating – one's self if no better victim offered – was not its rarest amusement.' Alan Priest indulged in the pleasure of hating with a virulence worthy of medieval Florentines. If he loved himself in

252

Peking, he appeared to hate himself and others in New York. Sometimes we had sessions of sympathetic hatred. He made one aware of the aesthetes' struggle with a hostile universe. His few joys were related to a China that was in swift disintegration. Mine were fortunately deflected and enhanced by Italy.

Others I met in New York and saw more of in the following years were old friends from Eton, Oxford and Paris: James Stern, Wystan Auden and Pavel Tchelitchev. New York was their temporary anchorage. Auden had become acclimatized, but in spite of certain Americanisms, which he pronounced as if they were in inverted commas, I considered him a product of cultured Oxford; he was a born teacher as well as a poet, and his research work into word combinations kept him boyish under a premature network of wrinkles. He captured live images in mid-air, entranced by phenomena that irritated Evelyn Waugh – by the racy slang, the garrulous cab drivers, the jets of steam in the streets, receptive to ideas, generous in reading his latest poem aloud, diffident about his celebrity. He had remained true to his poetic self though querulous youngsters might carp at what they called his betrayal of the Marxist attitude.

James Stern was more *dépaysé*, and he made me realize that I might become a fish out of water if I stayed on. He had written some of the best English short stories of his generation but he was too fastidious for a sensation-seeking public and perhaps too bitter. His experience had been varied, for he had travelled in Africa and Hawaii, he had visited unemployed coal-miners in Wales and Derbyshire, and the ruins of Germany just after the war – his book *The Hidden Damage* is a masterpiece of tragic irony and compassion. He had been brought up by fox-hunting parents in Ireland but he had broken away from that horsy world whose limitations he understood thoroughly. Edwardian parents expected their children to conform, and it cannot have been easy for him to leap over the hedges and ditches of the Irish countryside into the field of letters. His handsome features were signed with the strain of his divided allegiance. Like Somerset Maugham he could make you see persons and places in primitive isolation, but he penetrated the loneliness and frustration of individuals more deeply than Maugham, without that slick artifice which makes you exclaim 'How clever!' and forget them. The reverse of facile, he had to wrestle with his material. He and his wife Tania seemed more isolated in New York than other Europeans.

Pavel Tchelitchev had lived with and among Americans since I met him in the twenties, and an American, Gertrude Stein, had been his chief sponsor in Paris. He was the typical dramatic Russian *émigré* who never pierced the surface of the soil where he had pitched his tent. America suited him as well as any other country, for he had plenty of friends and admirers in the so-called art world. If Gertrude Stein had helped to launch him, Edith Sitwell had bolstered his belief in his own genius. He told me that he had a trunkload of letters from her, and that these were his dearest possession. I suppose each acted as a stimulus on the other. Tchelitchev needed a poet as Edith Sitwell needed a painter, and their friendship was fruitful to both. But as La Rochefoucauld observed: 'We are more prepared to love those who hate us than those who love us more than we would wish.' And perhaps Edith loved him more than he would wish. With Gertrude Stein, who preferred her own sex, he felt safer, though he was often incensed by her rough and ready criticism of his work. Edith was content to admire and feed him with fresh images.

A gifted draughtsman with a skilful technique, he was always searching and twisting in different directions, as if he were afraid of dropping behind the times. His designs for scenery, especially for *Ode* and *Ondine*, had been memorably beautiful, yet he deliberately turned his back on this branch of his talent. He would also have been a splendid illustrator of books. But ambition impelled him to paint in oils, and his canvases were a succession of cerebral experiments, often interesting, strange, suggestive, but seldom to my eye completely realized. If we bear in mind the perspective drawings of Paolo Uccello such as the veined and dissected chalice in the Uffizi, or the sixteenth-century *Bizarie* of Gio. Battista Bracelli, there was nothing arrestingly novel in his treatment of these inventions. His transparent skulls and foetuses floating like jellyfish reeked of Central European Expressionism.

In Edith Sitwell he had found his ideal model. Her alabaster features, especially the long thin nose and green-gold hair, were a benison to any portrait painter, and she posed for him with patient sympathy, amused and startled by the pirouettings of his Slav temperament. She was the answer to his prayer for a 'new vision', new words and colours and forms; and even when his English was rudimentary he was convinced that he understood her better than anyone else. When he was not painting Edith he went through dark patches of doubt and depression which left their mark on his careworn features. Though Gertrude Stein changed her mind about his work, Edith Sitwell believed steadfastly in his greatness and took pains to organize his first exhibition in London and procure commissions for him. Edith saw him with the eyes of a poet.

Had he given rein to his natural talent instead of trying to force it for the sake of modernity he might have become a great painter. No more than a writer should a painter be too preoccupied with his 'greatness'. Let him concentrate on his work and 'greatness' will look after itself. In his effort to evoke 'the unattainable, the beyond', Tchelitchev despised the French Impressionists as photographers, but while he inveighed against them and the preposterous prices they fetched now that they were dead, I recalled Monet who had lived entirely for his work, 'an unceasing production, and an almost unvarying degree of excellence', as George Moore wrote, from sunrise to sunset, summer and winter, until he was eighty-two and his eyesight failed him. Sacha Guitry has related how he called on him and found him sitting alone before his palette in his studio. In deep distress he groaned: 'I can no longer see yellow!'

Monet had known poverty, indifference and contempt: until the age of forty-seven he said he had never sold a picture for more than fifty francs, yet he was free from bitterness. His flowers consoled him. Even when he became affluent his garden was his only luxury. He did not try consciously to suggest 'the unattainable, the beyond', but he suggested it sometimes without apparent effort.

Edith Sitwell never quite forgave my failure to appreciate the genius of Tchelitchev. In 1948 she came to New York with Sir Osbert for the first of a series of joint readings and lecture tours, and it was gratifying to see genuine originality recognized wherever they went. No literary brother and sister of equal distinction had lectured in such a manner before. Apart from their writings, they made a tremendous impression as personalities, and they were sufficiently young in spirit to relish the ovations that greeted them. Their voices, so full of colour and charm, were raised in the cause of pure art, and those who prate about 'social awareness' and insist that our social upheavals should be the substance of poetry, are the enemies of art. The peevish hypocrites who resent the publicity given only too seldom to writers of real merit are neurotically eager to demonstrate, usually in protest, on public platforms. These receive more publicity than the Sitwells ever did, and they go to indecent lengths to obtain it.

The Sitwells were welcomed in America as few poets had been in England. Though Edith was already fragile she put every ounce of energy into her recitals. Her Gothic appearance, her capes and gowns and turbans, her exquisite hands with huge aquamarines on the tapering fingers, fascinated the eye as her voice fascinated the ear. After the years of retirement at Renishaw it was physically fatiguing to shake so many hands and answer so many questions, yet I had never seen her look so happy. The only flaw was that all this popular acclaim aggrieved Tchelitchev. He bore writers a grudge since he imagined that words came easily, whereas the painter had a constant struggle with his medium. His picture 'Hide and Seek' in the Museum of Modern Art seemed to me to express this struggle: it reduced Edith to silence when he expected a paean of praise. Tchelitchev was hurt and showed it. Yet silence can be a greater compliment than gush. 'Don't spoil me!' said Edith to a woman who told her that she had 'read one of her books'. People who make this remark to authors suppose they are conferring a special honour.

Remembering the slights and insults Edith and Osbert had suffered when we were all younger, I rejoiced at their trans-atlantic triumph. It was noticeable that American critics were free from the perverted class prejudice of their English col-leagues. There seemed to be an Anglophil wave, on the crest of which Stuart Preston and George Dix were pre-eminent. They had been rivals in the affections of London hostesses during the war, and this gentle rivalry persisted among the hostesses of New York. As an art critic on the *New York Times*, Stuart was con-sulted about pictures and he cultivated the younger painters, most of whom were more agreeable than their productions, which had to be seen through a metaphysical mist to be understood. On our visits to the modern galleries that were cropping up like mush-rooms I was disarmed by his kindly tolerance, his readiness to detect virtues in what were mere daubs to me. No wonder the painters loved him.

My older friend Carl Van Vechten had given up writing for photography. Though his novels had enjoyed a vogue in the 1920s, he belonged to the 1890s. He should have been a wasp-waisted dandy, but he was big and burly with porcelain eyes of deceptive innocence. An eclectic dilettante with a flair for originality in literature, he was among the first to praise Faulkner and introduce Ronald Firbank to American readers; above all he was a devotee of Gertrude Stein. Though sensitive Negroes distrusted him on account of *Nigger Heaven*, he did more than anyone else to promote their arts. He appreciated them without condescension but with too hungry a curiosity, so that some felt that they were being exploited. Obsessed with every form of Negro self-expression, he was too prone to interpret their talent as genius. He pressed on me many a Negro novel whose chief merit was its musical rhythm and strong local colour. Recently he had returned from Haiti. 'You must go there immediately,' he said. 'It is the only place in the world where you will find a modern renaissance. It is a paradise of poets and painters. The painters are superb, they cannot help painting beautifully. Black rhythm is transformed in glorious masses of colour.'

'But I've just been to Mexico. There they also talk of a painter's renaissance. I confess I was disillusioned.'

'I promise you that in Haiti you will find the genuine article. It is a land of magical adventure.'

His apartment was a highly personal bazaar. There were cats by Steinlen, for he was a great cat lover, a bust of Paul Robeson by Epstein, a self portrait by De Chirico when young, and a whimsical jumble of folk art and Mexican toys. His photography was more than a hobby: it was a therapeutic occupation. The examples he showed me were quite eloquent. There was Reggie Turner chuckling against a background of hydrangeas, and a series of portraits of Gertrude Stein, each more monumental than the last. The best of his photographs recorded her opera *Four Saints*, for which Virgil Thomson composed the music. It had been performed by a coloured cast, thus emphasizing the link between Carl and the author of *Melanctha*, the story of a Negress, which Gertrude had never excelled.

Carl invited me to pose for him, but I am not photogenic and he never showed me the results. He who used to sit up late carousing in Harlem nightclubs drank scarcely at all these days. He had become a quieter person under the influence of photography. Perhaps this was also due to his wife Fania Marinoff, one of those actresses who act better off the stage than on it. Their life together had been a succession of storms and reconciliations, which might account for his mask of impassivity. They took me to dine at the Woman's Exchange, a restaurant buzzing with elderly ladies. The genteel waitresses were most attentive to him and Fania, who were evidently favoured clients, so different from the others. As Fania sipped her coffee between mouthfuls of chicken salad I was amused to remember wilder occasions when she had screamed and Carl had barked like a bulldog, distributing sharp bites as if he had caught rabies. Now he toddled soberly to bed at nine-thirty.

❧ 15 ❧

Instead of proceeding to Haiti I went to Boston, since my mother's closest friend, Florence Crane, had invited me to Castle Hill near Ipswich on the 'North Shore' (the Massachusetts coast north of Boston), a tranquil summer resort. Florence was a chauvinistic Chicagoan. Her husband had bought this handsome estate of three hundred acres without consulting her, and he had commissioned a leading Bostonian architect to build the mansion on a panoramic hillside at vast expense. When he took her to see it her silence was disconcerting. 'Well,' he asked nervously, 'what do you think of the place?' 'I don't like one thing about it,' she replied. So the house was demolished and a more classical residence of pink brick imported from Holland was built farther up the hill by David Adler, the doyen of Chicago architects. It was splendidly furnished in Queen Anne style, seven of the fifty-two rooms with panelling from Hogarth's London house, and ancestral portraits by Lely, Dance and Joseph Wright of Derby adorned the walls. The sporting and marine paintings interested me less, but I coveted Zoffany's portrait of Lunardi the Balloonist at Windsor. Sumptuous editions of the classics gleamed on the shelves of the library transported from Essex House. From the terrace where exquisite humming-birds sipped the tiger lilies a wide grass mall flanked by high hedges and Venetian statues at regular intervals rolled up and down to the sea. No hunting was allowed on the estate, and hundreds of deer sought shelter in the park.

Mrs Crane had lived alone here since her widowhood. Though extremely hospitable she had strong prejudices. Having entertained some titled Englishwomen during the war who had never

259

troubled to thank her, she had a poor opinion of our manners. However, she liked her English maid and butler. 'What about me?' I asked. 'You're American,' she replied. Of all Americans, the Bostonians were the most English in manner and intonation and they lived more soberly than the denizens of other resorts, indifferent to fashion and averse from ostentation. Florence Crane had caused offence by demolishing the work of their architect Coolidge but she was so candid and lovable in her quiet way that they forgave her. She needed my protection, she remarked with a smile, as she was being courted assiduously by an elderly general who bored her to tears. I felt sorry for the venerable suitor, who was disappointed to find me always blocking his path. Florence was vexed by his showers of flowers and exorbitant gifts: she was inclined to refuse them, but I dissuaded her, for at least they gave him pleasure. She was one of the few who preferred giving to receiving.

Her daughter, known as 'little Florence' though she was taller than her mother, lived in an older house near by called Labour-in-Vaine farm. Having married a Russian of the old regime, Prince Serge Belosselsky, she had become more Slav in appearance than her husband, who bred pheasants as a hobby. The keeper of these birds was a colossal bearded moujik who spoke no English. Apart from this couple and their cherubic daughters, few of the neighbours were under seventy, but how strenuous they were, especially the widows! Mrs W. H. Moore, who had a Colonial mansion at Pride's Crossing, was eighty-nine yet she conducted us personally round her large estate, through hot-houses full of fuchsias and begonias, past lotus pools with rare Chinese goldfish and a long willow-covered walk to the sea. She had planted the elms herself in 1900. Her love of Chinese art was as strong as ever.

Mrs Endicott, who lived at Danvers, was slightly younger, but her sister-in-law Mrs Carnegie was at least ninety: in her youth she had been the wife of Joseph Chamberlain and had married Canon Carnegie of Westminster after his death. Tall as a grenadier, she was so uncompromisingly British that she even maintained the superiority of English cooking to that of Massachusetts. 'And the English diet is far more wholesome,' she said. 'Here the food is too rich and liverish – waffles and maple syrup at breakfast! I'm sure most people die of indigestion.' No wonder she had kept her slim figure. Like the old residences of Salem and Newburyport, the Endicott house had been furnished by its owners instead of by interior decorators, and it had a mellow long lived-in air, with porcelain brought from the Far East in pre-Treaty Port days and other relics of early trade with Cathay, Chinese and Empire wall-papers and eighteenth-century furniture made in Salem: the rooms were redolent of maritime adventure. The garden contained a graceful summer pavilion by Samuel McIntyre, who had built several neo-classical houses in Salem in the 1780s.

These ladies were devoted gardeners, and I fancied it must be their passion for horticulture that kept them so young and rosy-cheeked without the aid of cosmetics. In reality it was due to their puritan upbringing. Having sublimated or eliminated what is now generically called sex, they had settled down to cultivate 'gracious living'. The Garden Club was a perennial resource, and at one of its meetings I was privileged to attend Mrs Ellery Sedgwick delivered an erudite lecture on the wild flowers and exotic plants which had sprung up among the ruins of the London docks, their seeds wafted from distant lands and continents. Another lady discoursed with emotion on the tea gardens of India and Kashmir. Flower nurseries put other nurseries in the shade.

When my hostess invited me to contribute to the Ladies' Reading Circle I proposed to read a story from *Glue and Lacquer*, translated from the Chinese. Since it had amused Mrs Berenson, who had been brought up as a Quaker, I thought the ground was safe. The elegance of its style, moreover, mitigated its naïve sensuality. But Florence, who knew the ladies better than I did, took the precaution of scanning it in advance and she vetoed the very idea. So I read them a chapter from my memoirs which mentioned the beautiful Francesca Braggiotti who had married a

Bostonian patrician, John Lodge, who became Ambassador to Spain. 'Mr Sedgwick should publish it in *The Atlantic Monthly*,' said one of the ladies. But Mr Sedgwick had retired from the editorship of that journal and his successor was not interested.

Of the many gardens I saw in the vicinity it was hard to decide which was the most alluring. Ellery Sedgwick's tree peonies, Chinese roses and day lilies were peculiarly fragrant, but so was the Crowninshield rose garden at Peaches Point, Marblehead, where the sailing ships took one back to the nineteenth century. Frederick Bartlett's sphinxes with periwigged heads framed in orange and vermilion foliage, his Empire statues and gay gazebo at White Hall, Beverley, also had its charm to which the catalpas, yuccas and smoke trees contributed. He had formed a unique collection of early nineteenth-century hats and parasols. The furniture was mostly Biedermeier with neo-Classical obelisks and medallions by Thorvaldsen. Venetian blackamoors and chandeliers were arranged to harmonize with Chinese landscapes and a Kanō screen. But Bartlett's superb collection of French Impressionists had been presented to the Chicago Art Institute in memory of his first wife. A Scottish butler wearing a tartan kilt piped the guests in to dinner, since when I have thought bagpipes an excellent appetizer.

Even on the North Shore the temperature stood around ninety, but the sea was too cold for leisurely swimming and green-head flies stung me viciously when I dashed for my towel. Boston was broiling. Most of the day was spent in the museum, which contained some of the finest Chinese paintings to be seen anywhere, and the Winthrop collection in the Fogg Museum at Harvard was of superlative quality. Paintings were usually shown to greater advantage in American museums and collections, for they were cleaned and cared for and hung with a discrimination we have at last begun to emulate. Outside China and Formosa the best art of Old Cathay was to be seen in America, and there was a continuous emigration of masterpieces from Europe.

This was the first of many post-war visits to America which strengthened my ties with relations and friends there. But

Florence Crane's circle at Castle Hill and my mother's friends in Chicago were fading fast. They represented a style, a standard, a way of living from which our present time has degenerated. It was a prolongation of the Edwardian era without its vulgarity. These gentlefolk, all born in the last century, had retired from the turmoil of the market-place to cultivate their gardens. Fastidious about their persons and formal in their manners, they offered hospitality without pomp or parvenu pretentiousness. They made me feel instantly at home.

The dearest of my former pupils and collaborators, Chen Shih-hsiang, was teaching in Berkeley, California, and I was not surprised to find that he had endeared himself to the faculty of that pleasantly situated university, not only as a ripe scholar with a remarkable command of English but as an enlightened humanist. He had adapted himself to an environment totally different from North China without any spiritual compromise. (The large Chinese colony of San Francisco consisted mostly of southerners, who are as unlike northerners as Sicilians are unlike Piedmontese.) Having realized his vocation, to interpret Chinese culture and keep it alive when its foundations were threatened from within, Shih-hsiang had overcome his homesickness. In 1948 his luminous study and English translation of Lu Chi's *Essay on Literature* was published for the semi-centennial anniversary of Peking University under the title *Literature as Light against Darkness*.

Lu Chi had composed this essay in poetical form in A.D. 300 – three years before his execution in a period of convulsion, yet, as Chen wrote, 'it set up new standards of value for creative literature'. Consciously or not, Chen must have discerned a parallel between Lu Chi's predicament and his own. Lu Chi remained a Confucianist when his contemporaries were turning towards Taoism and Buddhism: he continued to believe in the humanities. Chen's faith in literature 'as light against darkness' gave him courage when he was uncertain as to whether he should go home or stay in California. I urged him to stay: in Berkeley he could keep the torch of Chinese culture burning. His translation of Lu Chi's essay seemed to me more valuable than the ephemeral polemics about China. Here was criticism inspired, as he wrote, 'by the contemplation of creation at a sublime hour of detachment from the world's chaos and gloom'. The wisdom it embodied was ancient, and it had become a classic often quoted and paraphrased in China, hence it was in danger of being wiped out by the Communists. Chen toiled at the revision of his translation, seeking the utmost degree of expression for every sentence. To recapture the thought and imagery of a man writing in A.D. 300 and reconcile medieval Chinese with modern English was an exacting venture, and I think it was crowned with success. I was often consulted about some elusive shade of meaning.

After the great speedways with their avalanche of traffic, the sprawl of Oakland with as many garages as houses of similar type, and the forests of ugly poles carrying utility wires, Chen's wooden house was a cloistral refuge. But San Francisco was the most diversified and bracing of American cities, tolerably warm in the daytime and cool at night. Owing to the distances to be traversed, a car was a necessity, and Chen had become an accomplished motorist. He thought nothing of driving for hundreds of miles and, thanks to the freeway, most of the distance could be covered at sixty miles an hour. He often took me to the Chinatown, which recalled old Hong Kong with its ideographic advertisements and bazaar-like emporiums so scintillating at night. The Chinese settlers had transformed this part of the city and made it their own, including a theatre free from alien influence. Though the theatre was Cantonese, its traditions were similar to those of Peking; the scenery was more realistic but the costumes, with their wealth of embroidery, spangles and plumes, were equally sumptuous. The restaurants teemed with prosperous gourmets enjoying their native delicacies.

Most of the visitors from China I met with Chen were alarmed by the drift of events at home. The National Government had become foolishly repressive, so that the people were ready to welcome any change. Large American-trained regiments fully equipped, having been divided among the armies of corrupt and inefficient provincial generals, were defecting to the cannier Communists, who provided them with a positive ideology. Inflation was so rampant that scholars who lived on modest salaries were the hardest hit. The victory over Japan was turning into defeat.

Flaubert once wrote that 'the only way not to be unhappy is to shut yourself up in art, and count everything else as nothing'. The art of translation is more difficult and perhaps more exacting than original composition, and it became Chen's chief solace until he found an ideal wife. Together we tackled *T'ao Hua Shan* ('The Peach-blossom Fan'), a long classical drama which also had a bearing on recent history since it dealt with the decline of the Ming dynasty. The result gathers dust in my cupboard, but I do not regret our efforts, for in spite of *longueurs* it is one of the finest Chinese dramas after *P'i-pa Chi* ('The Story of the Guitar'), of which there are several European versions. We often worked on the grassy slope of the university campus where thrushes hopped about pecking for worms and squirrels came up to peer at us; or at Carmel, where we sat with our books on the beach among driftwood like abstract sculpture, long ropes of seaweed and stranded jellyfish. Occasionally we were interrupted by the visiting professors from China who would call on Chen and remain talking for six hours at a stretch, as in Peking. These were scholars who questioned authority but respected tradition, and I often wonder if they have been brainwashed since. They tried to persuade Chen to return. The temptation was great but he resisted it.

In the mornings I wrote *Prince Isidore*, a Neapolitan fantasy based on Dumas *père's* account of the evil eye in *Le Corricolo*. While writing it, in a mood half nostalgic, half ironical, I had a premonition that I would write more about Naples in future. Conversing with Chen's compatriots, I realized that I could never return to the halcyon life I had led in Peking before the war, at any rate not in my present incarnation.

'Absence weakens ordinary passions, but inflames great ones, as the wind extinguishes a candle, but fans a fire' – and absence had inflamed my passion for Italy. There the Muses eternally young awaited me. Much as I appreciated American dynamism, I felt at a loose end among the Titans of American technology. Unduly susceptible to physical surroundings, I was horrified by the implications as well as the sheer ugliness of a sprawling city like Los Angeles, which seemed to be made for machines rather than for men. The implications were of spiritual and cultural starvation. Engineers were replacing architects, and new jungles of metal and concrete would continue to devour the world's surface, a nightmare prospect. Viewed from above, New York was a strident symphony of soaring towers, but from the street the effect was generally impersonal and drab: the very skyscrapers seemed vacant-minded when I compared them to the buildings of Florence, the miracle of Venice, the magnificence of Rome, the voluptuousness of Naples, and countless other Italian cities comparatively small but noble in conception, the harmonious creations of individual genius. I was still as homesick for cypresses as in my schooldays. Ruskin would have understood this for he had written: 'The man who possessed not, among the many spirits of the woods, the special spirit of the cypress, assuredly could not spiritually paint the country of the hill-village, the belfry, the gold-white simple walls, the pure and remote sky pricked with delicate and upright forms on the hill-edge, the country of soft dust and of old colours, which is Italy.'

Florence remained a fortress of beauty that did not overwhelm the beholder. Time had not marred its essentials, not yet . . .

So electric was the air of New York that I could seldom obtain my normal quota of sleep. I was charged with a nervous battery that prevented me from relaxing. The crystallized fireworks of Broadway, the illuminated sky-signs flickering and rotating, tempted me to wander among the milling crowds who never seemed to tire in their quest for communal togetherness, yet I felt as alone as the solitary drinkers who sat screwed to their glasses, seeking self-oblivion in alcoholic stupor. At night New York wears all its jewellery. Impossible to concentrate on a book with this extraordinary spectacle round the corner, the rampaging radio next door; and the wailing of fire engines was so frequent that one was wakened almost as soon as one dozed off. How authors contrived to write amid so many distractions puzzled me, yet several assured me that they could work better in New York than elsewhere. They must have cut off the telephone, whose persistent note seemed to dominate every building. Cocteau's play *La Voix Humaine* belonged more to New York than to Paris. People communicated more by telephone than in proximity. Wherever I went I caught snatches of excited monologues. But when I tried to telephone I had to repeat the number, for though my articulation was clear my accent bewildered the operators, who suspected me of mocking them.

The dependence on mechanical contrivances depressed me, and I dreaded the possibility of being marooned in a skyscraper. It was a relief to climb the stairs of a private house, and to enter a sitting-room without abstractions on the walls.

The vogue of abstract painting had reached its apogee. Almost everybody's aunt, and many a spinster who would have been wiser to stick to her embroidery, was 'going abstract'. Children were encouraged to do likewise with painting materials, perverted by schoolmistresses who scolded them if they strayed towards naturalism, though their instincts were to depict something seen and known, a pussycat or a steamer. Monkeys at the zoo were given brushes and paint to vie with the *avant-garde*. On a side-walk in Greenwich Village an enterprising girl demonstrated a device for producing your own abstracts with the slogan 'You too can be a Picasso'. You applied the paint to a sheet of paper and she pressed a switch. The paper revolved and scattered the paint in the manner of Pollock rather than of Picasso, and all for fifty cents. It might be fun, but one shuddered at the contingency of its mass production. Watching this trend towards abstraction, it became conceivable that mankind might outgrow its need for art. Fortunately a spirit of revolt was endemic in artists, who were likely to plump for the figurative if only from boredom. But I could appreciate the convenience of abstract painting for interior decorators, since serious art is rarely adaptable to a modish colour scheme. Between photographers and interior decorators the role of the serious artist had been reduced.

I discerned a parallel between New York publishers and interior decorators. I could no more adapt myself to the demands of the former than figurative artists to those of the latter. In fact I had only written letters with an eye on the reader. No doubt this was a mistake but I could not help it. I felt guilty of wasting the time of my literary agents, as if I had been weighed in the balance and found wanting. I even began to doubt if I should write at all, for I had ceased to recognize myself. 'Neither fish nor flesh, nor good red herring,' I muttered. Yet in London I had never failed to find a publisher.

After a while my benevolent uncle agreed that it might be awkward to emigrate at my age, as Florence was bound to be my ultimate home. My parents and my worldly property, all my deepest interests were there. California could not rejuvenate me as it had rejuvenated my uncle. It made me feel like one of the acrobats in *Les Forains*, packing up to move elsewhere after trying to entertain a scanty audience.

Once off the ground at La Guardia airport, I succumbed to a delayed reaction from the tension of New York, prolonged by the incessant announcements of flight after flight. Fatigue crept like a paralysis through my veins.

On my way home I stopped in the middle of Ireland, since Michael and Anne Rosse had invited me to Birr. Thanks to these beloved friends, I see it always through a mist of poetry, for they have made it a castle of flowers, a garden within and without. Though the castle foundations and keep are medieval the present gothicized structure dates from the 1620s, its severity softened by so many levels of green terraces and sloping banks, so many combinations of colours and such varied fragrance that the nose is as enchanted as the eye, and the plash of a waterfall soothes the ear. Each view has its singularity: the castle seen from the lake, the river from the park, the river garden across a suspension

bridge built before 1824, with St Brendan's well on one side of
the waterfall and a tunnel of bamboos on the other. And what an
abundance of trees indigenous and exotic! Many had been
planted in the eighteenth century, but they had been multiplied
by Michael and Anne. Besides regal specimens of oak, ash, beech,
copper beech, magnolias and yews, gnarled Japanese cherries
flourished as in Kyoto; there was a Himalayan juniper with a
spread of over forty feet and a gorgeous ginkgo, the maidenhair
tree that used to be held sacred in China where it flourished near
temples. This 'living fossil', the sole survivor of prehistoric
plants, had beautiful fan-shaped leaves which evoked the
vegetation of Eden.

There was also a rock garden, and some distance from the
castle a formal garden was separated from the park by a stone
wall with a wrought-iron gate: this contained intricate box
parterres and alleys of hornbeam based on a seventeenth-century
design. But Mr Lanning Roper and other experts have described
the botanical wonders of Birr in worthy detail.

Most singular in the midst of the park were the crenellated
walls of an observatory built in the 1840s by the 3rd Earl of
Rosse, one of the leading astronomers of the nineteenth century.
This had contained the largest reflecting telescope in the world
until 1917. The Earl had been experimenting with telescopes
since 1827, and all the machinery and instruments were made to
his order by the workmen on the estate. A contemporary painting
portrays the astronomer in top hat and tails climbing a ladder to
the observation platform of his enormous telescope, dwarfed by
its immensity. The vast wooden tube hooped with iron (56 feet
long and 7 feet wide) still stands between the two walls like
Gothic battlements, but the telescope was dismantled and the
speculum removed in 1914 to the Science Museum in London.

Like other Irish castles Birr has survived many turbulent
episodes, including fires and sieges which left cannonball scars: it
was restored during the eighteenth century by Michael's ancestors
but the Gothic style prevails, so delicate in the saloon and
dining-room as to suggest a Nordic rococo. The town nestling

outside the castle walls – once known as Parsonstown, so much it owed to Michael's family – was neat and unspoilt; the cosy houses had an early Victorian gentility. The bogs beyond it provided that peat which fills the air with musty incense and flavours Irish whisky. All this was a restful contrast to New York.

A radiant aureole surrounded Anne, who had come to meet me at Shannon airport. It was an aureole of happy fulfilment. Lightness and grace and vitality – how she and her children shone apart from the crowd waiting behind the barrier! Little William and Martin had such beautiful manners that for once I wished I had children of my own, but the wish faded when I considered that they might inherit my features. I read poems to them and they were an ideal audience. Soon they were joined by their half-brother Tony Armstrong-Jones: fresh from Eton, he was already an accomplished young man of the world with fine eyes full of promise.

On Friday mornings the whole floor of the entrance hall was carpeted with flowers which Anne arranged for the vases all over the house, opulent harmonies of colour and form, and as she separated the lilies from the ferns and blended them in graceful clusters her voice trilled like a lark. She had a way with flowers and they had a way with her. This was extended to her decoration of the rooms, of the dinner-table. Her personal touch with *objets d'art* never allowed them to congeal as in a museum.

From Birr we drove to many romantic houses which had survived 'the troubles' of patriotism run amok – to Abbey Leix, the home of Michael's mother and stepfather, with an Italianate garden, Adam ceilings, and architectural panels by Pannini to give a foretaste of Italy; to Belvedere at Tullamore, packed with precious bibelots and historic silver (what rich accumulations of heirlooms these houses possessed, but would the younger generation cherish them as Michael and Anne did?); to Shelton Abbey near Arklow, a gem of Strawberry Hill Gothic soon to be destroyed by dry rot; and to such sinister ruins as those of Leap, which truly sent cold shivers up one's spine. The stone hedge country, Galway with its purple mountains and black oxen, the farmland and cattle-fairs exactly as depicted by Jack Yeats, the deep gorge like a Norwegian fjord near Leenane, all that I saw of the country had a penetrating quality of romance, yet nearly all the people I met seemed to live for sport – hunting, shooting and fishing. This had not always been so, for the Irish or Anglo-Irish had been discriminating collectors of painting in the past as well as builders and gardeners on a lavish scale. Dublin's National Gallery contained rare Tuscan Primitives as well as masterpieces of the seventeenth and eighteenth centuries, but it was invariably empty except for its genial director George Furlong, who was too sociable to enjoy his comparative isolation. For me it was a luxury to see pictures without a mob. Of a lusciously Arcadian Poussin, 'The Marriage of Thetis and Peleus', Shane Leslie had told me that it had been relegated to an attic as indecent, and I wondered how many attics in Ireland concealed similar indecencies.

Saturated in George Moore's Irish writings during adolescence, I became aware that the easy informality of Dublin life continued almost unchanged though in a minor key, since there were few survivors of the original Celtic Movement. I had always loved Yeats but I had to admit that George Moore's anecdotes about Lady Gregory and Synge and his other collaborators were more instructive and amusing than their literary creations, which I had conned when I should have been studying Virgil at Eton. They had followed a precocious predilection for the Nineties, but in spite of their racy idiom I had found them monotonous. Their peculiar flavour still clung to the discussions of Dubliners, always generous with their time and conversation. George Moore's crony Dr Richard Best, an affable Irish scholar now in his eighties but as rosy-cheeked and clear-eyed as I remembered G.M., revived my curiosity about Synge, A.E., and the rest of them. He evoked their eccentricities, and I have seldom been so amused by anecdotes of people who had been little more than names to me but who had played prominent roles in the literary life of Dublin. It gave me the same sensation as when I read

Aubrey's *Brief Lives*. And I was touched when he told me bashfully: 'You know, Oscar Wilde took a fancy to my pink cheeks.'

The Kildare Street Club was equally fascinating in its way, for it was the stronghold of the Anglo-Irish squires, many of whom resembled the strange antlers and trophies that adorned the front hall. These reminded one that in spite of the rapid strides in industry, Irish country life had changed little since Christine Longford satirized it in the thirties. Many a village was still 'just a few houses and a shop at a crossroads'. Houses were still tinted blue and green, and obelisks were often to be seen in the centre of squares – at Birr there was a handsome column whence the Duke of Cumberland's statue had been banished – and walls with shaggy loungers leaning against them who saluted as we passed. I was much taken with the politeness of local speech, the obliquity of the conditional mood as in: 'Would you be taking the morning train, sir?' But with Michael and Anne I saw everything *couleur de Rosse*, even under the soft rain which might have depressed me elsewhere. One of the amenities of Peking had been the punctual behaviour of its climate. There it never rained outside the rainy season, for which one was prepared. Before it started I fled to a drier zone.

After tea we would cut bamboos or saw and trim branches by St Brendan's wishing well. What delicious draughts of pure water I drank there, wishing always to return to such dear friends. And after the water and the wishes, what delicious draughts of wine! All my weariness had left me when I flew home to Italy

❀ 16 ❀

Until Naples and the Bourbons engrossed me, I spent much time lecturing and writing articles and reviews. Was the time wasted as I sometimes feared? Not altogether, for lecturing enabled me to travel, revise my opinions, modify impressions, and meet a variety of people, some of whom were discovering new aspects of English literature for themselves. I was often surprised by their choice of subject: thus in Chiavari a demure young schoolmistress was devoted to D. H. Lawrence, the daughter of a restaurant keeper in Parma had a partiality for Norman Douglas, whose *Venus in the Kitchen* had not yet been published, and together we sent him a postcard, hoping to whet his appetite with Parmesan aphrodisiacs. Professor Attilio Bertolucci of Parma was an admirer of Evelyn Waugh. In Reggio Emilia, where Communism was gaining ground and one of my hosts shocked me by lighting a cigarette in the Cathedral — I had to beg him to put it out — I found a fan of Osbert Sitwell. The most diverse English authors seemed to have votaries as unlike themselves as possible in every Italian city.

Prince Isidore was published with spirited decorations by Feliks Topolski, and as usual I had to be content with the plaudits of the few, for it lacked that earnest social consciousness for which the critics pined. I was accused of 'fine writing', a heinous offence in their eyes. When the Italian translation appeared several pages were omitted by the printers and the whole edition had to be recalled by the publisher. On seeing me he made the sign against the evil eye as if I had assumed the mantle of my hero.

My *Memoirs* had been more kindly received, but several readers discerned malice where none was intended. Cyril Connolly would not speak to me for years in consequence, and Peter Quennell became ill at a country-house party when he found the book in his bedroom: a doctor had to be summoned from afar. My account of his poetical precocity had upset him, and I was blamed for spoiling a convivial week-end. My *Memoirs* was the record of a life already buried. I never reread it, though I often revisit the past, as I am doing now.

My earliest impressions of Naples go back before the First World War and I can only recapture them when I listen to the songs I heard then – *Dicitencello Vuie, Maria, Mari, Santa Lucia Luntana, 'O Marenariello*, and others whose mere names it is a pleasure to transcribe, so potent is their evocative magic. I know they are despised by musicians, but the feeling behind them is genuine, and they could have sprung from no other soil.

For me it was the harmony of sea and city, the poetry in the air, that constituted the principal charm of Naples. Every walk was an architectural adventure. Yet in recent times, until the advent of Norman Douglas and the Sitwells, the average Englishman took Baedeker's dictum on trust: 'In historical and artistic interest this part of the Italian peninsula is singularly deficient.' Most Angry Saxons, as Berenson dubbed them, went to Naples to nurse a weak chest or recuperate from an illness. They arrived with puritan misgivings, prepared to shudder at superstition and the immorality associated with a balmy climate. They seldom ventured to explore the city. Since Gladstone had given it a bad name many authors had chosen it as a background for lurid episodes: Joseph Conrad's *Il Conde* (ironically subtitled *Vedi Napoli e poi mori*) is a notable example, the pathetic story of an elderly invalid who was driven away by the threats of a young *camorrista* after being robbed by him in the Villa Nazionale, the public park. To an older generation the fact that Oscar Wilde rejoined Lord Alfred Douglas there after his release from prison had a sinister significance. He recovered a remnant of his golden humour at Posillipo, where he put the final touches to *The Ballad of Reading Gaol*. But his euphoria was ephemeral, for Lord

Alfred soon lost patience with his poverty. Left alone, he confessed that he missed an intellectual atmosphere, and was tired of the Greek bronzes that strolled about at night. He left Naples to die in Paris.

Norman Douglas, who had a villa at Posillipo at the same period, was vexed to be mistaken for Lord Alfred. He moved to Capri, which inspired his most famous book, and it was to Capri that he returned in November 1946, where Kenneth Macpherson, a younger fellow Scot, gave him a private apartment in his Villa Tuoro. There I found him goose-stepping on the sunny terrace in obedience to his female doctor's orders. He complained of giddiness but he looked robust with his ruddy complexion and shock of yellow-white hair. We goose-stepped arm in arm as on the deck of a steamer, and he talked of mutual friends – a trifle impatiently of Nancy Cunard's 'graphomania' and the latest bee in her bonnet about the exploitation of Venetian gondoliers – she had asked him to draft an appeal to the mayor of Venice, why couldn't she mind her own business? – of Charles Prentice who had been his publisher as well as mine, a gentle scholar and sponsor of literary talent whose death we both regretted.

One could argue with Norman more freely than with other lions of his ripe age. We were able to disagree on many subjects and yet remain good friends. 'I like somebody whom I can dislike, at least with whom I can quarrel,' he wrote. He also said: 'I like to taste my friends but not to eat them.' His strictures on the Bourbons of Naples were vestiges of the Gladstonian Liberal tradition to which he belonged, but I felt he should have extended his vindication of Tiberius, who had also retired to Capri in his declining years, to these relatively modern rulers who had been as grossly maligned. At present he was not writing: the inclination, never strong unless he was in love, had left him. He cared for few contemporary authors. 'Why waste time over humbugs?' he asked; the classics were good enough for him. He remained loyal to W. H. Hudson, much of Conrad, and some of Gissing, but, like Conrad's *Conde*, he made one feel that he was marking time, that his only business was to wait for the unavoidable: at the age of eighty freedom from physical pain was an important matter. In spite of being hampered by arteriosclerosis, the spark had not gone out of him: it could still fly upward. He was glad to see me and there were flashes of his juvenile fun.

At the Villa Tuoro he was well looked after, and the light raillery of Kenneth Macpherson and Islay Lyons made him chuckle like a schoolboy. Even if he were glum his spirits soon rose at a savoury meal in youthful company, and even if he had not been the literary founder of 'a whole Capri school', as Graham Greene remarked, he would have impressed one as a vigorous and independent personality with a *soupçon* (he was fond of this word) of the pedagogue. To me he always seemed to increase in stature. In Capri he was on soil that he had populated with characters beside whom the newcomers were humdrum. Through the scramble of trippers, he saw the island with historical, geological and botanical eyes. Few of the islanders knew it so intimately.

David Jeffreys, then acting as Vice-Consul in Naples, was solicitous in providing him with the pipe tobacco, snuff, and minor comforts by which he set great store. In doing so David assimilated his mannerisms, his staccato 'Hah!', his 'Pah!' of contempt, and the clichés he had made his own, such as: 'What next!' 'Uphill work!' 'Can't be done!' 'Peace with or without honour', and the final 'To Hell with it!'.

In mid-November, the weather was still warm enough to lunch out of doors, looking over the garden towards the cluster of Capri, and a great platter of ravioli was set in front of Norman, who put on his spectacles as for an incunabulum. 'Swimpish' or not, his appetite was hearty, and Kenneth had a worthy cook. David Jeffreys assumed the role of Denis in *South Wind*, ever ready to play parlour tricks with corks and matches, while Islay Lyons was busy with his camera. Norman turned his back on the sea, which he pretended to dislike. A recent trip to Sant' Agata had disgusted him with the mainland: for him it had been spoilt. 'Never again!' he pronounced. 'Not even the threat of an atom bomb will dislodge me from this island.' He was a literary *pleinairiste* who preferred the remote countryside to urban architecture.

Though the last war had dealt devastating blows to Naples and the speculators were inflicting additional damage, there was plenty to enjoy in the midst of its teeming disorder. Many of the finest palaces and convents were hidden in narrow streets; many a splendid façade, a cloister, a courtyard with a flamboyant staircase, was crumbling away in a slum. How strange, for instance, was the Anticaglia, its massive walls of brickwork pierced by two arches which had connected the public baths and the theatre in Graeco-Roman times. Such antique remains had been grafted on to later buildings with a melodramatic effect. Cross currents from Greece and Spain mingled in architecture as in the blood of the population. So different were the Neapolitans from the Florentines that I felt I was in a separate country.

More and more I was drawn to Naples. On landing there from one of my visits to America, the ship was besieged by frantically gesticulating porters, mendicant friars and nuns rattling money-boxes, beggars waggling withered claws, women holding up their babies, waving relatives and friends of fellow-passengers. Maybe the *lazzaroni* were extinct, but the spirit of Pulcinella was alive. Near by stood the tomato-tinted building of the Immacolatella Vecchia, with Vaccaro's graceful statue of the Virgin and chubby cherubs crowning the eighteenth-century façade. Only the singers and guitars, the trumpets and drums were lacking. I welcomed this impromptu performance, this explosion of vitality, after the dull sea voyage. But a Tuscan fellow-traveller looked on with frozen face. 'What scum!' he exclaimed. 'And to think that these are also Italians. *Che vergogna!* It oughtn't to be permitted.' And another rejoined: 'To come home to this! It might be the shore of Africa. I've been away for years but I feel inclined to turn back.'

Being English, perhaps I was too detached to feel affronted by the exhibitionism of people determined to squeeze every drop of drama from the occasion. Though nobody had come to meet me, the general air of festivity cheered me up. I was even amused by the cheek of the customs official who filched two packets from my carton of cigarettes with a garlicky grin, observing that Christmas was coming. He slipped them deftly into his pocket as if to say: 'my reward for not rifling your baggage.' Haggling with a rascally porter afforded another diversion. To persuade me to double his tip he showed me a snapshot of his wife and children – so many mouths to feed!

As the train puffed out of the station, my Tuscan friend sighed: 'Thank God we're out of the sink at last. What a relief it will be to enter the real Italy! Don't mistake Naples for Italy. I'm afraid many foreigners do.' My defence of the place was dismissed as sentimentality. 'Oh, you Northerners!' In fact his was the stubborn prejudice of North against South. He would have agreed with Ruskin that Naples was 'the most loathsome nest of human caterpillars I was ever forced to stay in'. For me the caterpillars had turned into delightful butterflies.

Each of my visits to Naples became more protracted and prolific of ideas. In comparison with other Italian cities, it had been woefully underrated and misunderstood, and even now the glamorous bay of the tourist brochures at one extreme and the squalid rookery of the post-war films at the other obscured the Protean reality of the ancient Bourbon capital. At the risk of being called perverse and paradoxical, I hoped to throw fresh light on this reality. I was drawn there by instinctive sympathy for Neapolitans in general, apart from the aesthetic fascination and prodigality of nature in their background. Since Peking was lost to me, Naples became a substitute. For better or for worse, the Bourbons had identified themselves with it more than any other ruling dynasty. Wherever I looked their monuments predominated, beginning with King Charles, who had inherited his ancestral passion for building on a grand scale. Fortunately he was endowed with taste and a flair for good architects, whose plans he encouraged with his own fruitful suggestions.

Through this growing affection my work was cut out for me: I would write a history of the Neapolitan Bourbons. I was an amateur consumed by a curiosity which was almost as physical as it was intellectual, and true amateurs, even in the field of athletics, were getting scarce. Fully aware of this, and that the very word, like aesthete, had fallen into disrepute, I was buoyed up in moments of self-doubt by a passage in Burckhardt's *Reflections on History*: 'in learning a man should be an amateur at as many points as possible, privately at any rate, for the increase of his own knowledge and the enrichment of his vision. Otherwise he will remain ignorant of any field outside his own special area and perhaps, individually, a barbarian. The amateur, because he loves things, may find points at which to dig deep in the course of his life.'

Perhaps, in a world of jet-propelled specialists, I belonged to an obsolescent species. I could not lay much claim to disinterested curiosity. I want to touch the past, inhale it, swim in it, bask in it. Mere peeps and glimpses and whiffs do not suffice me. I must join the tarantella at Caserta or the minuet at Versailles, attend the gala for the King's birthday at the San Carlo, and hear the Abbé Galiani bandy words with the *philosophes* in Madame Necker's salon. And as Carlyle wrote in one of his flashes of deeper insight: 'History after all is the true Poetry: Reality, if rightly interpreted, is grander than Fiction; nay even, in the right interpretation of Reality and History, does genuine Poetry lie.' As to the right interpretation opinions continue to differ, but a certain serenity and tolerance seem essential, and these eighteenth-century virtues have been lacking since the nineteenth century. Incidentally it was Gladstone who asked Tennyson whether he did not consider Carlyle to be a true poet. Tennyson answered: 'Certainly he is a poet to whom Nature has denied the faculty of verse.'

In order to write the history I dreamt of I divided my time between Florence and Naples. My visits to Naples often coincided with Berenson's. At the age of eighty-five he was still an inveterate sight-seer, and to drive with him to Cumae and scramble about the acropolis was to visualize the first Greek colony in Italy through ruins that were otherwise mere heaps of stone. Juvenal had described the desolation of Cumae in his time, for it had been founded in 1050 B.C., yet its acropolis retained a military importance until the Neapolitans destroyed it in 1205. B.B. pointed to the finely hewn rectangular blocks of tufa as original Greek work, and he could trace the line of the city walls as far as the amphitheatre. Below the rocky pile was the grotto of the Sibyl, whence the oracle boomed forth in Greek hexameters. Apollo had granted her the gift of prophecy and as many years as the grains of dust in her hand, but she forgot to ask him for youth. The pioneer of rare book dealers, she must have been very decrepit when she sold her books to Tarquin the Proud. Evidently she travelled far or had deputies in different places. Whether there was trickery or not in the 'maddened voice that reached a thousand years', one could imagine its awe-inspiring effect on the consultant. The deep cleft whence it issued was still wrapt in archaic mystery, of which B.B. and I were conscious as we stood there, regretting that there was no Sibyl to consult. We visited Capodimonte when it was still a down-at-heel palace, which Professor Bruno Molajoli was about to transform into the loveliest museum in Italy. Together with Nicky Mariano we were stuck in the antiquated lift, and while we were bottled in that restricted space I admired B.B.'s imperturbable calm, for he continued discussing the Goya portraits until with a jerk or two the lift decided to jog on. I remembered that when a lift stopped between floors in a Florentine palace the women began screaming as if they were imprisoned for life. The American Consul, Mr Waller of Alabama, who was present with his aged mother and sister, soothed their nerves by singing Negro spirituals until the apparatus was mended.

Only once could B.B. be inveigled into lunching with me in an open-air restaurant at the point of Posillipo: he was enraptured by the scenery but deafened by the singers and mandolins. He preferred his friends to lunch with him in the carpeted quiet of his hotel. Nicky invariably accompanied him with scarves and shawls and other accessories, and we advanced in a measured procession towards his table with waiters bowing on either side, while other clients dropped their knives and forks to stare and whisper to each other: who was this important little personage? Some exiled royalty perhaps, or a famous virtuoso. And Nicky, wreathed in smiles, resembled a benevolent Grand Duchess. A frequent guest was B.B.'s Neapolitan Egeria, Clotilde Marghieri. When he mused on the maternal devotion of younger women for much older men as a beautiful subject for fiction, it was not only Nicky he had in mind. Clotilde bore a striking resemblance to Bronzino's portrait of Laura Battiferri, the poetess who married the sculptor-architect Ammannati, with sensitive aquiline features, brilliantly intelligent eyes, and a languid voice and manner until some topic excited or amused her. Her features were wistfully pensive in repose, imbued with the sense of tears in mortal things.

Clotilde lived in a Vesuvian villa not far from the house where Leopardi composed his *Ginestra*, among straggling vineyards and pine groves, the volcano behind and the spectacular gulf in front. Berenson wrote that he had never stayed anywhere that made him feel so much as if he were 'living in the Antique'. The black cindery soil, so rich in vines and fruit trees, had rolled down as incandescent lava aeons ago, and the life of the peasants retained the primitive pattern of religious feasts accompanied by fireworks and the popping of petards. Clotilde invited me to this idyllic retreat until I found a suitable apartment in Naples. Most willingly would I have stayed on there, for it deserved its name *La Quiete*, but it was too remote from the libraries and archives. Her mother Donna Giulia Betocchi, a white-haired matriarch whose intense black eyes flashed joy and sorrow, and who could weep and laugh almost in the same sentence, lived in a larger house behind it. We became such friends that she allowed me to use the jealously guarded library of her son, whose death was a permanent grief to her. This contained many Neapolitan publications which had long been out of print.

In the sprightly pages of her book *Vita in Villa*, Clotilde has sketched this Vesuvian colony, presided over by her neighbour the Marchesa Eleonora de Cillis, whose weekly 'At Home' was the social event of the parish: a *monaca di casa*, or lay nun of uncouth aspect, distributed the cakes while the hostess poured tea, insulated from the outer world until she introduced television into her drawing-room. Television hypnotized her, and eventually she could not tear herself away from it. An ardent monarchist, she throve on her memories, surrounded by nostalgic bibelots and fading photographs in tarnished frames. Her rustic tenants cheated her and she knew it, but she maintained that they upheld the good old customs and traditions. They kissed her hand and called her 'Your Excellency' with unction.

The Marchesa had a rugged grandeur, and owing to her prestige in pious circles she introduced me to convents which were then closed to the layman. To accompany her was like taking part in a triumphal progress. She conducted me to San Gregorio Armeno, whose Abbess not only showed me the phials containing the dried blood of Saint Patrizia but caused the precious substance to liquefy from dusty brown to bubbling crimson, after which she remarked that we must be unusually devout, for the miracle had worked in record time. The nun who clasped the phial had an unearthly pallor while she mumbled in prayer and sweat poured down her forehead. The nuns' rooms – too large and airy for cells – opened on to balustraded balconies around the cloister garden, where a marble fountain sculpted with sea horses and masks was a Baroque glorification of the well of Samaria. On either side of it were life-size statues of Our Lord and the Samaritan woman by Matteo Bottiglieri (*circa* 1730). The cloister had preserved its monastic seclusion and I thought it even more beautiful than that of Santa Chiara, famed for its majolica-tiled pergola and benches. The adjoining church is a gorgeous example of Neapolitan Baroque frescoed by the ubiquitous Luca Giordano, who portrayed himself in a scene representing the arrival of the Armenian nuns at Naples. The street outside was monopolized by shops selling figures for Christmas cribs and artificial flowers, and one could see the artisans modelling inside them as in the middle ages – one of the few streets unchanged since the *Risanamento*, when the antique centre was disembowelled after the cholera epidemic of 1884.

The Marchesa also took me to her splendid family chapel in the crypt under the Duomo. It had been built in white marble for her ancestor Cardinal Oliviero Carafa by Tommaso Malvito of Como in 1492: His Eminence was realistically portrayed kneeling in prayer beside the tomb of San Gennaro (Saint Januarius), the most popular patron of Naples, whose body he had brought here from Montevergine above Avellino. Of course we lingered in the Cappella del Tesoro, where the miraculous blood of the Saint is kept in the tabernacle of the high altar, but this blood usually liquefies thrice a year, during May, September and December, in full view of a vast congregation which is often worked up to a hysterical pitch of excitement, especially when there is a long and anxious delay. Domenichino, who frescoed the cupola, was frightened away in the middle of his work by the *camorra* of his Neapolitan rivals. Lanfranco finished it rather frigidly, but it is the holy relics, the silver bust of the Saint in cope and mitre, the phials containing his blood, that warm the chapel and make it a centre of pilgrimage. Anyone named Gennaro is almost certain to be a Neapolitan

My majestic guide did not mind walking for miles, never squeamish about the bad smells and squalid details that would have shocked a genteel stranger. It was pelting with rain when she took me to tea with her brother Antonio, the Duke of Andria. Though she had shared my umbrella, we were both dripping. In this plight I was shy of accepting a seat on the sofa, but I could see no alternative and sat uncomfortably on the edge of it, one eye on the rivulet my shoes were creating. Her brother was too urbane to notice my embarrassment and his conversation soon made me forget my predicament, for he was a Greek scholar. His gods were those of Hellas, and he smiled cynically at his sister's Roman fervour. For him the achievement of the age of Pericles was unparalleled: he preferred Pindar to Leopardi, many of whose manuscripts were in his possession. The Marchesa pointed proudly to the bust of their papal ancestor Paul IV, but her brother admitted that he felt more sympathy for his later ancestors Ettore, Count of Ruvo, the fanatical republican who was beheaded in 1799, and the Carafa sisters called *Madri della Patria* (Mothers of the Fatherland) because they had supported the revolutionaries and suffered exile in consequence. 'I'd prefer their company to that of Pope Paul,' he said. Their portraits simpered; the Pope's frowned. The Marchesa looked reproachful. No doubt she prayed earnestly for her brother's conversion.

Antonio Carafa had the cosmopolitan polish of the Neapolitan aristocracy blended with an erudition which he aired somewhat diffidently in esoteric essays and pseudo-Grecian dialogues. His blonde little wife seemed more French than Neapolitan, and in fact she usually spoke to me in French, perhaps because we often met at the house of Professor Jean Pasquier, who ran the French Institute as a branch of Grenoble University and invited me to lecture there. I chose Beckford as my subject, since he had written *Vathek* and usually corresponded in that language.

With Jean I enjoyed many architectural excursions, especially to the catacomb district of the Sanità where the living seemed more alive in contrast with their surroundings. No doubt we, as two foreigners, suggested lottery numbers to those who stared at us so inquisitively. The poorest of the poor went about with their heads full of numbers, analysing this or that event in relation to the lottery ticket they hoped to buy. Every dream, chance meeting, accident, had its corresponding digit: and if they were uncertain about it they could consult the *Smorfia*, a book which gave the numerical significance of almost everything. Newspapers were scanned for clues: births, marriages, deaths and murders were totted up and analysed. Deathbeds might yield a fortune, and last words were weighed with minute attention as most likely to provide the lucky cipher. Betting in England is not nearly so imaginative or intellectual.

More often I wandered alone, pausing to admire a graceful arch or the terraces of crumbling walls with steep steps climbing between them, surprised by sudden silences as when crickets are hushed after a shrill chorus. Time vanished as if clocks had never been invented. Cubes, oblongs, and rippling curves, art anonymous and unconscious, a hybrid of styles, enlivened

284

by lovers embracing and children playing in lava-cobbled lanes, an overflowing untidiness like the peeling of innumerable oranges: it was all a visual vacation after the classical discipline of Florence, whose history was simple compared with that of Naples.

Many a street scene was more operatic than theatrical, for the voice of a florid tenor was seldom absent and life was lived chiefly out of doors. More than once I heard screams and saw knifings, with knots of bystanders on one side and others running like hares while the victim lay groaning in a rivulet of blood, and from snatches of gossip I gathered it was some 'settlement of accounts' between members of the *camorra*. I saw harridans pulling each other's hair and intrepid peacemakers mauled for attempting to separate them; pompous funerals followed by cabs of wailing women; urchins rolling tyres filched from a motor-car; and rats as big as cats, often bigger, for the average cat was half-starved. Most pathetic were the old men and boys collecting cigarette stubs, their eyes fixed so intently on pavement and gutter that they risked being run over. At night the street shrines glowed in dark corners and the palaces of the winding Monte di Dio were revealed in full magnificence under the moon, but then one was tempted towards the bay, to contemplate a panorama of which I, for one, never wearied though it has been multiplied in reproduction and description. 'A sort of intoxicated self-forgetfulness' – Goethe had described the sensation. He felt that Naples had altered him, almost guilty 'to enjoy rather than to learn and to do'. But here one could learn in the midst of enjoyment.

Beside the intense open air life there was an intense indoor life in archives and libraries, of scholars, historians, philosophers and jurists who were among the most learned in Italy. As if to vindicate the reputation of their fellow-citizens for shallow cleverness these, with few exceptions, were rigidly methodical in their researches, models of precision often verging on pedantry. They collected fascinating anecdotes and wasted them in the telling, as if it were their duty to dehydrate them. Benedetto Croce and Fausto Nicolini were the salient exceptions. Croce has confessed that even as a child he was thrilled by the smell of paper and printer's ink. His whole life was dedicated to study. It was necessary to investigate what was certain and concrete in the past, he said, whereas the future was uncertain and abstract. Since the end of the nineteenth century Croce's influence had been growing and he infected his disciples with his fever of industry. Scholarship had kept him young in spirit but he was the Grand Old Man of Neapolitan letters. He had launched Fausto Nicolini and many others on a literary career. At first Nicolini had wanted to be a musician, but having inherited the bulk of the Abbé Galiani's manuscripts he was urged by Croce to publish them. He studied Galiani as if he were his next of kin and developed a passion for historical research. After Galiani he worked on a critical edition of Vico's *Scienza Nuova* and devoted so many years to that obscure philosopher that he was nicknamed 'Vico's nephew'. A friend who saw him quarrelling with a railway porter said to the latter: 'Fie, don't you know that this gentleman is the nephew of Giambattista Vico?' And the illiterate porter was so impressed that he doffed his cap and apologized saying: 'Excuse me, sir, I didn't recognize you.'

Nicolini became Inspector General of Archives in Italy but he never lost his Neapolitan wit, which excelled when he crossed swords with Marxist writers. He played many a practical joke on pedantic rivals, as when the lost books of Livy were supposed to have been discovered by one of those impostors who crop up in the academic world, a farce worthy of Eduardo De Filippo. The publications of the *Archivio Storico per le Province napoletane* are apt to be ponderous but Nicolini had a light touch derived from his contact with the Abbé Galiani. Croce said of him: 'In all orderly houses there is a lumber room in which odds and ends are stored. Nicolini is the reverse: with him all is confusion, but he keeps one room in perfect order, which is his brain.'

I was chary of inflicting myself on these celebrities but I saw them now and then to shake hands with on formal occasions. Their public faces were friendly and they wished me good luck: *Buon lavoro!* I knew Count Riccardo Filangieri, the Director of the State Archive, rather better though he was extremely reserved and so restrained in speech and gesture that he could have been mistaken for an Englishman.

During the last war Count Filangieri had removed the most precious contents of the Archive for safety to a distant house in the country, but before leaving Naples the German troops had gone there and set fire to them on purpose, one of those acts of vandalism for which there was even less excuse than the destruction of the Florentine bridges. Count Filangieri spent the rest of his laborious life tracing and gathering transcriptions and photostats of the documents destroyed.

In 1949 he was still repairing the havoc in the vast building which had formerly been a Benedictine convent. It had three cloisters, one of which was filled by a colossal plane tree a thousand years old: this was said to have been planted by St Benedict himself, whose life story was depicted by Andrea Solario in another courtyard. In the monastic silence of his study Count Filangieri struck me as a modern saint. I often met him on solitary walks, ruminating before some relic of the past. He could see the past in the present, Boccaccio and Petrarch in San Lorenzo Maggiore. The Gothic of the Angevins appealed to him most strongly, but in Naples even the Gothic aspired towards the Baroque, as in the doorway of the Pappacoda Chapel with its elaborate triangle of outspread wings.

On a more mundane level Salvatore Gaetani, Duke of Castelmola, was a perambulating repository of Neapolitan anecdotes. He haunted the National Library where I worked, but he was also to be seen at every social function hovering – except that hovering suggests lightness and his tread was elephantine – in the precincts of the buffet, a paunchy figure with protruding eyes and heavy jowl, his plate heaped with a variety of dainties. He contributed chatty articles to the *Mattino* in which he assumed the pose of a Parisian *flâneur*. In reality he was a D'Annunzian romantic and he required the presence of ladies to ignite his remarkable memory. I relished his anecdotes of Neapolitan eccentrics, such as the young Count Balsorano who wondered what sound his family piano would make if it were pitched into the street. His younger brothers encouraged the experiment. The palace porter warned foot passengers to keep out of the way while the servants dragged the piano to the terrace and pushed it over the parapet. When the old Count came home and saw a crowd round the wreck of his piano, he asked what had happened. In fear and trembling the porter explained. 'What a pity,' said the Count. 'I'm so sorry to have missed it!'

Of that staunch old Bourbon legitimist the Duke of Regina, he used to relate that on his deathbed, after receiving Extreme Unction, he slept for a couple of hours. Opening his eyes, he asked: 'Has the catastrophe occurred?'

Often gesture sufficed in Naples, as if speech were superfluous, but when the language of gesture became articulated in words it had a style of its own which defies translation. The dialect is melodious with a humorous, whimsical twist, naïve with a dash of guile, rich in fantasy and suggestion. And the prevalence of grand gesture, perhaps derived from Spain, was illustrated in Salvatore Gaetani's stories. Soon after the Allied landings Prince Francesco Ruspoli stopped his smart limousine before a fishmonger with a basket of fresh lobsters, but the fishmonger refused payment when the Prince wanted to buy one. 'Sir,' he objected, 'you have paid me the honour of stopping here with this gorgeous automobile, so why shouldn't I offer you a lobster?' Equally characteristic was his story of the beggar who was accustomed to receiving fifty lire from the Duke of San Pietro. On being given ten lire by mistake he protested: 'From now on, sir, you must find yourself another beggar.'

Claiming descent from Pope Boniface VIII, Gaetani could be tedious about genealogy. How sonorously the sesquipedalian titles rolled off his tongue! Yet he was too fascinated by their psychology to be called a snob, for the snob is devoid of humour. Most Neapolitans had a romantic feeling for the aristocracy, due to pride in their past, for their prestige had vanished with the kingdom. There are so many branches of the Caracciolo, Carafa and Pignatelli clans that they fill pages of the *Libro d'oro*, the peerage which Gaetani must have known by heart. For a foreigner they are apt to be confusing.

One of Gaetani's most characteristic stories was about an impoverished Neapolitan marquis who went to stay with a great Sicilian family. The family lived on a feudal scale with dozens of retainers, and the three luxurious months he spent with them were only troubled by the thought of the tips he would have to leave. On the day of his departure the whole staff stood at the door, from the majordomo to the fourteen-year-old groom. The marquis had just enough money for his train journey but he did not lose heart. Smiling with the suavity of an ambassador offering his credentials, he held out his hand to the steward and said: 'Francesco, you are absolute perfection. Never in my life have I met so masterly a majordomo, not only a brilliant manager but endowed with the tact and resourcefulness of an experienced diplomat. Congratulations. I thank you with all my heart.' Turning to the footman with the same radiant smile and out-stretched hand he said: 'Gustavo, my suits were pressed better than in London; my bath was always the right temperature. I'll always remember you as a champion footman.' For each of the servants he had a suitable compliment accompanied by a friendly handshake. When he came to the little groom he gave him a hug and said: 'As for you, you deserve a kiss.' Whereupon he climbed into his carriage, leaving the whole staff as happy as if he had tipped them.

Fancying himself an epicure, Gaetani loved to describe the good dinners he had eaten. But as far as I could see he was more of a *gourmand* than a *gourmet*, with a preference for greasy concoctions. To me he recommended a restaurant whose speciality was a tepid mass of fried egg plant, peppers, tomatoes and *mozzarella* cheese, flavoured with garlic and swimming in oil. I could picture him spreading his napkin and lapping it up.

Salvatore Gaetani was typical of certain survivors of the *ancien régime* which lingered like the glowing embers of an extinct volcano. For these dwindling survivors Naples was still the capital. They did not emigrate to Rome or Milan like their impetuous offspring. Their palaces might need repairs and they could ill afford a motor, but they were members of the *Unione* whose waiters knew their foibles and flattered their ears with *'Eccellenza'*. Never in a hurry, they were always ready to join you for a cup of that delectable coffee which they imbibed at all hours of the day, and their conversation transformed the simplest meal into a banquet. They believed that punctuality was the thief of time.

The ladies were usually more royalist than their husbands: not a few travelled second class all the way to Portugal to attend some private celebration of the House of Savoy. In other circumstances they seldom strayed far from Vesuvius. A large proportion of the people were monarchists, like the mayor. A cousin of mine, the son of an admiral, would have risen high in the navy if he had not refused to swear fealty to the republic, an act of self-sacrifice rare outside Naples. His brother Ferdinando encouraged me to write about the Bourbons and he lent me some invaluable documents from his war-battered library in the Palazzo Cellamare. The former Acton palace on the Riviera di Chiaia, a white neo-Classical building standing alone in a green park evocative of Kew, now belonged to Princess Rosa Pignatelli who bequeathed it to the State. A vivacious old dame with a gay past, she had acquired a taste for French popular songs, for Piaf and Charles Trenet. 'Perhaps because of my name my favourite is *La vie en rose*,' she told me. Ninette Pasquier brought her the latest gramophone records from Paris.

For several years I spent part of each summer at Ischia, less frequented than now and less built over. The passage from Naples was always an enchantment: the villas and gardens of Posillipo rising dreamily from the sea, the classical harbour of Miseno and the promontory beyond it, named after Aeneas's trumpeter who was drowned there, the opalescent tints of Procida under the grim castle-prison, and then the cosy circular harbour of Porto d'Ischia which Norman Douglas called 'one of the few pleasing memories of Bourbonism'. Past flowering oleanders, I drove to Forio, in full gala to celebrate its patron

Saint Vitus, who was also patron of dancers, actors, domestic animals, and those who found difficulty in early rising. Illuminated arches in the town, necklaces of twinkling lights along the hills, rockets and catherine wheels, a band playing *Trovatore*, and gently jubilant crowds: it was as if Saint Vitus gave me a personal welcome.

The Chinese used to say that wine enables one to enjoy scenery more intensely, but it rather depends on the vintage. When Norman Douglas waxed lyrical over 'the golden torrents of thousand-vatted Forio' I had suspected him of pardonable exaggeration. But as I broached a second bottle of Forian ichor I swore I had not tasted so ambrosial a nectar out of Burgundy, and the lights along the hills glittered more gaily, reflected in the black mirror of the sea.

The rollicking strains of *Trovatore* mingled with the metallic voice of Eduardo Bargheer. Eduardo was Forio's adoptive painter, as Wystan Auden was its poet laureate, and his voice resounded above all others wherever he happened to be. The place had so hypnotized his vision that he painted endless variations of its multicoloured mosaic: it had entered into his bloodstream. To stroll with him was to be greeted incessantly by old and young. 'Ciao, Don Eduardo.' 'Ciao, Tonino.' 'Ciao . . . ciao . . .' He behaved as he fancied he was expected to behave, gesticulating frantically, shouting instead of speaking, and laughing uproariously, yet the islanders were more grave and sedate than the Neapolitans: they kept their distance with strangers and they smiled hesitantly. Don Eduardo's approach was a gust from his native Hamburg.

Next morning I rose at six and walked through the hamlet of Monterone to soak in hot mineral water. The air was exhilarating at that early hour and I met only a few goats on their way to be milked at different houses, their bells as clear as the air. Auden lived in a neighbouring house with Chester Kallman, a young New Yorker who wrote poetry and cooked poetically. Their factotum seemed only to be interested in his painting, and the rooms were a muddle of saucepans and messed-up canvases.

Wystan was absorbed in composition most of the day: he and Chester were collaborating on the libretto of the *Rake's Progress* for Stravinsky, an opera I greatly admired when I heard it in Venice. In the evening they relaxed outside Maria's bar, Wystan patient and avuncular with the aspiring authors who hung on his words, already the professor of poetry he was to become at Oxford.

Maria's was the one café on the main piazza of Forio where you were bound to meet old acquaintances and fresh arrivals. Maria herself was a dumpy matron whose dyed black hair had a snow-white parting, and she was an acute psychologist who quickly discovered the secrets of her clients, tolerant of their frailties and ready with practical advice, assisted by the male members of her family, dusky lads with Coptic faces and a bawdy sense of humour. Eduardo sat at one table discussing Klee; Wystan at another discussing Dylan Thomas. The local inhabitants paraded to and fro studying the foreigners with overt curiosity. They would stroll to the little white church of Santa Maria del Soccorso on a raised platform jutting out into the sea, whence the sunset was scanned for its famous 'green flash'. This invariably offered a pretext for conversation: youths leaning over the parapet became voluble; cigarettes were exchanged; and the new friends wandered off to discuss more intimate matters.

It was rumoured that one or both of the 'missing diplomats', Burgess and Maclean, had taken refuge in Forio, since Burgess was vaguely associated with Wystan Auden, and another poet, Stephen Spender, had been gossiping with press reporters a little too freely. Whenever an obvious Anglo-Saxon appeared – as conspicuous as a broiled lobster among the sun-tanned natives – 'There's Burgess!' somebody exclaimed. Wystan's house was subjected to special scrutiny and Archie Colquhoun, outspokenly Communistic, courted the gravest suspicion as a joke. But Forio was no place to hide in, for everybody knew everybody and even the rocks had eyes. What was not known was invented.

As I sat on the terrace of the Torrione restaurant, having taken a room in the old watch-tower, I was admiring the fish brought in by the brawny fisherman, a silvery and golden variety of mullets, sea breams, sardines and vicious-looking *scorfani* or sea scorpions, when Archie Colquhoun appeared in shorts and sandals, his toilet necessaries tied up in a grubby towel. He had crossed over from the mainland with Norman Douglas's itinerary, on which the best vintages were marked.

I had not seen him since, still in uniform, he had called on me with Sylvia Sprigge just after the war. He had been a liaison officer with the Italian partisans, who had converted him to Communism. His conversion had been more emotional than intellectual, for he told me they were more handsome than the bourgeoisie and entirely free from middle-class prejudice, 'the salt of the earth and the honey'. So far so good; I was glad he had enjoyed his war experiences. But my temper rose when he remarked: 'How lovely it will be when your villa and garden are handed over to the proletariat!' I could picture them stoning the statues, wrecking the flower beds, killing the goldfish and running bicycle races through the box hedges as in the public garden – if garden it could be called in its derelict plight – at the foot of the hill. 'But you would be employed as caretaker,' he said to soothe me, 'if you behaved yourself.' Later he had tried to smuggle some letters from Harry Pollitt to Communist agents in Madrid and been ordered to leave Spain. I had heard of him last in Venice, where he was arrested for assaulting some Capitalistic film operators. When he told the police that he was translating Manzoni's classic *I Promessi Sposi*, a police officer retorted: 'And now you'll have to translate *Le Mie Prigioni*' – a book equally famous in Italian schools. Presumably Manzoni kept him out of further mischief and influenced him, after a while, to return to his original faith.

Before the war he had lived at Ponte d'Ischia, and he wished to revisit the scenes of his heedless youth. He disliked the changes he saw, which at least were signs of growing prosperity. Porto was teeming with new hotels, neon-lit bars and boutiques: soon it would vie with Viareggio, whose magnificent pine grove was also threatened, but Ponte was practically unchanged. Archie knew the owner of its ruined castle, a lawyer who had bought it for a song, but bad luck had pursued him relentlessly since his purchase. Apart from domestic misfortunes he had gone blind. He occupied a cottage among the ruins of the Aragonese castle, a pile more imposing from a distance than when Archie and I clambered through steep tunnels to the tottering church, whose damp crypts and chapels were in the penultimate stages of decay. Fragments of early frescoes peeped through the peeling plaster and one vault still contained a few bones of nuns who had dragged themselves there to die – dogs had carried off the rest. Some of the courtyards and a hexagonal chapel were remnants of the period when Vittoria Colonna had lived there as a bride and during her widowhood. As her husband, Ferrante d'Avalos, Marquis of Pescara, was a general of the Imperial forces, she corresponded with him more often than she saw him, in high-flown passionate verse. After his death of wounds received in battle she wrote over a hundred sonnets to his memory. Evidently she idealized him during his absence, for she had a deeply spiritual character. Her poems were admired by contemporaries for their sweetness and purity of language, but now she is more famous as the mature enchantress of Michelangelo, whose sonnets have made her immortal. He was sixty-three and she was nearly forty-eight when they met, and in those days people tended to age prematurely, which makes their relationship more poignant than if they had been juveniles. They lived on a loftier plane than most of us. But there was no trace of the great lady in the crumbling castle where she had held court. Only the view was the same, and it was a relief to inhale the sea breeze after trudging through so dank and desolate a ruin.

Wherever I went some saint's anniversary was being celebrated, and the festival at Ponte in honour of Saint Giovan Giuseppe della Croce was the most spectacular, for the whole sea was tremulous with the flickering flames of boats under the black skeleton of the castle. The saint's relics together with his effigy and a statue of the Madonna were carried in procession to an illuminated barge for a tour of this part of the coast. Lily-white girls and choirboys with banners followed with the Bishop and clergy chanting hymns. The population streamed towards the foot of the castle-rock where a patch of waste land was covered with stalls of watermelons, iced drinks, pink nougat and other sweetmeats, curiously shaped balloons, rattles and tambourines, and fortune-tellers with caged canaries. The crowd was serene in its sobriety: there was no pushing and scrambling, no rowdiness, while cascades of fireworks lit up the sky and plunged into the sea.

Slowly the procession returned, the Bishop and clergy drooping with fatigue, and the band wheezing out of breath. When the crowd dispersed a lone *carrozzella* rattled down the cobbled street: its young Jehu, with a blood-red rose in his mouth, stood up like Phaethon driving his chariot through the clouds. He had a wild gleam in his eye but he kept his balance. Only the mule seemed tipsy. At the end of the street he halted, and when I passed he called to me: '*Signurì*, may I offer you a lift?' 'Not at your break-neck speed. I want to reach Forio all of a piece.' 'Hop in, sir. I'll drive you anywhere fast or slow. I like your face.'

The invitation was irresistible. I hopped in and had no cause to regret it. Vito was as radio-active as the air and from him I learned more about Ischia than from any scholarly treatise. He was always ready to take me on scenic drives to Barano, Sant' Angelo, the slopes of Epomeo, where his parents poured their best wine for me, and to various beaches, then almost private, where even the sand was reputed to cure aches and pains since time immemorial. From palest aquamarine to deepest sapphire, the sea was crossed by warm currents that precipitated pregnancy in women and potency in men. Such was their legendary fame, and I was ready to believe it as I lay on my back lapped by the crystalline water, which fortified flesh and spirit and banished anxiety.

❧ 17 ❧

The apartment I eventually found at Posillipo had no intrinsic beauty to recommend it. The rooms were ill proportioned and mediocrely furnished, but their high windows opened on to the whole bay of Naples. I could have dived from my balcony into the sea below, which curled and uncurled, crawled or cantered according to the season. The rollers and breakers could become very boisterous in winter when the spray rose near my balcony. In summer they became the smoothest of playgrounds where boys and girls shouted happily and dived and swam the livelong day from overcrowded boats, and the latest song-hits of Piedigrotta, amplified by loudspeakers, were wafted from the tourist steamers gliding to and fro, churning a foamy passage through the blue-green brine, leaving a line of silver in their wake. Large ocean-bound steamers tossed the tiny boats and sent waves scurrying against the rocks to splash the excited children.

I never tired of the spectacle from my windows, and if it distracted me from my work, it was only to fill my lungs with purer air and my eyes with such light that I returned to my work refreshed. The house was next to the Grotta Romana which in summer became an open-air night club and bathing establishment whose combined cacophonies were ultimately to drive me away. It was already winter when I moved in: except for an occasional ocean liner or cruiser in the distance there were only a few fishing boats. At night their orange lamps were reflected in the rippling blackness; the fishermen's raucous voices called in the pearl-grey dawn. It was like living on an anchored ship. The bay was nearly as broad as the Channel between Dover and Calais but owing to the clearness of the atmosphere in fair weather distances were deceptive, to such an extent that Capri looked within walking distance when the sea resembled a smooth silk carpet. Hence I gazed outward rather than inward, and whenever I could I sat on my balcony with a pile of books. On arriving from Florence my first movement was towards the marine balcony. There I lost count of time in wonder at the vast orchestra of colour before me, always varying against the same graceful outline. It was restful to return to from the city, and as a contrast to Florence, where I was constantly interrupted by visitors who expected me to show them the house and garden.

My landlady and her husband, a retired engineer, lived next door. This had its advantages, for they kept an eye on the rooms and on every knife and fork. The wife's nosiness did not disturb me, as she had an unusual mania for cleanliness and order. More unusual for a Neapolitan, she was a strict Protestant. She hated the sea since her only son, a naval officer, had been drowned during the war, but she could not afford to move elsewhere. Condemned to live with the element she loathed, she was consumed with bitterness. Her sunken eyes were those of a tragedy queen; her smile was a wry grimace. An obsession with astronomy consoled her grizzled husband for being henpecked. He had fanciful notions about flying saucers, which he was convinced were planetary messengers to warn us of our impending doom. A devout monarchist, he could never forgive the French for their revolution: they had set the rest of the world a pernicious example. Afflicted with hypochondria, his wife gradually lost all interest in living. She retired to bed, and her husband's attempts to make her leave it led to furious altercations which reverberated through the walls. Faith-healers and pastors prayed with and for her but she refused to speak, refused to eat, and willed herself to die. This cast a certain gloom over the sunny apartment. But when I brought flowers to the invalid I noticed something like a mischievous gleam in her cavernous eyes as they followed her aged husband round the room. He, poor man, had to nurse her night and day without a word of thanks. It looked as if she were avenging her private misery on him. Fortunately he had the constellations to cheer him. Now and then he would invite me to peer through his telescope.

My neighbours were more hospitable than our richer Florentines: Prince and Princess d'Avalos farther up the hill were intensely musical and their son Francesco was a promising composer whose *Hymn to Night* won the Marzotto prize. They had a huge collection of gramophone and tape recordings which constituted the old Prince's chief hobby. Musicians forgathered in this cave of harmony by the sea: Hans Werner Henze, the prolific young *avant-garde* composer who was going through a less frigid Neapolitan phase after his *Boulevard Solitude* and *Dance Marathon* which I heard then and there, as cold as Henze seemed warm, and perhaps a little too cerebral; his talented protégé Di Maio; and various pianists and conductors whose conversation was stimulating. The Greta Garbo of duchesses, Minervina Riario-Sforza, lived beyond, and on the tip of Posillipo Baroness Gabriella Barracco entertained half Naples at the coralline Villa Emma when she was not supervising her husband's estate in Calabria: the Baron was kept away from it by his horror of the parish priest. On his romantic isle of Gaiola, Paolo Langheim emulated an exclusive Capri in miniature. These neighbours gave me an illusion that Naples was still a self-contained kingdom.

From 1950 on I commuted between Florence and Naples, with occasional excursions to Paris, London and the United States. The placid international life of Florence was diminishing year by year. Currency restrictions affected English travellers more than others, and people I scarcely knew appealed to me for inconvenient loans. In one case my loan enabled an acquaintance to escape from the Grand Hotel without paying his bill. He had given my name as a reference to the manager, whom I had innocently assured of his solvency. Women I had not seen for years expected me to pay their dressmakers in return for post-dated cheques that were of little use to me. The most brazen dunned me on the strength of letters of introduction from somebody who had once been invited to tea, and that once had been sufficient. The Edwardian colony was evaporating. The furnished houses we had let to civilized foreigners before the war were occupied by psychiatric patients or neurotics: the largest of them had been converted from a wartime hospital into a pension where several friends chose to stay though it had no pretence to modern luxury.

To my great joy Osbert Sitwell returned to Montegufoni, the fortress-villa his quixotic father had bought as a plaything, to transform and furnish as it might have been when the powerful Acciaioli had lived there. Sir Osbert has related its history in his masterful autobiography. Although it had been used as a repository for some three hundred paintings from the Uffizi and other galleries; occupied by German paratroopers and SS groups, and later by Indian and New Zealand troops; its solid structure had survived the war. Assisted by his resourceful majordomo, Sir Osbert had the arduous task of making it habitable again. From a distance it resembled a small fortified town aloof on its hill of cypresses and owls – whence its name – crowned by the medieval watch-tower that evokes comparison with the Palazzo Vecchio. Each generation of Acciaioli had left its character on the building from the fourteenth to the seventeenth century, when it was dominated by the Baroque embellishments of the cruel Cardinal who caused his nephew to be imprisoned in the dungeon of Volterra because he had married a widow against his will. A monumental habitation for a writer of monumental prose and a connoisseur of everything Baroque. Whereas Sir George had struck me as a spectral intruder from the middle ages, who looked askance at his children's activities and pottered about this historic labyrinth dreaming archaeological dreams, a bearded figure in a wide-awake hat lost among the elaborate scenery of an abandoned theatre, Sir Osbert humanized the place and warmed it up. Lady Ida had tried, for she loved to entertain the indiscriminate guests whose presence she was apt to forget, but she could never overcome her husband's indifference to strangers. Besides, he treated her as if she were not there, peering beyond her at the ceiling or the view, and she felt cut off without a telephone.

She was much happier in a Florentine hotel where she confided to me: 'The boys got their brains from me, but I can't imagine where poor Edith got hers from!' It was painfully evident that she failed to understand her distinguished daughter or appreciate her poetry.

The absence of a telephone protected Sir Osbert against the pressure of visitors to which we at La Pietra, a bare mile from the city, were constantly exposed. Montegufoni was sufficiently distant to daunt stray callers when petrol was scarce, so that its landlord was allowed to work in peace. Like Dame Edith, however, he was importuned by letters from cranks and unknown fans – letters so fantastic that they had to be seen to be believed. No doubt they were a tribute to his fame but they were also a nuisance, and Sir Osbert retaliated with a printed questionnaire which was a parody of those prevalent during the war: 'A. Name in full (Block letters as throughout). B. Specimen of usual signature. C. Passport number . . . (This must be accompanied by six photographs 2 inches by 4, and these must be signed both by a clergyman and by a Justice of the Peace. They must also have been taken within the last six months. Old photographs cannot be accepted.) D. Finger Prints number (if any). E. When were you born? F. Where were you born? G. How were you born? H. If not, why not?' The questionnaire ended with: 'Did you ever meet Burgess and Maclean, or anyone who ever knew them? This last must be accompanied by an attestation taken in the presence of a Commissioner of Oaths.' I should like to have seen the faces of the recipients.

Dame Edith came more often to Montegufoni to visit her brother. The overworked adjective fabulous applied to her in earnest: she emitted a stellar radiance. Her voice was as melli-fluous as in her youth but she had grown more fragile. The tall pale figure with flat fair hair from the Unicorn Tapestry now resembled Queen Elizabeth I, very regal and commanding though 'always a little outside life'. Her almond eyes under thinly pencilled brows observed life from her interior world with a compassion and humour entirely sui generis. Her posthumous reminiscences, written under strain when she was recovering from a severe illness, contain typical nuggets of this humour mingled with memorable images and flashes of insight. She enjoyed the breath of battle with her assailants. Fundamentally shy, she was more on the defensive with strangers in private than in her public recitals when, superbly self-confident, she became the perfect medium of her poems. To my mind she was the purest English poet since Yeats. She lived for poetry. This made her acutely sensitive to the slings of certain dons and journalists who, whatever their intellectual pretensions, were as remote from genuine poetry as from the moon.

All morning she worked in her bedroom, and I felt it cost her an effort to descend from 'pure fire compressed in holy forms' to the cold plane of social intercourse.

Slightly dazed yet very dignified, she advanced from her higher sphere, and there was a suggestion of the astronaut about her helmets and turbans and the monstrous multi-faceted aquamarines that protected her slender fingers. The latest absurdity of some poetry reviewer would soon launch her into a stream of comic fantasy which was a treat to listen to for its own sake even if one were ignorant of the Aunt Sally in question. Most of them were unknown to me except by hearsay, one of the advantages of living far from literary London with its hysterical bickerings and nervous breakdowns. But having met D. H. Lawrence, I was reduced to helpless laughter by her description of him and his spouse. Her definition of Lawrence as 'the head of the Jaeger school of literature' since he was 'hot, soft, and woolly', which elicited a mild protest from the Jaeger firm, was a healthy antidote to the hysterical adulation of his devotees. Her analogies were amazingly precise, though she seemed aloof from her surroundings. During meals the contents of her plate were invariably offered to the cats that proliferated under Osbert's benevolent eye. Of cats she was fonder than of most human beings. When she disapproved of a statement she would murmur 'Well, well, well!' with an expression half prim, half playful. Though far from pompous she usually referred to 'Mr Shaw, Mr Wells and Mr

Galsworthy' as if it were over-familiar to pronounce their Christian names or initials, and she insisted on being addressed as Dr Sitwell – until she became Dame Edith. Not that she minced her words: vowels and consonants were given their fullest value. Few women I knew had so articulate a sense of fun.

So majestic a figure was bound to attract publicity, and some of the hostility that goes with it. No lecturer at the British Institute in Florence has drawn a larger public. Even the room adjoining the lecture hall was packed, though the microphone failed to function. 'I couldn't hear a word,' said a member of the audience, 'but it was a pleasure just to see her. She looks every inch a poet, and she's such a *grande dame*. I had expected a female dragon.'

Nobody had done more than Edith and her brothers to rescue poetry from the village pub and cricket field, the homespun and briar pipe of the *London Mercury*, and now that the *Mercury* was dead and buried she insisted on the need for greater expressiveness, greater formality, and a revival of good rhetoric as opposed to the tuneless understatements and neutral tints of current poetasters and the 'sandy desert of Dr Leavis's mind'. I had known her and her brothers so long that I could not view them dispassionately. Consequently what seemed strange to others escaped me. Their best portraits are to be found in their writings. At Montegufoni they led a retired life, seeing only those friends who shared their interests.

I had always appreciated Osbert's great kindness, generosity, artistic integrity and ready wit, apart from the varied architecture of his writings, and I was to admire his courage and patience under a heavy load of infirmities all the more. His vivid panorama of a whole epoch is a formidable achievement. For a man of his energy and *joie de vivre* it was tragic to be stricken with Parkinson's disease while still in his prime but he did his utmost to defeat it: he even continued to travel and lecture for a while. He thought less of himself than of others and he tried to make light of the accidents that befell him. Edith confided to me: 'I'm not as lame as I seem to be, but I don't want Osbert to feel that I'm bursting with health when he's so shaky.' I was moved by their solicitude for each other.

Eventually Edith was bedridden and Osbert was practically alone in his domain. A Sardinian valet was engaged who seemed attentive and agreeable, but a series of calamities followed his arrival and he soon acquired the reputation of possessing the evil eye. The poultry perished on the farm, the cow had a miscarriage, the cats expired mysteriously, the wine turned sour and the olive oil turned cloudy, a plague of rats infested the granary, the cook collapsed and her son was paralysed from the waist down. Then Osbert had a dangerous fall and a bout of fever, his friend David Horner tumbled down a flight of stairs at night and remained unconscious till he was discovered lying in a pool of blood next morning, since when he has been partially paralysed; and finally the majordomo, a vigorous man in his early forties, was seized with excruciating pains and died of spinal cancer. The sudden pregnancy of several respectable girls in the neighbourhood might have been attributed to other causes.

Belief in the power of the evil eye persists in Tuscany as well as in the South, and those who laugh at it are careful to make the horn sign, the first and little finger extended while the others are closed. *Jettatori* are never mentioned by name and the subject is generally avoided, but Osbert's majordomo could not conceal his alarm. No doubt the valet had exerted his influence unconsciously but this type of *jettatore* is considered the most malignant. Though Osbert remained sceptical, he had to admit that the coincidences lent an air of plausibility to the ancient superstition. The valet had none of the hallmarks of his species: pallor, leanness, hooked nose, hollow eyes behind spectacles. On the contrary he was sturdy and inoffensive in appearance, but his eyes did strike me as peculiar. I was unable to see if he had double pupils, or a double pupil in one eye and the figure of a horse in the other, reputed most pernicious. He was tactfully dismissed, after which we heard he was killed in an aeroplane crash. A pastoral tranquillity returned to Montegufoni, as when Zocchi engraved it in the eighteenth century.

303

Osbert was always a munificent host, lavish with wine, good cheer and conversation. His wine, both red and white, was the purest in Tuscany, and many a Frenchman who turned up his nose at Chianti acclaimed its excellence. The musty aroma from the vats in his cellars greeted one like a bibulous crony. After the austerities of post-war Britain, English guests felt they had entered the land of Cockaigne, especially Evelyn Waugh, who arrived in April, 1950, fully equipped for a course of Tuscan gastronomy. He arrived in his happiest vein.

Prince Isidore had delighted him – 'a huge pleasure', he had written, 'and so much more welcome for being all against the spirit of the times'. But he had always been kind about my productions, even about those which had been slated by the popular reviewers, for though I considered myself modern I had never tried consciously to swim with the current. 'I am coming to Italy in Easter week to do my Holy Year duties in Rome,' he continued. 'After that I am alone, without plans and with a fair amount of funds. I thought of spending a week or two travelling about. I have not been to the country since it was a mass of soldiers and thieves and long to see it again. I never knew it well. Is there any chance of your joining me, perhaps in Venice? It would be such a treat . . . May you be guarded from all evil eyes.'

Not having seen him since our encounter in Hollywood, I revelled in his society. His moments of gaiety more than compensated for his gloom, his silence was more sympathetic than other people's chatter, and his sharp eye infallibly detected the humorous aspects of every situation. Romantic without sentimentality, he cherished his firm convictions without compromise. Unfortunately Florence did not appeal to him: he said it was too dressed up for tourists. Perhaps it struck him as too pagan after the pieties of Rome, though architecturally it is more austere than other Italian cities. Ruskin could not convert him to Florentine Gothic. On the other hand, he admired the landscape near Montegufoni, the undulating hills with their groves of stone pines and cypresses which Benozzo Gozzoli had painted so

Dame Edith Sitwell at the time of the first *Façade*

Sir Osbert Sitwell: at the end

minutely. And he enjoyed the food, especially the creamy sweets he called puddings.

Sinclair Lewis was then in Florence, having rented a tasteless modern villa in Pian dei Giullari. Lean and lanky, with a par-boiled complexion and prominent blue eyes, strongly opinionated yet still eager to learn and sensitive, for all his toughness, to the triumphs of the Florentine spirit, he seemed aggressively self-satisfied. According to him only America produced a galaxy of talent in the art of fiction: he thought, or pretended to think, that the English novel had decayed with the nineteenth century. There was no limit to the variety of experience offered by the last bulwark of free enterprise. This made sense to me, but why exclude the literature of the Commonwealth?

Of course he visited Berenson, who was agreeably surprised by his 'tolerable pronunciation', for B.B. was censorious of the accent of his compatriots though he did not go so far as his friend Edith Wharton, who preferred not to meet compatriots from the Wild West. Though Lewis could be quarrelsome, he and Berenson enjoyed questioning each other and their meetings passed without a skirmish. This was not so with Lewis Einstein, who had brought him to our house. Einstein was a retired American diplomat who had lived in Florence before the First World War and written a number of erudite books on the Italian Renaissance and the American Civil War. With his polished diction, his historical anecdotes and cosmopolitan urbanity, he was as great a contrast to Sinclair Lewis as Berenson. Ponderous in manner as in physique, he had a partiality for the Almanach de Gotha, which the other Lewis could not stomach. The crisis occurred when Einstein invited him to visit the Archaeological Museum before it was open to the public, since Lewis was anxious to inspect the Etruscan Chimera. Lewis arrived late with Mrs Powers (I forget if she was his mother-in-law) while Einstein was escorting a couple of duchesses among the sar-cophagi. Apparently Einstein was so wrapt up in his duchesses that he failed to notice Mrs Powers in exchanging introductions. Lewis walked out of the museum without another word, more purple in the face than usual. Probably Einstein failed to notice his abrupt departure. He was deeply hurt when Lewis proceeded to cut him in the street. 'I went out of my way to oblige the fellow,' he said sadly, 'and he isn't exactly *sortable!*'

At four o'clock one morning when Lewis was drunk, he decided to call on the American Consul Mr Waller, an old-fashioned gentleman from Alabama who was a great stickler for etiquette. He had spent many happy years in Luxembourg, which he compared with Periclean Athens. Mr Waller rose hurriedly and dressed, imagining that Lewis had some urgent communication at this ungodly hour, but Lewis had only come to tell him that he was 'a son of a bitch'. As Mr Waller never mentioned the incident, Lewis's account was its sole authority. On another occasion he got even with Lewis, who addressed him publicly as 'George' at the Florence Club. Mr Waller turned on him and said: 'Only the Grand Duchess of Luxembourg, Winston Churchill and Franklin Roosevelt address me by my Christian name.'

While Evelyn Waugh was dining with me in a quiet restaurant, Lewis loped diagonally across the room to our table and hailed him as a dear old pal. Evelyn looked startled – how well I knew that elevation of the eyebrows, the round stare of his wide open eyes, the pursed lips, as if he had been chilled by a sudden draught! He was irritated, moreover, because Lewis addressed him as Evelyn: 'Well, Evelyn, it's mighty good to see you here. How are the *Vile Bodies* – not so vile as they used to be or viler? A good title anyway. We must get together, Evelyn, the sooner the better, you say when. I can give you dinner at my house. It's nothing special to look at but the view's tremendous. I took it for that view. I'm writing theology now, at least the subject's theological. Let's make a date right now.'

I was afraid Evelyn would say 'I'm Mr Waugh to you', but he explained that he was going to stay with Osbert Sitwell at Montegufoni.

'The Sitwells are an autonomous kingdom, strictly feudal. Florence is a republic. You ought to stay with me.'

Evelyn demurred and the conversation did not flow smoothly, but having dined well he was in a conciliatory mood. We accepted Lewis's invitation for the following Friday. Afterwards Evelyn groaned: 'Must we do it? Really I'd rather not. Let's make an excuse, send him a telegram.' Personally I looked forward to a sparring match between two such incongruous champions and I persuaded him to keep the engagement.

After the velvety *volupté* of Osbert's company Evelyn was more reluctant than ever to be dragged to dine with 'Red' Lewis. We were met at the door by an English secretary-companion. He explained that 'Red' was about to finish a new novel and that whenever he wrote he could scarcely bring himself to eat. It was impossible to tempt him to swallow enough vitamins. On the other hand he had been drinking more than was good for him. 'In point of fact,' he said (ominous expression), 'I'm trying to keep him off the booze, so I hope you don't mind if there isn't much liquor in the home, unless you fancy a drop of white vermouth. In point of fact I've had to water the wine.'

Evelyn glared at me indignantly. He was accustomed to his apéritif and now he definitely needed one. 'Red' appeared rather hazy: he lacked the jauntiness of our previous encounter. He informed us that this was the first dinner he had given for several months, he had been working so hard at his novel, and before that he had nearly died of double pneumonia. Apart from an Italian girl called Titi who seemed to be running the house, the only other guest was a short-haired elderly dame in masculine attire. This was Una, Lady Troubridge, known as the Widow of Radclyffe Hall since she had lived for many years with the author of *The Well of Loneliness*. Though she discoursed about dogs and looked as if she had breezed in from some English vicarage, she did not help to put Evelyn at ease. It was no meal for an epicure. Evelyn toyed with the tepid spaghetti but he refused the veal. Our host scarcely touched the food but his stomach rumbled and he belched at regular intervals to make up for it. Evelyn flinched in his chair on the host's right with an expression of growing alarm. 'What is that frightful noise?' he kept asking me. 'Red's' speech was incoherent but at length he noticed that Evelyn was fasting and he urged him to taste the veal, the *spécialité de la maison*. Evelyn answered severely: 'It's Friday.'

Diverted by this, 'Red' prompted his companion, who had been an army captain serving in Trieste, to entertain us with the saga of his war exploits. 'I don't want to hear them,' said Evelyn. 'Oh but you must. They're absolutely hilarious. Tell Evelyn about the holy water font that was mistaken for a urinal.'

The captain, an ingenuous type, proceeded to spin his yarns, which convulsed 'Red' with guffaws interspersed with hiccups. Evelyn pressed his fingers to his ears and sat back with an air of weary resignation. Towards the climax he turned to me and asked: 'Has he finished?' When I nodded he removed his fingers and contemplated the table cloth. Lady Troubridge strove to remedy the gaffe but the dinner was a social and culinary failure. We adjourned for coffee, which Evelyn could not drink on account of his insomnia, to 'Red's' bedroom – the room with the view. Our host repeated 'It's intoxicating,' alas, in his case, too truly. Subsiding on to a deck-chair, he maundered on about how much he had enjoyed writing his last novel. 'It may be bad but it has given me lots of fun.' Evelyn did not mention that he had finished his beautiful book on St Helen of Egypt or that he was rewriting *Brideshead Revisited* – he was dissatisfied with the original version and wanted to make the narrative more direct. He seldom discussed his own writing and he discouraged others from doing so in his presence. Singularly free from the egotism of most writers, successful or unsuccessful, his estimate of his own work is embedded in *The Ordeal of Gilbert Pinfold*: 'He regarded his books as objects which he had made, things quite external to himself, to be used and judged by others. He thought them well made, better than many reputed works of genius, but he was not vain of his accomplishment, still less of his reputation.'

Provoked by his silence, 'Red' delivered a panegyric upon the vigour, the splendour, the creative genius of America, which was moving in the circumstances despite its platitudes. Nobody in

Europe had begun to appreciate the virtues of the little man from Main Street, his marvellous potentialities: he might seem dumb and crude but he was making a better world possible. That little man would conquer the moon and the stars. A paean to democracy followed. 'Red's' bloodshot eyes bulged, his fingers trembled clutching the chair, as he wound up with a denunciation of contemporary English literature. I was reminded of Walt Whitman's 'Placard "Removed" and "To Let" on the rocks of your snowy Parnassus'. For literature had been reborn in the United States. 'You Britishers will have to cross the Atlantic to learn how to write. We are rejuvenating the language. Have *you* added anything new to the English language, Evelyn? Your "bright young people" are not likely to be remembered. I guess they're already forgotten. But *Main Street* and *Babbitt* will be remembered, so will *Arrowsmith* and *Elmer Gantry*. And there's more to come.'

Evelyn reddened more with embarrassment than resentment but he endured it all most patiently and politely. I suspect he was aware of the pathos underlying this half-defiant monologue.

'I can't think what got into him,' said Lady Troubridge when we escorted her home. 'I'm afraid poor old Red is off colour. He doesn't usually behave like that, I assure you.'

'I rather enjoyed the latter part of it,' said Evelyn. 'I was only afraid he might burst a blood vessel.'

He might have held this distressing evening against me but the macabre element had saved it, from his point of view.

Instead of Venice I suggested that we go to Verona, within easy distance of Vicenza, Mantua, Parma and other fine cities unknown to Evelyn, and it proved a fortunate choice. Pisan Gothic, Romanesque, Renaissance, Baroque, almost every style was represented here and it was extraordinary how they blended in relatively limited space, as on the Piazza delle Erbe, surrounding the bright umbrellas of the market stalls. Its harmonies of faded fresco and marble, of softness and mellowness of colour, prepared one for the symphony of Venice. We found comfortable rooms, and the excellent restaurants catered to every palate:

Evelyn went so far as to declare that he 'preferred wop food to frog food, it lay lighter on the liver'. The Romanesque and quasi-Gothic churches, the eleventh century San Fermo, the twelfth-century Cathedral and San Zeno, the thirteenth-century Sant' Anastasia, pleased him better than the Florentine churches as he maintained their atmosphere was more deeply religious: of this he was a better judge than I, for he rose before I did to attend early Mass. He had already breakfasted on salami and wine when I joined him to see the sights. No companion could have been more appreciative, and I thought Verona satisfied him more than any other city we visited together. He was as enthusiastic as Ruskin about the Scaligeri tombs, and the medieval chivalry of Pisanello's fresco of St George and the Princess of Trebizond enchanted him.

In essentials he had not changed though he allowed himself to appear middle-aged, with a paunch that imparted solidity and dignity to his gait. Clad as an Edwardian country gentleman, he carried a stick 'to beat the Communists in case of assault', he explained. In his new role of crusty colonel he insisted on speaking English to Italians, who could not understand him.

Our arrival coincided with a festival in honour of Our Lady: San Zeno was brilliantly decorated and *Ave Maria* was written on the houses in the vicinity; paper garlands, flowers and lanterns hung from the doors and windows and crinoline balconies. Next Sunday the Cardinal Patriarch of Venice, the future Pope John, celebrated Mass in Sant' Anastasia: the ceremony for the beatification of the boy saint Domenico Savio was very solemn and gorgeous. I was exhausted with standing two hours in the dense congregation: not Evelyn, who listened with rapt attention to the Cardinal Patriarch's sermon, which lasted a good hour.

Our excursions were sprinkled with comical incidents. In the Palazzo del Tè at Mantua a custodian with the high-pitched voice of a eunuch fastened himself to Evelyn and trotted beside him with lecherous winks and nudges to draw his notice to the erotic details of Giulio Romano's ceilings. Evelyn's attempts to shake him off were unavailing and he accused me in jest of goading the creature on. Neither of us were sound sleepers, and the narrow street outside our hotel was noisy with revellers in the early hours of the morning. I peered out and shouted 'Basta!' till I heard a resounding splash. Evelyn dispersed them with the contents of his water jug.

This carefree holiday had a disconcerting climax. Before leaving Verona we returned to Evelyn's favourite restaurant. He was scrutinizing the trolley of *hors-d'oeuvre* when a gangling youth sauntered in, accompanied by a typical American matron and a bearded escort. The youth wore a flowery chintz-like shirt open at the neck without a jacket or tie, and as he passed us he picked up a couple of *grissini* from another table and shovelled them into his large loose mouth.

'Look, look, the Ape Man!' Evelyn exclaimed. Unfortunately the trio sat down at the next table. Perhaps the matron had not heard Evelyn's comment but she must have sensed an adverse wind, for she turned towards us and said: 'I guess my son should be wearing a coat and tie but we're from California, see, and our climate's so wonderful the boys don't need to wear them.'

'Madam,' said Evelyn sternly. 'We haven't been introduced and I don't care where you come from. When he enters a decent restaurant your son should be properly dressed.'

The matron goggled as if she had been slapped. She dabbed at her spectacles with a sight-saver, and remarked: 'Well, I guess that's what the Marshall plan has done for us. We pay eighty-five cents tax in the dollar for you folks over here and that's all the thanks we get. Nothing but high-hatting and rudeness. I guess you're English. You Limies will never forgive us for helping you win the war. From now on I'm an isolationist. What's being done with all the money we're giving you I'd like to know? I don't see much sign of progress.'

Evelyn turned to me in a rage: 'This is intolerable. And it's your fault. They spotted you as a fellow Yank. You deliberately enticed them here to annoy me.' He drew himself up to leave while I heard the boy protesting, 'He was only kiddin', Ma!'

311

I was not inclined to follow when Evelyn marched out of the restaurant. I apologized on his behalf, explaining that my friend was rather eccentric and that her son's comment had been correct: he had not intended to be insulting. Slightly mollified, the lady proceeded to tell me her life history. She was a surgeon's widow from Santa Barbara and this was her first visit to Europe in years. She had come over for her son's education. Already she was beginning to regret it. Such rudeness everywhere! Americans were not appreciated. They might as well spend their hard-earned dollars at home. The bearded companion was a Russian guide who spoke English . . .

In spite of this unpleasant epilogue for which I was held responsible, Evelyn bore me no grudge. He must have forgotten about it, for he sent me a heart-warming letter from Paris and a card inscribed: 'My love to Red Lewis, Mrs Walston and all stray Yanks. I was touched to learn that I gave the impression of industry during our lazy days in Verona.' When I reminded him of such incidents later he treated them as figments of my imagination.

Our next excursion was more amusing in retrospect than in reality, for his *Pinfold* period was about to incubate. In this age of comparatively harmless soporifics it was characteristic of Evelyn to resort to such Victorian drugs as bromide and chloral, which he combined with brandy and *crème de menthe* to camouflage the flavour. As he had also been taking pills for rheumatism, the mixture affected him with a sort of paranoia.

Early in March, 1952, he sent me a telegram proposing a trip to Capri or Palermo. I was feeling so run down after an attack of influenza that I fancied any change must be for the better, especially in Evelyn's company, and his arrival in Naples provided a welcome recreation. Neither of us was a picture of health. We had both injured our knees during the war, Evelyn on jumping from a parachute, and rheumatism had invaded the vulnerable joint: he relied on a stick to support him. In order to see the churches near Via Tribunali it was necessary to walk, and he hobbled so painfully that I found myself hobbling in sympathy. Even so he was a pertinacious sight-seer and I knew what was likely to interest him: the Surrealistic sculpture in the Sansevero Chapel, where the figures of Modesty and the dead Christ are visible under transparent marble veils and a man struggles out of a net, symbolical of sin; the ghastly skeletons of nervous systems in the crypt below; and Caravaggio's 'Seven Acts of Mercy' in the Monte della Misericordia, a painting in which it is difficult to detach one act of mercy from another. 'Feeding the hungry' and 'Visiting the prisoner' are combined in the startled woman feeding her old father in prison from her breast. A priest with a torch looms above her, no doubt connected with the projecting feet, all we see of a corpse – 'Burying the Dead'. Whose ear and whose leg emerge from yonder shadow? A plumed knight in the foreground doffs his cloak for a bare-backed beggar – 'Clothing the naked'. The shell in a hat is a symbol of pilgrimage or 'Sheltering the stranger'. Could it be Samson drinking from the jawbone of an ass or was it 'Giving drink to the thirsty'? Caravaggio himself stands sombrely in the left-hand corner. 'All very rum,' said Evelyn, puzzling over what Hinks called its 'structural equivocations', which he examined with approval.

He was not chary of wine in spite of his rheumatism, and he had an enviable appetite. Lunching at a restaurant which was patronized by 'Lucky' Luciano, I drew Evelyn's attention to the notorious gangster, who had been deported from the U.S.A. He resembled a bespectacled solicitor surrounded by shady clients, who crept in furtively to consult him during his meal. His expression was intelligent, even kindly, and he tipped the waiters lavishly with dollar bills. Evelyn had never heard of him but he was sure his son Bron had. To my astonishment he procured a picture postcard, walked over to Luciano, and asked him to sign it as a souvenir for his son. The gangster, equally astonished, obliged him with a flattered smile.

At this time Evelyn was my chief liaison with friends in England, and he regaled me with news of their recent activities, embellished with his inimitable fantasy. Thus one boon companion had brought an exotic animal called a coaita from Brazil, a cross between a monkey and a fox, which he had presented to Cyril Connolly. As if it realized that servants were hard to obtain, the animal promptly stepped into the breach: more agile than any kitchen maid, it scoured the dishes with its prehensile tongue. It drew the window blinds and wakened guests with early cups of tea. An invaluable acquisition of which the Connollys had every reason to be proud! If a guest looked lonely it was ready to hop into bed with him, and it had the great virtue of silence: it could not blab. Its only peccadillo was a tendency to tipple, and since Cyril had inherited many vintage wines from Dick Wyndham's cellar, several bottles of these had been swilled by the boozy beast, which was apt to snatch your glass at dinner unless you were careful. Alas, I have forgotten half the talents of this pet which Evelyn described with gusto.

About general conditions in England he was pessimistic. The Conservatives were exceeding the Labour Party in imposing restrictions, cutting down travel allowances, making the rich suffer in a bid for popularity. Ultimately he predicted a Labour dictatorship. 'We'll all end in a concentration camp,' he said.

Owing to his rheumatic knee, Palermo seemed more suitable than Capri, but after ten dismally rainy days we decided to cut our losses and return to Naples. The weather was a dire disappointment to Evelyn, who had brought his bathing trunks, expecting to swim and bask in the sun. His knee hurt him so that he refused to walk, and I developed an obstinate cold. Everything conspired to vex him. His letters had been forwarded from the Consulate to the wrong hotel, and he roundly berated the clerks for their inefficiency. When the Consul paid us a polite call he was snubbed outrageously. Conversation flagged under Evelyn's dudgeon, and the Consul remarking in a quaint *non sequitur*: 'I've a map of Mount Ararat which might interest you,' Evelyn replied: 'Why should it? Has the Ark been found?' Impatient of boredom, he raised an invisible barrier of barbed wire. Occasionally his rudeness was so extreme as to be fascinating, yet I regretted the impression he made on people who did not know him. One of the kindest and most generous of friends, he could exude such malevolence that it was startling. When I expostulated with him he retorted that I suffered fools too gladly.

I attributed his passing squalls to his state of health. With the Commandos during the war he had forced himself to be more robust than his physique. The epicurean had worn the mask of a stoic until he became one. But the strain of military life at high tension must have left a delayed reaction on his nerves. He told me he could not bear a garrulous person or a grinning face: he preferred people to look miserable. They had every reason to be in Palermo under the rain, among so many ruins left by the bombing of 1943. The lines of Prévert's *Barbara* recurred to me:

> *Il pleut sans cesse sur Brest*
> *Comme il pleuvait avant*
> *Mais ce n'est plus pareil et tout est abîmé . . .*

Brest had become Palermo as I tried to make out the once splendid quay called the Marina. The magnificent open staircase of the Palazzo Bonagia still stood, but it looked as if a breeze would send it toppling.

Our tour was not a total failure. Having greatly admired the waxworks by Gaetano Zumbo in the Florentine Bargello, representing scenes of the plague and putrefaction, with worms crawling out of ulcers and gluttonous rats, Evelyn was sorry to find no examples of his art in his native island, but Giacomo Serpotta's plasterwork, as gay as the waxworks were gloomy, provided a pleasing substitute. And indeed his stucco groups representing the mysteries of the Rosary had the smoothness of wax.

About a mile from Palermo on the way to Monreale we stopped at the Cappuccini convent where the dead friars used to be dried, dressed and placed upright in niches underneath the church so that their friends could visit them whenever inclined. Many not in holy orders had joined them – desiccated mummies of women and children, twins and dwarfs, standing, lying, crouching, grinning and scowling, the yellow skin adhering to the bones, like victims of a famine or Goya caricatures, coated with dust, their garments rotting away. When they collapsed they were bundled into sacks from which the hands and skulls protruded as if to preach or implore. Here was Donne's 'bracelet of bright hair about the bone' and here – an American vice-consul in evening dress, his hair, moustache and beard very neat and trim, less dusty than the rest in his glass coffin. The bodies had formerly been deposited in vaults behind iron doors for half a year, at the end of which they joined the majority. Altogether the catacombs contained some eight thousand natural mummies, though interment here was discontinued in 1881.

The monk who showed us round rattled off a facetious commentary in slangy English like a Shakespearian clown. Evelyn ordered him sharply to shut up. He spent a full hour examining the grisly relics with an expression akin to rapture. According to my guide book, 'the atmosphere of the catacombs is impregnated with a smell so offensive that it cannot be wholesome', but Evelyn differed. He announced that his knee was cured and left his stick in the taxi. Whether it was due to the dryness of the air or to the emanations of the mummies, he felt so much better that he would recommend it in future to sufferers from rheumatism. Turning to take a last sniff, he muttered 'Delicious!' as if it had been jasmine. He became more cheerful, in the right mood to relish the mouldering grotesques of the Villa Palagonia and the elegance of the other villas at Bagheria, which he pronounced 'buggery', formerly the resort of the Palermitan aristocracy.

The good Consul having prescribed Syracuse for 'p and q', meaning peace and quiet, we took an express train thither. The carriages were unusually crowded, and we discovered that there would be motor races in Syracuse next day and that every hotel would be packed. Until the races were over we were advised to stop in Catania. There we trailed from hotel to hotel but not a single room was available. Our last hope was Taormina, another hour's distance by train. Taormina was overrun with Scandinavians travelling in charabancs, and we were very tired and hungry after a second search when we were reluctantly conceded two cold and poky rooms in a pretentious caravanserai shortly before midnight.

Surrounded by tourists with cameras swinging from their necks, it was no pleasure to climb among the ruins of the much-publicized Graeco-Roman theatre or test its acoustics, and so many were taking snapshots of the view that we could not observe it with serenity: Etna shrouded in snow, beaches and headlands, how often seen in Victorian water-colours painted when Persephone had brought back the spring we sighed for. Where were the Grecian lovers and Uranians, those who came hither to cultivate '*Les Amitiés Particulières*' – the German baron whose photographs of naked boys emulated Tuke R. A., and the rest of them? The most ostentatious had been expelled by the Fascists; the others had emigrated to some other island. They had left no tell-tale trace. In my youth Taormina had been a polite synonym for Sodom: now it was quite as respectable as Bournemouth. Drab tourists as disconsolate as ourselves drooped in front of a shop window displaying an aspidistra and a placard inscribed 'Nice Cuppa Tea' in Gothic letters.

The weather was so warm in Naples that we were sorry to have left it. Evelyn was still dogged by petty vexations: his wife had not heard from him and he had no reply to an urgent wire he had sent; the proofs of *Men at Arms* might have gone astray since he was uncertain he had given the right address; he had not slept a wink in spite of his potion; and he complained of a stench of sulphur in the air. He longed to escape to the country.

We compromised by taking a boat to Sorrento. It was full of the same tourists we had seen in Taormina, and while he was exhilarated by the sea crossing he was enraged by a garrulous cab-driver whose manner seemed to him derisive, and by the swarm of touts and beggars. Among the latter was a ragged nun with a bristly face. With his usual generosity he gave her a thousand lire note. 'Too much,' I muttered. 'I never refuse a nun,' he said reproachfully. The creature grabbed his donation and ran off without waiting to thank him, betraying his sex with a pair of brawny calves. Evelyn was annoyed with himself for not detecting the transvestite.

Several friends who met him with me remarked that he was totally unlike the person they had expected from reading his books. They had expected – one wondered what? – presumably some modern version of Beau Brummell. Authors tend to disappoint their readers in the flesh. Perhaps because I had met him at Oxford when we were both young if not unfledged, his writings struck me as an essential part of him, even the black humour and vein of cruelty, sharpened by the failure of his early marriage. *A Handful of Dust* was written in his blood. He was primarily an artist in revolt against philistinism, and this was our lasting bond. Compassion is extraneous to the satirist, yet it is inherent in his later writings. If he lacked what is loosely called a 'social conscience', as he wrote in *Pinfold*, he was certainly philanthropic in a practical sense. His anti-Americanism was the only pose I considered unworthy of him, a futile gesture against what our friend Graham Greene described as 'the sinless empty graceless chromium world'. It has always seemed to me superficial as well as unfair to charge America with a monopoly of these negative attributes, which apply to modernism in general and to Communist countries in particular. But Evelyn's anti-Americanism was exaggerated for my benefit: as the boy in Verona remarked, he was 'only kiddin''.

Though everything had conspired against us in Sicily, we extracted much amusement from our mishaps in retrospect. Nothing could exceed the drollery of Evelyn's impromptu acts. John Sutro had coined the adjective 'Wavian', as Shavian applied to Shaw, and for me these were acts of a Wavian comedy. He walked on to the stage and without bothering to take part in the plot created a character which was an epitome of his humour, making a trenchant comment on this or that episode, and he walked off when we were hoping to hear more. Sacha Guitry once said that a good joke required three people to make it successful: the perpetrator, the person who can see it, and the one who misses the point. The pleasure of the person who appreciates it is

318

increased by the latter's bewilderment, and I often found myself in this position in Evelyn's company. While I simmered with laughter there were others who failed to see the point. And when that is instantaneous it is apt to dissolve in the process of elucidation. One had to know him well to savour the idiosyncrasies of his humour. Life seemed flatter and duller after he had left me.

❦ 18 ❦

Memoirs should concentrate on all that is vital and attempt to recapture the hours and moments of exaltation and delight, the friendships, colours and emotions that have intensified an existence and magnified it if only for the time being. Above all the friendships. A sigh often follows a memory, said La Bruyère, but so does a smile; and I would not underestimate the power of laughter even when it is mingled with tears. Pain, suffering and death are best left to the poets and novelists and philosophers, who read new meanings and mysteries into them; and art can sometimes sublimate them.

I have seen much suffering, but I doubt if anything that saps vigour of mind improves character or contributes to beauty. It was my fortune to live with people older and wiser than myself, yet they did not seem old to me, and their friendship was warmer and deeper than that of most of my contemporaries. To my own age I seldom gave a thought. The early loss of my hair added years to my appearance but kept it static. When I wore a wig at a costume ball I was not recognized.

My father kept his hair and a boyish spirit into his late seventies, but he grew old quite suddenly and it was distressing to witness the decline of a man who had been blessed with unusual energy. He was in his eightieth year when he died in 1953. During the last year of his life he had been kept alive by the doctors he consulted. Each had prescribed a different medicine, filling him with renewed hope, but the relief was momentary. With arteriosclerosis and a failing heart, he sank into a hopeless depression, Day in day out he had sat in his great armchair by the window. gazing mournfully at the garden he had created. At first he had

Harold Acton and Norman Douglas

Harold Acton

listened to the radio with faint interest: now he preferred silence. He once spoke of wanting to see George Kaftal's *Iconography of the Saints in Tuscan Painting*, but when I brought him the book and turned the pages for him, he closed his eyes. When visitors called on him he did not seem aware of their presence. The only thought he expressed as he sat in his enormous bedroom surrounded by his most precious Primitives was one of regret, almost in the same words as Cardinal Mazarin's: 'To have to leave all this!' Sometimes he would mutter *'Cimitero'*. Nothing my mother or I could say to distract his mind affected him in the least. He just sat with folded hands, enveloped in a fog of weakness and pain: now and then an alarming shudder would convulse him. He was so heavy that it was difficult to move him, and his body was full of sores. It was a harrowing life-in-death.

As an orphan he had been brought up by priests, but though he had a respect for the Church, he had lost his faith long ago. Surrounded by religious art, he remained an agnostic. When his condition seemed desperate I considered it my duty to fetch a priest, but by then he was only half-conscious: his head dropped down on his chest when he received Extreme Unction. He was so shattered that death must have come as a release.

My mother, who had been constantly beside him during his illness, vigilant and tender, running to forestall his slightest wish when the nurse was absent and even when she was present, had exhausted her own reserve of energy. Nobody would have suspected that she was older. Now she had only me to depend on, and I did what I could to relieve her of the numerous trials attendant on death. Our old servants, who took a sombre pleasure in funerals, gathered round the prostrate figure of the *padrone*, whose dignified features had turned to pale alabaster under the light of flickering candles. There was a quiet funeral in the beautiful Allori cemetery where my brother had been buried, but my mother had not the strength to attend it. From now on I seldom left her for any length of time

By my father's express wish I did not publish any notice of his death in the newspaper. Of course I was blamed for this when half a page of the *Nazione* is daily devoted to obituaries couched in such formulae as: *Munito dei conforti religiosi è serenamente spirato* . . . *Dopo lunga malattia è deceduto* . . . *E'mancato all' affetto dei suoi cari* . . . *Ieri cessava di vivere* . . . *E'spirato improvvisamente* . . . and so drearily forth. However, some unknown person did publish an obituary.

Time disperses, but my father had always assembled works of art, and his collection was a complete expression of his taste and discrimination. When he could no longer browse in the antique shops, he sat dreaming in front of a painting or a statue. These were his true companions. Now they have become mine, but in spite of the pleasure they afford me, human companionship is dearer and more necessary. My friends are sacred to me though my life in Florence has separated me from the majority. Unlike most of them, I had lived much longer with my parents, over-shadowed by my father's restless personality, and latterly by his portentous gloom. The whole house had revolved round him for fifty years, and I was nearly fifty.

Fortunately two of our relations chose this time to visit us and their natural joie-de-vivre was a tonic to my mother. My cousin Louise Dillingham had no patience with illness, her own or anyone else's, and she refused to talk about death. She communicated her brisk vitality to others and she stirred our somewhat stagnant atmosphere. My mother had never shared her fondness for promiscuous society, but her light gossip about feminine topics was a gay contrast to the whining widows she usually saw. Whenever she stayed with us she coaxed my mother out of her shell of retirement. As the leading hostess of Honolulu she had much to relate of the VIPs she had entertained: the Duke of Windsor when Prince of Wales, Will Rogers, Noël Coward, and other eminent entertainers. General Douglas MacArthur was the brightest star in her diadem of guests. 'His wife calls him The General. I call him Douglas,' she remarked proudly. As her husband Walter called him 'Mac', I wondered which of these appellations he preferred. To be on such intimate terms with public figures flattered, as the French would say, her little vanity. She hinted that they confided their secrets to her over cocktails: if so, she was the soul of discretion.

Louise took her responsibilities as a hostess seriously: she was an indefatigable organizer, never happier than when contriving happiness for others. In recent memoirs and diaries I have noticed a tendency to ridicule this vanishing species. Individual hostesses are being replaced by committees, but these are poor substitutes for a charming woman who introduces her guests to the people most likely to interest them and studies their predilections. As Maugham exclaimed: 'What would happen to the lions if there were no hunters to hunt us?' Louise made her friends feel like lions. But she made us smile when she observed that we were living in a backwater: it was all very beautiful, but how could we bear to live so much in the past? True, Florence was small but its range of intellectual interests was boundless. We could produce few public figures of international repute except in the field of art and scholarship.

Of course she visited Berenson, who welcomed her vivacity. Certain women stimulated him, he said, because with rare exceptions they remained adolescent-minded. Perhaps Louise would not have relished this explanation. With Francis Toye, then directing the British Institute of Florence, she failed to hit it off. Having written a popular book about Verdi, he remarked in his jocular tone: 'You know, I discovered Verdi.' 'How curious,' she replied. 'I've heard Verdi's music all my life but this is the first time I've heard of you.' Toye snorted with resentment: knocked off his perch, he referred to her as 'that intolerable American cousin of yours'. But I was grateful to her for liberating my mother from her inhibitions. Her taste had been influenced by Elsie de Wolfe, Syrie Maugham, and other hostesses who went in for interior decoration professionally. Their fads became hers – all white at one period, all beige at another. Her eagerness to keep up to date is reflected in a jingle which she sent my mother:

> I have only just a minute
> Only sixty seconds in it

Forced upon me can't refuse it
Didn't see it – didn't choose it
But it's up to me to use it
I must suffer if I lose it
Give account if I abuse it
Just a tiny little minute
But eternity is in it.

Louise 'warmed both hands before the fire of life', and her minutes were crammed with activity.

Outside La Pietra I oscillated between the different poles of Osbert Sitwell at Montegufoni and Berenson at I Tatti. In spite of his occasional murmurs of failing vigour, tired eyesight, hay fever, and other trials accompanying old age, Berenson was still alert and agile. He made the most of late and early hours between the fixed periods of his retirement to rest. Nicky Mariano ministered to his every want as she had done for the last thirty years or more. Every sunset ravished him with delight, and like *L'Étranger* of Baudelaire, he paused in ecstasy before the passing clouds: . . . *là bas* . . . *les merveilleux nuages*. And he deplored the poverty of paint, of language, to communicate the infinite wonder of nature. He cherished one superstition which I shared: he would try to avoid seeing the new moon through glass. Once when we gazed at the new moon together, its pale thin eyelash over a tree loaded with ripe persimmons glowing like lanterns on the bare branches, he remarked: 'For fifty years painting should be forbidden.'

Though he constantly reverted to art in conversation he preferred to talk of other subjects. More than ever susceptible to the charms of young women, he would stroke their hands, their hair. Some shivered at these ghostly caresses, for he seemed hardly flesh and blood. He liked to tell of the doctor who recommended a patient to give up wine, women and song. 'I'll begin with song,' said the patient. His memory remained phenomenal though certain names escaped him, and he worried until they returned like truant schoolboys.

Every time I called on him I met some writer or scholar exchanging news, answering questions, delivering messages, hovering over a hypothesis, analysing a publication or event, and inspecting the pictures under the guidance of Nicky or Luisa Vertova. So many regenerative afternoons and evenings! To the very young B.B. seemed formidable. His manner and delivery had the formality of an age when 'peace and leisure soothed the tuneful mind'. Though he deplored his lack of style in the writing of English he used to say that he should have been a novelist. Perhaps his friendship with Edith Wharton had encouraged this notion, for his career had been romantic and he had come in contact with bipeds of many classes and nationalities. In the plethoric variety of his reading he managed to find time for modern novels, and he was as eager to discuss the craft of fiction as that of painting with Percy Lubbock, a mandarin of prose who had sat at the feet of Henry James, with Somerset Maugham and Sinclair Lewis, and with younger writers like Mary McCarthy and Anna Banti. But he was essentially a critic, and when a mind is so copiously stored with classics live and dead as well as with a photographic memory, it is seldom apt to produce original fiction. Familiarity with too many languages can also be a disadvantage, for the word that fails to express the exact shade of meaning in one language crops up in another and spoils its rhythm. B.B. was fascinated by the soul of words and had a passion for the *mot juste*. The best writers I have known in French, Italian and English were monolingual. B.B.'s *Sketch for a Self-Portrait* and later writings testify to the wide range and keenness of his curiosity as well as to a dissatisfaction with himself, a haunting sense of failure. Dip into them, and I hear his quiet voice and see his smile, the twinkle of his Puckish malice. He shared the French liking for general conversation and discouraged the Anglo-Saxon duologue which isolates couples at the dinner-table and in the drawing-room. But on afternoon walks he would discuss what was uppermost in his mind, the book he was reading, the person he had been seeing, and his talk was diapered with anecdotes. Discussing an archaeologist we knew, he quoted a Florentine carpenter's definition, pithily Tuscan in its simplicity: *Vuole rifare un ombrello* – 'He wants to remake an umbrella'.

Bad translations often remind me of his story of the American lady who visited Victor Hugo when he was old and deaf. 'Tell Mr Hugo,' said the lady to the bard's interpreter, 'that I look forward to reading his book when I go home.' Turning to the poet, the interpreter shouted in his ear: '*Cher Maître, Madame vient de dire que vous êtes l'Aigle de la France.*'

Somerset Maugham was nearer his age than most of the writers who visited him, and it was amusing to see the two veterans side by side, both impeccably tailored, dapper and urbane. They watched each other shrewdly between the exchange of courtesies. Which would win the golden apple of longevity? Maugham was more attached to the luxuries of this world, but he was indifferent to the fate of his French property and art collection, assured that the essential part of himself would survive in his writings. B.B., who was fundamentally austere, hoped that his library and collection would be preserved for the students of his cherished university. Maugham remained a nomad, believing that writers should keep in touch with 'the stream of life, with people, with happenings of import', as he confided to his Boswell, Mr Garson Kanin. I Tatti was by no means cut off from people and the stream of life – happenings of import are relative – but B.B.'s aims were different: he sought information, interpretation, reflection. Though he had travelled far to see works of art in their own environment, he suspected that the same time 'could have been better spent in the library, with books and photographs. It is there, and not picnicking around, that scholarship is apt to be most creative and productive'. He described I Tatti as a library with living-rooms attached.

Maybe Maugham was a trifle more nimble in gait and gesture, for he had been a regular patient of Dr Niehans, the magical rejuvenator, but his face was more deeply wrinkled and when it was still his mouth drooped with discontent. His stammer was effective in accentuating a point, as when he complained of the b-b-boredom of excessive f-fornication in recent fiction. Adultery was all very well, but when little else happened except wife-swopping one could not keep up one's interest in the plot. B.B. suggested that the creation of character was the hallmark of great fiction – character so round and firm and clear that one forgot the literary context. Maugham objected that it would be hard to find twenty such creations in the whole of our literature. B.B. cited David, Saul, and Samuel, evoking the Rabbi who had taught him Hebrew in early childhood when he had identified himself with the heroes of the Old Testament. Maugham's stammer got worse. B.B. whispered to me: 'The poor old thing's worn out!' As B.B. was already in his ninety-second year it was hard to keep a straight face.

Maugham was complacent about his flair for painting, which was literary and commercial rather than aesthetic. His writing of *The Moon and Sixpence* had led him to Gauguin and his friend Alphonse Kann had led him on to the Post-Impressionists. His collection had been a profitable investment and he was much gratified by the result of its sale at Sotheby's. But B.B. noticed his lack of feeling for visual art when he showed him his own collection, and he remarked that Alan Searle, his secretary-companion, was infinitely more perceptive. This deficiency was also apparent in Maugham's descriptions of scenery. Maugham had travelled in search of copy for his novels and short stories: he detested sight-seeing. On the other hand B.B. was a passionate sight-seer and he published a book with that title: he had travelled less but he had seen and felt more. Maugham once asked me to read aloud his description of the Great Wall of China, in which he took pride as an example of sinewy poetic prose. It sounded well, the sort of passage a teacher might select for an English dictation, but it was as trite as one of Logan Pearsall Smith's *Trivia*. One suspected he was writing with eyes on the public instead of on the Great Wall. He could not help playing to the gallery he despised.

Alan Searle had much to put up with. Though he was not

tempted to be rejuvenated in the prime of life, Maugham insisted on his submitting to the same series of injections. Three weeks without a cigarette or a cocktail seemed to him a futile sacrifice, but the matter was clinched with: 'You'll get no Christmas present unless you keep me company.' So the lambs unborn were also pumped into Alan. 'And how did you feel after it?' I queried. Definitely uncomfortable, he replied, for he had to shave several times a day and he often found himself in a state of embarrassing excitement.

Though nothing save a drastic face-lifting could have smoothed Maugham's myriad wrinkles, he was athletic for an octogenarian, and Alan confided to me that during a recent trip to Egypt the lubricious natives had been magnetized by Mr Maugham – whereas nobody deigned to glance at his junior. Apart from this long-suffering companion, Maugham cared for few individuals. He was gregarious in Riviera fashion and enjoyed society as a sporadic peep-show. 'I like to feel I have friends and it's nice to see them occasionally,' he said, 'but I prefer them at a distance. I don't want them to fence me in.' B.B. begged to differ: he loved to have his friends around him and to see them often. When they were absent and out of reach he was liable to suspect that they had ceased to care for him. He maintained a voluminous correspondence and delighted in the long letters he received, which were often read aloud to his guests after dinner. (Had I realized this in time I'd have taken more trouble with the letters I sent him.)

As I was in the predicament Maugham preferred, I found myself in agreement with B.B. I saw my best friends too seldom, but it never occurred to me to doubt their loyalty. My social ideal was Parisian, since culture in France is or was an eminently social quality: as Edith Wharton observed, 'wherever two or three educated French people are gathered together, a *salon* immediately comes into being'. I, too, believe that intimacy and continuity, rather than perpetual novelty, are the first requisites of social enjoyment. B.B. provided the nearest substitute for such gatherings in Florence. The miracle of good talk was repeated with the regularity of the liquefaction of San Gennaro's blood at Naples. But the chance introduction of a name obnoxious to our host might prevent the miracle from happening.

Some considered him selfish for not marrying Nicky, who had been his companion for so many decades. It was scarcely an exaggeration to say that she warmed his wrist-watch for him. As an old friend I took the liberty to tease them about it, but each objected that marriage would have been absurd at their age. I was not entirely convinced: for Nicky the marriage would have had material advantages. How much she had done and was doing for B.B. was not realized by the average visitor to I Tatti. I am sure that he owed the prolongation of his life to her. Again and again he pays tribute to her in his diaries: 'In the last thirty years (he was then eighty-nine) I have been in love seriously once, and lightly a number of times, but have loved one woman only, and that woman is Nicky Mariano . . . I can't imagine life without her. My world would crumble, and leave me alive perhaps, as an animal, or even a vegetable, but not as myself, if she should die before me.' And yet, and yet . . .

Nicky was twenty-two years younger than B.B., but after living nearly twice that period with him what did the difference matter? She had been the hostess of I Tatti even when Mrs Berenson was alive. At Casa al Dono, the country house he gave her at Vallombrosa where they spent part of the summer, B.B. observed the same studious routine as at I Tatti, and fresh relays of books and periodicals were dispatched to and fro. It was a sheltered house with entrances on two levels. The back entrance faced a grove of fir trees and a narrow path over a babbling brook led to the rural hut where we sat after luncheon for coffee and later for tea, and I often smiled at the contrast between our talk, which ranged over every subject under the sun, and our rustic surroundings – B.B. in his smart Edwardian panama reclining on a chaise-longue wrapped in a rug, and a view of the silvery valley below shimmering in the heat.

The climb to Vallombrosa in August was an invigorating crescendo of coolness, of purer and purer air as we wound round and up and up; then instead of reaching the ancient monastery we dipped down between dense fir trees with the forest murmurs of *Siegfried* in our ears, for the house was hidden and solitary. Sometimes I had to escort elderly ladies there, former flames of B.B. who insisted on closing the windows of the car in their dread of *courants d'air*, and one would arrive gasping and half stifled to gulp the delicious freshness. Nicky arranged that there should always be somebody to entertain B.B. and quench his thirst for information. If his concert-going days were over, there was the wireless and gramophone and the chamber-music of conversation, the flute-notes of John Pope-Hennessy, the 'cello of Kenneth Clark, and various violins, to which eventually the plangent harp of Derek Hill and the clarinet of Willy Mostyn-Owen were added. Derek Hill was the resident artist as it were, who inhabited B.B.'s adjacent villino on the way to Vincigliata. When he was not painting the Tuscan landscape he was depicting B.B. in and out of bed. 'Please don't move. The light on your beard is too heavenly. I simply must capture it,' I heard him beseech, as we sat by the fireplace in the living-room. And B.B. posed for him like a matinée idol. Derek caught his likeness better than other artists at this period. Willy Mostyn-Owen moved into the villino after Derek, a willowy Ariel languid with solicitude, who compiled a bibliography of B.B.'s works for his ninetieth birthday. (I delivered a broadcast for the occasion but as it was given in London neither of us was able to hear it.)

Among the many distinguished visitors to Casa al Dono the theatre was represented by that Protean *diseuse* Ruth Draper, who could create the illusion of a crowded stage, impersonating the different members of a single family such as the three – or was it four? – generations of American immigrants. Without any external disguise, each performance was a transformation, for she was demure, stiff, even shy in casual intercourse. She told me that she had tried in vain to act in plays and monologues written by others: she could only interpret her own compositions. She could not even bring herself to act in a sketch Henry James had written for her, though she venerated that most decorous of novelists. When she was uncertain about her future career – whether to be an actress, a writer, or a monologuist – he admonished her (and she made the solemn enchanter relive in the measure of her diction): 'You have woven your own very beautiful little Persian carpet. Stand on it!'

The little Persian carpet was often unrolled for B.B. Before the summer house of Casa al Dono she conjured up the horticultural English gentlewoman displaying her garden and naming even the flowers that had not yet bloomed in her herbaceous borders. How often have I felt like that lady while showing the garden of La Pietra between seasons! Ruth Draper's was a very special art. Behind the prim spinsterish façade lurked the Henry James heroine with smouldering eyes. She had been in love with Lauro De Bosis, the poet who had been killed in 1931 when he had attempted to scatter anti-Fascist leaflets over Rome from a private aeroplane – a D'Annunzian gesture. The poems of De Bosis had got B.B. into trouble with the Fascist police, who had confiscated them from his library. A spy had denounced their presence: fortunately Ruth Draper's accompanying letter had served as an explanatory alibi.

B.B. had expressed a desire to meet Norman Douglas, but there were many hitches. Norman had not returned to Florence since the war. His decline into old age had been less placid. When he died at the age of eighty-three in February, 1952, he had been stricken with arteriosclerosis. The last time I saw him was at Capri in September, 1951. I had invited him to lunch with me but he was uncertain as to whether his legs could carry him and he had lost his appetite. However, his young friend Ettore persuaded him to make the effort. Some two years had passed since Norman's first encounter with Ettore in the Galleria of Naples, and this mercurial Neapolitan lad had conquered his heart. 'I cannot live without youth,' he told me. 'Without Ettore I should die.' As Ettore was only twelve at the time, this infatuation involved him in difficulties with the boy's mother. Having deserted her husband for another man, she had shown little interest in her son till she saw a means of exploiting him. She went over to Capri and lunched with Norman, and it seemed a festive occasion until she announced that she was taking Ettore home. The boy's father had raised no objection, but in Italy a mother is sacrosanct whatever her private morals, and Norman had to disburse rather more than he could afford in order to keep his protégé. My own impression of the boy was favourable in spite of adverse reports. He behaved as if Norman was his personal possession, the *grande scrittore inglese* of whose friendship he was proud. I found him packing empty gin bottles and other oddments into a battered suitcase, after which he tied a couple of flower-pots together with string as a present for his father. I remarked that the flowers did not look as if they would survive the voyage. Norman said it was worth risking. They would cheer the boy's father, who lived in a squalid hole near the railway station.

Laboriously we set off together from the Villa Tuoro, Norman, Ettore and I; and Norman's step became lighter when we reached La Pica's restaurant. His exuberance returned as soon as we were seated: he offered the traditional pinches of snuff and cracked salty jokes with the waiter whom he knew by name while adjusting his spectacles to examine the bill of fare. '*Culatello's* verboten but I'll filch a slice of yours,' he said with a wink. Ettore's appetite stimulated Norman's. 'Always take a *soupçon* of garlic with your salad and see that your partner does the same,' he said, 'especially if you want a frolic later on. Kisses are wet blankets if the garlic is unilateral.' The meal was punctuated with bursts of laughter and arteriosclerosis was sent to blazes. By the time we reached the funicular Norman was almost buoyant. In the mouldy café facing Naples he offered me another drink 'for the road' – in this case the sea, which he disliked. Ettore pressed on me a shiny tin cigarette-case '*come ricordo dell'amico di Signor Duglass*'. As I hesitated to accept a gift more valuable to him than to me, Norman said: 'Don't refuse it. Ettore likes nothing better than giving presents.' Not to be outdone by his junior, he slipped into my pocket the reprint of an article he had written ages ago about the blue Faraglione lizard. I invited him to visit me on the mainland, to sustain the illusion that he was neither old nor infirm. 'My travelling days are over,' he repeated. 'I shall not leave Capri again.'

This was my last sight of the rugged old stalwart, bidding us farewell from the top of the funicular. It was as if he had turned into a statue of one of the immortals. Standing there in his loose overcoat and shabby beret, he had the elegance of a Scottish Jacobite in exile. He was the most sanguine of the octogenarians I knew: his physique, like his intellect, belonged to the eighteenth rather than to the twentieth century.

John Davenport, who had hob-nobbed with him during the war years in London, proposed to write a book about him and he might have done it well. Not that Norman cared two hoots. 'Let 'em write what they like about me,' he said. 'I'm tough enough to stand it.' The book was never written.

Some years after his death John Davenport appeared in Florence with Douglas Cleverdon to produce a broadcast about him for the B.B.C. Together they had travelled from the South of France to the South of Italy, gathering personal impressions of Norman from people who had known him. They brought a recording machine which was turned on while these people, including myself, were prompted to air their views. Over a dinner-table, or rather a wine-table, for Davenport was a valiant votary of Bacchus, I remember answering many pointed questions. Davenport was an adroit questioner, and as Oscar Wilde said: 'Questions are never indiscreet: answers sometimes are.' Whether the answers of the other people interrogated were indiscreet I cannot judge, but Norman among the shades must have overheard them and decided to veto the broadcast. On returning to London my friends of the B.B.C. discovered that the recording machine had not functioned: some cog in it had become, as Italians say, 'enchanted'. Norman's spirit must have chuckled. I can hear his 'Pah, serve them right!' Eventually another broadcast was given, but in this case the compère had never met Norman and the answers must have been discreet enough to satisfy him.

The supreme producer of such portrait-programmes was Christopher Sykes, who succeeded in writing admirably solid and serious biographies at the same time. A Regency figure beaming with bonhomie, he had the gift of reconstructing complex personalities by means of imaginative sympathy – a rare gift among those whose labours culminate in the silent studio for the ears of innumerable listeners. His dramatization of *Prince Isidore* was in my opinion perfect, for he even introduced the national anthem of the Neapolitan Bourbons composed by Paisiello. We were both devotees of Max Beerbohm, whom he visited at Rapallo after staying with me. Having mentioned that he had seen Berenson in Florence, he was surprised when Max rejoined: 'And now I suppose you are going on to Cap Ferrat to see Somerset Maugham.' Christopher denied this: he had never met Mr Maugham. 'But you *must* be going to see Maugham!' Max insisted. Rather flummoxed, Christopher asked him why. Max explained that it was customary for people to call on him either on the way from Maugham to Berenson or on the way to Maugham from Berenson: he was but 'a wayside station'. Christopher assured him that for a change it was not the case. Max, secretly flattered, repeated incredulously: 'Fancy coming all the way here to see me!'

Now all are gone: Maugham, Max, and B.B., and I feel chilly at the thought of their departure. Maugham, who clung to life in spite of his professed disgust with it, was to survive the other prominent stations. Max Beerbohm I knew but slightly: he was brought up to La Pietra by Reggie Turner when I was an Eton boy, and I shall never forget his delicate choice of phrase and his suavely subdued eloquence, which had the same tone as Berenson's. In middle age (as he was then) he was still a dandy of the naughty nineties. In his youth he prophesied that 'the future belongs to the dandy. It is the exquisites who are going to rule'. A dandy and an exquisite he remained, wilfully isolating himself in semi-retirement from a world where dandies were demoted to Beatles and the exquisites were silenced or crushed by machinery. Already the main features of his character had been formed at Oxford, when Oscar Wilde remarked: 'The gods have bestowed on Max the gift of perpetual old age.'

The works of Pater, Henry James, and Oscar Wilde had all

contributed to his manipulation of English prose, and his domestic familiarity with the theatre had affected his outward manner. He entered a room like Algernon in *The Importance of Being Earnest*. One could imagine him asking: 'Did you hear what I was playing, Lane?' and settling on a sofa to devour fresh cucumber sandwiches. His half-brother Sir Herbert Tree was a famous actor-manager and Max had married an actress, Florence Kahn, whom he had admired prodigiously as Rebecca in Ibsen's *Rosmersholm*. 'In its appeal to the emotions,' he had written, 'Miss Kahn's acting is not more remarkable than in its appeal to the sense of beauty. Throughout the play, not a tone is inharmonious, not a movement without grace.' High praise from the caustic drama critic of the *Saturday Review*. Ada Leverson, however, remarked of Max's wife that she had left the stage before anybody realized she had been on it, so her performance in *Rosmersholm* must have been exceptional. She was said to suffer agonies of shyness, yet she talked and talked so breathlessly in a voice just above a whisper that I, who longed to listen to Max, became exasperated. She had the bottled-up intensity of a frustrated tragédienne, and I thought her tiresome as well as dowdy. Apparently Max was devoted to her. He had lived with his mother until she died, and his wife had become a second mother to him, cushioning his muted existence at Rapallo.

Maugham I knew better: he was also a friend of Reggie Turner and Ada Leverson, and he had often come to Florence with Gerald Haxton in the pre-war days when my parents kept open house. While Gerald painted the town red, Willie sat glued to the bridge-table – no galleries for him! I had stayed with him at the Villa Mauresque when he was a valetudinarian at the zenith of his popular success. Though he was kind to me superficially, his kindness had a jagged edge to it. When my father sought his counsel about my juvenile literary aspirations he advised him to give me a hundred and fifty pounds and tell me to go to Hell. Young writers should rough it, sail before the mast, and experience 'life in the raw'. Perhaps this was sound advice, but I did not relish it at the time. There was a Kipling ring to it, a tang of the rugger field. As Jules Renard observed: 'Some people give advice like a punch on the nose. One bleeds a little and replies by not following it.' And when my brother fell out of a window at Oxford, Maugham remarked with a mocking grimace: 'I suppose you were quite delighted.' He could not resist the slick rapier retort – *c'était plus fort que lui* – and this was his salient weakness as a writer. Life was less crude and criminal than it suited him to suppose. His wit, when witty, was as vinegar to the mellow vintage of Berenson's humanism or to Norman Douglas's invigorating *vin ordinaire*.

Norman, born to affluence, had turned to literature for a livelihood when he had lost his income, but his writing, no more than Max Beerbohm's, had helped him to build up a fortune. Max augmented his modest competence with the sale of his exquisite cartoons. For him and Norman enough was as good as a feast. Berenson and Maugham had been poor in their youth, and if B.B., spurred on by the demands of an exacting wife, had accumulated considerable wealth, he never mentioned money in all the years I knew him: the practical management of I Tatti was left to Nicky.

Maugham, on the other hand, enjoyed discussing the business side of his profession and was inclined to boast of the big sums he had earned. Compared with B.B., he was a hedonist on a sumptuous scale. B.B.'s table was seldom without guests; his food was copious and simple, but he was abstemious and he disapproved of hard liquor. Even so he was denigrated as a gross voluptuary by those who did not know him, and a puritanical professor wrote that his 'worldly aims soon contaminated his intellectual goals'. Maugham was also a light eater but he lived more luxuriously, accustomed to the richer French cuisine and crusted wine of legendary *cru*, though he broke the rules of French gastronomy by insisting on his preliminary cocktail, which had to be strong and cold – he was an expert on the subject – and he smoked incessantly. Of all the writers I knew he was the most mundane. Norman Douglas, the unabashed pagan who wrote 'Why prolong life save to prolong pleasure?' was in fact more spiritual in his approach to nature. He felt it more deeply, and his feeling led to a quasi-mystical comprehension. Maugham, whose mortal span was prolonged, like B.B.'s, beyond that of the majority, cosseted by all the creature comforts, was evidently unable to prolong pleasure. His laugh was strangely mirthless, his expression bleak. Graham Sutherland has recorded the latter exactly for posterity.

I was lucky to have known these men, who were incapable of dullness. 'My work will speak for me,' Maugham said, but I am glad to have heard him speak for himself, even when what he had to say was discouraging. At bottom he was an inverted senti-mentalist: his acid comments and withering retorts were derived from a study of such French dramatists as Henry Becque, renowned for their *mots cruels*, his prefabricated cynicism from Voltaire, but in him I was conscious of artifice, of a pose which had become natural: the moneyed malcontent. After all, Voltaire was a happy man. 'I'm so happy,' he once said, 'that I'd think myself wise if I dared to.' And again: 'Happy people are hated. I must ask M. Berryer to allow a placard to be put up in Paris: Voltaire warns all men of letters that he is not happy in the least.' Unlike Maugham, he had achieved serenity.

Many have compared Berenson's existence at I Tatti with Voltaire's at Ferney, and the analogy is not extravagant. Though B.B. had no ambitious plan of world reform, he had realized his ideal of life as a work of art. 'Paradise is where I am,' the patriarch of Ferney had declared; his library was 'a monument of taste'. B.B.'s was a monument of art history and aesthetics, iconography and the sociology of style, with all that these contribute to the development of critical values. As in the case of Voltaire, many visitors were more interested in B.B. as a person than in his works.

When I consider which of these old friends have influenced my life, I recall it was Norman Douglas who urged me to go to the Far East while the going was good. Before publishing *How about Europe?* in 1929 he said to me, almost in the same language: 'Go to the East, young man: leave behind you the frowzy and fidgety little hole called Europe . . . Rectify your values while there is still some flexibility in your mind.' Europe did seem frowzy and fidgety at the time and I am thankful I took Norman's advice, for the years I spent in China gave me self-possession as well as 'ease of soul'. Then after the last war, when life at home became a problem of which flight seemed the only solution, it was Osbert Sitwell who encouraged me to endure it. For this counsel, which helped me to make a decision when I was tempted to return to Peking, I have also cause to be grateful. And when I wrote my history of the Bourbons of Naples it was Osbert Sitwell who gave it the most honest praise.

From Max Beerbohm I learned to respect my limitations, to use my gifts, such as they are, discreetly without straining them. To Berenson I owe not only a deeper appreciation of the fine arts but indirectly a plan for the preservation of La Pietra, so that the garden my father created, the works of art he collected, and the adjoining property, may continue to delight and inspire future generations in so far as preservation is possible. If my father dreamt of any such plan it was never formulated, but my conscience tells me he would have endorsed it, and my mother in her wisdom and sympathy agreed.

It was my mother who finally reconciled me to this earthly Paradise of which I never feel worthy. I wake up every morning into a reality which is never quite real to me and contemplate a garden I have always known but which is always a visual surprise. But the sadder associations of the past crowd in upon me and the newspapers nag: 'You are one of the privileged. What have you done to deserve all this beauty?' I try to let others share it within reason. Seldom a day passes without visitors, and far more come to see the house and garden than to converse with the custodian-proprietor, which is doubtless salutary to my ego. But there are moments when the ego resents being treated as a mere occupant or amenable host. Twice a week the garden is open to the public during the season, and I am often forced to retire from their inquisitive gaping when I would sooner sit out of doors enjoying the sunshine.

I am aware of the hostile forces outside my gate. Dimly I hear the cries of the distant demagogues, of the new privileged class of politicians who preach like the Fraticelli in 1400: 'Repent, for the end of your world is nigh!'

According to the Japanese architect Kenzo Tange, we shall all inhabit a megalopolis in future and Florence may become part of one, whether its arms or legs or brain it is too early to predict – the brain is my guess. Such a trend looks plausible. No city, says Tange, will exist independently: the idea of a town centre is medieval, pertaining to superannuated structure or social hierarchy when cities developed slowly. Now they shoot up rapidly, and the architect's business is to control an energy that might become chaotic. The monuments of the past may survive, but little else, since everything modern is so easily built and demolished. The prospect is not inspiring. Perhaps even La Pietra will be absorbed by the octopus of the metabolic process. *Absit omen.*

❧ 19 ❧

When I finished the first volume of my history of the Bourbons of Naples I felt like dancing, and by a happy coincidence I was invited to a ball in Paris at this time. Marie-Laure de Noailles summoned her friends from far and near to celebrate the Mardi Gras of 1956 in the guise of a writer, artist or musician of their own nationality between the fifteenth and nineteenth centuries. For a change there were to be no Pierrots and Columbines and no disguise of sex, though Marie-Laure herself had once appeared as a reincarnation of Louis XIV.

Together with the invitation came an official passport to be delivered at the entrance of her mansion in the Place des États-Unis. Not the least of its attractions for me was the knowledge that artists, in the largest sense, were bound to predominate over the mere chic, the denizens of so-called café society who were soon to be dubbed the jet set.

For once I was offered a chance of concealing my baldness, but I could think of nobody in any requisite category to whom I bore a resemblance. Since I had been lecturing on William Beckford it occurred to me to go as the author of *Vathek*, which had been written in French. This enabled me to don a light wig with a costume of pale blue satin and silver and buckled shoes to match. For once I was not too displeased with my appearance.

Though I had contributed a lurid essay to James Laver's anthology of *Memorable Balls*, I had not attended any since the heyday of the Charleston, the Black Bottom, and the Blues – dances that scarcely harmonized with fancy dress. Marie-Laure's ball was memorable for the grandeur of the décor and the brilliant ingenuity of the costumes. It had been a freezing February day with snow glistening in patches like grazing sheep along the

340

Champs Elysées, and salt had been sprinkled on the boulevards to melt it. One stepped shivering into a current of semi-tropical warmth. A herald from the Comédie Française announced my name and Beckford's in stentorian tones before I climbed the grand staircase to the strains of festive music. In a billowing gown embroidered with gold and silver, her ebony hair scattered loose about her shoulders with an intricate coronet of golden vine-leaves, our statuesque hostess greeted her guests from the top of the stairs. She had chosen to be Délie, an anagram for *l'idée*, the half-imaginary lady – *objet de la plus haulte vertu* – who had inspired Maurice Scève, the precursor of Ronsard and Du Bellay; and it was a felicitous choice, baroquely allegorical.

After this solemn entry the centuries began to dissolve and intermingle. Leaving the future behind, as it were, one proceeded in a historical glow towards the salons, where three orchestras played all night. The rooms had been redecorated and filled with fragrant flowers. Spotlights had been cunningly concealed between the tapestries to illuminate the whirling couples with colours that varied with the music. One had often heard of champagne flowing: here it flowed copiously and there was plenty of thirst to slake in that ardent atmosphere. Such out-of-season fruit as ripe strawberries, bunches of grapes, pineapples and Sicilian mandarines were piled in pyramids in the dining-room. Altogether there must have been three hundred guests, but one soon detected old friends and acquaintances and discovered new ones, thanks to the licence allowed by disguise. My wig had wrought a flattering transformation. This was everybody's chance of being somebody for a night – not that there were nobodies present, but of this one could never be certain. No doubt many would have liked to be the people they represented, at any rate for a while, whatever good opinion they had of themselves. Most of the men considered their comfort and convenience, the women enhancement of their natural charms.

Georges Auric said he had chosen Balzac as it enabled him to wrap his portly figure in a florid dressing-gown. Other musicians came as musicians: Francis Poulenc as Chabrier, Raffaele de

Banfield as Mozart, Maurice Gendron as Berlioz. Writers seemed to be in the majority, and again I was impressed by the French attachment to literature – such a contrast with our indifference. Henry James had discerned a Chinese quality in the French writers he met, and he had met some of the greatest, including Flaubert. 'Chinese, Chinese, Chinese!' he had exclaimed. 'They are finished, besotted mandarins, and Paris is their Celestial Empire.' Their 'truly infernal intelligency of art, form, manner – their intense artistic life' fascinated him as it did me. Compared with ours they were still mandarins.

Most of the writers therefore came as writers: Marcel Achard as Stendhal; Lise Deharme as Louise Labé, the vehement poetess of Lyons who carried a sword to defend her lover; André Roussin as Alphonse Daudet – 'to pick up the Provençal accent he had lost in Paris'; Roger Peyrefitte as the Abbé Prévost (he could never shake off his ecclesiastical obsession); Jacques de Lacretelle as Lamartine – in this case because he resembled the poet and there was some family connection, while his wife, who was descended from Racine, came as Atalide, the heroine of *Bajazet*. Of the French beauties Denise Duval was dazzling in the role of Manon. Denise Bourdet appeared as Becque's *Parisienne* and Nora Auric as the Comtesse de Ségur, mainly because that author of pretty children's tales was of Russian origin like herself. There was a ravishing Madame Récamier, a Marquise de Sévigné, a Berthe Morisot, and Goya's Duchess of Alba, whose private identities escaped me.

In the English group Lady Diana Cooper was far lovelier than the Lady Blessington she had chosen; Pamela Churchill was a Queen Titania who would have converted all the fairies to sexual orthodoxy; Violet Trefusis was a haughty Lady Hester Stanhope, but she was not dressed as a Turk except for her turban. Characteristically she had declared that she would have to bring a camel with her in this role, hoping to smuggle in a friend who had not been invited. 'But who would be inside the camel? I should have to see his face,' said Marie-Laure. Anne Fleming was a coquettish Harriet Wilson, escorted by Patrick Leigh-Fermor as a sturdy Bulwer-Lytton. Together we toasted fantasy and bravura, for we were tired of the drabness of our social realists. Paul Valéry's son was overwhelmed by Paddy's panegyric of his father. Our French *confrères* were less exuberant than we.

There were several versions of Byron, but the most original was Peter Glenville, who came as Byron after swimming the Hellespont, with an effect of seaweed and brine still clinging to his close-fitting costume, which had been designed by Oliver Messel. Frank Giles strutted about in a red beard as Bernard Shaw. Poe had come with his raven; Petrus Borel with a wolf's head; and there was an uncanny image of little Toulouse-Lautrec among a posse of prelates. I looked in vain for John Betjeman, who should have come as a kind Anglican bishop. Paul-Louis Weiller was resplendent as François I, and the super-exquisite Baron de Rede seemed an Adonis from his native Lichtenstein in glittering Renaissance garb. That irrepressible nonagenarian Baroness Lo Monaco had flouted the rules by coming as Leonardo da Vinci, but no costume ball would have been complete without her.

For voluptuous beauty I would have awarded the palm to the Italians. Donna Cora Caetani was Lucrezia Tornabuoni in all her pure lineaments as depicted by Ghirlandaio; young Princess Ruspoli was the quintessence of all D'Annunzio's heroines in the black velvet gown her famous grandmother Donna Franca Florio had worn when she posed for Boldini's portrait; after which my memory becomes blurred, for these were classical goddesses who had stepped down from their pedestals. The very last to arrive, like bejewelled parrots from some exotic aviary, were Arturo Lopez and his wife as the King of Peru and La Périchole, but by then the ball was in full swing. To paraphrase Byron, three hundred hearts beat happily, and all went merry as a marriage bell. But a few ghosts flitted among the dancers: Étienne de Beaumont, who would have enjoyed it more than anybody, and Bébé Bérard, that masterly masquerader; and where was Jean Cocteau, so intimately connected with *Le Bal du Comte d'Orgel*? Jean was aweary: he preferred the solitude of Milly.

343

'*Un bal masqué démasqué*,' he had said; but this did not apply to me, for I entered into conversation with utter strangers and behaved with an abandon foreign to my nature. Perhaps it was the abandon of the Caliph of Fonthill.

Outside the fresh-fallen snow; inside *les neiges d'antan*. Marie-Laure had performed a spectacular conjuring trick. As in a mirror, even if distorted, here was a cross-section of that civilization which, according to Professor Arnold Toynbee, had been in a prolonged and convulsive decline since the sixteenth century, and one was almost 'rapt into a momentary communion' with bygone events like the professor – at any rate with bygone artists. No diplomats or politicians had joined the gathering. Those I met later complained that the time was ill chosen: the situation in Algeria was getting worse and worse, the whole world was going to pot, it was bad taste to fiddle while Rome was burning, and so forth. Their grumblings sounded like sour grapes to me, for come rain come shine, Mardi Gras had always been a popular festival, and they were eager enough to learn who was present and what costumes had been worn by whom.

Fresh from this carnival revelry, I returned to Florence to correct the proofs of my book. But the task I had set myself was by no means finished: there was a second volume to be written, more complicated because it involved digesting the cumbersome epic of the Risorgimento. I doubt if any subject since Napoleon has produced so copious a literature in which it is only too easy to wander off into bypaths and be swallowed up in a quicksand. No pamphlet concerning it could be too precious, no detail too minute. Garibaldi, Mazzini, and Cavour are the Three Musketeers whose exploits never pall, but I had to keep my eye fixed on their arch-enemy King Ferdinand II, for whom I developed an amused affection as a personification of the Neapolitan paterfamilias. He had been so unjustly maligned that it was a challenge. Until my second volume was published in 1961 I was submerged in the controversies of his reign and had to endure much tedium.

Naples was being transformed more rapidly than other Italian centres since the war. The city, containing one and a half million inhabitants, was inseparable from the vaster area of its background containing three millions. With Rome spreading towards Latina and Naples towards the North, one could foresee that the two capitals of Central and Southern Italy would merge eventually into a megalopolis. The *Autostrada del Sole* would hasten the process.

Looking down from the heights of Posillipo, the bay was as glorious as ever on the left, but on the right the awful expanse of Bagnoli, a pandemonium of cranes, sheds, smoke stacks with flames belching from furnaces night and day, was a vision of Hell on earth. This Gehenna was to promote prosperity: the huge ironworks were harbingers of progress, and the number of workers had doubled in the last ten years. Nitti's dream of Naples as the great factory and market of the South might soon be realized.

Corrupt politicians were the chief obstacle. The class of lawyers – the *paglietti* detested by Ferdinand II – magniloquent, gesticulating, bombastic, had risen to positions of power. They did not represent certain interests; they promoted them. Accustomed to defending delinquents, they continued, if not to defend, to turn a blind eye to their offences. The *Camorra* was still active in the countryside, where its bullies imposed their own prices on market products. The peasants, abjectly poor, had nobody to protect them. Those who rebelled would wake up to find their fields devastated in the morning. Sporadic murders brought some publicity to this state of affairs, as when Pasquale Simonetti, alias 'Pascalone 'e Nola', threatened Antonio Esposito's monopoly of the fruit and vegetable market. A fierce struggle ensued between the two factions and both the bosses were murdered. Esposito's widow obtained a post in the prefecture. When a central dairy thwarted the interests of other groups nails, mice, beetles and worms were introduced into its milk bottles.

Public sentiment was often on the side of the delinquents. This is amusingly illustrated in Eduardo De Filippo's play *Il Sindaco del rione Sanità* ('The Mayor of the Sanità district'), whose hero, Don Antonio Barracano, is a veteran *camorrista* with his own

345

code of justice, to whom the poor take their problems rather than to the law-courts. 'The law is well made but men devour each other . . . the cunning devour the ignorant. I protect the ignorant,' he says. How he does this and gets killed before retiring into private life is the subject of the plot. It is so specifically Neapolitan that it is unlikely to be appreciated outside Naples, but it is one of Eduardo's most stirring topical plays. Don Antonio Barracano's method of dealing with his defenceless clients reveals an intimate knowledge of their psychology.

The tragic aspects of Naples were perceptible behind the fluttering laundry of the Spanish *quartieri*, in the alleys of Forcella and the Sanità district, and nearer the sea in the Pallonetto di Santa Lucia and beyond the port; but it would be a mistake to lump all the inhabitants of the *bassi* together as hopelessly miserable, for many of those who leave them are homesick: they miss the drama and the entertainment of alley life. Father Mario Borrelli's 'House of the Urchins' (*Casa dello Scugnizzo*) was one of the brightest beacons amid this darkening of the local colour, never pitch dark owing to the Neapolitan capacity for joy. How this dynamic young priest obtained sanction to remove his cassock and live among the *scugnizzi*, meaning 'spinning tops', the homeless children of the streets, disguised as one of them, has often been told, most sensationally by Mr Morris West.

The *scugnizzo* was no recent phenomenon: he had been sculpted by Gemito and painted by Mancini, and Charles Grant had described him in 1882 in the *Cornhill Magazine*; but during the last war he had grown more sophisticated, a tough little Existentialist whose sole education had been on the streets, pimping, begging and stealing. Such an existence made cocky manikins of those who survived malnutrition and disease: despite all its hardships, especially in winter, they enjoyed its thrills, its camaraderie, and a sense of precocious virility. From his close association with them Father Borrelli could discriminate between the professionals and the dilettanti, those who were orphans and those who might well have been: to help them it was necessary to understand them. He had set forth on his mission in rags and he had had to play the role of gang-leader before he could induce eight of them to doss down in the shattered church which became their first home. Beginning with this small nucleus, he had collected more than a hundred when I met him. For the older boys a hostel was found with the Oratorians of St Philip Neri opposite the Cathedral – a stupendous edifice with two beautiful cloisters and a spacious terrace on the top floor with a superb panorama. At last they had found somebody to take a personal interest in them, to offer them a friendship that was sincere without any ulterior motive of exploitation.

Whenever I visited the children at Materdei they clustered round me, tugging at my sleeves, calling me Joe, pelting me with questions, inviting me to share their meal of beans and macaroni. Father Spada, who attended to the housekeeping and had been Father Borrelli's first collaborator, conducted me round the primitive premises. A whimpering child with a leg in splints clung to this gentle priest, and I was impressed by his ability to soothe him. Some of the boys were playing football in the dusty yard, in a corner of which a small hermit had built a hut. Since he had an aversion to society, this child had been allowed to live apart from the others. Dreamy and sullen, his ambition was to paint, and the wise Fathers encouraged him. Alone with his painting materials he was quite content. He was too shy to show me his work, but Father Spada showed me the Stations of the Cross he had painted in the chapel. They were naïvely naturalistic and very touching. The first instinct of these children when they came hungry to the house was to hoard the bread at meals as a squirrel hoards nuts, for fear of not seeing it again. In most cases it was their first solid meal. The habit of pilfering was so ingrained that they would filch the knives and forks, and door-knobs and electric bulbs, until they settled down. The temptations of vagabondage were not easily overcome.

After one evening when I supped with them, having brought some cakes and sweets to vary their diet, a gramophone was turned on and the boys all danced together with professional assurance and without self-consciousness. Two of the happy

347

waltzers were brothers. They had fled from their family hovel by the harbour and taken to the streets when their father had set himself on fire with petrol because he had caught his wife with a lover. Since their father had died of burns they had never forgiven their mother, and they refused to see her when she called at the *Casa*. These boys whose infancy had been so cruelly warped had the manners of little gentlemen. The tiniest tot there importuned me to be his dancing partner and whirled me round and round till I was winded. 'The wonder is,' as a shopkeeper remarked to Charles Grant, 'that there should be so much life in so little flesh.' Their astute little faces looked older and their bodies younger than their years, due to under-nourishment rather than to inveterate smoking. The cigarettes I had brought were more popular than the cakes. All of them smoked like chimneys. Catching some of the effervescence of their spontaneous gaiety, I enjoyed myself almost as much as at Marie-Laure's ball. The crippled ones were intent on a card game in the adjoining room. When they learned I was English they asked me for pictures of the Queen, which I promised to send them. 'I wish we had a Queen,' sighed one. Evidently these were instinctive monarchists. Outside their section of the grand old building the vast corridors and stairs were dimly lighted and there was no sign of life. My diminutive dancing partner escorted me to the outer door and suddenly kissed me goodnight.

A cultured English priest, Father Bruno Scott James, joined Fathers Borrelli and Spada as co-Director of this House of Waifs and Strays; older and taller than his colleagues, he was blessed with a whimsical sense of humour: he soon picked up enough Neapolitan slang to fill a dictionary, and it was startling to hear it pour from his chaste lips. He had seen the worst as well as the best of these people and he loved them. 'I think only the impossible things are worth attempting,' he told me, '*Credo quia impossibile est*. I want these people to find peace and joy and liberty and it is only the pure love of God that can bring this. All romantic nonsense? No, all hard sense. Mysticism? Yes, perhaps, but that is only another name for sense. However, there it is, sense or nonsense, that is why I am here and that is what makes me tick, as the Americans say.'

For a man of fastidious taste, who cherished his Cockburn 1912 port and his Ashendene Virgil, it required unusual courage to cohabit with waifs who had witnessed every sort of vice, who considered they could not become men until they had begun to live like animals; and Father Bruno's health was delicate. When I met him in the ramshackle Materdei he looked wan and bedraggled as if he too had been sleeping in the street, but he wore a grin-and-bear-it expression which was definitely English. His daily fare consisted of bread and cheese, an onion and a glass of wine, supplemented by tiny cups of coffee and cigarettes. In his modest autobiographical sketch *Asking for Trouble*, he admits that 'the constant noise, the lack of privacy, the lack of hot water, of all heating during the damp and cold of winter, the appalling moral and physical filth, the complete lack of amenities that even the poorest of us take for granted in England, several times nearly broke my resolution'. Most Neapolitans do not mind noise and lack of privacy; they even seem to like it: but for the founder of the Virgil Society and the translator and editor of the Letters of Saint Bernard of Clairvaux, accustomed to a quiet library and modern sanitation, these crude conditions must have been an ordeal. He endured them cheerfully for four years until he concluded that his talents might be better employed among the undergraduates of Naples University.

Sauntering through the slums, he was greeted by the neighbours as 'Padre Bru', and I am sure he was the only Englishman who came near to understanding Neapolitans, though he had a tendency to idealize them. One suspected that in material matters the *scugnizzi* knew how to look after themselves better than he did. From the 'House of the Urchins' and from the plays of Eduardo De Filippo one could learn much about the character of the poorer classes of Naples which even a megalopolis will not dilute, though the radio, television, the cinema, and popular journalism are accelerating a levelling process of manners, fashions and language from Piedmont to Sicily.

349

After working all day in the libraries it was refreshing to go to Eduardo's theatre, the San Ferdinando, where the demonstrative public added zest to each performance. Apart from his histrionic skill, Eduardo's success as an actor-playwright was due to the fact that he reflected the experiences of his audience and established a closer relation with them than any other writer in the vernacular. His was the last mask surviving from the *Commedia dell' Arte* – that of Pulcinella grown older, sadder and wiser. His humour was of the poignant kind that laughs at its suffering, a 'mixture of the appeal to the pity of things with the appeal to their absurdity', as Henry James remarked of the French comedian Coquelin.

Most of my younger Neapolitan friends had emigrated to Rome and Milan, which offered them wider scope if they were artists, and they returned to Naples intermittently to visit their relations. Most of my older friends had died, and my circle was dwindling amid an invasion of novelty. More and more ugly buildings were spoiling Posillipo. The sylvan Vomero of my childhood had become a city of concrete. These were some of the penalties of progress. The tourist region between Naples and Salerno was being exploited by Philistines from the North. Fortunately they could not mar the Amalfi coast, but the motor car had become an instrument of aggression. An *aliscafo* or hydrofoil whisked one to Capri or Ischia in half an hour, but why the hurry? I had always enjoyed the slower voyage to Capri by way of Sorrento, to Ischia by way of Procida. The spell of the siren was cracking. Finally the noise of the nightclub near my apartment drove me away, and my visits to Naples were curtailed.

During my other interludes away from Florence I travelled farther – to Tripoli and again to lecture in America, at Vassar and at Chicago University. My hostess in Tripoli, the Venetian Countess Anna Maria Cicogna, lived in a villa which her father Count Volpi had acquired when he was governor – an oriental structure adapted to western convenience, all its luxury hidden behind white walls in a suburban street. The living-rooms with their divans and heaps of cushions and rugs of rich design surrounded a columned patio with a majolica-tiled fountain evoking the Alhambra, beyond which was a parterre of palm trees and beds of flowers divided by channels of running water and a pond of water-lilies. There was also a delectable swimming-pool, for which one was grateful after shopping in the souks, where Nasser's image grinned from every other stall. The ladies of the party were beguiled by gaudy striped silks and woollen shawls and barbaric jewellery; the men by leather jackets, shoes and slippers with an overpowering smell. The vendors raced up and down the covered alleys cackling like hens. One rag and bone man had sacks full of big Venetian beads of intricate design which had been used as a medium of exchange among the Arabs some fifty years back. My hostess spent hours selecting the most lustrous for necklaces of her own invention

Except at Angkor I had never enjoyed the contemplation of ruins, perhaps because I had seen so many during the war, and all the clichés about the fall of the proud and the desolation of the powerful are summarized in Shelley's *Ozymandias*. But the ruins of Sabratha and Leptis Magna cannot fail to produce a strong impression of the magnitude of ancient Rome. The massive theatre of Sabratha by the sea-shore had been so carefully restored after thirteen centuries of burial in the sand that it could be used again. The mosaic pavement from a Byzantine basilica – a huge elaborate design of peacocks, trees and flowers – was one of the most perfect of its kind. Under the aegis of the Superintendent of Monuments, Vergara Caffarelli, I was able to see the wide streets and the moles of the Roman harbour with a reconstructive eye. His archaeological enthusiasm was infectious: even so it was difficult to make the Libyan authorities realize the value and importance of his excavations. Here I was constantly reminded of Shelley's lines:

> . . . *Round the decay*
> *Of that colossal wreck, boundless and bare*
> *The lone and level sands stretch far away.*

Unless the authorities paid more attention to them the sands of the desert would bury those ruins again. Some of the roads were already half smothered. Since the mass departure of Italian colonists the olive and fruit plantations had a forsaken air.

The more extensive ruins of Leptis Magna had been used as a stone quarry until the Italians disinterred and restored them under the expert guidance of Giacomo Caputo and Giacomo Guidi. Over six hundred marble columns had been removed by European consuls during the seventeenth and eighteenth centuries. Some had been sent to Paris and others to Virginia Water. Others adorned the local mosques: about fifty stood in the mosque of Tagiura, an austere relative of Cordoba Cathedral in an oasis of palm groves and fertile fields. The forum, the baths, the theatre, stage, orchestra and seats, and the well-preserved basilica of Septimius Severus which had the characteristics of the standard type of Christian basilica, the long nave ending in an apse, its walls resting on colonnades flanked by aisles – all these were eloquent of Roman enterprise and technical skill under an emperor who was born at Leptis and died at York. According to Gibbon, Septimius Severus was 'justly considered as the principal author of the decline of the Roman empire', but he seems to have converted his birthplace into another Alexandria. There was a touch of Byzantium in the decoration of pilasters and the drapery of statues, and the heads of Septimius Severus resembled Cellini's bust of the Grand Duke Cosimo I de' Medici in their *terribiltà*. Often he was portrayed as the Sun-god with seven planets round him; so were his sons Caracalla and Geta, of whom we know nothing agreeable. His Syrian wife Julia Domna, 'the patroness of every art, and the friend of every man of genius', prefigured the handsome dames of the early Renaissance. The whole family were sunworshippers.

A young Venetian of our party was immoderately excited by the phallic emblems scattered here and there. He drew out a note-book to sketch one, but no sooner had he copied it than he discovered another even bigger, and he ended with a considerable collection. The biggest of all he proposed to have reproduced by a goldsmith as a talisman for his future bride. 'Surely she should be satisfied with your own,' I remarked. 'I have chosen the closest resemblance,' he boasted.

Our imaginative hostess enabled us to visit the ruins by night as well as by day, and in spite of Septimius Severus and the sun-worshippers it was the moon that animated the inert masses of masonry. True, the stage, orchestra and seats of the vast theatre were empty, and perhaps this was as well in view of the blood-thirsty procilivities of its audience, but was this worse than that of our Theatre of Cruelty fans who deem themselves more civilized? Even in its present condition the building was more solid than our London theatres. But everything was too, too solid for my taste. It had an air of bloated materialism. Owing to a little knowledge of its history, it failed to raise my spirits like the ruins of Angkor. Technically, the plumbing of the public baths and latrines was remarkably efficient; the cement was more durable than ours and the secret of its composition had been lost, but the worship of Buddha had produced buildings in sandstone without the use of cement which seemed to me more wonderful. Caracalla's 'frown, and wrinkled lip, and sneer of cold command' was strikingly realistic, but I preferred the serene smile of Buddha. One may have a surfeit of mere animal energy 'bombinating in a vacuum', of the materialism that brutalized the Roman masses as in certain countries today, but modern Libya would benefit from a few injections of that energy. Tripoli owed such amenities as its elegant promenade by the sea to Italian enterprise: building the new city, they had respected the picturesqueness of the old.

There were loud screams when I lighted a cigarette in the drawing-room, and this was my introduction to Marina Luling, the sister of my hostess. Ignorant of her allergy to tobacco, I apologized profusely and we became fast friends. Were I asked which of the sisters I love best, I could not answer. Both are artists in living, generous hearted, endowed with abundant fantasy. As Anna Maria presides over her cultivated oasis in Tripoli, Marina is the ultra-hospitable châtelaine of Maser, which Palladio and Veronese combined to make the loveliest villa in Venetia. It is the union of these great artists in a harmonious landscape that gives Maser its special fascination. I would compare the two sisters to the Empress Julia Domna and Julia Maesa, both daughters of the high priest of the Sun-temple at Emesa, as Count Volpi di Misurata, *mutatis mutandis*, was high priest of Libya under Italian rule.

My visits to Maser, sometimes in a period of personal trouble and anxiety, have lifted me into a revivifying circle and an atmosphere of *luxe, calme et volupté* – though on second thoughts only the setting is calm, for the household palpitates with pleasurable excitement. Pekingese pets, a tiny Yorkshire terrier, a dachshund, a Mexican chihuahua, gambolling and yapping within; Irish hounds and a stable of race-horses without; a polyphonic aviary; a temperamental telephone; Valeria dashing about with a bunch of clanking keys; Diamante radiant on her way to the pool; Enrico whistling in his riding togs; Marina calling 'Papa!' and shrieking with laughter; and always music somewhere – maybe Nikita Magaloff practising a Chopin mazurka, sympathetic roulades from the birds in the branches, the cool trickle of water from the secret garden, and a distant church bell tolling ever and anon, footsteps pitter-pattering along the outer corridor, and now a guest being welcomed with embraces and exclamations: a realm of wholesome gaiety, of poetry, art and enjoyment, of life being lived spontaneously and intensely. You feel it is all as it should be: the vitality of Veronese's frescoes has been prolonged into the present age, especially in the Olympus room where the wife of Marcantonio Barbaro (for whom the villa was built) is depicted with her old nanny and one of her sons, who is peering at a parrot on the balustrade; there is also a pet spaniel and a monkey. But all the frescoes beam with light and air, and music vibrates from the Hall of Harmony.

It is the least pompous and the most cheerful of Palladio's buildings. The main house projects from the front façade, with four Ionic columns to support a sculptured pediment; arcaded wings on either side end in pavilions with sun-dials above a grassy knoll where linen was spread to dry – a pretty domestic touch – when I arrived. Behind the villa is the secret garden with an alcove carved out of the hillside, adorned with statues, sculptured cornices and festoons, and a grotto from which water flows into a pool. Here I have heard the Forelle Quintet and other haunting music which I shall always associate with that enchanting spot, transformed into a dream even while I listened, with sylphs in diaphanous gowns who had drifted in from Venice.

Every day at Maser was an adventure. There were minor crises as when a sobbing governess had been stung by a bee and Marina administered first aid, or when a cherished white Pekingese expired in Marina's arms; and there were informal glimpses of Marina in her dressing-gown over coffee in the morning when we would review the comedies of the previous day, and there were excursions to other Palladian villas, to Fanzolo and to Malcontenta and to Venice itself, through a landscape populated with charming country houses, many of them in a state of sad decay, the balconied windows shuttered, the statues mouldering. The war had done much damage, but since the eighteenth century the Brenta canal had ceased to be the resort of rich Venetians, who floated to their villas by house-boat – the leisurely *burchiello* – on which they supped and sang and played at cards. The villas along the Brenta had been miniature courts where there was a constant round of amusements, but they were abandoned when their owners were ruined by reckless extravagance.

One of the finest, the Villa Foscari at Malcontenta, second only to the Rotonda at Vicenza for its influence on Palladian architects (and they ranged from Russia to America), was crumbling most pitifully when Bertie Landsberg, a Brazilian in spite of his name, acquired it with the collaboration of Baroness Catherine d'Erlanger, a lady who shared his taste for fine décor. His restoration of the place was a true labour of love: he restored the faded frescoes himself and refurnished the kitchen and cellars in traditional style. Palladio would have been moved by the care he lavished on it, all the more so since he was far from affluent.

His cult of Malcontenta was religious. While he discoursed on its mathematical proportions one felt that every detail was divinely inspired, that it was 'frozen music' composed by Bach. Its projecting portico, reached by an external flight of steps on each side, is typically Palladian, yet it is not mentioned in his famous opus, *I Quattro Libri dell' Architettura*, which contains most of his designs.

The name suits it well, and one could readily believe the legend that a wanton daughter of the Foscari family had been immured there. My English friends rave about it, but I have always thought it oppressive with its weeping willows beside the stagnant canal. Such mansions were created for the Venetian nobility eager to display their grandeur: they are nostalgic anachronisms today. The same cannot be said of our more modest Tuscan villas, which are perfectly adaptable to modern requirements, as many Anglo-Americans have proved during the last century.

Palladio's inventiveness was such that he seldom repeated himself. In his description of Fanzolo, the stately home of Count Lorenzo Emo Capodilista, he laid stress on the fact that thanks to the covered arcades, 'people can go everywhere under shelter'. This is convenient in Venetia, but it would not suit a dull climate. By contrasting light arcades with plain and rusticated walling he achieved the three conditions of commodity, firmness, and delight laid down for good architecture by Vitruvius via Sir Henry Wotton. Daniele Barbaro, Patriarch of Aquileia, who supervised the building of Maser while his brother Marcantonio was abroad on diplomatic missions, had translated Vitruvius. He chose Palladio as architect and probably suggested the allegories for Veronese's frescoes and Allessandro Vittoria's sculpture.

Marina Luling is one of the few who recreate the splendour of the Venetian Renaissance without the tedium of pomp and ceremony, living there most of the year, visited by friends and relations. The Venetians of old were great gormandizers: their dinners were so long and the courses so numerous that three dining-rooms were often used in succession for the same meal.

Though we all eat less nowadays, the traditions of Venetian hospitality are kept alive at Maser. Swarms of guests are bidden for a family birthday or anniversary, and they overflow into Asolo, where rooms are reserved for them when the villa is crammed. Gargantuan meals are offered by neighbours from Vicenza to Venice, where the modern Doge Count Vittorio Cini showed us his sumptuous art collection and the cultural centre he has created on the island of San Giorgio Maggiore, in memory of his son who was killed in an aeroplane; thence to Count Brando Brandolini's palace to watch the regatta on the Grand Canal, or to the Palazzo Labia which Carlos de Beistegui had restored and redecorated, to admire the famous ballroom frescoed by Giambattista Tiepolo. These are the paragon of his profane decorations, inspired by the loves of Antony and Cleopatra: the melting of the pearl on one side, the meeting at the harbour on the other, with how many details which create a visual parallel to the poetry of Shakespeare and Dryden, the gallery of musicians above the banquet, the halberds against the sky, the curved prow of the ship with a carved triton, the inevitable greyhound restrained by a blackamoor. Here is Venice in all her pride. These were painted some two hundred years after Veronese's frescoes at Maser and the debt to Veronese is obvious. I felt equally indebted to Marina for some of the most poetical impressions of my life. To know her is indeed a liberal education.

'We've had quite enough of your Bourbons,' said my cousin Louise, pronouncing them like the Kentucky whisky. 'Why not give us something more actual, more exciting?' To me the Bourbons were actual, and they had provided me with as much excitement as I could bear while I wandered imaginatively in their footsteps. But I realized that I could not expect others to share this sensation, for one had to know Naples to feel it and to regret the passing of a great if eccentric dynasty. Its strain of eccentricity was part of its attraction.

One of the most touching ceremonies I witnessed there took place in the recently restored basilica of Santa Chiara when the remains of Ferdinand II's Austrian widow Queen Maria Theresa and the youngest of her eleven children Gennaro, Count of Caltagirone, were buried beside the other Bourbon princes, after lying for almost a century in a church near Rome. The ceremony was solemn yet intimate, and the congregation consisted mostly of people whose names had been famous in Neapolitan history, assembled to honour the memory of ancestors who had served the Bourbons, the ladies in heavy black veils. Those not in mourning garb had been lured by the sight of the great crowned catafalque outside the basilica.

The Bourbon princes who had come from afar were delayed by the dense evening traffic, all the denser because of the coming elections, the crowds of voters listening to political speeches magnified by microphones. But the big bare church was insulated from the hurly-burly: silence and prayer prevailed. The princes were led by the Duke of Castro, the second son of Alfonso Count of Caserta and a direct grandson of Queen Maria Theresa, a superbly dignified old gentleman with features of melancholy refinement, his Polish consort, *née* Princess Zamoyska, his son Ferdinand Duke of Calabria with his wife and other members of the family, including the handsome Duchess of Ancona and her sister Princess Urraca. The Duke of Ancona was a descendant of the House of Savoy, but time had levelled political differences and annulled dynastic rivalries. Two auxiliary Bishops of Naples celebrated Mass and a long procession of chanting monks and priestlings accompanied the celebrants to the catafalque for the benediction. At the end of the apse the effigy of King Robert of Anjou, much damaged by the bombardment of August 1943, which had destroyed most of the original structure, reminded us that there were worse calamities than the fall of dynasties. I could remember the interior as the eighteenth century had left it, with its gilded Baroque cages for the nuns above the arcaded chapels along the nave. It had been completely burnt out: only the Gothic skeleton remained as when it had first been built in the beginning of the fourteenth century. And the sad lilt of Michele Galdieri's song throbbed in my ears:

> *Munasterio 'e Santa Chiara . . .*
> *tengo 'o core scuro scuro . . .*

Napule comm'era – the Naples that had been – was embodied in the kneeling figures around me and my heart was darkened as in the song. Here all was reminiscence; outside all was anticipation: the bellowing of loud-speakers and the election crowds jolted me back into the nerve-racked present.

When the princes left the basilica a few loiterers cheered them. A woman remarked of the Duke of Castro: 'You can see he's royal by the way he raises his hat. If he stood for election I would vote for him.' He and his family resided in France, Princess Urraca in Austria, another sister in Ecuador, Prince Gabriel had settled in Brazil, where he had inherited a coffee plantation. None of them was opulent. Their ancestors had left their wealth and treasures behind. Like Santa Chiara, their innate dignity remained. It was a century since Francis II had lost his throne to his cousin the King of Sardinia. He had protested against this usurpation until he died; so had his more vigorous half-brother, the Count of Caserta; but after the unification of Italy such protests were futile.

For several days the princes were entertained with the affectionate warmth of a loyal people. Elsewhere these receptions might have been dull and pompous: here they were courtly yet informal. The pleasantest were given by my cousin Ferdinando and by the French Consul Pierre Claudel, the son of the ambassador-poet, in the Pavoncelli Palace by the sea. Peach-fed Virginia ham, which our host had brought from America, was served at a sparkling buffet, and this was a succulent novelty for the princesses, who ate with Bourbon relish. The sight of pretty women enjoying their food always stimulates me, and for once I was able to answer the innumerable questions that were put to me. Princes are great questioners: no doubt it is due to their training. I am sure they had never read Proust, for they were puzzled when I mentioned his reference to the last Queen of Naples in *La Prisonnière*. Having written about their ancestors, whose private letters and diaries I had pored over in the Archives, I was curious to detect any trace of their idiosyncrasies and to hear if, after so long an exile, they still spoke Neapolitan. A few local expressions remained, but their French and their German were more fluent. Talking of Proust, I remembered that Paul Claudel, whose complete works in a sumptuous edition such as only the French produce nowadays were shown to me by his son, had thundered against *Du Côté de chez Swann* as 'that world of snobs and lackeys'. Were we snobs? Not according to Proust's definition or to that of the *Oxford Dictionary*. We did not puff ourselves out or try to enhance our importance. I am only a snob in so far as I often want better company than my own. My imagination is historical, and as Doctor Johnson observed, 'Were it not for imagination, Sir, a man would be as happy in the arms of a chambermaid as of a Duchess.' A pithy saying if applied to brief encounters, but it demonstrates the lexicographer's ignorance of the French duchesses, who were accomplished amorists. Finesse may treble the bliss of an embrace.

When *The Last Bourbons of Naples* was published my dear cousin heaved a sigh of relief. 'Now I hope you'll get on to something more contemporary. Don't forget that we're living in an atomic age!' Others remarked, as if I had a one-track mind: 'I suppose you'll be writing about the Bourbons of Parma next. Give us the works.' The psychology of Charles Louis, one of the last Dukes of Parma, was comparatively modern: handsome, restless, intelligent, a good linguist, a student of biblical matters, yet incapable of concentration and lacking in self-confidence; and his dependence on Thomas Ward, the jockey from Yorkshire who was created a baron of the Austrian Empire, gave his career a musical comedy twist. But the political complexity of his background – since Lucca was converted into a duchy by the Congress of Vienna to compensate the Bourbons for the loss of Parma to Napoleon's wife, the ex-Empress Marie Louise – was out of all proportion to its historical importance. It was truly parochial.

This parochialism had a charm which is still potent. In the eighteenth century Lucca was considered a model state which had governed itself as a republic for several centuries. Mrs Thrale described it as a 'fairy commonwealth'. One of its contributions to culture was a second edition of the French Encyclopaedia re-edited and printed in seventeen volumes in folio. It remained peaceful and prosperous as a duchy but it became more cosmopolitan. As Charles Louis supported the Legitimist cause in Spain and France, it swarmed with diplomats and enigmatic adventurers. Bagni di Lucca began to flourish as a summer resort, and its atmosphere is preserved in Heine's *Reisebilder*. Shelley was ecstatic about its magnificent scenery, especially the *Prato Fiorito*, where jonquils bloomed in such abundance that their scent almost caused him to faint – a sensation he recorded in *Epipsychidion*:

> '*And from the moss violets and jonquils peep*
> *And dart their arrowy odour through the brain*
> *Till you might faint with that delicious pain.*'

Englishmen and Frenchmen outnumbered the other foreign

visitors, and a Casino was opened for their amusement in 1837 when gambling was authorized by Sovereign decree. There was also an English Club, an Anglican church built in 1839, and the Protestant cemetery where Ouida was buried. Now fashion passes it by: the Victorian hotels and the English Club have vanished, and the chemists no longer display the arms of foreign embassies. But my friend Ian Greenlees has fallen under the spell of this romantic valley and he may become the pioneer of a new English colony. Thanks to his efforts, Ouida's tomb has been repaired, and he has organized a congress which met in the old Casino to celebrate the fiftieth anniversary of the British Institute of Florence, which he so brilliantly directs.

For me the chief merit of Charles Louis, Duke of Lucca and Parma, was his supreme consciousness of being a Bourbon. 'What a family of gentlemen ours always was! How it has changed both in fortune and in *heart*, that is to say, fallen into decay,' he confessed to Baron Ward. Having written about the fall of the Medici and the Bourbons of Naples, I had no desire to become a specialist in dynastic decay. Recently so many English writers and scholars have chosen to settle near Lucca, including Vernon Bartlett, John Fleming, Hugh Honour and Professor Michael Grant, that I am sure one of these will bridge this hazy gap. As for me, I was tempted to return to the freedom of fiction, and the theft of the Duke of Wellington's portrait from the National Gallery prompted me to write about a stolen picture in a novel that shocked my most serious friends, though it distracted my mind from illness and gnawing sorrow.

My mother's last years were tormented by the pain of incurable arthritis. She resisted it gallantly but I knew that she suffered more than she would admit. I was worried on her account and dreaded an accident. For both of us this was an unconscious strain. Her expression of sadness and resignation when she thought I was not looking wrung my heart. She had kept her delicate beauty and her soft youthful voice, and even when she was approaching ninety nobody would have guessed her age, which she never divulged. She became more ethereal in her fragility and when she smiled the years fell away from her. In her Chinese coats of cut velvet and flowered brocade she enhanced the beauty of every room she entered. To live with a companion of such grace and sweetness was an incomparable privilege. She had survived her best friends and at her age one does not make new ones, but she welcomed mine however strange some of them seemed to her. She even shook dry Martinis for them, not trusting the potency of mine. Fortunately her eyesight was good: she remained an omnivorous reader with an unflagging interest in current affairs. I showed her what I was writing and she was my most enlightened critic. Her historical memory was more acute than mine, yet her culture was in a sense domestic, for she had never attended a university.

Though we could not entertain on the scale to which my mother had been accustomed, we gave frequent luncheons and visitors came to see the house and garden almost every afternoon, as they still do. So long as she could walk, my mother accompanied them. Sometimes it was a waste of her time and energy, as when she took a couple all over the garden, which is more famous for its statues than for the reproductive organs of its plants. The couple glanced round superciliously; they smoked cigarette after cigarette, stamped them out in the grass and said nothing. Finally they explained: 'Old sculpture doesn't mean a thing to us. We collect pure abstracts.' And these people had come with an introduction from a near relation. Thanks to her sense of humour, my mother could laugh at such episodes, but she confessed that she often felt she was a mere pretext for seeing the garden. All my friends appreciated her wit and singular charm. Our dovetailed memories of another Florence were a frequent theme of conversation.

How many of the villas once occupied by friends had been converted into schools and institutions: the Finaly and Costantini villas farther up the Via Bolognese; Myron Taylor's Schifanoia; the Franchetti and Huntingdon villas at Bellosguardo; Charles Loeser's La Gattaia; Lina Waterfield's Poggio Gherardo. Berenson's villa of I Tatti was next in line, and eventually, after my death, La Pietra, which I hope will become a centre for the study of Florentine art and history. When Henry James revisited Florence in 1877 he wrote: 'If one is a stranger half the talk is about villas. This one has a story: that one has another; they all look as if they had stories. Most of them are offered to rent (many of them for sale) at prices unnaturally low . . . Their extraordinary largeness and massiveness are a satire upon their present fate. They were not built with such a thickness of wall and depth of embrasure, such a solidity of staircase and superfluity of stone, simply to afford an economical winter residence to English and American families.' In fact they had been built for rich bankers and merchants, most of whom had risen to high positions in the government. Many still belonged to the descendants of their original owners, of the Antinori, Gondi, Guicciardini, Ricasoli, Rucellai, Serristori, and other ancient families, who continued to produce excellent wine and olive oil. The wines of those who live in the Chianti region are sold all over the world. Though the vintage of our own *podere* is inferior, the peasants continue to produce it with profit to themselves. When I was a child they crushed the grapes in enormous vats with their bare feet to the accompaniment of laughter and song, but now more mechanical methods have been introduced and the occasion has lost its primitive gaiety.

The tide of foreign residents had ebbed while the tourists multiplied. On the whole the former had been suavely civilized: they wrote, they painted, they composed, they collected works of art like my father and cultivated their gardens. Berenson at I Tatti, Vernon Lee at Maiano, Lady Sybil Lubbock at Fiesole, held gatherings where literary and aesthetic problems were debated as earnestly as at the Platonic Academy of the Medici. Janet Ross wrote on Florentine history and supervised her farm at Poggio Gherardo, to be succeeded by her niece Lina Waterfield, whose vermouth, distilled according to a Medicean recipe, was sold in London at the Army and Navy Stores; Edward Hutton produced his invaluable guide-books at the neighbouring Casa Boccaccio; Mabel Dodge presided over

Bohemia at the Villa Curonia. The art historians quarrelled over their theories and attributions with the ferocity of the early Florentines. Many had become national monuments.

In the 1920s a younger generation of writers, Aldous Huxley, D. H. Lawrence, Richard Aldington, Scott Moncrieff, became temporary residents. E. M. Forster's *A Room with a View*, Edwardian *avant-garde*, had given way to *Aaron's Rod*, which evokes cosmopolitan Florence between the world wars. Somerset Maugham, a regular visitor at the Villa Spedaluzzo next door to La Pietra, frequented the frivolous set of fox-trotters and bridge-players. Mrs Keppel cultivated the ambassadors at L'Ombrellino; Reggie Turner kept up the gay persiflage of Oscar Wilde; and Norman Douglas, who was printing his books privately for the bibliophiles, scoffed at the art critics and damned the Cinquecento. Radclyffe Hall personified the *femme incomprise* in masculine attire, very proud of the laurel wreath presented to her in honour of *The Well of Loneliness* by D'Annunzio, which she kept under a glass dome. Ever and anon, the three Sitwells visited their formidable father at Montegufoni. They brought young painters and musicians with them: Gino Severini, who frescoed a room in the castle with scenes from the *Commedia dell' Arte*, Lord Berners, who painted and composed and wrote fanciful novels, and William Walton, who was setting Edith's *Façade* to music.

Maybe because I happened to be young, it seemed to me that we all breathed an atmosphere of lyrical creativity, and that the arts played a more vital role in our society. Now the main accent is on specialization, which too often means limitation. Having chosen some obscure painter or humanist for his thesis, the research student is unable or unwilling to look much further. One said to me frankly: 'I don't care much for X's paintings but at least they offer fresh territory for research. There is so little left to write about. The artistic personalities of Y and Z have been thoroughly exhausted.' But there is always more to be said and rediscovered about Italian painting, before Cimabue and after. A good eye is the first requisite, and I noticed that most of these students wore dark glasses through which it must have been difficult to distinguish subtle tones and contours. It is absurd to compete with computers, yet that is what many of them seem to be doing – unless it be hunting for some *Amico di Nessuno*.

Berenson's death on October 6, 1959, deprived me of my oldest Florentine friend, for he was ninety-four. Latterly a swelling in his mouth had prevented him from expressing himself except with gestures, though fever had made him lucid and he longed to speak. Like a little monk carved in ivory, wrapped in a light white woollen shawl, he lay in his beloved library among masses of flowers with the sun streaming through the windows. He used to say: 'If survival after death were conceivable, I should like to be the guardian spirit of my house and library.' He would have enjoyed the sight of his own funeral, the long winding procession from I Tatti to the typically Tuscan church of San Martino a Mensola, with the bright gonfalons of Florence and Fiesole borne by standard-bearers in medieval costume and half the population led by seminarists in white vestments carrying torches downhill and uphill between the silvery olives. One was inevitably reminded of Benozzo Gozzoli's frescoes in that crystalline air. B.B. was buried beside his wife in the small chapel near the entrance to I Tatti. As the climax of a long life dedicated to Italian painting, it was in harmony.

From this moment I was made more poignantly aware of how irrevocably my whole background had changed. It was not only the end of a chapter, for one hoped that the next chapter when Harvard inherited I Tatti would continue as B.B. had willed it, and that other students would enrich their values and insights in the library and garden he had animated. The final curtain had fallen on a figure who had contributed more than anyone since Ruskin and Pater to our appreciation and understanding of art. In an age of destruction it was necessary to remember that man is a creator and that 'the human past, long before history begins, is strewn with figured records of his love of beauty and testimonials to his genius as a creator'. B.B. had been a humanistic sage.

Among distinguished foreigners the greatest acquisition to Florence since the war, a most considerate friend and a discriminating connoisseur of the fine arts, was Prince Paul of Yugoslavia, but alas, even as I write, his splendid property of Pratolino is being sold. Prince Paul inherited it from his maternal aunt, Princess Abamalek-Lazareff, *née* Demidoff, who had lived on the vast estate like a retired empress with a great reputation for old Russian lavishness. All the Demidoffs had been lavish, since the founder of the family fortune had re-organized the production of firearms during the reign of Peter the Great. His great-grandson became Russian Minister to the Tuscan Court. According to Stendhal, he 'collected heads by Greuze and relics of St Nicholas, and while in Rome kept a company of French actors who performed the comedies of the Parisian Gymnase in the Ruspoli Palace where he resided. Un-fortunately a character in one of these vaudevilles was called Saint-Ange and the exclamation *Pardieu!* was noted in the course of the dialogue. These circumstances deeply offended Cardinal della Genga (entrusted by Pope Pius VII with the duties of Bishop of Rome). Subsequently under the reign of Leo XII Mr Demidoff's actors, with typical French flightiness, made the mistake of producing a vaudeville with a character called Saint-Léon. The last straw was when a performance given on a Thursday did not end till a quarter past twelve, encroaching on Friday by a quarter of an hour . . . These incidents drew all the vexations of the police on Mr Demidoff, and in this country it still has the terrible forms of the Inquisition. Consequently this benévolent Russian, who supported several hundreds of paupers and gave two amusing entertainments every week, went off to settle in Florence.' Stendhal also relates that he wanted to remove the ten or twelve feet of earth covering the pavement of the Forum, from the Capitol to the Arch of Titus, and build a canal for conducting rainwater into the *Cloaca Maxima*, but that these laudable projects failed 'because a character in a vaudeville had been called Saint-Léon'.

Florence benefited largely by this emigration, for Count Nicholas Demidoff, as he became, lived in munificent splendour with a hundred retainers and the same company of French actors for his private theatre. Not only did he entertain on a more extravagant scale than the Grand Duke but he gave so much to charity that his alms were said to have demolished beggary in Florence. He founded a school, a hospital and an orphanage. When he died in 1828 his two sons Paul, Governor of the Ukraine, and Anatole inherited his immense fortune and estates. Anatole, who was born in Florence, was given the Tuscan title of Prince of San Donato. He married Princess Mathilde Bonaparte, daughter of Jerome, King of Westphalia, and Princess Catherine of Württemberg, but his reputation suffered as a result of this marriage. The Goncourt Journal and the Memoirs of Viel-Castel depict him from Princess Mathilde's point of view as a boorish monster, but he had literary ambitions, artistic taste, and copious charities. Even if he had a liaison with the Duchess of Dino, Princess Mathilde had given him ample cause for jealousy with Baron de Poilly, Captain Vivien, and Niewerkerke, and she had some of the greatest of French writers as partisans. The marriage culminated in a public scandal. While a ball was in progress at San Donato, Prince Anatole strutted up to her and slapped both her cheeks. She locked herself in her bedroom for the night, and left next day for St Petersburg. The Tsar Nicholas I sympathized with her, granted her an annuity and disgraced Prince Anatole, forbidding him to live within a hundred miles of her. In 1880, ten years after his death, San Donato was sold with most of its precious contents, except for some that were moved to the villa of Pratolino, which his nephew Prince Paul Demidoff purchased in 1872. These are now being sold by Sotheby's.

The marvels of Pratolino, with its statues, grottoes, fountains and water-spouts, have been described in detail by Montaigne, Richard Lassels and John Evelyn, and depicted in the etchings of Stefano della Bella. Francesco I de' Medici commissioned Buontalenti to design it for his adored Bianca Cappello in 1569 and, as Montaigne remarked, 'the Grand Duke has used all his five senses to beautify it', but the villa and most of the garden were destroyed by the Austrian Grand Duke Ferdinand III, who wanted a hunting park. Giambologna's colossal statue of the

Apennine, built of large blocks of stone above a small lake, is one of the few relics of the original garden. The present villa was formerly the *paggeria* or pages' quarters, enlarged and modernized by Prince Paul Demidoff.

An enlightened connoisseur like his ancestors, Prince Paul of Yugoslavia would have liked to restore the garden as it had been before it was blown up, but the expense was prohibitive. He filled the lake with gorgeous lotuses and improved the decoration of the house, adding choice pieces from what remained of his own collection, though the great music room with its elephantine furniture in late Victorian style was more than even he could cope with. Yet the life-size portraits in their ponderous frames had a definite 'period' charm. Among these Prince Anatole's displayed the most flamboyant personality: in one he was shown as a naked cupid armed with bow and quiver astride a tiger, teasing the fierce animal's nostrils with a mischievous hand; in another as a dandy in Circassian uniform on a prancing steed, the personification of a dashing Ouida hero. One could imagine that he had broken many a heart in his rakish youth. Prince Paul defended him against the calumnies of Princess Mathilde and showed me an imposing book he had published called *Voyages dans la Russie Méridionale et la Crimée*, recounting a journey through Hungary, Moldavia and Wallachia to the Crimea, to study the flora and fauna and the mineral resources: the painter Auguste Raffet and several naturalists had joined the expedition. The painting of Princess Mathilde, who was reputed to have been a beauty, was heavy and dull in comparison, but a marble bust of her by Hiram Powers was slightly more flattering. A picture of Paul Demidoff, plump and bespectacled in a plum-coloured coat and top hat, evoked Mr Pickwick.

The pink villa with its long corridors lined with marble busts and portraits and inlaid chests, the meandering park with its venerable oaks and Jersey cows and flocks of pheasants, were more suggestive of a remote estate in the Hungary of the *ancien régime* than of Tuscany. Though Pratolino was only six miles beyond La Pietra, I always felt I was entering another country in another century when I passed its gate. Apart from his innate flair for art and literature, Prince Paul's courtesy was almost too exquisite for this ill-mannered age. He made light of favours when he conferred them, and seemed to be receiving when he was giving. He had loved Oxford and most of his friends were English: he had too much good sense to bear us a grudge for his maltreatment by ignorant journalists. His outspoken sympathy for England and opposition to the Tripartite Pact when he visited the Berghof on March 4, 1941, was overlooked, whereas his reported visit to Hitler on March 18 was a fabrication, of which there is no record in the German Foreign Office files. All who wish to understand his hideous dilemma as Regent of Yugoslavia till the *coup d'état* of March 27, 1941, should consult Dr Jacob Hoptner's well-documented book, *Yugoslavia in Crisis, 1931–1941*. This should remove the vulgar slur upon his regency.

As a lifelong friend of Berenson, who had been his guest in Yugoslavia, he was provoked to find no mention of the fact that it was he who had arranged B.B.'s visit to Queen Marie-José of Italy in exile, so casually referred to in his diary *Sunset and Twilight* – all the more so since while in South Africa during the war Prince Paul had received a telegram from Pope Pius XII (who had been accused of anti-Semitism) assuring him that the veteran art historian was safe in Florence. The omission seemed to have invidious implications at a time when Prince Paul, an ardent anglophil, had been taunted with anti-British prejudice, but I suspected it was merely the oversight of a tired octogenarian.

Prince Paul and his wife Princess Olga used to spend the summer at Pratolino with their grandchildren and if the art of pleasing and doing good to one another is, as Fielding wrote, the art of conversation, they possessed it to a consummate degree. Queen Helen of Roumania and her sister Duchess Irene of Aosta, and the late Princess Marina, Duchess of Kent, whose nobility was printed on features of the utmost refinement, were the most frequent visitors I met there, and all were endowed with a gallant sense of humour which enabled them to rise above misfortune. Prince Paul's wit was French and he had a rich fund of historical anecdotes. He was perfectly at home in the eighteenth century, but he also had many good stories about modern politicians. About Clemenceau, for instance, I remember his telling me that when he was appointed Home Secretary he turned up early next morning to inspect the offices of his department. His chief of staff escorted him and opened all the doors. Office after office was empty – not a soul stirring. Finally they came to an office where a man was sound asleep. The chief of staff rushed forward but Clemenceau stopped him. 'No, don't wake him,' he said. 'He might leave.' This occurs to me now that Prince Paul has left Pratolino, for I fear that the restricted society of Florence – even more restricted for royalty in exile – sent him to sleep when he preferred to keep awake.

For me one of the most memorable evenings of these years was the concert given to celebrate Edith Sitwell's seventy-fifth birthday in October, 1962, at the Festival Hall in London. Robed in red velvet with a hat like a golden helmet, Edith read some of her latest poems from a wheel-chair, since she had had an accident. Her contralto voice rang out deep and clear, oracular, sibylline, full of fire. 'Still falls the rain,' perhaps the only great poem inspired by the air-raids of 1941, was sung superbly by Peter Pears to Benjamin Britten's music, which interpreted every inflexion of its desolate rhythm.

It was almost forty years since I had heard Edith's own recitation of *Façade* to Sir William Walton's music. Full of the sun of Ischia, the composer conducted it again to a vast packed hall – how unlike the New Chenil Galleries in Chelsea where I had heard it last in the twenties! The audience were hungry for these rhythmical pyrotechnics, and they responded enthusiastically with wild applause. Irene Worth and Sebastian Shaw declaimed the poems with professional brio and sonority, and their verbal virtuosity was more than matched by the kaleidoscopically shifting moods of William Walton's accompaniment. The atmosphere it created was so purely English that it had no counterpart in any other music of this quality. One had to be familiar with the poems of Lear and Lewis Carroll, as most of us are in childhood,

371

to savour all the fun of this unique production. Edith was greeted with a jubilant ovation: the box in which she sat with Osbert and Sacheverell was floodlit while the whole audience turned towards it rapturously. I am sure no other poet has experienced such popular acclaim after a début of ridicule and abuse. Edith called it her Memorial Service and in a sense it was.

A supper party followed but half the guests – so many brilliant, witty, handsome friends I remembered in their prime – were tottering in various stages of decrepitude, and the contrast between the concert and the supper was rather gruesome. The figure of Carson McCullers, twisted and jerky in a fur coat with carpet slippers, the face still young but partly paralysed, was grotesquely tragic. At moments I thought I was in an orthopaedic hospital. Edith's poems had exhilarated us and quickened our blood, but in other respects the ravages of time were manifest under the harsh electric light in bald heads, white hair, and stooping shoulders. The lines of *Façade* which Evelyn Waugh and I had recited with such gusto in the quadrangles of Oxford – Sir Beelzebub who 'called for his syllabub in the hotel in Hell'; 'the navy-blue ghost of Mr Belaker, the allegro Negro cocktail shaker'; 'Daisy and Lily, lazy and silly'; and the 'Trio for Two Cats and a Trombone', echoed in my ears long after, and together with the mantilla'd ladies flirting their fans on the balconies of Seville, mocked Time as it fled. Sir Beelzebub roared in vain for his rum. 'Gone was the sweet swallow – gone Philomel.' I saw Edith again, not as a bespectacled sibyl in a bath chair but as a tall lithe Gothic 'nymph as bright as a queen' in a gown of green brocade, followed by a satyr train led by Lytton Strachey piping through his russet beard. I remembered the farcical charades in Osbert's house after the performance: how vivid were the impressions of colour, psychedelic before the word was invented, that still remained! And to make myself clear to the younger generation, let me add that she possessed a genuine charisma.

Evelyn Waugh had not been present, though it was the sort of occasion he would have relished. Before I returned to Florence he dined with me, and he asked me avidly for details about the performance and who was there. Only his lack of musical ear would have been a handicap: this deprived him of much enjoyment as he grew older. When it suited him he pretended to be deaf. We were staying in the same hotel and he joined me in boisterous mood, having quaffed copious draughts of champagne with one of his old comrades-in-arms. Though the dining-room was quieter than most, he complained of the hubbub. A page was summoned to fetch the ear-trumpet from his room. The trumpet was brought ostentatiously on a salver, a formidable instrument which he must have disinterred from some county junk shop. Having dusted it tenderly with a silk handkerchief, he flourished it in the direction of each of his interlocutors with, 'Sorry, can't hear you. Speak up!' All of us had to shout at him, and as we were sitting in the middle of the restaurant our loud voices and laughter caused consternation among the other diners. John Sutro and I played up to his act, but under the arrows of disapproving glances we felt a trifle selfconscious. We were the last to leave, and the waiters fidgeted around our table a little too persistently as we sat over coffee and liqueurs. Evelyn liked to linger over a Churchillian cigar. 'It's no good your fussing,' he snapped at a waiter. 'You're not going to make me budge till I have finished. Bring me another crème de menthe!'

My mother died a month after my return to Florence. She had had pneumonia during the previous summer and, now in her ninetieth year, she suffered a fatal relapse. Her mind had never grown old and to me she was eternally beautiful. This is the greatest grief I have endured and still endure, and I am unable to put it into words. My only consolation is that her spirit is with me bidding me take courage. I struggled against my sorrow, continued to write and lecture and act as cicerone to visiting guests, but often I felt like an automaton, hearing myself repeat the same words, the same gestures. My own illness leading to a severe operation could be of no possible interest to others, but of course it left its mark.

Heaven touches me in Florence, but so occasionally does Hell. On the night of November 3, 1966, I was dining with friends at

Fiesole, even higher than the hill on which I live. It had been raining steadily for a month but I had just returned from London and felt impervious to bad weather. The downpour increased in violence, and the courtyard of the villa where I was dining was deep under water when I bade my hosts goodnight. Some of my fellow guests floated paper boats merrily on this improvised lake, little dreaming of what was happening in the city down below. All too soon when Florence was waterless in spite of the flood – water, water everywhere but not a drop to drink or wash in – the same guests were to come to this villa begging for the boon of a hot bath, as Fiesole was still favoured with running water. And soon sensational accounts of the catastrophe of that night in Florence were to reach the ends of the earth, the vicissitudes of some twenty thousand people suddenly homeless, of thousands of shopkeepers ruined, of the ravenous Arno at forty miles an hour, the invasion of blackened mud, the wreckage of so much beauty. All this was rendered more actual by television and photography, by Franco Zeffirelli's film *Florence, Days of Destruction*, with Richard Burton's voice reciting Dante's lines:

*'Nel mezzo del cammin di nostra vita
mi ritrovai per una selva oscura . . .'*

('In the middle of the journey of our life I found myself in a dark wood'), and a sound-track of bulldozers and scraping shovels and scraps of Tuscan talk, rising ironically to Handel's Hallelujah Chorus when the devastation of Santa Croce was revealed.

The destruction of magnificent libraries and works of art was as great as, and in some cases greater than, that caused by the war, but it was as much of a natural catastrophe as an earthquake or volcanic eruption. It was an act of God which could not have been prevented by man. In impotent rage and despair, there is a tendency to seek a scapegoat and there were many complaints that no official warning had been given. Some argued that the hydro-electric dam some thirty-eight miles above Florence might have been opened earlier and by slow degrees. Certainly its abrupt opening increased the violence of the torrent, but had the dam burst the situation would scarcely have improved, and if the alarm had been spread in the early hours of November 4th by loudspeakers and the pealing of bells there would have been a madhouse panic, as when there was another flood scare in December.

Overwhelming calamities can exert a morbid fascination, and the catalogue of disasters was swollen day by day. But the Florentines proved that they had not lost their willpower. Haggard and sleepless and hungry, they got down to work. At first their efforts to clear their houses and shops from the invasion of oily mud looked hopeless: everywhere the deposit of thick black oil above doors and windows, sometimes high over one's head, and the stench of ooze and mould which lingered for many a month, the sewers vomiting their contents, shops gutted, metal shutters crumpled like tin foil, the battered and overturned cars, the huge trees and oil drums piled by the chaotic torrent against the bridges, and men and women with buckets and shovels and brooms, some of them singing.

Within a month the most conspicuous part of the débris had been removed and when the shops opened again, some after a year or more, they were neater and pleasanter: they had been given a 'new look'. But the whole district of Santa Croce where our mayor lived, the sanguine, sensible and eloquent Piero Bargellini, had been atrociously shattered and befouled. This and the National Library, which was closer to the river, had borne the full brunt of the avalanche. So many treasures had been kept on ground floors and in basements, in the restoration laboratory opposite the Uffizi for instance, and the most damaged were moved to the large greenhouse in the Boboli gardens, transformed into a temporary hospital for pictures, which lay on rows of metal frames bandaged in rice paper, the temperature controlled by a rumbling machine. One of the worst victims was Cimabue's great Crucifixion, which would have been saved had it remained in the Uffizi. Unfortunately the Franciscan friars wanted it in their own museum beside the cloister, which was filled with eighteen feet of muddy water. For seven centuries it had been intact: now seventy per cent of its surface was destroyed. 'But enough of Cimabue's Christ: now we must think of the poor Christians!' said the practical mayor. In the better equipped restoration laboratory of the Medicean Fortezza da Basso, it is still lying on its back, and short of repainting most of it, it will have to be left as a relic of the catastrophe. But the indomitable doctors in white under the guidance of Dr Umberto Baldini are determined to persevere: 250 paintings on wooden panels, by far the most vulnerable, and some thousands of canvases are still being treated, and this is one of the wonders of Florence since the flood.

In certain cases the process has revealed the original beauty of the object, as in some of the sculpture of the Bargello. Donatello's St Mary Magdalene has returned to life as it were, for the ugly brown varnish which had covered it for at least a century has at last been removed, showing the delicate modelling and latent colour, the pink of the arms, the gold on the ragged smock. And the eyes in the emaciated face are no longer blind. The funds for this meticulous labour are being wisely spent, and many of the paintings are in fresher condition than before, but many are lying like layers of skin detached from their wooden bodies, while others are still being dehumidified under tents of plastic. The treatment of panels whose paint bubbled and burst over the warped wood before Japanese rice paper had been available is painfully slow: the plight of these is the most critical. To restore the ancient furniture from churches and museums, pieces of wood of the same age and species are selected to fill in the intricate patterns of inlay. But it will take decades to repair the damage. Over a million books were submerged at the National Library, apart from those at Vieusseux's and other libraries.

Ten thousand automobiles were wrecked with claxons uncannily keening, but in no time their number was doubled, and the prostitutes (so numerous since the closure of 'houses of tolerance') were back on the avenues outside the stricken centre. One in a scarlet mini skirt offered a special discount for the flood victims. The rumourmongers talked of typhus and tetanus, but probably the ubiquitous fuel oil had killed the bacteria as well as horses, cattle, dogs, cats, and a few human beings, old cripples trapped in basements. Helicopters had rescued several from rooftops in the country.

A pointillistic amber mist full of floating particles hovered over the valley and the stench of fuel oil even reached me at La Pietra: it clung to my clothes whenever I returned from wading through the streets, since the ground floor and basement of my property on Lungarno Guicciardini had been wrecked and the porter had narrowly escaped drowning.

Help was urgently needed, and it came from many countries outside Italy. Britain was among the first of these and our Consul, Christopher Pirie-Gordon, with a posse of strenuous assistants, surpassed himself in distributing supplies to the homeless. Aircraft were flown in with the foremost necessities and an army of students appeared from nowhere – some to reinforce the expert restorers of books and works of art, others to clear up the shambles. These long-haired, quaintly garbed boys and girls toiled cheerfully without being asked, some for fifteen hours a day in the mud-choked basements. As one of them said, he felt that Florence 'belonged to the world'. Winning their haloes as 'angels of the mud', they showed the Florentines that they were not alone, and that deeds were more precious than the words of politicians. James Fenton, the winner of the Newdigate Prize at Oxford, was among them. He had fallen in love with the City of the Lily – still blossoming from the mire.

'I believe in the rebirth of Florence,' wrote Franco Nencini in his chronicle *Firenze: i giorni del diluvio* – a best-seller to be seen on every other sitting-room table as a grim memento. And in a sense Florence was reborn after its ordeal. Previously the Superintendent of Fine Arts, Professor Ugo Procacci, as well as the directors of museums and libraries, had been profoundly dissatisfied with their working conditions. 'After my generation,' he had said, 'there will be a void. None of the university graduates are attracted to this underpaid profession. Prestige won't feed a family.' Restorers had been scarce: those who could earn a living moved elsewhere. While one fresco was being restored two others were crumbling away. Besides, there was the lack of personnel. Who cared about the artistic heritage? he asked bitterly. 'We have so many works of art that it doesn't matter if some of them are ruined. We can always rely on what remains, and on our congenital reputation for immortality. The problem is not only one of survival: it is to have a sense of the future, a definite aim and hope.'

One of the effects of the flood was to comfort and reassure him. The international experts who came to assist the restorers, including Mr Kenneth Hempel of the Victoria and Albert Museum, and a team of fifteen from the British Museum led by Mr Peter Waters to operate on the books from the National Library, supported by hundreds of student volunteers, gave a considerable boost to Florentine morale. On many sedentary professors their strenuous exercise in salvage acted as a mud cure. The colour returned to their cheeks. Professor Procacci's question had been answered, for the world of culture had been mobilized to save these treasures. The fine arts and cultural 'assessor' of the Commune was aptly named Hope – Avvocato Speranza.

Yes, there has been an awakening. Before the flood too many Florentines took their heritage for granted. Their monuments had seemed so solid. Having been forced to realize their fragility, they are devoting more time and thought to their conservation. This also applies in a modest way to me. Since my father's death my chief aim has been to keep La Pietra and its garden, which is visited by hundreds of tourists every year, in the best possible state of preservation, to keep it all alive. Sometimes I feel I am hardly more than a custodian, and as expenses mount and taxation increases I wonder if I might not renew myself with greater profit elsewhere while I am free to travel. For I am a writer, and such a property makes heavy claims. But here I was born, and I believe, like Candide, that we ought to cultivate our garden. I consider myself lucky to have a garden to cultivate. I am aware that I am privileged, that I belong to a vanished period: entangled in the past as I am, I have no desire to belong to any other –

unless it were the middle of the eighteenth century. In the constant flux of those fashions and systems which the impotent try to foist on us I have kept my independence: I have not attempted to force fresh flowers from the modish manure and twist myself into the latest trendy postures. We must be true to our own vision of this world. My own vision has been enhanced but also circumscribed by La Pietra.

14 April, 1969.

Index

Russell, Lord Bertrand, 71
Rutter, Owen, 88

Saint-Exupéry, Antoine, 124
Sainte-Beuve, C. A., 91
Salvemini, Gaetano, 77
San Donato, Anatole Demidoff, Prince of, 368, 369
San Donato, Paul Demidoff, Prince of, 368, 369
San Francisco, 264
Santa Chiara, Neapolitan basilica, 358, 359
Sarcey, Francisque, 2
Sartre, J.-P., 105, 157
Satie, Erik, 36
Sauguet, Henri, 151, 170, 177, 182
Scott James, Father Bruno, 348, 349
Scott Moncrieff, C. K., 365
Searle, Alan, 327, 328
Sedgwick, Ellery, 262
Sedgwick, Mrs, 261
Septimius Severus, Emperor, 352, 353
Serpotta, Giacomo, 53
Sert, José-Maria, 75
Sert, Misia, 76, 156, 161
Seurat, Georges, 218
Severini, Gino, 365
S.H.A.E.F., 139, 147, 151, 165, 181, 199
Shankar, Uday 29
Shantiniketan, 126
Shaw, G. Bernard, 23, 318, 343
Shaw, Sebastian, 371
Shelley, P. B., 361
Sheriff, Rothwell and Mary, 249, 250
Sickman, Laurence, 135, 220, 221
Siqueiros, 232, 233
Sitwell, Dame Edith, XIV, XV, 29, 174, 179, 254–257, 300–303, 365, 371, 372
Sitwell, Sir George and Lady Ida, 299
Sitwell, Sir Osbert, 86, 146, 179, 205, 206, 222, 256, 257, 273, 299–307, 338, 372
Sitwell, Sir Sacheverell, 227, 240, 372
Sitwell Society, Oxford, 48
Siva, 114, 121
Smith, Arthur H., 70
  Logan Pearsall, 71
  Professor J. A., 56
Snow, Edgar, 122
Soriano, Juan, 236
Spada, Father, 347, 348
Spencer, Beatrice, 36
Spender, J. A., 46
Spender, Stephen, 292
Speranza, Avv. Edoardo, 378
Sprigge, Cecil, 44, 45, 55, 57
Sprigge, Mrs Cecil (Sylvia), 293

Stefan Batory, S.S., 103–105
Stein, Gertrude, XIV, 72, 161, 166–169, 171–176, 199, 219, 254–258
Stein, Leo, 172
Stendhal (Henri Beyle), 45, 50, 342, 367
Stern, James, 253, 254
Stilwell, General Joseph W., 109, 111
Stoclet, Adolphe, 187, 188
Strachey, Lytton, 26, 37, 372
Stravinsky, Igor, 292
Strong, Mrs Arthur, 25, 194, 196, 197
Summers, Romney, 108
Sutro, John, 19, 83, 84, 318, 373
Sutro, Mrs John (Gillian), 83, 84
Sykes, Christopher, 96, 166–169, 333, 334
Synge, Patrick, 199

Tagore, Rabindranath, 126
Tamayo, Rufino, 233
Tangmere, R.A.F. station, 95, 96
Taormina, 316, 317
Tchelitchev, Pavel, 75, 253–256
Tegetmeier, Denis, 88
Temple, Reginald, 63–65
Tennyson, Alfred Lord, 279
Thomson, Virgil, 258
Thorpe, Courtenay, 23
Tiepolo, Giovanni Battista, 357
Tirumala Nayak, 121, 122
Titian, 170, 195, 241
Toklas, Alice B., 166–168, 171–174
Topolski, Feliks, 273
Torrigiani, Marchesa Lulie, 67, 68, 200–202
Toulouse-Lautrec, Henri de, 13, 343
Toye, Francis, 47, 194, 323
Trabia, Princess of, 54
Tredegar, Lord (Evan Morgan), 29
Trefusis, Mrs Violet, 183, 342
Trilussa, 49
Tripoli, 350–353
  Sabratha, 351
  Leptis Magna, 352
  Tagiura, 352
Trott, Adam von, 6
Troubridge, Una, Lady, 307–309
Turner, Reginald, XIV, XV, 62–65, 143, 258, 334, 335, 365
Tzintzuntzan, Patzcuaro, 241

Valéry, Paul, 179, 343
Vallombrosa, 329–331
Vansittart, Lord, 31
Van Vechten, Carl, 223, 257, 258
Van Vechten, Mrs Carl (Fania Marinoff) 258
Venice, 40, 58, 159, 357
Verney, Sir John, 91

387